AF352661

"Fr. Emmanuel Durand is among the most vital voices within Roman Catholic (and Christian) theology today. Francophone readers have been able to learn from him these past few decades. It is very good to know that, with this publication, English-speaking readers can now profit from his insights. This is the kind of theology we need today: deeply attuned to contemporary concerns (for instance on the question of divine suffering and anger), constantly engaged with the scriptural witness, and steeped in some of the most significant theological and philosophical works (ancient and modern). If you wonder where Roman Catholic theology might be (fruitfully!) headed these coming years, look no further!"

—CHRISTOPHE CHALAMET, UNIVERSITY OF GENEVA

"This book is a model of 'Thomistic ressourcement.' Not only does Emmanuel Durand offer a profound reflection on the attributes of God, on God's action, on Christ, and on salvation, he also formulates a quite exemplary method which brings together Sacred Scripture, the Fathers of the Church, Thomas Aquinas, and contemporary theology. The close attention Durand gives to Sacred Scripture and to the employment of analogy, together with a keen sense of God's mystery and the singularity of Christ, allows him to offer a fresh reading of Thomas Aquinas on issues which are of utmost theological relevance today. This book is an exemplar of how to do theology."

—GILLES EMERY, OP, UNIVERSITY OF FRIBOURG, SWITZERLAND

"This volume is not only deeply instructive, but has the merit of showing in practice how theology can only be enjoyed when it is conceived in unity with life and the profound questions it poses to us. Following in the footsteps of Aquinas, Emmanuel Durand proves in these pages to be a true master of theology."

—GUILIO MASPERO, PONTIFICAL UNIVERSITY OF HOLY CROSS, ROME

Divine Speech in Human Words

Divine Speech in Human Words

Thomistic Engagements with Scripture

EMMANUEL DURAND, OP

EDITED BY MATTHEW K. MINERD

The Catholic University of America Press

Washington, D.C.

The paper used in this publication meets the minimum
requirements of American National Standards for Information
Science—Permanence of Paper for Printed Library Materials,
ANSI Z39.48-1984.
∞

Cataloging-in-Publication Data available
from the Library of Congress
ISBN: 978-0-8132-3536-3
eISBN: 978-0-8132-3537-0

supported by a grant

Figure Foundation

lettered to be

To the friars, colleagues, and students

of the Dominican University College of Ottawa,

with esteem and gratitude

Contents

PART 2. ANALOGY, TRINITY, AND
CHRIST THE SAVIOR

Acknowledgments

Chapter 1. This prologue chapter is original.

Chapter 2. An earlier version of this chapter was delivered as a lecture at the University of Geneva, June 2, 2018, as part of the symposium "Nommer Dieu aujourd'hui. Approches contemporaines des attributs divins" and was then published in *Modern Theology* 34, no. 3 (2018): 419–33.

Chapter 3. An earlier version of this chapter was delivered as a lecture at the Pontifical University of Saint Thomas Aquinas (Angelicum) in Rome, February 22, 2018, as part of the symposium "Theological Exegesis: Scriptural Theology," and was then published in *Nova et Vetera* (English Ed.) 18, no. 4 (2020): 1235–46.

Chapter 4. An earlier version of this chapter was published in French in *Nova et Vetera* 94, no. 3 (2019): 221–35.

Chapter 5. An earlier version of this chapter was published in French in Durand, *Les Émotions de Dieu, indices d'engagement* (Paris: Cerf, 2019), 165–211. © Les Éditions du Cerf, 2019.

Chapter 6. An earlier version of this chapter was published in French in Durand, *Les Émotions de Dieu, indices d'engagement* (Paris: Cerf, 2019), 213–35. © Les Éditions du Cerf, 2019.

Chapter 7. An earlier version of this chapter was delivered as a lecture at the Pontifical University of Saint Thomas Aquinas (Angelicum) in Rome, October 3, 2019, as part of the symposium "Thomas Aquinas on Nature and Creation," and was then published in *Nova et Vetera* (English Ed.) 20, no. 1 (2022): 159–78.

Chapter 8. An earlier version of this chapter was published in *The Thomist* 78, no. 4 (2014): 519–36.

Chapter 9. An earlier version of this chapter was published in *Science et Esprit* 73, no. 3 (2021): 375–94. A first sketch of the second part of this chapter was previously published in French in *Recherches de Science Religieuse* 106, no. 4 (2018): 539–54.

Chapter 10. An earlier version of this chapter was published in French in *Science et Esprit* 71, no. 3 (2019): 401–20.

Chapter 11. An earlier version of this chapter was published in French in *Nova et Vetera* 80, no. 1 (2005): 7–22.

Chapter 12. An earlier version of this chapter was published in French in *Transversalités* 110, no. 2 (2009): 103–24.

Chapter 13. An earlier version of this chapter was published in French in *Revue des Sciences philosophiques et théologiques* 92, no. 2 (2008): 209–23.

Chapter 14. An earlier version of this chapter was published in French in Durand, *Dieu Trinité. Communion et Transformation* (Paris: Cerf, 2016), 189–219. © Les Éditions du Cerf, 2016.

Chapter 15. An earlier version of this chapter was published in *The Oxford Handbook of the Trinity*, ed. Gilles Emery and Matthew Levering (Oxford: Oxford University Press, 2011), 371–86.

Chapter 16. An earlier version of this chapter was published in French in *Revue thomiste* 108, no. 4 (2008): 467–96. It was also published subsequently in a rearticulated form in Durand, *L'Offre universelle du salut en Christ* (Paris: Cerf, 2012), 183–211.

Chapter 17. An earlier version of this chapter was published in French in *Nova et Vetera* 94, no. 1 (2019): 3–26. It was also delivered as a lecture at the Pontifical Academy of Saint Thomas Aquinas in Rome, June 15, 2019, as part of the symposium "San Tommaso et la salvezza."

Chapter 18. An earlier version of this chapter was published in French in *De Jésus à Jésus-Christ II. Christ dans l'histoire*, ed. Vincent Holzer and Jean-Louis Souletie (Paris: Desclée-Mame, 2011), 91–109. A much-enriched version was published subsequently in Durand, *L'Offre universelle du salut en Christ* (Paris: Cerf, 2012), 361–419.

For his unique support as the main translator and official editor of this book, I am deeply grateful to Dr. Matthew K. Minerd as well as to his wife, Courtney. I wish also to warmly thank the translators Jeremiah

Batram for chapter 7, Matthew Jarvis, OP, for chapter 8, John Baptist Ku, OP, for chapter 14, and Thomas Joseph White, OP, for chapter 15. I am also indebted to many friars, colleagues, students, and friends for support, conversations, and inspiration over the course of two decades, especially in Paris, Ottawa, Rome, and Fribourg. I will undoubtedly have forgotten some interlocutors, but I would like to record my special thanks to Maxime Allard, OP, Joseph d'Amécourt, OP (†), Lewis Ayres, Camille de Belloy, OP, Gilles Berceville, OP, Serge-Thomas Bonino, OP, Benoît Bourgine, Didier Caenepeel, OP, Christophe Chalamet, Guillaume Cuchet, Alexandra Diriart, CSJ, Jean Doutre, OP, Gilles Emery, OP, Michel Gourgues, OP, Jean-Miguel Garrigues, OP, Christine Gautier, OP, Vincent Holzer, CM, Louis Roy, OP, John Baptist Ku, OP, Matthew Levering, Marie de Lovinfosse, CND, Pierre Magnard, Bruce D. Marshall, Terrence Merrigan, Jean-Christophe de Nadaï, OP, Adriano Oliva, OP, Michał Paluch, OP, Patrick Prétot, OSB, Jean-Pierre Sonnet, SJ, Marc Vial, and Thomas Joseph White, OP. I also thank the peer reviewers of the initial manuscript for their shrewd comments and helpful advices.

For permissions and rights, I thank Cerf Editions, Fleurus-Mame Editions, and Oxford University Press, as well as the directors of *Nova et Vetera* (Fribourg), *Nova et Vetera* (English Ed.), *Recherches de Science Religieuse*, *Revue des Sciences philosophiques et théologiques*, *Revue thomiste*, *Science et Esprit*, *The Thomist*, and *Transversalités*.

Abbreviations

AHDLMA	*Archives d'histoire doctrinale et littéraire du Moyen Âge*
CCC	*Catechism of the Catholic Church*
CCSL	*Corpus Christianorum Series Latina*
Denzinger	*Enchiridion Symbolorum (ed. Hünermann)*
NPNF-II	*Nicene and Post-Nicene Fathers of the Christian Church, Second Series*
RSPT	*Revue des Sciences philosophiques et théologiques*
SC	*Sources Chrétiennes*

Works by Thomas Aquinas

SCG	*Summa contra Gentiles*
Sent.	*Scriptum super libros Sententiarum*
ST	*Summa theologiae*
Sup. Eph.	*Super Epistolam ad Ephesios lectura*
Sup. Heb.	*Super Epistolam ad Hebraeos lectura*
Sup. Io.	*Lectura super Ioannem*
Sup. Mat.	*Lectura super Matthaeum*
Sup. Phil.	*Super Epistolam ad Philippenses lectura*
Sup. Psalmos	*Postilla super Psalmos*
Sup. Rom.	*Super Epistolam ad Romanos lectura*

1

Prologue
Searching for God through Theology

Talking about God with young philosophy students has revealed to me that their horizon suffers from a great absence: God himself is, as it were, "the great absent one" for them. Our conversations remain focused on religion, conceived of as a collection of irrational myths, a structure of oppression, or an existential crutch for the weak. Even if some young people question this outlook, which they have received from their parents and teachers (themselves baby boomers), in order to search for other points of reference, God remains absent from the newly-composed perspectives that they recast in the course of this search.

Hence, I have felt the presence of a fundamental question pressing insistently upon my own awareness: what is the proper perspective to take up when faced with the question of God, so that he may be considered as an acting subject and a living interlocutor, and not a conceptual or religious relic? Where are we to start and how are we to proceed if we are going to speak of God as a real person? The purpose of this prologue is to discern the most relevant registers of speech for our discourse about God. In short: how can we venture to speak anew about God—or, even, facing God—in a befitting way?

A THEOLOGY WITH OR WITHOUT
ETERNAL LIFE?

In the midst of his meditations upon the impasses arrived at by the
Roman religion in *The City of God*, Augustine refers to an ancient
classification of theology into three branches.[1] He relies on the Roman scholar Marcus Varro (116–27 BC) while also criticizing him.
Varro uses a traditional distinction between "mythical theology,"
"natural theology," and "civil theology." While he criticizes the fab-
ulous theology of poets and values the theology of philosophers,
Varro cautiously spares civil theology, which undergirds public worship. Augustine unveils, however, the stark reality: there is no real
difference between the gods of fables and those of the city cults.
Varro does not dare to openly criticize civil theology. Nevertheless,
he suggests to his readers that myths and cults correspond to one
another, so that civil theology is no better than the fables of poets.

Only the "natural theology" of philosophers is noble, for it deals
with the nature of the gods, with things as such. It raises the right
questions:

… what gods there are, where they are, what their origin is and what their
nature, that is, whether they were born at a certain time or have always existed, whether they are of fire as Heraclitus believes, or of numbers as Py-
thagoras thinks, or of atoms as Epicurus says. And there are many other
such points, which our ears can endure to hear better within the walls of a
school than outside in the marketplace.[2]

All these investigations, despite their groping and the disagree-
ments stemming from human weakness, bear witness to an authentic quest for truth.

However, Augustine sets another criterion than reason alone for
evaluating the true nature of theology: hope for felicity and obtain-

---

1. See Augustine, *De civitate Dei* VI.5–9, trans. William M. Green (Cambridge, Mass.:
Harvard University Press, 1988–97); Werner Jaeger, *The Theology of the Early Greek Philosophers* (Oxford: Clarendon Press, 1947), 2–4.

2. Augustine, *De civitate Dei* VI.5 (2:309–11). Augustine quotes here the *Rerum hu-
manarum et divinarum antiquitates* of Marcus Varro.

ing eternal life. Here, civil theology indeed proves to be completely impotent, for it wanders about just as much as does mythological theology. Civil theology cannot lead anyone to eternal bliss, because the gods dealt with by this theology do not bestow happiness upon human beings.

This criterion, namely an effective orientation of "theology" toward eternal life, also reveals, in a muted fashion, the glass ceiling of philosophers' theology. Some of them, like the Neoplatonists, perceived something of the immutability and simplicity of the divine, but they could not offer the means for reaching immortal and blessed life.[3] Through his long personal quest, Augustine discovered and experienced that only Christ is the true mediator of eternal life.[4]

At this point, let us remember two key points. First, rational theology operates as a second-order form of discourse that presupposes the transmission of memory, myths and narratives, cults and practices, as well as the activities of legislators, priests, and prophets. Second, in order for theology to be a form of wisdom, it must enable man to truly gain access to God without merely succumbing to empty and futile discourse about him. This represents a serious challenge, especially in our own era when theology survives mainly in academic settings, themselves subject to industrial or commercial standardization, begetting a culture of "intellectual production." Such conditions are not conducive to learning theology as a spiritual exercise and quest for wisdom.

3. See Augustine, *De civitate Dei* VIII.6; *Confessiones*, trans. Maria Boulding (New York: New City Press, 1997), VII.9.13–15, 20.26–21.27. However, it is possible to develop a more positive vision of philosophy in the ancient world; see Michael Pakaluk, "Philosophy as a Path of Salvation in the Ancient World," in *San Tommaso et la salvezza*, ed. Serge-Thomas Bonino and Guido Mazzotta (Rome: Urbaniana University Press, 2020), 13–29.

4. See Augustine, *De civitate Dei* IX.15; *Confessiones* III.4.8, V.13.23, VII.5.7, 18.24; *De Trinitate* XIII.8.11–10.14. A similar perspective can be found in Thomas Aquinas, *Summa theologiae* [hereafter *ST*] III, prol. Unless otherwise noted, all citations from *ST* are drawn from the English Dominican Fathers' translation (Westminster, Md.: Newman Press, 1952).

BACK TO THE PRIMARY QUESTIONS

In a confessional environment, it would be almost easy to assume that God's identity is his trinitarian mystery: God is the creative and saving Trinity; he is Father, Son, and Spirit in unity and communion. This is perfectly true, but clarifying faith's convictions concerning such matters requires many explanations:

- What does the word "God" mean? Does it mean the same thing to everyone?
- Why is the knowledge of God so elusive from humanity?
- Can a transcendent God intervene in this world?
- Does a transcendent God care about humanity?
- Is God in relationship with human beings considered as individuals?
- Does God experience the suffering that affects his creatures?
- If God is almighty, good, wise, and just, why is there so much suffering in the world?
- Does God change his will in accord with the prayers addressed to him?
- Is God's power limited by human free choices?
- Does God exercise sovereignty over human history? How?

All these questions are crucial for Christian faith. They call for collaboration between faith and reason. To deal with these issues in an appropriate manner, we must mobilize, at once, a firm confidence in a common tradition alongside the human ability to exercise rational discernment. Such a task necessarily takes place in the collective context of dialogue with one's predecessors and contemporaries, in a spirit of receptivity, debate, and a mutual willingness to adjust one's theological positions.

To enter into theological discourse concerning God, precaution is required from committed Christians from the outset. It would be illusory and univocal to wish to draw all knowledge of God from Jesus of Nazareth, even though he is the summit of God's revelation in history. An utter and exclusionary priority of Jesus' humanity over any possible true knowledge of God is not sustainable for two main reasons. On the one hand, the recognition that the man Jesus of Nazareth is the Son of God requires a certain preconception of God, transmitted by biblical revelation and confirmed by natural reason.[5] On the other hand, any theology open to possible dialogue with all presupposes some common meaning of the word "God" which is given in culture. One should then promote a theology that speaks of God from the ground plowed by human reason and biblical tradition together.

REGISTERS OF SPEECH *VIS-À-VIS* GOD

Theology undertakes human discourse concerning God. A confessional theology is based on the ecclesial faith of a given community, supported by a specific tradition. Faith is a response to the word of God, creative and revealing, prior to any human, theological speech concerning God. As regards human speech, it is useful to make some preliminary distinctions in order to identify various registers of speech within theological discourse.

According to the famous linguist Roman Jakobson, different functions of language are more or less involved in every form of verbal communication.[6] Such linguistic functions can be delimited as follows:

- Referential or denotative: some description of the world, context, reality
- Emotional or expressive: the speaker's attitude toward the object being discussed
- Incentive or conative: some action on the recipient, a request for him or her

5. This has been well argued by Wolfhart Pannenberg, *Systematic Theology*, vol. 1, trans. Geoffrey W. Bromiley (Grand Rapids, Mich.: Eerdmans, 1991), 63–73.

6. See Roman Jakobson, "Closing Statement. Linguistics and Poetics," in *Style in Language*, ed. Thomas A. Sebeok (Cambridge, Mass.: MIT Press, 1960), 350–77.

- Phatic: effect on the channel, contact maintenance, code verification
- Poetic: modulations of the form of the statement or the beauty of the language
- Metalinguistic: description of the language, instructions for using the code

Some of the functions of human language are naturally found in theology, through various registers of words. Let us expand on at least three of them.

Speaking about God. Most of the time, theologians compose propositions and chain them together in the form of descriptions or arguments. This register of speech corresponds first and foremost to the referential function of the speech. Here, the dominant parameters of one's statements are the objective adequacy of thought in relation to reality, along with the internal coherence of one's discourse. The other functions of theological language are not significantly mobilized here, at least consciously. Although the speaker's unique identity is inevitably engaged, it remains latent and abstract, only intervening in the discourse in a muted way.

Speaking of God. While, in the previous register, discourse is exclusively concerned with aiming at the referent, in this register, one's emphasis is turned to a kind of triangulation. For example, St. Dominic spoke of God to the Cathars. The "God" reference-frame remains the most decisive parameter of the discourse, the one Dominic was speaking of, but the unique identity of the speaker and the condition of the recipients also shape the discourse in question. St. Dominic often bore witness to God among the Cathars, paying great attention to their own concerns. Speaking of God in this way implies a mission and beneficiaries.

Speaking to God. In this third register, the situation or the state of the speaker, as well as an action or attitude addressed to God as the addressee of the words all have a primary role to play. Here, the expressive and incentive functions of language are mobilized as a priority. For example, Job did not speak about God, or even of God, as his friends could, but rather, spoke directly to God. He did not intend to speak to God in a fine and proper manner, but rather looked to express his incomprehension and his cry to God, so that he would hear it, respond to it, and justify it.

Where should theology be placed among these various registers of human speech? It is always a secondary form of discourse because it is reflexive. In my opinion, theology navigates between speaking about God and speaking of God. It oscillates between referential objectivity and addressed testimony. It should not be reduced to only one of these two registers.

Systematic theology has the task of proposing and explaining the intelligibility of revelation. The referential function of the discourse remains dominant. Nevertheless, theology must also take into account the contexts and dispositions of its immediate or potential addressees. At times, it nearly takes on the character of testimony or preaching. Finally, theology is not a form of human speech directly addressed to God. However, it benefits from listening to the way humble believers speak to God in the form of invocation, complaint, revolt, etc. To enhance theology, in both accuracy and profundity, the theologian must hear in what ways, and under what modulations, our predecessors and contemporaries address God in the midst of their real, often-trying situations, indeed sometimes beyond theological guidelines.[7] In ancient Jewish tradition, psalms are a living expression of theology in action, often addressed to God. Articulated theology always presupposes such a form of address expressed to God. Before beginning to speak of God, one should always seek him at length, listen to him in his word, and speak to him as a humble creature and poor sinner.[8]

---

7. Among our contemporaries, the prior of the monks of Tibhirine, Christian de Chergé, might have been ahead of the Catholic theology of world religions. In his long-term acquaintance with Muslims and Algerian Islam, he wanted above all to join in God's gaze on the hidden meaning of the practices and beliefs of others. See Christian de Chergé, *L'invincible espérance* (Paris: Bayard-Centurion, 1997).

8. See Jean-Yves Lacoste, "*Ressurectio carnis.* Theological Study and Knowledge in Worship," in *The Appearing of God*, trans. Oliver O'Donovan (Oxford: Oxford University Press, 2018), 185, echoing Kierkegaard's *Edifying Discourses*.

FIVE CRUCIAL QUESTIONS

First and foremost, "God" is a proper name, both in day-to-day language and in the language of faith. When a literary café host asks a famous writer, "Do you believe in God?," there is no ambiguity concerning what this question means. The answer does not require prior clarification concerning what it signifies, except for the sake of intellectual elegance. God designates the unique and transcendent principle of all things. At first glance, the word "God" has the same meaning for the believer, the atheist, and the person who is indifferent in matters of religion. Even people from very different backgrounds, cultures, or religions, such as a Vietnamese Buddhist, a Senegalese Muslim, and a South African Lutheran, can answer the question because they understand the discriminatory minimal meaning of the word "God." The way that this simple word, "God," a proper name, refers to what it signifies is operative, whether or not the latter actually exists, whether he is known or remains unknown, etc. The common meaning of the word "God" makes possible several fundamental questions concerning that which it signifies.

DOES GOD EXIST?

This question can indeed receive an uncertain answer, one remaining in the form of a mere opinion. For example: "Yes, God must exist, since so many religions and witnesses speak of him through the ages." Or the other way around: "No, in view of all the woes existing in the world, I cannot accept the claim that God exists." These opinions are not compelling. They are fragile. It is also possible to dare a more committed response in the form of a conviction: that of the believer or that of the atheist. For example: "I have been convinced that God is my Lord and Savior since my conversion at St. Augustine Church in Paris." Or the other way: "I am firmly convinced that God is only the inverted projection of human beings, who deceive themselves by wanting to go beyond the boundaries

that hem in their finite and limited condition." Such statements may
be very convincing, but their subjective justification is not compelling when presented to another human subject.

Philosophers or theologians usually try to answer this question
in a different register than pure opinion or conviction. In philosophy, rational arguments have been developed in favor of God's existence; currents of thought in the Enlightenment, and thereafter,
often took their own shape in deconstructing such reasonings. The
basis for such arguments is provided by some external experience of
the world or by the internal experience of oneself, more or less formalized. Despite multiple refinements in the profiling of these arguments, they have remained fundamentally the same since the time
of Christian antiquity.[9]

In confessional theology, biblical revelation and ecclesial faith
are presupposed. Nevertheless, in the Catholic tradition, it remains
possible and necessary that one construct an argument to show that
it is rational to believe in God on the basis of his revelation and his
creation. Some even argue that it is absolutely necessary for theology
to be able to "demonstrate" the existence of God by means of natural
reason, in order to ensure that human intelligence has the capacity to
pass from phenomena to their transcendent foundation. However,
this remains a point of debate, particularly between the disciples of
Henri de Lubac and those of Thomas Aquinas.[10] In my view, the affirmation of what well-trained minds should know by natural reason
is as decisive as the identification of the cultural conditions favorable to such knowledge,[11] as well as that of the existential obstacles

9. See Wis 13:1–5; Rom 1:20; Plato, *Timaeus* 28c–30a, and *Laws* X; Athenagoras, *Apologia pro Christianis* IV.2; Theophilus of Antioch, *Ad Autolycum* I.4; Irenaeus of Lyons, *Adversus haereses* IV.4.6; Athanasius of Alexandria, *Contra gentes* 38; Clement of Alexandria,
Stromata V, XII.87.1–2; Basil of Caesarea, *Hexaemeron* I.11; Gregory Nazianzen, *Orationes*
28.6, 32.7; Gregory of Nyssa, *Oratio catechetica*, prol. See Anne Richard, *Cosmologie et théologie chez Grégoire de Nazianze* (Paris: Institut d'Études Augustiniennes, 2003), 35–62.

10. See Aquinas, *ST* II-II, q. 109, a. 1. For a strong argument in this direction, see Denys Turner, *Faith, Reason, and the Existence of God* (Cambridge: Cambridge University
Press, 2004).

11. See Serge-Thomas Bonino, "Vertus sociales et sens de Dieu," in his *Études thomasiennes* (Paris: Parole et Silence, 2018), 423–37.

to true recognition. The second aspect was illuminated with a bright light by the Apostle Paul in Romans 1.

The central conviction of this Pauline epistle is that the Gospel, and not the Law, is "the power of God for salvation to everyone who has faith, to the Jew first and also to the Greek" (Rom 1:16).[12] Correlatively, "the righteousness of God is revealed through faith for faith" (Rom 1:17). From this point on, Paul intends to show the universality of sin, in which both the Gentiles and the Jews remain exposed to God's judgment. The Apostle thereby intends to manifest the universality of grace, along with the gratuitousness of justification, accessible to all by faith.

Let us consider how Paul characterizes the sin of the Gentiles in terms of disregard of God and abuse of the truth. By way of contrast, the letter also reveals some of the requirements for having true knowledge of God. The genealogy of sin attributed to the Gentiles does not apply in each of its stages to each individual Gentile. It is an etiological account, along the same lines as the narrative of sin in Genesis 3. Observing the confusion into which the Gentiles are plunged, Paul constructs a theological archetype of the sequence leading to such a situation, thus deriving darkness, idolatry, confusion, and inversions from an inexcusable first act: the refusal to give back to God in proportion to his gift, as a response to his manifestation.

The decisive thesis of Paul's argument is that the sin of the Gentiles is that they hold the truth of God captive by adhering to an injustice (Rom 1:18). The latter is first of all theological in nature, and then ethical. The injustice in question is the opposite of the condition of those who are justified. Paul shows here that the Gentiles are in default as to the justice that proceeds from faith. The same will apply to the Jews.

What grounds the statement that the Gentiles have such a truth in a hidden though silent form, as it were, neutralized by

___

12. All scriptural quotations are taken from the *Revised Standard Version, Second Catholic Edition*, unless otherwise noted.

their injustice? In short: an objective economy of the manifestation (Rom 1:19). God is the author of an act of manifestation of the truth about himself in creation: the invisible attributes of God himself, his power and divinity, are reflected in his visible and tangible works (Rom 1:20). Therefore, on account of this objective economy of manifestation of God in his works, Paul considers the Gentiles to be inexcusable. Their guilt is due to the gap between what is known and what is rendered: they knew him and did not give him glory and thanksgiving (Rom 1:21). The current economy of giving and counter-giving lies in the give-receive-repay sequence. The pivot of any response or non-response lies in the way of receiving the donation.[13] The emergence of any kind of giving in return depends on the freedom of the one who receives the initial gift: will his or her manner of receiving develop into gratitude or not? If the Gentiles knew God's manifestation without giving him glory, the root of their sin lies in the way they receive the manifestation. Where the reception of the gift could (and, indeed, should) have turned into gratitude, what we find, instead, is that they lacked a due spirit of thanksgiving.

It seems that the Gentiles have been positively rejected, leading to a state of complete disorientation: loss of meaning, darkening of the heart, an inversion between wisdom and madness. Hence, by inverting the incorruptible and the corruptible, idolatry arises with all of its senseless practices: instead of worshiping the glory of God to them manifested in his works, they enslave themselves to simple images of ephemeral or vile creatures (Rom 1:22–23). Enslavement to lusts and impurity is then presented as a judgment by God, in the form of the (temporary) abandonment of the Gentiles to their disoriented hearts, with the host of disordered and dehumanizing practices that follow (Rom 1:24). The source of all inversions of right order is located in the human heart. The Gentiles have reversed the truth of God and thus live a lie by giving to the creature what belongs to the creator (Rom 1:25). Therefore, the inversion of

13. See Paul Ricoeur, "La reconnaissance mutuelle," in *Parcours de la reconnaissance* (Paris: Stock, 2004), 221–355.

values and widespread confusion become the prevalent state of affairs, leading all relationships to sink into various forms of alienation.

Denial, lies, madness, lusts, inversions ... all this is derived from a kind of suffocation of the truth in the heart. The truth of God, although manifested, remains unknown or bypassed in order to leave the field open to injustice. Ethical alienation is denounced as a serious consequence of an even more serious theological injustice, located in their relationship with God himself.

Paul achieves a theological *tour de force* here. In the face of pagan ramblings, he does not stop at the symptom, namely ethical disruption, but presses on to the very root of evil, namely, a refusal to give glory to God in response to his self-manifestation. This ultimately amounts to a refusal to respond to God in faith. To give glory to God in response by faith to his new manifestation in Christ is the only thing that might reintroduce justice—both theological justice and ethical justice—into the warp and woof of a now-pagan existence. Basically, according to Paul's interpretation, the typical Gentile—who does not always correspond to the real pagan—voluntarily stops along the path of knowing God, because it would require him or her to place himself or herself entirely under the sovereignty of God, with all the ethical consequences entailed by such submission.

Let us now turn to the rational arguments in favor of God's existence. The point of arrival for this type of argument remains quite circumscribed and limited. It consists in arguing, for example, that it is highly probable that God exists, or that it is necessary to affirm that God exists. It represents a kind of conquest, reaching a point of cognitional stability, and some would say that it is a prerequisite for any possible rational theology. Such statements about the existence of God are qualified by modalities (convergence, probability, necessity) that attest to the limits of reason when left to its own resources in this matter.

The *a priori* (from cause to effect or from essence to properties) and *a posteriori* (from effect to cause) demonstrations applied to the existence of God have been vigorously criticized in modernity by

David Hume and Immanuel Kant.[14] However, such criticisms are not decisive for those who support a rational argument for God's existence. Nevertheless, the emphasis has shifted.

First, contemporary philosophers who present arguments in favor of the existence of God hold that they are probable, parsimonious, convergent, or coherent.[15] As a general rule, they do not claim a binding demonstrative value for each of their arguments taken in isolation. Rather, they present a set of arguments with a high probability or a compelling convergence.

Second, the debate has partly shifted from a review of arguments to an epistemology of beliefs. The objective of the latter is to show the legitimacy and rational validity of theistic or Christian beliefs.[16] The guiding perspective has thus become apologetic in the proper sense. Here, the aim is to show that a belief, regardless of whether or not its object can be demonstrated, can be legitimate and guaranteed, in particular by the practice of certain intellectual virtues and by respect for certain cognitive procedures. Such statements defend the rational legitimacy of believing against prohibitions or disqualifications of religious beliefs as projective, infantile, oppressive, etc.

From an epistemological perspective, one may ask why good arguments in favor of God's existence only very rarely call into question the previous convictions of both parties.[17] Such a lack of existential efficiency does not, however, take away their value as good rational arguments.

An argument always presupposes primary certainties, which cannot (and will not) be demonstrated. Any argument thus makes sense on a specific background, which is not itself demonstrated. A conclusion is accepted because of the value of the argument, which

14. See Immanuel Kant, "The Ideal of Pure Reason I–VII," in *Critique of Pure Reason* (Cambridge: Cambridge University Press, 1998), 551–623 (A568/B596–A704/B732).

15. See Alvin Plantinga, "Two Dozen (or so) Theistic Arguments," in *Alvin Plantinga: God's Philosopher*, ed. Deane-Peter Baker (Cambridge: Cambridge University Press, 2007), 203–27.

16. See Alvin Plantinga, *Warranted Christian Belief* (Oxford: Oxford University Press, 2000); Roger Pouivet, *Épistémologie des croyances religieuses* (Paris: Cerf, 2013).

17. See Pouivet, *Épistémologie des croyances religieuses*, 53–59.

depends on its degree of consistency with the subject's primary certainties. When an argument is rationally compelling, pressing against the prior convictions of a particular person, he or she remains free to question (or not to question) his or her prior conviction on the basis of that argument.

For example, an atheist may very well acknowledge the metaphysical validity of the theistic argument built on contingency and necessity, while remaining unable or unwilling to question his or her presupposition of atheism. In most cases, given the great and demanding costs involved in reworking one's prior convictions, such worldview reconstruction is not consented to by the mere recognition of the validity or convergence of rational arguments. Such alterations would have such existential consequences for the subject that he or she should be forced to consent to it through some other power than that of argumentative reason. This sometimes happens under the shock of an event: an unprecedented encounter, a serious illness, the loss of a loved one, a confrontation at an impassable limit, etc.

Most rational arguments in favor of the existence of God, whose name is derived from religious traditions, can be rationally questioned or even challenged.[18] However, even if "God" is denied or rejected by reason, he remains fundamentally a question, concern, or enigma for human intelligence, whether in the form of expectation, atheism, or uncertainty.

From a theological perspective, such arguments and discussion concerning them attest to the possibility that human intelligence is open to God, even if this possibility remains hemmed in by many doubts and possible errors. Openness, however, is decisive, for it represents the anthropological foundation for the possibility of reasonably believing.

---

18. See, for example, the difficulties or uncertainties raised by Fernand Van Steenberghen, *Le problème de l'existence de Dieu dans les écrits de saint Thomas d'Aquin* (Louvain-La-Neuve: Institut supérieur de philosophie, 1980), 235–44; John F. Wippel, *The Metaphysical Thought of Thomas Aquinas* (Washington, D.C.: The Catholic University of America Press, 2000), 497–500.

Thus, rational arguments in favor of the existence of God do have a function, albeit a limited function. On the one hand, they reinforce the previous convictions of those who adhere to theistic or Christian beliefs, demonstrating the rationality of such beliefs. On the other hand, they make it possible to maintain toward nonbelievers that it is not irrational or irresponsible to believe, without this being sufficient, however, to convince a nonbeliever that it is right and good to believe.

WHAT IS GOD?

Such a question may have two different meanings, depending on the depth of one's questioning. On the one hand, the solution is simply to clarify the common meaning of the term "God." As I have already stated, the signification of the word is commonly clear and available, both to those who assert it and to those who deny it. God is the unique and transcendent creator of the whole world.

On the other hand, the question concerns the essence of God, what he is in himself. In the tradition of the Church Fathers, most famously in the East,[19] this is not within reach of our human intelligence. No proportion exists between, on the one hand, our ability to apprehend or conceive and, on the other, the essence of God. We can understand the meaning of the word "God," but not his essence. Some rationalists thought that it was possible to have an immediate evidence or intuition of God, from which would flow the certainty of his existence and a vision of all things from him. But such knowledge is not, in the end, intramundane. To overcome our inability to do so requires us to travel indirectly upon byways. Although we are unable to conceive God's essence, we can, for example, discard a number of properties that do not suit him (e.g., corporeality, lying,

19. Among the Cappadocian Fathers, in response to the excessive claims of Eunomianism, see Basil of Caesarea, *Letter 234*, 2; *Contra Eunomium* I.12. Likewise, see Clement of Alexandria, *Stromata V*, X.71.3; Philo of Alexandria, *De posteritate Caini* 168; *De specialibus legibus* I.32–40; Plotinus, *Enneads* V.3.14.

or shame).[20] At least this prevents God from being understood in a manner unworthy of his eminent dignity.

We can also infer some segmented determinations of his essence from his effects in creation. For example, the beauty, order, and excessive grandeur of a starry sky at night elevate the soul, leading it to feel reverence in the face of God's greatness, however little circumscribed the latter may be. To define God's essence lies beyond the scope of our powers of conception. Therefore, we must proceed by means of negations and inferences, while cultivating the meaning of its excess—in other words, its eminence.

WHO IS GOD?

"Who is a God like you"? (Mi 7:18). Such a question seems more decisive than the two previous ones, which are nevertheless essential to the truth of this one. Surprisingly, the question of "who" has been little formalized in classical theology, as if it were presupposed, obvious, or offscreen. However, it is directly raised by some saints or witnesses. Thus, according to oral tradition, Francis of Assisi asked God: "Who am I? Who are you?"

Certainly, the difference between "what?" and "who is this?" does not refer to a real distinction on God's side. Unlike humans, in whom essence and subject are really distinct (the essence being shared with all other humans), deity and God are not really distinct. God is not composed of essence and subject (*suppositum*), nor of abstract and concrete.[21] The difference between "what is God?" and "who is God?" is entirely a matter pertaining to our human way of knowing. From this perspective, the distance separating the two questions is significant, on the one hand, because of the fragmentary nature of our knowledge of God and, on the other, because of

20. See Gregory P. Rocca, *Speaking the Incomprehensible God: Thomas Aquinas on the Interplay of Positive and Negative Theology* (Washington, D.C.: The Catholic University of America Press, 2004); Thierry-Dominique Humbrecht, *Théologie négative et noms divins chez saint Thomas d'Aquin* (Paris: Vrin, 2006).

21. See Aquinas, *ST* I, q. 3, a. 3.

the different ways that the questioning person finds himself or herself thereby to be involved on these two fronts.

To ask the question "who?" is identical to seeking to know God as the personal subject of his own actions and of his original mode of manifestation. Indeed, a subject is revealed by his or her operations and actions. Action reflects the personal identity of the person who performs it. To the question "who is he?" or "who are you?" responds a unique story, such as a narrative of projects, actions, and commitments.

Here again, a logic of inference has a role to play, though it is more personal in nature than what we find in the ascent from the properties of the created to the unknown properties of God. Moreover, the effects on which it is based, leading to knowledge of God within the regime of grace are "more numerous and more excellent."[22] Through God's actions in the history of the covenant, we acquire knowledge of the subject thus engaged. The passage from action to the author is intuitive, especially because God acts in a unique way, with actions that are enlightened by his word.

By the question "who is he?" we identify God as the one who initiates the word of creation, election, and covenant. At the same time, we recognize him as our potential interlocutor, as the one to whom we can address our prayers and to whom we can give our entire confidence. The question of the "who" ultimately implies the framework of a possible, expected, and hoped-for dialogue or covenantal relationship.

At the beginning of his *Confessions*, Augustine develops a brief theology of God's invocation, in practice.[23] While addressing God directly, Augustine explores how his desire to praise and invoke God develops and justifies itself. Augustine immediately addressed God in the form of "You." For this, he is freely inspired by the Psalms, taking up the direct invocation of the Lord in his greatness (see Ps 48:1, 96:4, 145:3). Before pondering the act he is performing (praise and invo-

22. See ibid., q. 12, a. 13, ad 1. See chapter 11 of this volume.
23. See Augustine, *Confessiones* I.1–5.

cation), Augustine is actually performing it as his truest and most spontaneous way of speaking, not *of* God, but *to* him.

The impulse of praise, the willingness to praise, is the focus of reflection only thereafter. Augustine wonders about the profound appeal of praise. The first qualification of the person who wills to praise is that he or she is an "ordinary part" of creation. Two aspects can be discerned here. First, because they are a part of creation, it is normal and expected that human beings praise God, their creator, as every creature does in its own way. Second, like any part of creation, one part among many, what is the great impulse driving the human will onward to praise God? The properties of human beings then mentioned—mortality and sin—might be understood either as additional reasons for praising God or as obstacles to be overcome in order to praise God. Mortal and sinful, human beings can easily turn against their creator and repress the impulse of praise within themselves. This entails flight from God in the form of a kind of death spiral. On the other hand, precisely because they are mortal and sinful, human beings have every reason to want to be in contact with their creator through praise, for without him they are lost.

According to Augustine's judgment, the desire to praise God is an ineradicable element of the human heart. Mortal and sinful, he or she nevertheless remains more radically a part of creation and, as such, he or she is animated by an irrepressible desire to praise God, the creator. This is an essential property of the creaturely condition. Human beings can frustrate it, but they cannot extinguish it.

The human will to praise God can also be directly related to God's action. Augustine does this in the form of a word addressed to God: "You arouse us so that praising you may bring us joy, because you have made us and drawn us to yourself, and our heart is unquiet until it rest in you."[24] The creator excites in human beings the desire to praise God through the mediation of spiritual delight (*delectare*). This is an indication that the activity of praising is marked by its own sort of finality.

24. Ibid., I.1.1 (39).

The delight of praising God is a sign and property of human beings' positive orientation toward God, imprinted upon them by the creator. The other sign, one even more profound than the latter, is the anxiety of the heart which affects human beings as long as they do not find rest in God, fixing in them their unstable will, leading them to errantly wander about, unmoored from any truly stable points of reference.

Augustine then wonders, in dialogue with God, about the order found between invoking, praising, and knowing. It seems that invoking is the first step of praise, so that the discernment focuses here on the order between knowing and invoking. On the one hand, it seems that we must first know in order to be able to invoke. On the other hand, we might invoke in order to know, driven by our desire to know. The dilemma is not resolved by any autonomous dialectic. It falls to the biblical word to untie this knot. Augustine quotes Romans 10:14 ("How shall they call on [the Lord] in whom they have not believed?") and Psalm 22:27 ("they shall praise the Lord those who seek him"), and using the latter as a basis, he suggests the following solution: invoking is a way of searching. Hence the sequence: search (= invoke) → find → praise. Invocation comes before praise. Here Romans 10:14 intervenes. Invoking does imply a certain mode of knowledge, that is, of believing. And belief in turn presupposes having heard, in other words, having been preached to. Preaching is an accomplished reality for Augustine. Indeed, he was preached into the faith. He relates his faith to God himself, while emphasizing that this gift has been accomplished through mediation: the preaching of the Son in his humanity. The preacher is Christ himself.

Invocation is therefore the first step toward praise. It represents a concrete expression of the quest for God inscribed in the heart of every human being by God himself. We might invoke God in order to know him even more, but invoking him already implies that we believe in him, as a gift received from God in synergy with the preaching of Christ.

This argument is followed by Augustine's meditation on the paradox of calling God, by invocation, to come into him when God is already in him, for otherwise Augustine would not be present at all. God cannot be contained by anything, though indeed he fills everything.[25] From the paradox of this calling, Augustine is finally led to the even-deeper paradoxes of God's own modes of being.

Four questions open up this meditation on God. The first two ask "what?" (*quid*), the last two "who?" (*quis*). These questions are not about God considered in an abstract and nonrelational manner, but about "my God" and "our God." At the heart of these questions lies the exclusive identity of the Lord (*Dominus*). A sequence of variations, either superabundant or paradoxical, answers both types of questions: that relating to essence (*quid*) and that relating to identity (*quis*). Essence is first and foremost equated to a number of eminent qualities:

You are most high, excellent, most powerful, omnipotent, supremely merciful and supremely just, most hidden yet intimately present, infinitely beautiful and infinitely strong, steadfast yet elusive, unchanging yourself though you control the change in all things, never new, never old, renewing all things yet wearing down the proud though they know it not; ever active, ever at rest, gathering while knowing no need, supporting and filling and guarding, creating and nurturing and perfecting, seeking although you lack nothing.[26]

This list refers to the paradoxes of the divine essence and sequences involved in the divine action toward creation. On the other hand, identity is given its full expression through a series of statements beginning with the personal pronoun "you":

You love without frenzy, you are jealous yet secure, you regret without sadness, you grow angry yet remain tranquil, you alter your works but never your plan, you take back what you find although you never lost it, you are never in need yet you rejoice in your gains, never avaricious yet you demand profits. You allow us to pay you more than you demand, and so you become our debtor, yet which of us possesses anything that does not already belong to you? You owe us nothing yet you pay your debts; you write off our debts to you, yet you lose nothing thereby.[27]

---

25. See ibid., I.2.2–3.3.
26. Ibid., I.4.4 (41).
27. Ibid.

These paradoxical statements accentuate the personal traits of the divine physiognomy. Finally, Augustine returns to the status of his own speech. He tried to say things worthy of God, but they remain mere words about God, whereas he was seeking above all to speak to God. It is to God himself, his sweetness and his life, that he in the end expresses both the inadequacy of his own words about God and the need to speak in this way, so as not to endlessly prattle by speaking about everything but God.

Within theology taking on the form of a personal confession, the construction of human discourse should remain ideally driven by the ultimate question: who are you? The horizon of research and discourse is to foster listening to the word of God and the human person's response. Such a confession is mediated through various registers of human words: praise, supplication, thanksgiving, doxology. Dialogue with God goes far beyond theology, but it also outlines its possible horizon.

WHERE IS GOD?

Without a basic underpinning of metaphysical insight, the question "where is God?" could reflect a latent confusion about the possible localization of God as a hyper-object situated somehow above the world. In order for the question of "where?" to take on a relevant meaning, one must first clarify some characteristic features of God's transcendence, without falling into the dead ends of Deism or into the prohibitions against the possibility of his presence.

In any case, in our own days, the question "who?," directly related to the identity of God, has been replaced by a painful question that is felt to be more urgent: where is God? This is connected to a loss of evidence that there is any room for "God" in the world as it is and below our horizon of existence.[28] Since the seventeenth century, westerners have been living under the primacy of human au-

28. See Eberhard Jüngel, *God as the Mystery of the World*, trans. Geoffrey Wainwright (Edinburgh: T and T Clark, 1983), 49–104.

tonomy, in the related fields of religion, action, politics, conscience, knowledge, technology, etc.[29] This situation, no longer immediately needing God to ground sciences or to fill the gaps of human knowledge, naturally enough leads men and women to live as though God did not exist, as though he were not a given within human existence. Such autonomy can be interpreted as representing a form of progress or, by contrast, nothing more than a mirage. The fact is that it leaves the question of "where is God?" hanging in this human world which functions without God. The question is not only concerned with the possible localization of God, but also with the discernible or undetectable reality of his presence and action, or even his intervention, in the world.

Even more vividly, such a question stems from the scandal experienced when facing unbearable evils, which evacuate or annihilate any image of "God," because he is not compatible with such evils perpetrated before our eyes. The emergence of the question, "For God's sake, where is God?," was told in a shocking way by Elie Wiesel, in the context of death camps, when facing the prolonged agony of a teenager hanged too lightly to die quickly. The reply was heard as a voice that rose from the depths in the narrator's soul: "Where is he? This is where—hanging here from this gallows …"[30] Wiesel's inner voice leads to various interpretations, undecided and contiguous, all concerned about what happens here on earth: God is not here, God is dead, God does not exist, God hangs there, God is innocent, God is present, God is crucified … all these possibilities do however refer to the question "who is God?" Is it our own image of the "merciful God" who died? Who is God to be hung on the wood with this child? Even if God were powerlessly located here below, his identity would still be at stake. This poignant story became a prototype of the questions raised after Auschwitz.

29. See Wilhelm Dilthey, *Weltanschauung und Analyse des Menschen seit Renaissance und Reformation* (Stuttgart / Göttingen: B. G. Teubner / Vandenhoeck and Ruprecht, 1964), 246–83; Dietrich Bonhoeffer, *Letters and Papers from Prison* (New York: Touchtone, 1997), letter of July 16, 1944.

30. Elie Wiesel, *Night* (Toronto: Bentam Books, 1986), 61–62.

The statement of the question includes a reminiscence of the Book of Psalms: "Where is your God?"[31] It would be a pity to dismiss the question "where?" by attributing it exclusively to skeptics and opponents, as it is *de facto* the case in the aforementioned psalms (see also Mi 7:10). The possible meanings of such a provocation must be honored in various contexts of application.[32] Nevertheless, beyond irony or derision, the question also has a positive value because it requires us to thwart our attempts to construct false localizations for God and to seek true attestations of his presence.

Facing scenes of evil, here and now, it seems indecent to answer, without further comment: "Our God is in the heavens" (Ps 115[113]:3). This could be understood as a terrible admission of God's absence or as the full license granted to human beings to manage their affairs and misfortunes without God.[33] However, we can refine our interpretation of the psalmist's response to the question "where?" When he comments on Psalm 42(41):5, Thomas Aquinas narrates the quest of the soul that tends toward God without stopping at the wrong place: it finds only traces of God among creatures without reason; God does not reside permanently in the intellectual powers of the soul. According to the psalmist, God is present in a tent and in a Temple, where one can only pass through. Indeed, these places signify the present church, which itself refers to the only stable house of God: the admirable tent prepared for the saints in eschatological heavens.[34]

31. See Ps 42:3, 10; 79:10; 115:2.

32. For example, Thomas Aquinas explores three possible configurations underlying Ps 42:2: a question addressed by pagans to catechumens, or by an unfaithful Jew to a converted Jew, or by a sinner to a just afflicted person; see Aquinas, *Postilla super Psalmos* [hereafter *Sup. Psalmos*] 42:2. A similar question is put on Job's lips by his friend Elihou; see Jb 35:10: "ubi est Deus qui fecit me?"; Aquinas, *Expositio super Iob ad litteram* 35:10 (ed. Leonine, 186). A similar provocation is also found in the mouth of the Pharisees in John 8:19: "ubi est pater tuus?"; see Aquinas, *Lectura super Ioannem* [hereafter *Sup. Io.*] VIII, 19, ed. Marietti (1952), no. 1159.

33. See John Locke, *The Second Treatise of Government*, chap. 5, §25, in his *Two Treatises of Government*, ed. Peter Laslett (Cambridge: Cambridge University Press, 1994), 285–86.

34. See Aquinas, *Sup. Psalmos* 42:5.

HOW LONG, LORD?

This other question is much more direct. It involves the person and is addressed to God himself. Like the previous one, it is found several times in the Book of Psalms: "How long, O Lord? Will you forget me forever? How long will you hide your face from me? How long must I bear pain in my soul, and have sorrow in my heart all the day? How long shall my enemy be exalted over me?" (Ps 13:1–2). In the Psalms, it is most often the praying person who directly addresses God with the question "How long?"[35] However, God also calls out to human beings or pagan princes in this way (Pss 4:2, 82:2). The question arises time and again in the Bible, either because the Lord thus calls out to his people (Nm 14:11, Jer 4:14, Hos 8:5) or a prophet (1 Sm 16:1), or because the people (Jer 4:21) or prophets (Is 6:11, Jer 12:4, Hab 1:2) challenge God to answer the same question.

Some people access theological questioning through this kind of direct questioning, and truth be told, they thereby find themselves to be closer to the experience of the people of the Bible than the conventional form adopted by Western theology. There is no theoretical atheism in the biblical tradition, but some address their existential questions to God, while others prefer to avoid such a confrontation and live as though God did not exist.[36]

Psalm 88(87) is unique in the Psalter and practically in the whole Bible (with the exception of Jb 16:7–14), for the psalmist addresses God as though he were his persecutor, his direct and personal enemy who reduces him mercilessly to suffering, solitude, death, and darkness. With the exception of the initial call, which is full of mean-

---

35. See Ps 6:4, 13:2, 74:10, 79:5, 80:4, 89:46, 90:13, 94:3. It also happens that the prayer launches invectives at enemies or false friends by means the same question; see Ps 62:3, Jb 19:2. Joshua and Elijah thus challenged the rebellious or undecided people; see Jos 18:3, 1 Kgs 18:21. In the Synoptics, Jesus similarly expresses his exasperation toward "this incredulous generation"; see Mt 17:17, Mk 9:19, Lk 9:41.

36. See Jacques Vermeylen, "Le fou dit dans son cœur: pas de Dieu! Comment le Premier Testament parle-t-il de l'incroyance?," *Mélanges de Science Religieuse* 63, no. 3 (2006): 7–20.

ing in such a context—"God of my salvation"—the psalm contains no positive note about God's action toward the psalmist. The situation in which the praying person is locked appears to him as though concrete reality is asserting a denial of his faith. He opposes the God of his faith with the distorted image of an evil God with whom he struggles in his ordeal. Theologically, this psalm suggests that prayer can express directly to God, in the form of protest and complaint, qualifications that one could in no way attribute to God in the form of theoretical discourse about him.[37] Direct address provides the only context in which such words are true and revelatory.

God is directly called upon as the author of the evils afflicting the psalmist, but he is called upon within a prayer in the form of crying, lamentation, and supplication. Like Job, the praying man is sure of his innocence in the midst of his misfortunes and that he cannot attribute them to anyone other than God. The psalmist can no longer be satisfied with mere perseverance in trust. He demands a recovery that does not come. Therefore, in this psalm, there is great tension between God as he can be characterized from the desolation to which the praying person is reduced and God as he remains the one who is both believed and challenged within this situation. Nevertheless, the expression "God of my salvation" bears witness to the psalmist's faith at the very depths of the ordeal. By the leap of faith that allows him to address his complaint and revolt to God in the form of prayer, the psalmist gives God the opportunity to reveal himself to him as he is believed and hoped for, and no longer as the situation portrays him, namely as a merciless enemy. In other words, we here see the gulf which separates God considered as the concluding terminus of an inference from the condition of an overwhelmed creature—the context in which the praying person is enclosed—and God addressed as being the only one capable of reversing the intractable, closed-off situation in which he is infinitely distressed.

At the center of his plea, the psalmist draws on the biblical con-

---

37. See Bernd Janowski, *Arguing with God: A Theological Anthropology of the Psalms,* trans. Armin Siedlecki (Louisville, Ky.: Westminster John Knox Press, 2013), 222.

viction that God himself suffers a loss every time a dead person falls into oblivion, for a potential witness to God's wonders thereby disappears.[38] All the distress thus expressed before God, including when it is expressed in the generalized form concerning the dead, has the value of an *ad Deum* argument, so that God may intervene for his supplicant and at the same time save his own image, the only true one, to which the praises of the living respond for his wonders. At the end of the Book of Job, while the latter had designated God as his enemy and aggressor, God rehabilitates and justifies him by affirming twice, against his friends, that Job spoke of God with righteousness (Jb 16:7–14, 42:7–8). It is an extrinsic confirmation of the legitimacy of Psalm 88 in its invective addressed to God.

The language of the Psalms embraces the whole of our own language during our time as wayfarers. These are the words of proven faith. Such words are true by way of first intention. They have a coefficient of truth closer to real life and determined faith than the derivative language belonging to discursive theology. More generally, it is important not to separate intellectual questioning about God from our relational dispositions toward him. This is also a requirement of intellectual honesty, because our own orientation in relation to God constantly influences the way we think about him.

A WELL-GROUNDED CONFESSING THEOLOGY

More radically, how might we ground the possibility of any human discourse that fits God's uniqueness? Does the incommensurability between God and man disqualify from the start any human discourse about God? It is easy to believe this and to relativize traditions, doctrines, and theologies in their claim for truth. As the only and transcendent creator of all things, God is so radically different from man that human words seem, at first sight, powerless to offer any truth about God or to establish real communication with him.

38. With Ps 88, see Ps 6:5, 30:9, 115:17; Sir 17:27–28.

Are we then condemned to wander about and make mistakes about God, as our contemporaries often think? Yet believers confidently raise their prayers to God and Christians receive the scriptures as the fruit of prophecy.

Prayer and prophecy attest that communication with God is possible in both directions: from human beings to God and from God to human beings.[39] This opens the possibility of uttering human words that are true and meaningful regarding God, even though they remain merely human. Indeed, both prayer and prophecy fulfill an unexpected translation: human expectations and desires are presented to the divine attention through prayer, while God's gaze, word, and design are translated into human language through prophecy. This double movement is accomplished in the very person of Jesus, true God and true man, ensuring a two-way mediation, from human beings to God and from God to human beings.

Prayer attests that human words can reach God in some way. Prophecy is a manifestation of how the divine word is addressed to mankind in human language without being betrayed. Prayer and prophecy open the way to theology. They guarantee that it is possible to speak to God and to speak of God in truth. Certainly, this remains a challenge for any theology. Its reliability should be assessed according to its impregnation by or exclusion from the word of scripture. For theology to remain aware of this in the long run, the labor of human discourse must be anchored both in an ecclesial practice of prayer and in a careful listening to scripture, which is the fruit of prophecy.

To know the living God, several approaches are possible and might be combined. We shall discover them in action and integrate them through our theological investigations. At this preliminary

39. See Adrian Schenker, "De la validité de l'exégèse croyante de la Bible," *Revue des Sciences philosophiques et théologiques* [hereafter *RSPT*] 97, no. 4 (2013): 449–57. For Aquinas, the principles of the *sacra doctrina* are received by the mode of revelation on the part of the ones who communicate them, like the prophets, and by the mode of prayer on the part of the ones who receive them, like the psalmists; see Aquinas, *Scriptum super libros Sententiarum* [hereafter *Sent.*] I, prol., a. 5, resp.

stage, we merely need to identify the multiple points of support that a theology as confession might use.

First, through the testimony of the Old Testament, a memory of God's commitments and achievements in Israel's history is transmitted: election, creation, exodus, the gift and renewal of the covenant, etc. A confession of faith joins together these actions into a common narrative. The events of salvation are celebrated, recapitulated, and constantly renewed in the Jewish-Christian tradition. For instance, Wisdom 10–19 amplifies and universalizes the memory of the exodus. The mighty deeds of salvation are often read as being the mirror image of God's creative work, or even as a new creation. Through them, God reveals himself as the unique author of all things.

Second, through his advent, his public ministry, his trial and his passion, and then his apparitions as the risen One, Jesus made liberating and unprecedented gestures, pronounced teachings imbued with a new authority (*exousia*), accomplished overwhelming signs for their beneficiaries and witnesses, etc. The four Gospels present the testimony of those who gathered these actions and words as a full and definitive revelation. Jesus' concrete humanity, with its filial expressiveness led onward to its paroxysm by the passion, is God's presence among human beings. Since Pentecost, the church has been preaching and transmitting this very gospel.

Third, through their structural and distinctive polarities (carnal and spiritual, man and woman, knowing and willing, autonomous and dependent, etc.), human beings reveal the profound aspirations that constitute and lead them. These polarities are both a source of dynamism and a factor of fragility, internal conflicts, and even complete collapse. Through the tension between undefined desire and tested limits, human beings long for the infinite Other. With wills that are, in fact, oriented toward infinity, they often suffer from wanting the finite objects of a limited will. By faith, such a gulf can be related to the condition of a creature made in the image of God, as a capacity unable to achieve its own fulfillment by itself.

Fourth, human beings are often confronted with the enigma of their own condition. At times, they remain obscure or opaque to themselves. Like Paul or Augustine, they experience the fact that they are a question or a mystery in their own eyes. Through the resources of mind and reason, human beings seek the truth. They do not accept payment in the form of lies. They seek reliable statements, true testimony, and valid arguments. Even disillusioned, skeptical, or indifferent people expect the truth from their spouses and children. Without being entirely self-confident, the human capacity to reach the truth is an ally in seeking God. If we seek a hierarchy of approaches, the quest for truth is not in itself higher than the undefined desire that troubles the human heart. Rather, it is a specific modulation of it. Still, the quest for truth often seems more determined than unfathomable desire, which is more easily trapped in its attachment to its immediate object. As the *Confessions* of St. Augustine testify, we often have to go through dissatisfactions and disappointments if we are to have access to our deepest aspiration toward God.

Fifth, the order and beauty perceptible in the universe and in nature commonly elevate the human soul toward God and lead it to a kind of contemplation. This represents a positive aspect to which individuals are more or less sensitive. Wonder felt before infinite vistas like mountains, oceans, deserts, and starry skies draws the soul to God or turns it toward an unknown transcendence. However, we know how easily one stops on this path (Wis 13:1–8), or even willingly restrains oneself, refusing to render glory to God through true, self-oblative contemplation of him (Rom 1:18–25). The testimony of creation also entails another dimension, one that is less serene, though more effective. The profusion and disproportion of the cosmos seize human beings or lead them to experience vertigo, and this can lead them back to a fully-acknowledged dependence on God, as in the words of the psalmist: "When I look at your heavens, the work of your fingers, the moon and the stars which you have established; what is man that you are mindful of him, and the son of man that you care for him?" (Ps 8:3–4).

CENTRAL THESIS AND GENERAL METHODOLOGY

The central thesis of this volume is that the portrait of God revealed in scripture is fundamentally intelligible. As expressed in this introduction, the book seeks to address our contemporary culture's profound sense, one felt most keenly in academic milieus, that the biblical God is a weak concept that cannot be taken seriously by those wishing to reflect rationally concerning God's existence, nature, and relations with creation. In the following chapters, I will address a number of problems or questions that arise when one attempts to think about the God of biblical revelation. Generally, I approach these topics by laying out certain questions or apparent contradictions surrounding the human understanding of God as revealed, attempting to articulate such concerns in a sympathetic and thoughtful manner. In general, I then introduce certain philosophical distinctions drawn from the Thomistic tradition as aids for thinking through the given issues under discussion. Such philosophical instruments can indeed open pathways toward a solution; however, they are not sufficient by themselves.

Thus, the reader will note that, throughout my reflection, I feel the need to move on to a properly theological mode of reflection, considering the question from the perspective of biblical revelation. Such engagement with key biblical passages and/or events from both Testaments helps to facilitate the discovery of a more fruitful path forward for thinking through the issue at hand. These theological issues cannot be solved by means of logic alone but, rather, call for the use of sapiential argumentation and metaphysical considerations, illuminated by the light of faith. These instruments enable us to think through the given biblical issue in a way that admits the tensions which exist in our understanding of God. Such tensions are typically addressed in the biblical witness, especially when received with Aquinas's presentation of *sacra doctrina* and theological language. The book's key contribution to contemporary discussions is to show how a thoughtful Thomistic practice of theology can enable one to navigate through theological problems (both contemporary and perennial ones).

The biblical witness is received as a truly intelligible and truthful manner of speaking of God, who himself speaks to us through this witness. Collaborative volumes classified as "Biblical Thomism" usually study how Aquinas reads and uses scripture in his works.[40] In the essays gathered here, I attempt to offer a contemporary way of achieving this same goal, according to a mode of thinking inspired by Aquinas, though not always seeking after his own literal position concerning topics related to the contemporary questions that I raise herein.

The overall trajectory of the essays gathered in this volume can be summarized as follows. Chapter 1 is a prologue for the whole book. Chapters 2 to 10 deal with names or attributes of God through a bifocal approach, at once scriptural and sapiential. Metaphysics and narratives, as well as invocations, seem to be mutually exclusive. My goal in these chapters is to explore the fruitfulness of a simultaneously biblical and metaphysical theology for considering God's holiness and transcendence, the passions of the biblical God, divine immutability *versus* God's lament, almightiness facing the impossible, divine providence and prayer, the modes of divine action according to the Creed, and the extension of God's saving will in view of human freedom. Chapters 11 to 18 trace the lineaments of a theology—here focused on Trinity and Christ—that is at once rigorous and spiritual, rooted in the economy of revelation. I develop arguments about the epistemol-

---

40. See Michael Dauphinais and Matthew Levering (eds.), *Reading John with St. Thomas Aquinas: Theological Exegesis and Speculative Theology* (Washington, D.C.: The Catholic University of America Press, 2010); Dauphinais and Levering (eds.), *Reading Romans with St. Thomas Aquinas* (Washington, D.C.: The Catholic University of America Press, 2012); Matthew Levering, Piotr Roszak, and Jörgen Vijgen (eds.), *Reading Job with St. Thomas Aquinas* (Washington, D.C.: The Catholic University of America Press, 2020); Piotr Roszak and Jörgen Vijgen (eds.), *Reading Sacred Scripture with Thomas Aquinas: Hermeneutical Tools, Theological Questions and New Perspectives* (Turnhout: Brepols, 2015); Roszak and Vijgen (eds.), *Towards a Biblical Thomism: Thomas Aquinas and the Renewal of Biblical Theology* (Pamplona: EUNSA, 2018).

ogy of Catholic theology, the illuminative function of trinitarian faith, the ultimate position of God the Father beyond the divide between Christocentrism and theocentrism, the unique way by which Christ transcends the world he enters into, the multi-faceted "conversation" of Christ with his contemporaries, as well as the universal amplitude of a singular event—the incarnation—for the sake of our salvation.

PART 1

The Holy One and His Providence

2

God's Holiness

A Reappraisal of Transcendence

In the Hebrew Bible, God is often designated as the Almighty One. God is located in heaven, or even beyond the heavens (Ps 115:3). God exceeds and watches over God's entire creation. God sits in heaven on a lofty throne (Is 6:1). God thus seems to have the features of separation and hierarchy which are valid among beings in our world: altitude, distance. However, the Hebrew Bible never expresses God's elevation in a way that might contradict his proximity to those who are humble: "For thus says the high and lofty One who inhabits eternity, whose name is Holy: 'I dwell in the high and holy place, and also with those who are contrite and humble in spirit, to revive the spirit of the humble, and to revive the heart of the contrite' (Is 57:15)."[1] The true God is both very high and very near, different and intimate, free and committed, especially toward those who are humble.

In this chapter, I will try to articulate, in a nontechnical manner, the following thesis, which will be enriched along the way: God's revealed holiness enables us to critique a superficial conception of transcendence, understood as a kind of projective difference. Where

---

1. See Richard Bauckham, "God Crucified," in his *Jesus and the God of Israel* (Grand Rapids, Mich.: Eerdmans, 2008), 35–37.

such a misconception is held, it is a symptom of some form of Deism that has been assimilated by our imagination.

When we think of God's holiness, we cannot escape the injunctions of Leviticus. Holiness requires separated spaces, as well as rituals of consecration and purification. God alone is holy, undoubtedly; however, God invites the members of his people to become holy as well, through all kinds of practices and observances. The major justification of those practices proves to be highly theological: "For I am the LORD your God; consecrate yourselves therefore, and be holy, for I am holy. You shall not defile yourselves with any swarming thing that crawls upon the earth. For I am the LORD who brought you up out of the land of Egypt, to be your God; you shall therefore be holy, for I am holy" (Lv 11:44–45).[2] The entire pedagogy of ritual holiness is related to the exodus, the salvific event which grounds the covenant, along with its requirements in terms of membership. God's self-designation as being holy makes use of an abiding paradox: holiness requires separations and, at the same time is marked by the tendency to be shared.[3]

Let us keep in mind the prescriptive character of ritual holiness, while paying attention to specific narratives of holiness: Isaiah 6 and Exodus 3. We must first sketch out the problem in philosophical terms, though its ultimate resolution will be presented in theological ones.

AN APORIA AND PHILOSOPHICAL APPROXIMATIONS

Contemporary continental philosophy shows both concern and embarrassment when dealing with God's transcendence. How are we to consider it properly? How far should we push it? A somewhat perverse outcome is to make God completely external, or even contrary,

2. See Lv 19:2; 20:7, 26; 22:33; 25:38; 26:45; Ezek 40–48.

3. See Walter Vogels, *Célébration et sainteté. Le Lévitique* (Paris: Cerf, 2015), 113–44, 174–75.

to our field of existence and perception. Let us consider two examples and a counterexample.

According to the philosopher of religion Ingolf Dalferth, God cannot be present in the world due to his difference, except by the mode of a total worldly absence. To be present in some coordinates of the world would be contrary to God's very nature. This thesis might represent a philosophical integration of an effective revelation of the divine in the form of its opposite.[4] However, by establishing such a strict equation between divine presence and worldly absence, must we not thereby implicitly admit that God cannot combine his divine presence with *any* kind of intraworldly presence, insofar as God's utterly singular mode of presence enters into conflict with *all* the modes of presence of the subjects or objects of this world? God and the world are mutually exclusive. Paradoxically, such an outlook assumes that God is still considered as a subject or an object belonging to this world. God has been removed from the world and, consequently, is unable to come into this world without being in direct competition with other subjects or objects of the world.

According to Jean-Luc Nancy, a friend of Jacques Derrida, the divine is never given under the mode of presence, but is, rather, like an echo, at the time of a passage or event: the footstep of the person passing by in the hallway (*le pas du passant dans le passage*).[5] The discourse of transcendence is eventually shaped into a post-Heideggerian poetry of the ineffable, with a prohibition against drawing any connection between God and being or presence. Again, any presence of God in this world is to be excluded. Nevertheless, something divine continues to provoke disquietude in the thinker.

***

4. See Ingolf U. Dalferth, "God, Time, and Orientation. 'Presence' and 'Absence' in Religious and Everyday Discourse," in *The Presence and Absence of God. Claremont Studies in the Philosophy of Religion: Conference 2008*, ed. Ingolf U. Dalferth (Tübingen: Mohr Siebeck, 2008), 1–20. For a subtle dialectic of presence and absence, see Eberhard Jüngel, *God as the Mystery of the World*, esp. 54, 61–63, 103–4, 182–83, 348–49. See also Anthony J. Godzieba, *A Theology of the Presence and Absence of God* (Collegeville, Minn.: Liturgical Press, 2018).

5. See Jean-Luc Nancy, "On a Divine *Wink*," in *Dis-Enclosure: The Deconstruction of Christianity*, trans. Bettina Bergo (New York: Fordham University Press, 2008), 104–20.

The refusal to turn the "divine" or "grace" into an object does not equate to an affirmation of pure absence.

On the other hand, there are currently some other philosophical attempts to approach God's transcendence in such a way that his infinite qualitative difference does not exclude every sort of presence whatsoever. To take one example, according to Jean-Yves Lacoste, we are familiar with some things that transcend their present mode of appearing. Perceiving implies a synthesis of adequate and inadequate perception. Perfect and integral perception is only an ideal, as we always perceive phenomena in temporal and partial ways, by multiplying visual angles and by superposing memories. That which appears to us always leaves some space for what does not appear at all or does not yet appear. "There is no perception of the visible without a simultaneous perception of the invisible," contends Lacoste.[6]

Relying on such a qualification of ordinary perception, it becomes possible to consider that God cannot be labeled only as "wholly other." Admittedly, at the present time, we do not have a direct intuition of God, one which would make God familiar to us, "phenomenologically" speaking. Such an "intuition" would coincide with the eschatological "vision." However, it is possible that God may appear and make himself present to our conscience or in the world, while remaining invisible and transcendent, because God is perceptible first of all as lovable, and is always greater than any of his modes of manifestation.

Out of this brief philosophical *status quaestionis*, I gather some hope that God may not be condemned to be the opposite of the world. However, we still have to elucidate, in some way, the precomprehension (or, implicit nexus of meaning) which inclines moderns to exclude God spontaneously from the world or to prohibit God from being present therein.

6. See Jean-Yves Lacoste, "Perception, Transcendence, and the Knowledge of God," in his *The Appearing of God*, 19–38, at 24.

IMAGINATIVE TRANSCENDENCE:
RESIDUAL DEISM

From the seventeenth century onward, there has been a tendency to think of transcendence as meaning separation and distance from the world. This would constitute the opposite of immanence: the more God becomes transcendent, the less God is close and intimate. The qualities of the wholly Other are then likely to be simple projective negations. Such a precomprehension is probably rooted in a univocal representation of being, valid both for God and the being common to all created entities, or in a univocal conception of God's attributes and of the world's properties. As soon as God and the created realm fall into a common genus, God's transcendence is represented as being a kind of exclusion from this world.[7]

Our imaginary Deism represents a coherent translation of the equation: the being of God is likened to a separated being which, however, lacks true transcendence and in fact conforms to the character of intraworldly beings. Detached from the world, God is described, as in a mirror, as some hypertrophied worldly object, extracted from the world. His autonomy is ensured by distance and disconnection. The criteria of transcendence are altitude, separation, dissociation of places, absence of contact, self-sufficiency, independence, etc. In order to free God from any relation with the world or action in the world, our imagination projects upon God a mode of worldly existence, pushed to maximum isolation.

Such an understanding of transcendence is called "contrastive": transcendence becomes the opposite of immanence. This view stems from a projection upon God of the mode of being belonging to this-worldly realities, which cannot simultaneously exist outside of

---

7. See William C. Placher, *The Domestication of Transcendence: How Modern Thinking about God Went Wrong* (Louisville, Ky.: Westminster John Knox Press, 1996), 111–27; Kathryn Tanner, *God and Creation in Christian Theology: Tyranny or Empowerment?* (Oxford: Blackwell, 1988), 89; Olivier Boulnois, *Être et représentation* (Paris: Presses Universitaires de France, 1999), 223–91.

and inside of another this-worldly reality.[8] Such a projection made upon God is radically false. Augustine of Hippo, Thomas Aquinas, and John Calvin spontaneously conceived of God's transcendence while correlatively holding that he is intimately present within any creature and intimately active within the freedom of the righteous.

This is not my principal concern here, but I could illustrate this correlation by showing that in the *Prima pars* of the *Summa theologiae*, the question dealing with God's presence in all things mirrors the question concerning God's simplicity. The sharpest form of transcendence gives rise to the sharpest and most active intimacy, and vice versa.[9] Thanks to his transcendence, God acts in the innermost depths of creatures without entering into competition with their own autonomy in being and acting. One and the same effect can be entirely established by divine action *and* entirely result from intraworldly causality, without needing to erect any partition between the two forms of efficient causality. This is what happens in petitionary prayer. The divine activity should not be equated with a kind of first-order, intraworldly causality; it is an action of another kind, of an incommensurable effectiveness, traversing without confusion all the causal chains of the world, whether they are necessary or contingent.[10]

A requalification of God's transcendence needs to be freed from the paradigm whereby transcendence and immanence are held to be opposed alternatives. Several approaches are possible to address the imaginary Deism which overpowers language about God. However, I will now set aside this philosophical debate, for I would like to pay attention to some testimonies concerning God's holiness, drawn from the Hebrew Bible. If God's transcendence is requalified

8. The participation theory might bypass what remains, at first sight, a worldly impossibility; see Aquinas, *In II Metaphysicorum*, lect. 2, ed. Marietti (1950), no. 292.

9. See Aquinas, *ST* I, qq. 3 and 8; q. 43, a. 3, resp.; II-II, q. 1, a. 2, ad 2; q. 17, a. 5, resp.; q. 23, aa. 3 and 6.

10. See Aquinas, *Summa contra Gentiles* [hereafter *SCG*], trans. Anton C. Pegis (Notre Dame, Ind.: University of Notre Dame Press, 1975), III.70 and 72; Pasquale Porro, "*Lex necessitatis vel contingentiae.* Necessità, contingenza e provvidenza nell'universo di Tommaso d'Aquino," *RSPT* 96, no. 3 (2012): 401–50.

in terms of holiness, it stands forth as a divine self-declaration which initiates the deployment of specific narratives. Our working hypothesis will be that the revelation of God's holiness is correlated to his commitment, presence, and mission.

**FROM HOLINESS TO TRANSCENDENCE,
IN TWO STAGES**

Let us focus on two biblical accounts of holiness: Isaiah 6 and Exodus 3. Our aim will be to discern how some parameter of "transcendence" intervenes and functions in these two narratives. We are led to recognize that God does not reveal his holiness in an isolated way, simply in itself; rather, holiness steps in like one of the features of God's relational identity, for the sake of an interpolation or a mission which directly matters for God's partners.

The Function and Transfer of Holiness in Isaiah's Calling (Is 6:1–13)

Let us consider the vision which is usually referred to as the "calling of Isaiah," where God's holiness and glory intervene. We focus on the sequences of narration and action; for Joseph Blenkinsopp, the scene begins by setting forth the mandate given to the prophet for a specific mission in the context of the threat of an imminent invasion (i.e., the Syro-Ephraimite War). This political and religious mission is doomed, but the vision and the dialogue reveal that this failure is anticipated and controlled by God.[11] In the long run, a radical purification of Judah, which probably hints at the double deportation, will make possible the resurgence of an authentic holiness (Is 6:13) by once more bringing about the separation of Israel from other peoples (see Ezr 9:2).

The death of King Uzziah acquires a symbolic value of pride and

---

11. See Joseph Blenkinsopp, *Isaiah 1–39* (New York: Doubleday, 2000), 223–24. His interpretation on this point differs from that found in Jacques Vermeylen, *Le Livre d'Isaïe. Une cathédrale littéraire* (Paris: Cerf, 2014), 61–70. Vermeylen considers that the original text stops at v. 9 and that the mission was at first depicted as a positive one.

suspension of human royalty (Is 6:1; 2 Chr 26; 2 Kgs 15:1–7). The only kingship which holds fast is that of the Lord, and the prophet is made the witness of this. The revelation of God's holiness and glory is highly dramatic. The effect of remote distancing is accentuated by the solemnity of the framework, the elevation of the throne, the mediation of seraphim, and the theophanic demonstrations (see Ex 19:18).

> In the year that King Uzziah died, I saw the Lord sitting on a throne, high and lifted up; and his train filled the temple. Above him stood the seraphim; each had six wings: with two he covered his face, and with two he covered his feet, and with two he flew. And one called to another and said: "Holy, holy, holy is the Lord [Yhwh] of hosts; the whole earth is full of his glory." And the foundations of the thresholds shook at the voice of him who called, and the house was filled with smoke. (Is 6:1–4)

Responding to the unveiling of God's holiness and to the saturating effect of divine glory, the remote distancing is transposed in the conscience and the speech of the seer: conscious of the gulf between his vision of the holiness of God and his own sinful condition, he is seized by fear (Is 6:5). His impurity is incompatible with the vision. To gaze at what he sees requires a purification of his lips and exposes him to death. This is consistent with the mandate which he is about to receive, requiring him to prophesy in dangerously truthful speech. The word of the prophet cannot adjust by itself in conformity with the vision. He must experience a kind of therapy, one that is simple but external to him, so that his words can fearlessly flow forth anew: a burning coal touches the lips of the prophet (Is 6:7).

These various, nearly-crushing effects of God's holiness and transcendence are oriented toward a direct dialogue, a face-to-face conversation (Is 6:8–13). The revelation connected with the vision has been indirect, being mediated by the seraphim; however, the Lord's voice, though high and exalted, calls out and awaits a response.[12] The question launched by the Lord is disconcerting, compared to the

---

12. Thanks to his purification, the prophet might attend a divine council; see Vermeylen, *Le Livre d'Isaïe*, 66.

sovereignty expressed just before through the vision: "Whom shall I send, and who will go for us?" (Is 6:8). The Lord's voice is addressed to the seer; it establishes a relation that the vision and the theophany, as such, do not authorize.

In a new way, when the voice takes over a visual theophany, the revelation of holiness and glory becomes the background for the covenantal mission, as well as a warrant for the envoy's authority. This appears all the more necessary as the mission consists of an announcement of seclusion and misfortune: "Keep listening, but do not comprehend; keep looking, but do not understand" (Is 6:9). According to human standards, such a mission will lead the prophet to inevitable failure and rejection.

In other words, the economy of holiness and divine transcendence (understood in terms of loftiness and glory) is ordered to a covenantal mission that requires a human response. The response comes from a man who has become aware of his distance from God, when faced with the saturating effect of God's holiness. The very holiness of God has been manifested in order to give way to a simple dialogue and a dangerous mission. The mission happens to be so harsh and trying that it requires an emphatic preliminary warrant in order to be embraced in the face of predictable human and religious failure.

By the end of this sequence, the depiction of Isaiah's mission hints at some purification of the remnant of the people, which would once again be capable of encountering the holiness that comes from God. Just as Isaiah had to be purified, the people will be purified by God, beyond their deafness and closed minds which seem to prevail and block God's work. The adjective "holy" (*qadosh*) comes back significantly at the end of the Lord's response to Isaiah's question, "How long?"

Then I said, "How long, O Lord?" And he said: "Until cities lie waste without inhabitant, and houses without men, and the land is utterly desolate; and the LORD removes men far away, and the forsaken places are many in the midst of the land. And though a tenth remain in it, it will be burned again, like a terebinth or an oak, whose stump remains standing when it is felled." The holy seed is its stump. (Is 6:11–13)

Surreptitiously, a transfer and communication are considered: from God's holiness on his lofty throne to the people's holiness, though the latter has been reduced and stripped on several occasions, to the point of utter destitution. An astonishing and demanding correspondence is established between the proclamation of God's holiness, the prophet's mission, and the remote horizon of that mission as the transformation of God's people.

If the reader looks at the narrative from a distance, two interwoven displacements are revealed. On the one hand, the extinction of the ambivalent kingship of Uzziah makes room for a full manifestation of the true divine King. On the other hand, the grandiose proclamation of the holy One grounds and anticipates a resurgence of holiness, one that is still remote, in the ultimate remainder of the people, radically purified from sin. These two movements are tightly knit together in Isaiah's vision. Though they are highly elevated, God's kinship and holiness are connected with Judah's tribulations and vocation.

The Excess of Divine Names in
Moses's Calling (Ex 3:1–15)

If we return to the Pentateuch, using Isaiah 6 as our hermeneutical criterion, we may note that the first occurrence of *qadosh* employed to mean "holy" places the reader in front of the burning bush.[13] The account of Moses's vocation, in Exodus 3, can be analyzed by following the sequence of God's actions and his interaction with the prophet.

Intrigued by the flame of the bush, Moses does not recognize the angel of Yhwh at first sight. He comes closer with inner questions about this "great sight" (Ex 3:1–2). From there, the divine questioning introduces a dialogue. "Moses said, 'I will turn aside and see this

---

13. See the article "*qdš*" in *Theological Dictionary of the Old Testament*, ed. G. Johannes Botterweck (Grand Rapids, Mich.: Eerdmans, 2003), 12:521–45, at 529.

great sight, why the bush is not burned.' When the Lord saw that he turned aside to see, God called him out of the bush, 'Moses, Moses!' And he said, 'Here am I.' Then he said, 'Do not come near: put off your shoes from your feet, for the place on which you are standing is holy ground'" (Ex 3:3–5). From the start, the account of Moses's calling sets up a relation, by means of question and response, providing the basic framework wherein the utter uniqueness of Yhwh stands forth. If we call it transcendence, this singularity is not a pure distance, but rather a personal difference, one that is somewhat enigmatic, revealed as a parameter of the relation that God establishes with his envoy, for the sake of his people: "I will send you to Pharaoh that you may bring my people, the sons of Israel, out of Egypt" (Ex 3:10).

The narrative sequence shows the rich and integral depths of the revelation of the divine "I am." The name expressing the excess of the divine "I am" is preceded by two relational statements of the same declaration. First of all, God depicts himself by his predilection and election in relation to the patriarchs: "I am the God of your father, the God of Abraham, the God of Isaac, and the God of Jacob" (Ex 3:6a). Then he presents himself by his relation and commitment in respect to Moses: "I will be with you" (Ex 3:12). The identity in excess, sealed by "I am who I am," breaks through as the ultimate ground and warrant of an identity which is both relational and committed.

The expression "I am who I am" in reality can have several meanings ascribed to it, and we cannot choose any one of them in an exclusive manner—a refusal to reveal himself beyond what is necessary for the mission: I am who I am; a self-declaration of transcendence which legitimates the sending: I am that which is; and a self-declaration of eternity in the form of an active promise: I will be who I will be. It would be misleading to think of the third reading as dismissing the second one. The enigmatic character of the divine name indicates his identity by way of excess, far surpassing what we would know of him either from a functional approach or an ontological one. The reiteration of "I am who I am" in the simple form of an absolute "I am," without any predicate, is significant. It suggests that the ontological dimension has priority over the functional one, given that the former is the foundation and the warrant for the latter. Thus, the whole economy of the scene justifies the articulation of these two dimensions.

While the divine "I am" is a name which overflows in meaning, probably combining absolute existence, withdrawal, and promise, the Tetragrammaton is delivered as being equivalent to a "personal name" belonging to an utterly unique case of self-presentation. Within the framework of a first encounter, to answer the question "what is your name?," it would not be fitting simply to reply "I am human" (a name expressing an essence), or "I am who I am" (a unique and sealed existence). I would also have to deliver my very first name: "Emmanuel," because my first name indicates my incommunicable and irreplaceable singularity. The communication of the (vocalized) Tetragrammaton to Moses conveys a similar unveiling of God's singularity, without recourse to formal signifying content.[14]

At the end of the narrative, God presents himself again as the God of the patriarchs. Ultimately, several designations are closely interconnected: "I am who I am / I am," "Yhwh," "the God of your father / the God of your ancestors," "the God of Abraham, the God of Isaac, and the God of Jacob." These names are of various origins.[15] Beyond the identification of the subject receiving these different names, which one of them is meant for invocation? According to Hosea 12:6, the name of God's singularity, Yhwh, is to be used

14. See Aquinas, *ST* I, q. 13, a. 9, resp. (*in fine*): "However, if there were a name imposed to signify God not on the part of the nature but on the part of the *suppositum*—i.e., insofar as he is thought of as a this-something [*hoc aliquid*]—then that name would not be shareable in any way at all, as perhaps is the case with God's four-letter name (tetragrammaton) among the Hebrews." See also q. 13, a. 11, resp. and ad 1; Thomas Joseph White, *Exodus*, Brazos Theological Commentary on the Bible (Grand Rapids, Mich.: Brazos, 2016), 39–44.

15. See Thomas Römer, "The Revelation of the Divine Name to Moses and the Construction of a Memory About the Origins of the Encounter Between Yhwh and Israel," in *Israel's Exodus in Transdisciplinary Perspective*, ed. Thomas E. Levy (Heidelberg: Springer, 2015), 305–15.

as God's invocation.[16] The stage of the absolute "I am" is one moment, a decisive but non-isolable one, within the context a more complete revelation. It breaks through in the history of the covenant, with the election of the fathers. Its first aim is to convince and equip Moses for his mission for the sake of the people. For Moses, God's self-revealed identity is not limited to his transcendence. The enigmatic singularity of God is brought forth for the sake of covenant and mission. It is framed by the memory of the election and a promise of fidelity.

BACK TO REVEALED TRANSCENDENCE

Through Isaiah 6 and Exodus 3, we have detected certain modalities of God's self-presentation and commitment in relation to the theme concerning his holiness. Let us consider, consequently, an adjusted qualification of transcendence in the field of systematic theology. The two narratives have something to do with prophecy and worship. How should we move from these contexts to some kind of rational discourse? Though theological thinking has some specificities, it should not become alien to modes of discourse drawn from prayer, invocation, and worship.

From a theological perspective, God's transcendence is something that is revealed, not something postulated or reached by way of intuition or argumentation. Admittedly, it is possible to reach some truth about God's transcendence *via* philosophical or experiential routes. For example, think of the various types of rational arguments that seek to prove God's existence.[17] However, by means of natural reasoning, one might never form a true idea of the divine transcendence. This has become obvious in the residual Deism that under-

---

16. According to Gn 4:26, the Tetragrammaton is first employed by Seth to invoke God. From a narrative perspective, see Jean-Pierre Sonnet, "*Ehyeh asher ehyeh* (Exodus 3:14). God's 'Narrative Identity' among Suspense, Curiosity, and Surprise," *Poetics Today* 31, no. 2 (2010): 331–51. The author sheds some light on the *idem per idem* self-presentation, which entails either indetermination or intensification.

17. See Plantinga, "Two Dozen (or so) Theistic Arguments," 203–27.

lies our own imaginative thinking as late moderns. We tend to project a god detached from this world as if he were a hypertrophied object extracted from the world, along with all the features befalling intraworldly separations: distance, exclusion, abstraction, nonrelation, etc.

In order to foster our theological discourse concerning God's transcendence, it is best that we build our reflection upon a decisive and self-obvious event: God's transcendence is revealed by himself through words and theophanies which are addressed to real human beings. This means, from the start, that transcendence is not posited in terms of pure separation; otherwise, it would not be concerned with God's self-communication addressed to humans. As it is revealed, transcendence matters greatly for those to whom revelation is addressed. It has a decisive connection with how they relate to God, along with their life lived out in the midst of a secularized world.

In the two narratives of vocation, that of Isaiah and that of Moses, God's holiness or identity is revealed as one parameter of his singularity within the framework of covenant and mission. God's self-presentation or self-designation is one decisive moment of God's covenant with his prophets, in order to ground, qualify, and warrant their missions. The unveiling of God's concealed identity has neither the first (nor the last) word in the economy of revelation. It presupposes election and it strengthens the covenant. It is highly fitting that God draws close and introduces himself as the God of the fathers, so that the accentuation of his enigmatic transcendence could not be reduced to a pure negative conceptual moment.

The transcendence thus expressed in the context of the covenant, and for the sake of the covenant, can be precisely called a "relational transcendence," distinct from an "absolute transcendence" which would involve pure distance from the world and would eventually be reduced to a "contrastive transcendence," a false opposite of immanence.

Seeking to reach a proper theological appraisal of God's transcendence, the route suggested in this paper supports the following assertions:

- Transcendence is not the separation of a divine "object" that has projected out of the world
- Revealed transcendence is relational, within a reciprocal though asymmetrical relation
- God communicates himself as the creator and redeemer of Israel
- When God reveals a facet of his holiness, he expects and causes a response
- God's holiness calls for separations which aim at the transformation of those thus separated
- Divine holiness and "I am" are the ground and warrant of highly difficult missions
- Transcendence is one parameter of God's revealed identity, not the whole of it
- Election and covenant establish the framework for a right apprehension of transcendence

Finally, by considering God's transcendence through the lens of holiness, we thereby raise a recurring question concerning the best "use" of biblical revelation. As westerners, we are drawn to question God's essence, existence, and identity from a theoretical angle. We are satiated with theological and epistemic concerns about God. With such an orientation, we tend to regard revelation as a window on the divine realm and to interpret it as an unveiling of God's intimacy.

In other cultural spheres, biblical testimony is questioned differently, starting from traumatic collective stories which are closer to those of the chosen people: oppression, precariousness, wandering, deportation, culpability, etc. What is at stake with the biblical testimony appears more practical than theoretical in these contexts.[18]

---

18. See Eep Talstra, "Exile and Pain: A Chapter from the Story of God's Emotions," in *Exile and Suffering*, ed. Bob Becking (Leiden: Brill, 2009), 161–80.

Thus, the quest for identity follows a more decisive question: to what extent is God engaged in relation to us in our own tormented stories?

This is primarily how biblical testimonies should be received. Nevertheless, God's identity is delivered as the warrant of God's steadfast commitment. This is the main conclusion drawn from our cross-examination of divine holiness and transcendence. To shed further light on the specifically Christian dimension of God's holiness, we would need to consider its incarnated figure and its trinitarian form.[19] According to John's Gospel, the "I am" of Christ was already present in the burning bush.

Along these lines, let us suggest the following conclusion. Briefly reflecting on the use of the word "holy" in the New Testament proves to be astonishing. In the Gospels and Acts, Jesus is designated as "holy" (*hagios*), though with limited extension: he will be called "holy" (Lk 1:35), he is identified as "the Holy One of God" by demons (Mk 1:24; Lk 4:34), and he is confessed as such by Peter (Jn 6:69); he is also designated as the "holy servant" of God by the same Apostle (Acts 4:27). The Father is called "holy" by Jesus in his last prayer (Jn 17:11). Then, one is forced to observe that the Spirit encapsulates holiness in the New Testament. The Spirit steps forward as the divine agent who bears and conveys holiness. As revealed by the initial blessing of Ephesians 1, the saints have been filled with all spiritual blessings in Christ. The Spirit of Christ is always the main agent of transformation for the elect.

What is God's holiness? According to both Testaments, it is the transforming power of God. Such a power entails a distance, but its deep reality is the very power which has raised Jesus up from the dead. God is the only One who calls into existence that which did not exist, grants life where death has overcome it, and sheds overabundant grace where sin abounded. These very acts designate who God is.

19. See John B. Webster, "The Holiness and Love of God," *Scottish Journal of Theology* 57, no. 3 (2004): 249–68.

3

God's Passions
Unfitting Attributes?

In Book V of his *Ethics*, Baruch Spinoza dismisses the passions and emotions (or affects) of God because they are inconsistent with his perfection.

Proposition 17: God is without passions, and he is not affected with any emotion of pleasure or pain.

Proof: All ideas, insofar they are related to God, are true, that is, they are adequate. Thus, God is without passions. Again, God cannot pass to a state of greater or lesser perfection, and so he is not affected with any emotions of pleasure or pain.

Corollary: Strictly speaking, God does not love or hate anyone for God is not affected with any emotion of pleasure or pain, and consequently, he neither loves nor hates anyone.[1]

We could spend much time, I suspect, refining the interpretation of this statement within the framework of Spinoza's own system. It might be an attempt to prune the biblical character of God to match the requirements of rational theism or a more radical denial dressed in a soft cloth of some gentle atheism. Radically, adequate ideas en-

---

1. Baruch Spinoza, *Ethics* V, prop. 17, in *Complete Works*, trans. S. Shirley and ed. M. L. Morgan (Indianapolis, Ind.: Hackett, 2002), 371; translation slightly adjusted.

tail actions, whereas inadequate ideas entail passions.[2] God has only adequate ideas, which exclude passions as such. Moreover, the passage from passivity to activity provides joy, whereas the passage from activity to passivity entails sadness. A perfect God cannot go through such changes. At first sight, this contention makes sense. If we accept the impassive God, how do we approach the somehow "passionate" God of scripture? Let me merely use Spinoza's statement as an intellectual springboard. We could find similar radical critics in contemporary atheistic literature.[3]

One linguistic precaution has to be taken into account from the start, however. Passions and emotions are not exactly the same. We may argue for a clear distinction of their descriptions—as Kant did for instance, stating that emotions shake us and are very limited in time whereas passions last much longer and are much more powerful.[4] Nevertheless, the biblical narratives reveal a God who has both passions and emotions. Therefore, I will treat both at once here, while distinguishing between them.

At least two basic reasons should restrain us from dismissing too easily the emotions of the biblical God: first, by himself and through prophets, God spoke a human language to human beings, addressing not only their intellect and will, but also their appetites and emotions; and, secondly, God the Son became man. Consequently, the emotions of the Son may have something unique to reveal regarding God's disposition toward us.

This will be one of my underlying assumptions: human emotions are not just perceptions of bodily changes and animal reactions.[5] They also demonstrate and signify specific modes of engaging with others and with the world. Thus, when the biblical God

---

2. See ibid., III, props. 3–15.

3. See, for instance, Valerie Tarico, "God's Emotions: Why the Biblical God is Hopelessly Human," in *The End of Christianity*, ed. John W. Loftus (Amherst, N.Y.: Prometheus Books, 2011), 155–77.

4. See Immanuel Kant, *Anthropology from a Pragmatic Point of View*, Book III, §§73–87, esp. §74.

5. Unlike reductionist views inspired by William James, "What Is an Emotion?," *Mind* 9, no. 34 (1884): 188–205.

reveals himself as having emotions, we learn something about the unique manner of God's engagement with his beloved creation and creatures.[6]

I suggest that we begin with Aquinas's treatment of the problem of God's passions in first book of *Summa contra Gentiles*, which leads to a different set of conclusions than Spinoza's. I will highlight the linguistic dimension of Aquinas's interpretation of how passions are attributed to God in a nonproper sense. He uses two different constructions of metaphors, giving way to two very different strategies of interpretation. I will then suggest that Aquinas's innovative insight concerning this matter can be unpacked thanks to Ricoeur's twofold characterization of metaphor, in rhetoric or in semantic. Regarding God's emotions, the semantic frame should be extended to include narrativity. Briefly at the close of this chapter, as well as in a later one, I will suggest one possible application of this line of investigation, to be applied to God's sadness. Overall, my approach requires us to slow down the process by means of which we interpret God's emotions.

AQUINAS ON THE LIMITED AND SIGNIFICANT FITTINGNESS OF GOD'S PASSIONS

Summa contra Gentiles I.89–91 presents us with a short treatise on God's passions. Aquinas starts by listing sound and compelling arguments which should prevent us from attributing any passion to God:

- Passions require senses and are rooted in sensible knowledge
- Passions entail bodily modifications of many kinds
- Passions draw people out of their natural and calm dispositions
- Each passion is directed toward *one* specific object
- Passions affect beings which are in potency

6. I have unfolded this insight in my *Les Émotions de Dieu, indices d'engagement* (Paris: Cerf, 2019).

For all these reasons, passions as such, according to the generic dimension of the concept, are inconsistent with the nature of God.

Aquinas then moves from the genus of the passions to their species, to investigate further possibilities. The proper meaning of a given, specific passion is drawn from its proper object and from the mode through which a patient or subject relates to this object. For instance, an angry man relates to some present disturbing evil by way of confrontation, disapproval, and possibly revenge. The loving woman relates to the object of her love through inner adequacy, attraction, tenderness, delight, or excitement. Nowadays, we call this mode of reference the intentionality proper to a particular passion. Abstracting passions from their common genus and considering them according to their specific intentionality opens new possibilities of fittingness, albeit limited in number.

According to Aquinas, most of the passions, even if we leave aside the genus and consider only their specificity, are not properly suited to God. He excludes the following:

- Sorrow and pain, whose object is some present evil
- Hope whose relation to its object is unmastered non-possession
- Fear, whose object is a threatening evil
- Regret (literally "penance"), a sadness entailing a change of will
- Envy, a sadness built on the perception that the other's good is an evil for the one who perceives it
- Anger, an appetite for revenge following a sadness about an injury from others

Nevertheless, a few passions can be properly attributed to God in respect to their specific manner of relating to their proper objects: joy (*gaudium*), delight (*delectatio*), and love (*amor*). Only these three are properly attributed to God.

Two further developments deserve particular notice here. First, among human beings, each of the passions of joy, delight, and love have a corresponding specific act of the will. In our experience, both registers (sensible passions *versus* rational will) are so intertwined that the same names are used to label both complex passions of the sensible appetite and simple acts of the will when it rejoices in, delights at, or loves someone or something. Thus, when applied to God, these passions signify simple acts of the divine will.[7]

Second, Aquinas provides a shrewd observation concerning human love, which is a unitive power[8]: the more extended are the activities shared by the lovers, the more intense is their love; and the more deeply rooted (in nature or in habits) is the source of some love, the stronger is this very love, as in familial bounds.[9]

Let me suggest a possible benefit to be drawn from this observation. Most of the time, intensity and stability go hand-in-hand in human experiences of love. Intensity is often a property of some passion, whereas the will is usually more determined, reasonable, and stable. As a consequence, once we deal with God's love in human language, it might be fitting to use both the register of passions and that of the will in order to signify the completeness of divine love: it is both intense and stable, because it is entirely actual. We know that God's love for his Son and for his creatures goes far beyond any passion, but this very love combines some properties, like intensity and stability, which are somehow divided between passions and acts of the will in human beings. From experience, we also know that a human love is more integral, durable, and perfect when it combines the intensity of passion with stability of will. Thus, we might need these two distinct perfections of created love if we are to properly signify the fullness and uniqueness of divine love.

According to this broad theological analysis of the limited fittingness of divine passions, which could be disputed in some of its anthropological assumptions,[10] most of the passions or emotions at-

---

7. See Aquinas, *SCG* I.90.3; *ST* I-II, q. 22, a. 3, ad 3.

8. This classical definition of love was drawn from Dionysius, *De divinis nominibus* IV, which Aquinas commented upon at length early in his career.

9. See Aquinas, *SCG* I.91.4.

10. I think of the discontinuous distinctions among passions and the object/patient conception of emotions, in comparison with contemporary psychology, which is more

tributed to God in biblical narratives, such as sorrow, anger, regret, or envy, are not to be understood as signifying their meaning in a proper sense. This does not mean that they are irrelevant but, rather, indicates that their mode of attribution is of a different kind. In addition to proper attributes, improper ones might be highly valuable and revelatory in their own turn.

My main interest is now to highlight two different schemata of metaphorical attributions made available by Aquinas for receiving and assessing those passions which are unbefitting for the biblical God. One of these schemata is traditional among Aquinas's predecessors. The other seems to be quite new. Let us consider this intriguing novelty.

AQUINAS ON THE TWOFOLD USE OF METAPHORS, OF WHICH ONE IS INTRIGUING

Regarding what the Bible says concerning those affections which cannot be attributed properly to God on account of the fact that they contradict his perfection—as Spinoza will later assert—Aquinas proposes that we must interpret them *metaphorice*: "It must be noted ... that the other affections which in their species are repugnant to divine perfection, are also said of God in Sacred Scripture, not indeed properly, as has been proved, but metaphorically, because of a likeness either in effects or in some preceding affection."[11] Aquinas's understanding of metaphors is subtle and not perfectly defined.[12] Most of the time, his notion of metaphor is qualified by

concerned with continuity in emotional valences, appraisal, and cognitive components of the emotions. See Gerald L. Clore and Andrew Ortony, "Appraisal Theories: How Cognition Shapes Affect into Emotions," in *Handbook of Emotions*, ed. Michael Lewis et al. (New York: The Guilford Press, 2008), 628–42; to be contrasted with Paul Ekman, "Basic Emotions," in *Handbook of Cognition and Emotion*, ed. Tim Dalgleish and Mick J. Power (Sussex: John Wiley, 1999), 45–60. Elementary emotions are listed by Ekman as follows: amusement, contentment, disgust, embarrassment, excitement, fear, guilt, pride in achievement, relief, sadness/distress, satisfaction, sensory pleasure, and shame.

11. Aquinas, *SCG* I.91.15 (trans. Pegis, 281).

12. See Gilbert Dahan, "Saint Thomas d'Aquin et la métaphore. Rhétorique et herméneutique" (1992), in *Lire la Bible au Moyen Âge: Essais d'herméneutique médiévale*

reference to some similitude, a proportion which is imperfect and limited, yet relevant and true. In the case of God's passions, such metaphorical attribution is said to operate in the following way.

First, such an attribution is possible because of a similitude between God's acts and some effects of the passion mentioned by scripture to signify such actions.[13] In this way, God's anger might signify some just and wise punishment. God's sadness when confronted by his creatures' misery might signify the action of relieving them of such burdens; and God's repentance might signify that he restores or destroys what he had previously done (or announced). The similitude on which the metaphorical attribution is built may apply not only to effects but also to properties. For instance, the audacity and strength of the lion justifies using that image for God in scripture. This line of explication is often used in Aquinas's writings, as it was among his predecessors.[14]

Second, such an attribution is also possible because of a similitude between such or such passion mentioned by scripture in a specific passage and another passion which is not expressed but precedes the one attributed to God in the text under consideration. Thomas explains this kind of metaphorical attribution:

And I say *in some preceding affection* since love and joy, which are properly in God, are the principles of other affections, love in the manner of a moving principle, joy in the manner of an end. Hence, those likewise who punish in anger rejoice as having gained their end. God, then, is said to be saddened insofar as certain things take place that are contrary to what he loves and approves, just as we experience sadness over things that have taken place against our will. This is apparent in Isaiah (59:15–16): God "saw, and it appeared evil in his eyes, because there is no judgment. And

---

(Geneva: Droz, 2009), 249–82. Dahan has revealed that the notion of metaphor has three constitutive elements: *similitudo, convenientia, analogia.*

13. See Aquinas, *SCG* I.91.16.

14. See Aquinas, *Sent.* I, d. 34, q. 3, a. 1, resp. and ad 2; a. 2, ad 4; d. 45, q. 1, a. 4, resp.; *Sent.* II, d. 13, q. 1, a. 2, resp.; *Sent.* III, d. 32, q. 1, a. 1, arg. 1 and ad 1; *SCG* I.91.11–12; *ST* I, q. 13, a. 9, resp.; q. 20, a. 1, ad 2; q. 33, a. 3, resp. [1]; I-II, q. 37, a. 2, resp.; q. 46, a. 5, ad 1. See also Gilbert Dahan, "Les émotions de Dieu dans l'exégèse médiévale," in *Émotions de Dieu. Attributions et appropriations chrétiennes (XVIe-XVIIIe siècle)*, ed. Chrystel Bernat and Frédéric Gabriel (Turnhout: Brepols, 2019), 97–121.

he saw that there is not a man, and he stood astonished, because there is none to oppose himself" [Douay-Rheims].[15]

In such occurrences, God's sorrow might be deciphered by taking into account another passion, here the simple passion of love, properly applied to God. Consequently, sorrow becomes a metaphorical expression of God's disapproval in front of the disfiguration (by sins or other damages) of those he deeply loves. The quotation of Isaiah hints at some astonishment on the part of God when faced with evil, along with a sorrowful reversal of his prior amazement in the face of such goodness.

In such a case, sadness is not to be interpreted in accord with the first configuration of metaphorical attribution mentioned earlier. In theory, sadness could have been interpreted in accord with some actions or effects we usually do or endure when we are saddened by something or someone: we tend to withdraw from reality, or we feel overwhelmed. But God does not do so.

To clarify the second possibility of metaphorical attribution, which may be more fitting and sound than the first one, we may need to introduce the category of narrative. Searching for an antecedent passion that is not identified in the text but nevertheless remains explanatory for an explicit passion entails some element of temporality and, therefore, a subtextual plot. The literary structure is somehow of a narrative kind.

We may also assume that the reference to an antecedent passion might be to one that can only be improperly said of God (anger, sorrow, repentance) or to one that remains proper (love, joy, or delight). However, it seems to me that, at some point, we would end up with love and joy, which are radical and final among the passions. In this way, metaphorical attributions would eventually be explained by reference to some proper attribution of simple passions signifying divine acts of will.

15. Aquinas, *SCG* I.91.17 (trans. Pegis, 282). On the genealogy of love in Aquinas's writings, see Emmanuel Durand, "Au principe de l'amour: *formatio* ou *proportio*? Un déplacement revisité dans l'analyse thomasienne de la *voluntas*," *Revue thomiste* 104, no. 4 (2004): 551–78.

From the start, Aquinas's main concern was to avoid confusion between these two registers, proper and metaphorical, as he thought that certain Jewish scholars were fostering confusion. These are the last words of his short treatise on God's passion in *Summa contra Gentiles*. We should bear in mind that the theological issue coincided with a heated historical sequence of Christian-Jewish theological controversies, which led to a form of trial, sadly coming to a close with the burning of copies of the Talmud in Paris, around 1242.[16]

METAPHORS, PLAIN OR UNENDING? RHETORIC VERSUS SEMANTIC AND NARRATIVE

I would now like to move further in the direction of the narrative use of biblical metaphors related to God. When metaphorical attributions are not just made according to effects or properties, it might be difficult to figure out what proper signification they both deliver and conceal. This problem can be clarified by calling upon contemporary philosophical discussion concerning the nature of metaphorical language.

Paul Ricoeur shed light on two typical metaphorical constructions in language.[17] The first one was defined by Aristotle in his *Rhetoric* and *Poetics*.[18] Let us call it a "rhetorical" use of metaphor. For the sake of convincing or charming, a proper word or expression is replaced by an improper one, having some imaginative power and connection with the term for which it is substituted. Some of these met-

---

16. See Aquinas, *SCG* I.91.18; Gilbert Dahan, "Textes et contextes de l'affaire du Talmud," in *Le Brûlement du Talmud à Paris, 1242–1244*, ed. Gilbert Dahan (Paris: Cerf, 1999), 7–20; André Tuilier, "La condamnation du Talmud par les maîtres universitaires parisiens, ses causes et ses conséquences politiques et idéologiques," in his *Le Brûlement du Talmud à Paris*, 59–78. Albert the Great, master at the university of Paris at that time, was one of the signatories of the condemnation. Aquinas was his student.

17. See Paul Ricoeur, "Metaphor and the Main Problem of Hermeneutics," *New Literary History* 6, no. 1 (1974): 95–110; Ricoeur, "The Metaphorical Process as Cognition, Imagination, and Feeling," *Critical Inquiry* 5, no. 1 (1978): 143–59.

18. See Aristotle, *Rhetoric* III.2.1405a3–b19, III.10.1411a1–b21; *Poetics* 21.1457b6–33. Aristotle explains the notion of metaphor by the one of analogy. For a counter-statement, see Donald Davidson, "What Metaphors Mean," *Critical Inquiry* 5, no. 1 (1978): 31–47.

aphors are so well known and commonly used that we do not pay any attention to them. "This man is a shark" means that he is so greedy that he will have no scruple swallowing your small family company. Most of the time, rhetorical metaphors can be immediately translated upon hearing or reading them. There would be no difficulty agreeing with others concerning the acceptable word or expression which would restore the proper meaning of the metaphorical terms.

Some metaphors, however, are much more intriguing and difficult to grasp. Let us think of a poem where a metaphor cannot be matched with a unique clear and proper meaning. We have to let it echo in our mind, allowing the poem's different allusions to interact with each other—as well as with our other more subjective words and emotions. Ricoeur calls such metaphors, which allow no one to claim hold of a definitive and settled meaning, "semantic." Substitutions may well remain possible, but interpreting them has almost nothing to do with restoration of a proper sense. Rather, here, one only looks for uncertain echoes. Think of Cavafy's poem entitled "The City":

> You said: "I'll go to another country, go to another shore,
> find another city better than this one.
> Whatever I try to do is fated to turn out wrong
> and my heart lies buried as though it were something dead.
> How long can I let my mind molder in this place?
> Wherever I turn, wherever I happen to look,
> I see the black ruins of my life, here,
> where I've spent so many years, wasted them, destroyed them totally."
> You won't find a new country, won't find another shore.
> This city will always pursue you. You will walk
> the same streets, grow old in the same neighborhoods,
> will turn gray in these same houses.
> You will always end up in this city. Don't hope for things elsewhere:
> there is no ship for you, there is no road.
> As you've wasted your life here, in this small corner,
> you've destroyed it everywhere else in the world.[19]

19. Taken from Constantin P. Cavafy, *Collected Poems*, trans. Edmund Keeley and Philip Sherrard, ed. George Savidis (Princeton, N.J.: Princeton University Press, 1992).

What does the "city" signify? Many possibilities remain open before us, not merely random in nature, though, nonetheless, it remains difficult to spell out which are acceptable. My home city? My inability to settle? My restless quest? My inner self? And so on. If we move from a poem to a narrative, some kind of plot or story becomes the frame for interpreting specific metaphors.

SLOWING DOWN IN INTERPRETING
GOD'S EMOTIONS

In his *De doctrina christiana*, Augustine states that an obscure sentence of scripture should, at the end of the day, mean something which is stated plainly elsewhere in scripture. In the first question of the *Summa theologiae*, Aquinas, following Augustine, applies this rule specifically to metaphorical terms in comparison with proper language.[20] This equation is true within the overall framework of the *analogia fidei* applied to the whole canon. However, an overly hasty application of this ultimate resource to singular items could lead to the loss of some pearls of biblical revelation. Explication is always an attempt to enlighten some unknown territories or uncertain enigmas by starting from clearer ground, but being too impatient in this kind of natural process would be unwise when the nature of God is at stake.

If we deal with biblical narratives involving God's passions or emotions, we come close to the kind of investigation that Aquinas proposed: we may have to search for something which is not immediately at hand in the text, enabling us to interpret such or such unfitting emotions as expressing God's own and true dispositions within the logic set forth in some complex narrative. As sorrow could be interpreted as a kind of disapproval grounded in amazing love, some cases of God's anger might be interpreted as bearing witness to his inability to accept evil as such, a radical incompatibility between God and sin.

20. See Augustine, *De doctrina christiana* II.6.8, 9.14; Aquinas, *ST* I, q. 1, a. 9, ad 2; *Quodlibet* VII, q. 6, ad 3.

However, I suggest that we should not move too quickly in interpreting God's passions. We should pay attention to each occurrence of sorrow or anger, heeding the way that they may play very different roles in diverse biblical narratives or sequences. Aquinas indicated that we should search for some prior passion which is simple and proper, providing an explanation for the one which is improper and metaphorical. He mentioned two possibilities: love as being the radical passion and joy as being the terminal one. Therefore, joy may not precede improper passions in the same way that love does. There is room for many different plots, here, I suspect. We may also imagine other configurations. The preceding passion may be an underlying passion, concealed through echoes and various verbal tricks.

For instance, what does God's sadness hint at in Genesis 6? This cannot be known by assuming that we know exactly beforehand what sadness is, either in its essence, its properties, or its effects. In meditating upon God's sadness, we must slow down in order to hold together what we experience in human sadness and the unusual sequence of divine action (love, amazement, sadness, repentance, etc.) in which this very sadness of God is enshrined as a profound mystery to be approached with awe and wonder.

SKETCHING OUT THE METAPHOR OF SORROW IN PROPER TERMS

In order to capture the proper signification of God's sadness in conceptual terms, I suggest that God's sorrow is a compassionate love in relation to the self-disfiguration of his creatures. If God were not immutable, his sorrow would belong to the same genus as human sadness. The difference would be merely one of degree, not of nature. His immutability is what makes his sorrow such a profound mystery. God's passions provoke our amazement as they seem to contradict his immutable nature and magnitude, but such awe and wonder on our part presuppose that we do not dismiss God's immutability.[21]

---

21. With others (more qualified in this field than am I), I believe that this is the right

According to our human experience, sadness is a derivative passion, one which presupposes the fact that we have invested our love in something or someone. Thus, obstacles, hindrances, losses, or injuries become harmful for the one who loves, for they harm or remove the one who is loved. God invests an overflowing love in his creatures through creation and election. His love creates its objects and their proper goodness, as unique and singular as they might be. This divine intentionality of love is the ground for attributing sorrow to God.

Even though God remains inalterable in himself, vulnerability in love is a human perfection derived from God's exceeding perfection. As pure act, God embodies in himself the fullness of what we ourselves experience in the form of fragmented, positive affective dispositions: sensibility, benevolence, attention, care, vulnerability, and compassion. All these qualities of ours preexist in God in a simple, unified, and perfect state.

Because he is pure act, God is not disfigured in himself by the evils, sins, and sufferings which affect his free creatures. When a human being is betrayed in his or her love, two aspects might be taken into account: the humiliation of the one who is offended and the self-disfiguration of the offender. When we endure such situations, we experience a mixed sort of sorrow: for ourselves and for the other. Most of the time, the personal wound overcomes the concern for the offender. In some cases, human parents are capable of being almost exclusively concerned with their child's self-destruction, leaving aside, at least for a while, their own anger, distress, and pain, all for the sake of rescuing their child drawn into addiction, for example. This kind of experience is imputed to God in Hosea 11, where God overcomes his own anger and offense when confronted with

---

reading of the amazement expressed by Origen at the *passio caritatis* of the Son and that of the Father prior to the incarnation and the passion of Christ; see Origen, *Homilies on Ezekiel* VI.6; Samuel F. Eyzaguirre, "'*Passio caritatis*' according to Origen in *Ezechielem Homiliae* VI in the light of *DT* 1, 31," *Vigiliae Christianae* 60, no. 2 (2006): 135–47; Thomas G. Weinandy, *Does God Suffer?* (Edinburgh: T and T Clark, 2000), 99–100. More is to be found on this issue in chapter 6, below.

his rebellious children, in order to let his compassion and love over-flow. In this way, God appears exclusively saddened by his creatures' self-disfiguration, rather than sad in himself. In the end, we see that his sorrow is, in fact, exceeding love, pure compassion.

Divine love is continually exposed to rejection, denial, betrayal, and irrational hatred, all of which originate in the inner will of his creatures whom he has endowed with freedom. The self-destruction is theirs. Nevertheless, God's sorrow is a metaphorical expression of an overflowing compassionate love. It remains proportionate to the loving amazement that God experiences as their creator.

4

The Love of God
Radical Asymmetry Overcome

In the Book of Hosea, various terms drawn from the language of human love are mobilized in dramatic terms in order to embody or express the Lord's relationship with his people. Thus, we find ourselves faced with two different scenarios regarding the divine love, awaiting an ultimate resolution. Hosea sets the scene regarding God's love for his people by using the prophet's own marriage, along with the vicissitudes involved in his conjugal union with Gomer, his dissolute wife. The prophet's life is presented as a living parable for how God is related to his people. A second image is added to this first, namely, that of parental love for a rebellious son. The divine love is tested in both of these domestic-conceptual registers, though it ultimately emerges victorious. God would have every reason to withdraw his love from his people, but he does not do so. His love trumps his anger, even if certain punishments are real and effective, aiming at curative ends. God ever wishes to win back his people through the ways of love, applying a kind of detox treatment for their sin.

This study will begin by singling out some unique characteristics of the divine love, such as it is set before us by the prophecy conveyed to Hosea. The physiognomy of this love is quite unique: it is terribly clearheaded and confronts infidelity and hostility without, however, becoming discouraged. Quite to the contrary, through its very sovereignty, God's love emerges as something radically asymmetrical, indeed so much so that it runs the risk of seeming unilateral. Can the beloved really be rehabilitated while also preserving true reciprocity in such love? In order to respond to this aporia,[1] we must meditate on the meaning of the incarnation and of the passion, for the New Testament theology of the divine love offers us a superior resolution to the question facing us here. There, in the mystery of the redemptive incarnation, we discover that God has drawn so close to man that he can, in quite human terms, truly enter into covenantal reciprocity.

A CONJUGAL LOVE THAT IS NO LONGER SELF-EVIDENT (HOSEA 1–3)

When God asks Hosea to take a prostitute as his wife, this represents the beginning of Hosea's conjugal story. Although Hosea's story is, in fact, the symbolic representation of God's own history with his people, the two tales present their main players at different stages in their respective relationships. Hosea's journey with Gomer begins here, whereas God's journey with his people already has involved a lengthy history. Prior to his people's infidelities, God's own primordial election of his people made them his own for many years already (Hos 11:1), despite the fact that they have ceaselessly scorned his covenant.

Gomer's prostitution represents the people's own infidelities. Even when this prostitution comes to an end, the three children whom she bears for Hosea are marred by her sin. They are called "children of prostitution" even though they were born of Hosea and Gomer's legitimate marriage. Their names express punishments and

---

1. The aporia also has a philosophical side: if it is too greatly accentuated, asymmetry seems to make reciprocity impossible or at least impracticable. In reality, most human relations attain true reciprocity against the backdrop of an asymmetry that is taken up. Here, I share the judgment expressed by Yves Labbé, "Apologie philosophique de la réciprocité," *Nouvelle Revue Théologique* 131, no. 1 (2009): 65–86.

a kind of abandonment of love by God: Izreel, "not beloved" and "not my people." However, as soon as these names are given to these children like so many expressions of disappointment, an announcement sounds forth, telling of a divine reversal of their fortunes, turning this disappointment into a blessing (Hos 2:1–3:25).

It seems that Gomer did not remain faithful to Hosea. In any case, this is the dramatic situation of Israel in relation to God. Nonetheless, through the trial, public humiliation, complete deprivation, and loss of her lovers, the unfaithful wife becomes aware the vanity of her conduct.[2] Hindered in her search for her lovers, she ends by saying, "I will go and return to my first husband, for it was better with me then than now" (Hos 2:7). This word of wisdom and disappointment portend a human conversion.

However, God is not content with the contrite return of the wandering and unhappy woman. He intends to win back his unfaithful spouse. Here, the Hosea-Gomer couple clearly fades away behind the God-Israel couple: "Therefore, behold, I will allure her, and bring her into the wilderness, and speak tenderly to her" (Hos 2:14). The wife will respond with the full and vigorous impulse of her early youth. The spousal covenant will be restored: "You will call me, 'My husband,' and no longer will you call me, 'My Ba'al'" (Hos 2:16). "Ba'al" was a generic name at once designating the master of a household (including women) as well as Canaanite divinities.[3] Replacing an alienating relationship with the Ba'als, the covenant will be reestablished in its full truth.

Thus, we are here faced with the recreation of the couple and not a kind of mere bandaging over its wounds. The partners will once more pass through their betrothals: "And I will espouse you forever; I will espouse you in righteousness and in justice, in steadfast love [*checed*], and in mercy [*rachum*]. I will espouse you in faithful-

2. For a critical evaluation of these metaphors in relation to masculine projections involved therein, see Susan E. Haddox, *Metaphor and Masculinity in Hosea* (New York: Peter Lang, 2011).

3. See J. Andrew Dearman, *The Book of Hosea* (Grand Rapids, Mich.: Eerdmans, 2010), 124.

ness; and you shall know the LORD" (Hos 2:19–20). The gifts sealing the betrothal are not external affairs. They coincide with the very attributes of God we find expressed in Exodus 34:6: "The LORD, the LORD, a God merciful and gracious, slow to anger, and abounding in mercy and faithfulness." This establishes the possibility of true knowledge, along with the connotation of conjugal intimacy (Gn 4:1). Betrothal presupposes that the future bride is an undefiled virgin. For Israel, this is no longer the case, given her infidelities. And nonetheless, the Lord's conduct attests to a new beginning and a full restoration: courtship, betrothal, and (re)marriage.

God alone can do this. Hosea cannot. Nonetheless, God calls him to use his own conjugal life to set the scene for God's own winning back of his people. Through the scorned husband's renewed attentiveness, the divine love shines forth in full radiance and truth:

And the LORD said to me, "Go again, love [*aheb*] a woman who is beloved of a paramour and is an adulteress; even as the LORD loves the people of Israel, though they turn to other gods and love cakes of raisins." So I bought her for fifteen shekels of silver and a homer and a lethech of barley. And I said to her, "You must dwell as mine for many days; you shall not play the harlot, or belong to another man; so will I also be to you." For the children of Israel shall dwell many days without king or prince, without sacrifice or pillar, without ephod or teraphim. Afterward the children of Israel shall return and seek the LORD their God, and David their king; and they shall come in fear to the LORD and to his goodness in the latter days. (Hos 3:1–5)

Hosea redeems his wife at the cost of a slave. We can accept the narrative hypothesis that the same woman, Gomer, is always involved in the tale, for otherwise the living parable would no longer be relevant.[4] Affectively and economically, the woman henceforth seems completely alienated and indebted. In absolute terms of economic valuation, she probably is "worth" the average price of a slave. The prophet is commanded to act out his love for her by means of this redemption, thus clearing her debt.[5]

---

4. See ibid., 80–85.
5. See ibid., 135.

He imposes a period of abstinence on his wife, withdrawing marital relations, just as the children of Israel were deprived of the kingship, public worship, and oracles. God still loves his people, even while they wander about in their adultery. Nonetheless, the persistence of the divine love does not suspend the *ad hoc* punishments through which Israel receives the prolonged cure she needs. This is directly attested to by the historical experience in the midst of which Hosea's own preaching took place. Such deprivations will arouse a new trembling search, one lacking in self-assurance, seeking after the Lord God and David. This implies that the one true worship and legitimate kingship will one day be restored to all of Israel.

Despite his people's repeated infidelities, God still loves them, purifies them, and renews the overtures that he makes toward them: courtship, betrothal, and (re)marriage. There is nothing airy or romantic about the divine love. It is an attentive and combative love, wherein everything is brought to the relationship by him who first loves. Even though it may be betrayed, this love is renewed in the gift of the covenant, though such a renewal must begin with a time of healing and purification. God perseveres in his free love for his people, even when they hand themselves over to other gods. God's love is neither aroused nor conditioned by his people's goodness or conduct. Through all things and despite all things, this love goes out to meet them, not only to purify them but also to win them back. This is what is most astonishing: not only is God faithful but, going far beyond such "mere faithfulness," he continues to love with such intensity, audacity, and freshness even after the first marriage's failure. Nothing can surprise him, for he has chosen the people with wide open eyes, just as he asked Hosea to wed Gomer with such full awareness, not only the first time but also the second.

A PARENTAL LOVE PUSHED TO THE
BREAKING POINT (HOSEA 11)

"When Israel was a child, I loved him, and out of Egypt I called my son" (Hos 11:1). After being symbolically represented in terms of a turbulent spousal covenant, the Lord's love is then set in relation to his primordial act of electing the people of Israel. In the narrative recounted in Exodus, the unique relationship of paternity and filiation existing between God and Israel is revealed (Ex 4:22–23). In this way, the hidden motive and sole reason for the election are unveiled: God's free preference which posits no prior requirements on the side of the beloved. Ample development of this theological theme emphasizing the fact that God's election is a form of love can be found in the Book of Deuteronomy.[6]

Israel's own behavior is incomprehensible against the backdrop of this election, namely, such an absolutely freely given primordial calling: "The more I called them, the more they went from me" (Hos 11:2). The chosen people were so carried away into idolatry and infidelity that they perceived the reiteration of the call by the prophets—in other words, by the Lord himself—as being something repulsive.

The description of the divine love is accented in ways that are at once paternal and maternal, with great tenderness and closeness. God taught his people to walk; he hugged them close to his cheek; he leaned over them in order to feed them (Hos 11:3–4).[7] The evocation of this tenderness in former days makes the enunciation of the verdict all the more startling. The people will not return to Egypt,[8] from which God has drawn them once and for all; instead,

---

6. See Dt 4:37, 7:7–9:13, 10:15, 23:16. Alongside these texts see the debates mentioned and comparison provided in Carsten Vang, "God's Love According to Hosea and Deuteronomy: A Prophetic Reworking of a Deuteronomic Concept?," *Tyndale Bulletin* 62, no. 2 (2011): 173–94.

7. According to Dearman, on the basis of the Hebrew text of the fourth verse, it remains difficult to distinguish between parental imagery and that of animal breeding. See Dearman, *The Book of Hosea*, 282–85.

8. Here again, this is one of the possible readings of the Hebrew. See ibid., 285.

they will know a new form of slavery, one that is no less heavy: "Assyria shall be their king, because they have refused to return to me" (Hos 11:5). Once again, love does not preclude punishments that are curative in nature. While the new exodus remains an object of hope, these punishments are indeed keenly felt through Israel's own historical experience.

However guilty the people may be (and, therefore, deserving of punishment), God cannot bring himself to annihilate his son Israel, like a father whose heart and very innards turn back from the idea of destroying that which is most dear to him:

How can I give you up, O E'phraim! How can I hand you over, O Israel! How can I make you like Admah! How can I treat you like Zeboi'im! My heart [*leb*] recoils within me, my compassion [*nichum*] grows warm and tender. I will not execute my fierce anger, I will not again destroy E'phraim; for I am God and not man, the Holy One in your midst, and I will not come to destroy (Hos 11:8–9).

Admah and Zeboi'im were destroyed at the same time as were Sodom and Gomorrah (Dt 29:33). In line with the image of paternal love, God cannot bring himself to execute a punishment that is justified but destructive. Even though it is not likely that such prescriptions were actually applied, Jewish Law required human parents to punish their errant sons up to the point of death by stoning in cases when he would not repent (Dt 21:18–21).[9] God experiences a kind of interior reversal: his parental compassion takes precedence over his anger, even though the latter is well-founded and legitimate.

Whereas love provides a platform for comparing human and divine sentiments, the case of anger here calls for a carefully articulated differentiation between the two cases: "for I am God and not man [*enosh*], the Holy One in your midst, and I will not come to destroy" (Hos 11:9). The quite human thing to do would be to allow one's anger to run wild, against the intimate suasions of parental love. In his

9. See Marvin A. Sweeney, *The Twelve Prophets*, vol. 1: *Hosea, Joel, Amos, Obadiah, Jonah* (Collegeville, Minn.: Liturgical Press, 2000), 112–16; Bo H. Lim and Daniel Castelo, *Hosea* (Grand Rapids, Mich.: Eerdmans, 2015), 171.

anger, God's appearance is quite different from that of human beings: "his anger is but for a moment; his favor is for a lifetime" (Ps 30:5).

However, God's holiness disposes him in an utterly different way toward his unfaithful people. As an explanation of the divine reversal from wrath to mercy, "the Holy One in your midst" is affixed to the words "I am God and no mortal." Beyond the difference between God and human beings, holiness is revealed as the most positive index of God's identity. Surprisingly, in Hebrew, "the Holy One" is introduced by "in your midst" (Hos 11:9). This declaration is of high density, tightly weaving together four different elements together: the divine "I am"; holiness as a nominalized adjective; God's dwelling in the midst of his people; and his renunciation of destructive wrath.

From a narrative perspective, God's holiness dispossesses divine anger of its potential excess. Holiness turns God toward his people in an unexpected manner. Beyond the punishments weighed out by his love, the Holy One is in the midst of accomplishing an enlarged reiteration of the exodus, not the destruction of his people. This new exodus will not only be accomplished by bringing the people out of Egypt but will also bring them forth from Assyria (Hos 11:11). The sons of Israel will be gathered together from all the nations where they have been scattered and alienated (Is 11:11–16 and 19:23–25).

In short, the story presented in Hosea 11 is founded on a confrontation between God's disappointed love and his anger toward his people / rebellious son. The resolution of the conflict is clear: love prevails over anger.[10] The justification of love overcoming anger delivers a striking theological equation: "I am God and no mortal [= qualitative difference], the Holy One in your midst [= indwelling]." "The Holy One" corresponds to "I am God." Holiness is the peak of God's identity. At the same time, the assertion of difference is worked out right away in terms of presence and indwelling.

---

10. This contention is valid in the frame of this narrative. It could not be extended as a general theological principle, for at least two reasons: (1) in some narratives in the Old Testament, divine wrath prevails over mercy or comes back later; (2) as long as the final judgment has not taken place, an "eschatological reservation" has to be maintained, even though theological boldness finds a firm foundation upon the cross and resurrection.

RADICAL ASYMMETRY AND

DIFFERENCE OF NATURE

Within the prophetic perspective elaborated by the prophet Hosea, the divine love possesses the following characteristics (Hos 14:5):

- It is primordial and creative, without prior goodness on the side of the beloved
- It is fully aware of the beloved's infidelity and unlovable character
- It is a preferential love, a free election
- It involves exclusivity and the requirement of a spousal love
- It involves the cares and vulnerability of a parental love
- It incorporates emotional components into itself: tenderness, anger, compassion
- It supplants and controls the potential excesses of anger
- Instead of being destructive, the divine love imposes detoxifying cures
- In a surprising way, it reengages the phases of courtship and betrothal
- It ultimately shows itself able to overcome infidelity

In order to assess the quality of God's love for his people, we must recognize that God would have every reason to hate his faithless people. Exposed to the possibility of utter contempt, this love is threatened by hatred: "Every evil of theirs is in Gilgal; there I began to hate [*sane*] them. Because of the wickedness of their deeds I will drive them out of my house. I will love [*ahabah*] them no more; all their princes are rebels" (Hos 9:15). The prophet's denunciation of evil is aimed, in particular, at the "princes" of the people, whether for their seditious machinations or for their religious transgressions (Hos 4:15). Gilgal calls to mind the people's crossing of the Jordan under Joshua's leadership, as well as the circumcision of the generation born along the way in the desert (Jos 4:20–5:9). By way of contrast, this remembrance of salvation and the people's commitment to God emphasizes their current infidelity. Gilgal also indirectly calls to mind the collapse of the kingship, which was entrusted to Saul there (1 Sm 11:14).

With no small regularity do we find the prophets presenting God as the subject of the verb "to hate" (*sane*), most often in relation to his people's corruption.[11] However, it turns out that we can discern the register of the hatred mentioned in Hosea 9:15–16 with remarkable accuracy. In the Deuteronomic code, the verb "to hate" occurs several times in order to describe conjugal relations that are in disarray. In the case of polygamous marriage, even if the firstborn is the son of the woman whom the husband hates (in contrast to her whom he now loves), the husband still cannot deprive the firstborn of his rights (Dt 21:15–17). When a marriage completely falls apart, the fact that a man falls out of love with his wife is also described as hatred (Dt 22:13). When such a repudiation of marriage has occurred, if the second husband of a woman who was already repudiated by another man now himself ceases to love her as well (literally, "to hate her"), he can in turn repudiate her in good form and drive her out of his house (Dt 24:3). The conjunction of hatred and this action of driving her away calls divorce to mind. Now, these two terms are specifically articulated in Hosea 9:15–16: Israel can be compared to an already-divorced wife who has failed the man who had nonetheless wed her, to the point that he hates her and drives her out of his house.[12] Thus, we can easily follow the thread of the marital analogy deployed in Hosea 1–3. Humanly speaking, Israel is no longer worthy of love in God's eyes, like Gomer in Hosea's. God has good reasons to hate his wife and divorce her.

Yet, in his unchanging wisdom, God does not experience hatred for any of his creatures, even for those that are sinful or corrupt: "You love all things that exist, and you loathe none of the things which you have made, for you would not have made anything if you

---

11. In particular, see Is 1:14, 61:8; Jer 12:8, 44:4; Am 5:21, 6:8; Zec 8:17; Mal 1:3.

12. Also see Gn 29:31–33 and Jgs 14:16. Here, we follow the line of explanation developed in Dearman, *The Book of Hosea*, 255–57.

had hated it" (Wis 11:24). Nonetheless, in the prophets' language, the possibility of hatred expresses the value of the love experienced, maintained, and offered anew. Divine hatred is not something metaphysically realizable. For this reason, what corresponds to it in reality is something completely situated on the side of the creature that is deserving of hatred, namely, the deformity of its wicked actions. However, the unrealizable possibility of hatred expresses the positive act of will by which God chooses to love those who are no longer loveable, like a repeatedly unfaithful wife or a son hardened in his rebellion against his parents.

The extraordinary character of the divine love, carefully described in this way, reveals a qualitative difference between, on the one hand, God who loves and, on the other, his beloved people. On account of this difference, God can take up to their bitter end the failures and disfigurations of his people or his creatures. His love calls for a response, but the awaited reciprocity can only be realized against the backdrop of a recognized asymmetry.

However, God faces more than a qualitative difference. He must overcome the fact that the beloved pushes back against him. The sound qualitative asymmetry between God and the creature comes to be deformed and aggravated by the deformity and antagonism established in the sinner.[13] Left to themselves and wandering about in their sin, the people have become resistant to the love offered to her. The more God calls them, the more the people draw back from him. To the sinner's diseased heart, God's demonstrations of love provoke an effect opposed to what he desires. The closer God draws to his people, the more do they flee from him. The sinner avoids him who lovingly calls him back to holiness. He rebels against the manifestations of this love.

The aforementioned qualitative difference, as well as the sinner's own pushback, both still await a resolution. Therefore, how will he

13. Along the same lines, see John Chrysostom, *Trois catéchèses baptismales* III.1, Sources Chrétiennes [hereafter SC] 336 (Paris: Cerf, 1990), 213–15. Likewise, see the analyses by Alexandra Diriart, "La dimension nuptiale des catéchèses baptismales. Entre similitude, circularité, et dissymétrie," *Nova et Vetera* 93, no. 1 (2018): 25–45.

handle this affair without towering over the beloved from the great heights of his incommensurable difference from the creature? What is the appropriate action for him to take in order to thwart the sinner's flight from the testimonies of his love and his appeals, urging the sinner to return to him? God cannot be deprived of his radical transcendence without also thereby qualitatively changing the very character of the loving relationship which exists between himself and his people. Therefore, God would need to remain himself while simultaneously approaching his people in a new way. In order for love not to subjugate the beloved, making her lose the truth of her condition, perhaps it would be appropriate, in the final analysis, for God to truly lower himself, taking on the full gravity of human existence, in order to stand at the humble level of the beloved.[14] It would be suitable that God could encounter his people on their own level. Indeed, as dangerous as it would be for the person who would take up such a task among men, on this same level, God would need to be able to confront the deception, caricature, and hatred imprisoning his people through the distorting lens of their sins.

Without annulling it, the New Testament steps outside of the framework of immeasurable qualitative difference expressed by God's love in the Book of Hosea. The incarnation places God's love within the range of the human encounter with Jesus of Nazareth without, however, destroying the qualitative difference between God's love and man's response. Here, a new and decisive threshold is crossed in the covenant between God and humanity, for it is no longer only a question of filling a dizzying distance or manifesting the highest degree of love. An even starker challenge is offered: the overcoming of the unfaithful people's hostility, subverting an irrational hatred merely by means of the weapons of truth and love.

14. On love as a resource in the midst of the asymmetry experienced in the face of that which is utterly incomprehensible, see the meditation of Søren Kierkegaard, "The God as Teacher and Savior," in his *Philosophical Fragments*, ed. and trans. Howard V. Hong and Edna H. Hong (Princeton, N.J.: Princeton University Press, 1985), 23–36.

HISTORICAL EXCESSES AND
ETERNAL SOLIDITY

Understandably disappointed with his disillusioned people, God astonishingly responds with an excessive love: the gift of the beloved Son himself (Mk 12:1–12, etc.). In the New Testament, God's love is *agapē*, a gift beyond every reasonable calculation we could tabulate. In St. Paul, this love is addressed to the elect; in John, it is addressed to the world to be saved. God's love involves a kind of folly, a salvific providence taken to the very extremes of the gift that is given. Through what he has done in history, God's love for humanity manifests its intensity and displays a twofold excess: that of the passion (in Paul) and that of the incarnation (in John). From both perspectives, God's love is attested to by the incarnate Christ in history.

"While we were yet sinners Christ died for us" (Rom 5:8). According to St. Paul, God showed his love for his faithful through the ultimate witness offered in the passion while they were still alienated from him:

> But God shows his love for us in that while we were yet sinners Christ died for us. Since, therefore, we are now justified by his blood, much more shall we be saved by him from the wrath of God. For if while we were enemies we were reconciled to God by the death of his Son, much more, now that we are reconciled, shall we be saved by his life. Not only so, but we also rejoice in God through our Lord Jesus Christ, through whom we have now received our reconciliation. (Rom 5:8–11)

Such love exceeds all human wisdom. In the end, God's love does not presuppose any prior quality in those whom he loves. This is why this love proves to be unwavering: "What then shall we say to this? If God is for us, who is against us? He who did not spare his own Son but gave him up for us all, will he not also give us all things with him" (Rom 8:31–32). Beyond every possible shade of doubt, the historical manifestation of the divine love reveals to us the eternal solidity of this love which prevails over all time and over all circumstances. By interpreting the words "[God] did not spare his own Son" in a way that coheres with our trinitarian faith, we thus avoid positing any kind of distorted dramatization of the relationship between the Father and the Son in the work of salvation. We must not think that, faced with sinners, the Father and the Son take up two opposite attitudes, the Father being filled with wrath and the Son paying the necessary price for the restoration of peace.

Even before the Reformation, dramatic representations of this kind were expressed in northern European Catholic piety. A notable example of this can be seen in a manuscript illumination describing a dispute between justice and mercy in the depths of the Trinity, Catherine of Cleves's Book of Hours (ca. 1440), which is preserved in the Morgan Library in New York. In the miniature image, scrolls place words on the lips of each of the three Persons who together sit upon the divine throne. God the Father states: "Adam will die, along with his entire line." The Holy Spirit compassionately pleads: "If Adam does not receive mercy, then, Lord, your mercy will perish." Embracing his sacrificial mission, Christ has the last word: "Let this be a good death, and let him obtain what he asks for."[15]

Far from espousing such theatrics and overwrought dramatics, St. Augustine in his own era spelled out the eternal priority of peace and love over the drama of the passion:

But what is meant by "justified in his blood" (Rom 5:9)? What power is there in this blood, I beseech you, that they who believe should be justified in it? And what is meant by being "reconciled by the death of his Son" (Rom 9:10)? Was it indeed so, that when God the Father was angry with us, he saw the death of his Son for us, and was appeased towards us? Was then his Son already so far appeased towards us, that he even deigned to die for us; while the Father was still so far angry, that except his Son died for us, he would not be appeased? And what, then, is that which the same teacher of the Gentiles himself says in another place: "What shall we then

15. See the *Book of Hours* of Catherine of Cleves, Morgan Library, New York, Ms. M.917/945, ff. 81v–82r. I was able to look with my own eyes on the splendid folios in this book of hours while at the Morgan Library in 2010. A website commemorates the exhibition and gives access to each of the numbered folios in thumbnail format; see themorgan .org/collection/Hours-of-Catherine-of-Cleves.

say to these things? If God be for us, who can be against us? He that spared not his own Son, but delivered him up for us all; how has he not with him also freely given us all things?" (Rom 8:31–32). Pray, unless the Father had been already appeased, would he have delivered up his own Son, not sparing him for us? Does not this opinion seem to be as it were contrary to that? In the one, the Son dies for us, and the Father is reconciled to us by his death; in the other, as though the Father "first loved us," he himself on our account does not spare the Son, he himself for us delivers him up to death. But I see that the Father loved us also before, not only before the Son died for us, but before he created the world; the apostle himself being witness, who says, "According as he has chosen us in him before the foundation of the world" (Eph 1:4).[16]

With an exceptionally sure exercise of judgment, Augustine is clear that the guiding principle in theological discussions of soteriology must be the priority, constancy, and resolute character of the Father's love for sinners, however alienated they may be from him. He then goes on to specify that the Son was not handed over against his will, as is attested in Galatians 2:20. The trinitarian rule of Catholic faith thus finds a confirmation: the three Persons always harmoniously act together in equality.[17] In conformity with the fundamental principles of Catholic scriptural exegesis, when he was handed over, the Son was able to accomplish the historical reconciliation of humanity with God only by acting in communion with the eternal love and abiding peace in which the Father, Son, and Holy Spirit ever remain in relation to sinners. The priority and asymmetry of the undeluded but nonetheless tireless divine love holds true at the most important moment in the trinitarian economy of the reconciliation.

Without the trinitarian rule of faith, we would remain uncertain

16. Augustine, *De Trinitate* XIII.11, trans. Arthur W. Haddan, ed. Philip Schaff, in Nicene and Post-Nicene Fathers of the Christian Church, Second Series [hereafter NPNF-II], vol. 3 (Buffalo, N.Y.: Christian Literature Publishing, 1887), 175. A number of contemporary exegetes impute a kind of enmity to both God and men. See Thomas Schreiner, *Romans* (Grand Rapids, Mich.: Baker Academic, 1998), 264; James D. G. Dunn, *Romans 1–8* (Dallas, Tex.: Word Books, 1988), 258.

17. See Augustine, *De Trinitate* XIII.15 and I.4, where Augustine develops the rule of faith, received from the Fathers, in virtue of which he prepares to refute Arian interpretations of scripture.

concerning the scope of the divine "reversal" from anger to compassion attested to in Hosea 11:8–9. Does God really experience a drama in his intimate depths, along with an interior reversal? Is he disturbed in himself or is he disturbed only from our perspective? Through our convictions about the Trinity, we hold that the Father and the Son retain harmony and peace in relation to sinners. Instead of shifting the tension and repayment into God, we should understand his "reversal" as something witnessing to the value of his mercy. Where hatred and anger rightfully could prevail, God still chooses to love, so great is his primary fundamental mercy in relation to his justice.[18] This reversal from anger to compassion is the sign of God's unflagging commitment to his creatures, whom he loves with so great a love. Instead of reifying the conflict between anger and mercy by placing it in God himself, as though salvation unfolded as a kind of an eternal drama, we should instead turn toward the passion and contemplate it. It represents the paradigmatic scene of sin and the historical resolution of the conflict: "While we were yet sinners Christ died for us" (Rom 5:8).

"God so loved the world that he gave his only Son" (Jn 3:16). According to St. John, God's love is revealed by the gift of the only Son to the world: "God so loved the world that he gave his only-begotten Son, that whoever believes in him should not perish but have eternal life" (Jn 3:16). The coming of the Son proceeds from the Father's unconditional gift which is fully taken up and conveyed by the Son:

- The incarnation: "My Father gives you the true bread from heaven. For the bread of God is that which comes down from heaven, and gives life to the world" (Jn 6:32–33)
- The passion: "I am the living bread which came down from heaven; and the bread which I shall give for the life of the world is my flesh" (Jn 6:51)

18. It turns out that mercy is prior to justice in God's relation to his creatures, for everything that is owed to God presupposes a primordial creative gift, to which God's mercy remains directly related. See Aquinas's discussion of this in *ST* I, q. 21, a. 4, resp.; q. 25, a. 3, ad 3.

- The Eucharist: "unless you eat the flesh of the Son of man and drink his blood, you have no life in you" (Jn 6:53)

The narrative arc of the incarnation extends from Christ's coming into the world (Jn 1:14) to the Eucharist (Jn 6:53). It is brought to its fulfillment in the passion—which for St. John is already Christ's exaltation—and the body that has been thus handed over continues its work, transforming his disciples through faith and the Eucharist. Akin to a gift flowing downward like a waterfall from on high, access to eternal life is thus opened up for every believer (Jn 1:12; 6:29, 40). Here again, we find that the divine love is primary and foundational, having no prior expectation.

The ultimate gesture of the divine love takes on a human form or, rather, the condition of a slave: "[Jesus], having loved his own who were in the world, he loved them to the end [*telos*]" (Jn 13:1). Here, looking on Christ, laying aside his garments, girding himself with a towel, and then kneeling down to wash the feet of his disciples, including the feet of him who would betray him, we have an explanatory embodiment of the passion. Jesus did not simply bend down from the heights of his human grandeur or the heights that he occupied precisely as the disciples' master. No, he lowered himself from the heights of his divine majesty.[19] He who lovingly assumes the position of a slave is the Word made flesh, the Son given to the world. He washes the feet which soon will flee from him. He completely washes them all, cleaning all the way to the heel of the friend who has already turned against him: "Having loved his own who were in the world, … loved them to the utter end"; his own utter end, the utter end of the other, the utter end of *man*, of every man, even the man who immediately thereafter will go out into the night after receiving the morsel of bread, his feet still cool from having been washed. Several verses later, John will recall the words of Psalm 40: "He who ate my bread has lifted his heel against me!" (Jn 13:18). He lifts this

19. On the humility of God involved in the incarnation, see Augustine, *De Trinitate* XIII.22.

heel that just had come forward to be washed. You see, then, who it is who gets up.[20]

These gestures of salvific love are at once fully human and fully divine. Their divine depths are lodged in their human eloquence. In his *Lectura super Ioannem*, Thomas Aquinas expresses a realistic insight concerning the educational value of this exemplarity. Following the washing of the feet, Jesus enjoins his disciples to follow his example and imitate his own conduct in their relations with one another "because in human actions examples are more powerful than words." There is always much more value in practically showing the good to be chosen than in merely teaching it theoretically. Nonetheless, in the end, merely human examples, by themselves, are insufficient. "This is why we are given the example of the Son of God, who is infallible and suffices for all things." What is the source of such rectitude and such fullness? For St. Thomas, Christ's unique exemplarity is founded on his very identity, that is, on his eternal relation to the Father: "For he himself is the art of the Father, so that just as he was the exemplar of creation, so too he was the exemplar of our justification."[21] Then he cites 1 Peter 2:21: "Christ died for us, leaving us an example so that we may follow in his footsteps." Christ's ethical and theological exemplarity is definitively founded on an ontological exemplarity: he is the Father's art, that is, the operative model of the divine actions in the orders of creation and salvation. This is why, in the final analysis, through his words and deeds, Christ is the concrete parable of the divine love in the flesh.

For St. Thomas, one of the recurrent motifs of the incarnation comes from a kind of emotional pedagogy. The extreme love testified to by the Son's coming in the flesh is fit for arousing men's own love in turn, for they themselves love more easily when they first are presented with evidence of a love that is great. At the same time, in the order of knowledge, contact with Christ in the flesh enables

20. Christian de Chergé, "Le 'martyre' de la charité," in *L'invincible espérance*, 226.

21. Aquinas, *Sup. Io.* 13:15, ed. Marietti (1952), no. 1781; see Pawel Klimczak, *Christus Magister. Le Christ Maître dans les commentaires évangéliques de saint Thomas d'Aquin* (Fribourg: Academic Press, 2013), 168–71.

man to draw close to God and become accustomed to him through what is bodily and sensible.[22] Christ is the way in act. He shortens the path and adjusts God's contact with us, adapting it to the human condition, with its cognitive and affective requirements. Through his proximity and his interactions with us, Christ offers the greatest of incitements for man to love God. In this way, he makes possible the reciprocity of charity between men and God. He is the agent, at once human and divine, of the mutual friendship proper to the covenant between God and humanity. The radical asymmetry between God and man remains, but here we have a definitive offering of reciprocity.

LOVE AS INCARNATIONAL

The New Testament does not present the divine love as a kind of abstract essence. According to 1 John, "God [*ho Theos*] is love" properly means "God [the Father] is charity." This unique love is revealed historically in the flesh through the sending of the Son and through his self-offering in expiation for our sins (1 Jn 4:8–10). The trajectory of *agapē* is fulfilled in "us" through the effective establishment of mutual love in the Christian community (1 Jn 4:11–12).

Yes, God's love is eternal. Nonetheless, its own proper nature can only be discerned through God's interventions in history: his steadfast election of the people of Israel, his love for a faithless people, his full awareness of the fact that they are not loveable, his renewal of his loving conquest, the sending of the Son, Christ's passion as the ultimate witness to this love, and the sending of the Spirit underlying the charity which now is finally rendered possible in the Christian community. Such love at once has an eternal solidity and a kind of excess stretching through all of history.

Drawing toward his passion, Christ invites his disciples to love

---

22. See Aquinas, *Sent.* III, d. 1, q. 1, a. 2, resp.; *SCG* IV.54, §5–6; *Compendium theologiae* I, chap. 201; *ST* III, q. 1, a. 1, s.c.; a. 2, resp. and ad 3. The two principal reasons from fittingness for the incarnation are tightly woven together in *De rationibus fidei*, chap. 5. See chapter 17 of this volume.

one another as he himself has loved them (Jn 13:34). If we reconnect the ultimate testimony of the incarnate love to the ancient parables of the divine love encountered in Hosea, the new love taught by Christ incorporates properly divine traits into itself. Through the grace of the incarnation, man finds that he now is able to love with the divine love. Through grace, Christ's disciples are invited to embrace love's priority over the beloved's qualities, and to love repeatedly and unendingly him or her who no longer appears to be loveable. Moreover, they must lovingly journey through the asymmetries that are accentuated by sin, aiming at a rebirth and growth in reciprocity that is received as a gift, though ever imperfectly lived. Even though it is vigorous in its discernment of reality, "[charity] keeps no record of wrongs" (1 Cor 13:5).

5

Retracing the Plotlines of God's Anger

When perusing the Hebrew scriptures, we find ample testimony to the motif of God's anger, and indeed, it remains like a kind of suspended eschatological threat in the New Testament. But what is the meaning of the proposition, "God's anger was inflamed against his people"? Such a claim remains supremely opaque. Does this mean that God punishes his people, that he vigorously disapproves of their conduct, or that he is gravely offended? Are we sufficiently acquainted with the reality of the divine anger such that we could interpret a given biblical statement when taken in isolation? Certainly not. We cannot content ourselves with a generic meaning for the divine anger, whose character is, *a priori*, so unclear. Rather, in order to decipher the meaning of God's anger, we must consider the various cases bearing witness to it, such as they are staged out within specific plotlines presented in the narratives recounted in scripture.

In order to put our finger on this obscure aspect of God, we will here reflect on his anger from the perspective of the divine repentance, considering it as being a kind of reversal on his part. Nonetheless, from the start of our reflections here, let us take care to remember that such divine "conversions" do not universally take place as events pursuant to his anger. Indeed, such reversals are, at times, expressions of his sorrow or disappointment, as we see in the well-known accounts presented in Genesis 6:6–7 and 1 Samuel 15:11. Other cases follow upon unexpected conversions undergone by those who receive his word, for example, in Jeremiah 26 and Jonah 3.

In this chapter, we will begin with a reflection on the polysemy of human anger itself, a semantic multivalence that is expressed in everyday language. Following this, we will then provide a kind of first sketch of the divine anger itself. In order to reassess the divine anger by retracing some of the plots recounted to us in scripture, we will extend our reflection to a motif that is connected with that of God's anger, namely, that of the divine repentance, first considering it in light of points made by Augustine of Hippo and then in light of themes expressed in contemporary biblical exegesis. Together with Jean-Pierre Sonnet, we will read Exodus 32 as providing us with an exemplary narrative concerning the reversal of God's anger, in a plot that reveals the very identity of the God of the covenant. By briefly extending our investigation to texts drawn from Jeremiah, Jonah, and Joel, we will begin to glimpse the first lineaments of a theology of the divine mores considered from the perspective of God's anger and repentance. Ultimately, our reflection in this chapter will provide clarification regarding three typical scenarios, along with a concise theology of God's anger, which we will summarize in four propositions at the conclusion of our reflections.

THE POLYSEMY OF HUMAN ANGER

Our task requires us to provide a kind of first cataloguing of the various semantic registers involved in the phenomenon of human anger. Such semantic reflection will help us to have a meaningful command of the words that can clad the realities which we experience, thereby also enabling us to translate the meaning of biblical texts. The vocabulary involved in describing anger is varied in nature and cannot, *a priori*, be limited to a single, generic term. A whole host of words gathers around this emotion as we try to express its multiform character. There are some synonyms for anger which express an intensification of this emotion: wrath, fury, rage. Moreover, anger manifests itself in irritation, irascibility, exasperation, indignation, frustration, disputatiousness, protestation, and conflict. Certain terms evoke the idea of repressed or suppressed anger, while others signify the eruption of anger or the actions that follow upon it, such as confrontation.

In any case, one thing is quite clear: anger is a particularly strong human emotion. In a difficult or oppressive situation, it is distinct from sadness having the form of despondency and submission. Anger strains against the unbearable and intolerable weight of the yoke which we feel to be crushing. Instead of suffering the evil in question, anger turns back against it and confronts it head on. Thus, anger plays a capital role in human life, for it intensifies the vitality needed so that we may not merely passively suffer all situations, indeed, perhaps enabling us to reverse them. Here, in the domain of anger, we see rather clearly that our emotions exist on the very borders of passion and action. In order to become angry, we must first be affected, sometimes for a great length of time. Then, at last, with great power, our anger swells up, giving us the strength to act and confront the evil before us. Like a thunderclap, the words burst forth from our lips: "That's enough!"

Anger also has a social dimension. First of all, the anger of a crowd or of a class of people can be united into a single impulse, providing a kind of force-multiplier for the possibilities of this group's activity—both positively and by way of excess. Moreover, it is often the case that the day-to-day relations found in groups of men and women include an implicit form of blackmail inspired by anger. By creating an environment that is constantly threatened by the possibility of angry outbursts, a dominant or insecure personality can easily manipulate the relationships in a given group. Anger can forever drift in the direction of such manipulative excesses. While this emotion is noble insofar as it provides springs for action, it sometimes can be perverted. Anger is one of the principal factors underlying unjust domination and submission found in various social hierarchies. However, the indignation and protestation of inferiors in such hierarchies functions as a kind of check, pushing back against the excesses of the powerful.

A FIRST APPROACH TO GOD'S ANGER

When biblical revelation presents God in his anger, a great deal of ambiguity remains, given the ambivalence involved in human anger. Indeed, transferred to God, the threats and consequences of man's finite anger seem to undergo tremendous enlargement.[1] Is God justly angered? Or is his anger a form of terrifying blackmail? Is his anger a permanent threat or is it, rather, a characteristic moment in a turbulent relationship? In order to respond to such questions, we need to come down from the clouds of generality and consider particular cases of anger attested to in various biblical narratives, attempting to understand the scenarios that we find presented there. First, however, in order to clarify the matters at hand, let us a sketch out a basic schematic overview of the theme of God's anger.

A first description of his anger has a very anthropomorphic character. Such anger is presented as though it were a form of rage or fury. Thus, it is depicted like a lively emotion which enkindles one's face (Ex 4:14). All of a sudden, it takes possession of God and sometimes overwhelms him. At times, God's anger is presented as being a kind of force that is distinct from him, administered by angels or personified scourges. These mythological depictions are commonly found in the cultures of the ancient Near East. They are found in various apocalypses, even among those included in the New Testament.[2]

In the scriptures, God's anger often has scourging effects, bring-

1. See Tarico, "God's Emotions," 155–77.

2. See Lam 5:1–22; Is 64:8–11; Ps 78:59–64; Rv 15–16. See Christophe Nihan, "Excès et démesure de la colère divine dans la Bible hébraïque," in *Colère et repentirs divins*, ed. Jean-Marie Durand et al. (Fribourg / Göttingen: Academic Press / Vandenhoeck and Ruprecht, 2015), 89–107.

ing about destruction and extermination, indeed with a cosmic or warlike ferocity. These are often interpreted by God himself, his prophets, or its witnesses as being a divine punishment for sins committed by peoples or individuals. In his anger, God destroys, punishes, and chastises. Sometimes, however, the education and salvation of the chosen people is the ultimate reason for the chastisement of their foes. Such is the case during the exodus, as we see in the rereading of this event presented in the Book of Wisdom (10–19). Conversely, when God gives free rein to his people's enemies, he does indeed chastise his people, though without always presenting the fury of these enemies as though it were legitimate (Is 10:5–19).

The correlation between God's anger and its effects is not a mere necessary, syllogistic deduction, and prophetic discernment is indeed necessary for interpreting this connection. Moreover, the divine anger is often connected to historical scourges which technically could be explained without having recourse to God. Thus, it presents us with an open question: does God's anger simply give free rein to utter chaos, or does he administer justice while holding scourges in reserve?

What are the objects of God's anger? Through it, God is opposed, in particular, to the oppression of the weak, as well as to infidelity to him.[3] Like a threatening storm cloud, the divine anger hangs over the heads of all evildoers, oppressors, and sinners. God demands even more of his chosen people and his servant than he does of others. Idolatry committed by the holy people or infidelity committed by his elect are particularly intolerable in God's eyes. To the degree that God has invested more love in his covenantal relationships, so too does his anger have a greater vigor.

Epistemologically speaking, we can consider the divine anger as being a metaphor, according to the rhetorical meaning of the term. Notwithstanding the immeasurable difference between humans and God, anger is imputed to God because certain effects of his action

---

3. For oppression, see Ex 22:21–23. For infidelity, see Ex 32:10; Dt 7:3–4, 11:16–17, 31:16–18; Jos 23:15–16; Jg 2:11–23, 3:8, 10:6–8; 2 Kgs 24:20.

resemble effects or consequences of human anger: irritation, irascibility, spite, destruction, vengeance, punishment, etc. However, the Bible takes care to point out the notable differences involved here. For example, God's anger does not endure forever (Ps 30:5); God "avenges" himself when he metes out recompense to the wicked, though without giving in to the deadly urges which we see in human vengeance (Nah 1:2–8); in relation to his own, rebellious people, God's compassion prevails over his anger, for he is God and not man (Hos 11:8–9).

Human anger is a kind of derivative emotion. It does not have the simplicity of desire, disgust, or sadness. It implies a paradox and overcomes the natural flight-response that we feel when faced with an evil, a feeling that is more immediate than the upsurging of anger. The same holds true for God. The divine anger likewise has a kind of derivative character. Presupposing prior loves, covenants, expectations, or engagements, it arises as an intense response to unacceptable behaviors. In relation to his creatures and his children, God experiences disappointments and frustrations which lead to various cases of anger that are proportioned to how much he has personally invested in his relations with them (Hos 11:5–6).

Early on in God's history with his people, in the Book of Exodus, we find his anger arising not only as a kind of law against the mistreatment of widows and orphans (Ex 22:21–23) but also as a tale following upon the people's infidelity committed through their worship of the golden calf (Ex 32:10–14). The possibility of integrating God's anger into the Law suggests that this divine emotion plays a regulative role in the living out of the covenant. The retribution of oppressors provides a sign of God's dedication to widows and orphans.

Before coming to consider an exemplary account of the divine anger (Ex 32), which we will decipher within the very context of the plot presented there, we should first integrate into our reflection the possibility of a divine "reversal" from his anger, something traditionally called "repentance" (*paenitentia*) in Latin translations of the Bible. A rich and complex host of such cases exists. The way that the divine repentance is presented in contemporary biblical scholarship becomes quite eloquent if we consider certain patristic outlooks concerning this motif, using them to sketch out a suitable background context for such contemporary considerations. The ancients were not lacking in hermeneutical finesse, whether textual or doctrinal.

AUGUSTINE ON THE DIVINE REPENTANCE AS A RHETORICAL METAPHOR

For forty years now, the divine repentance has been the subject of renewed interest in biblical scholarship. Renowned exegetes have called into question certain normative presuppositions involved in the traditional doctrine concerning God.[4] Succinctly stated: the conviction holding that the biblical data must be interpreted strictly within the framework of the theism coming from ancient culture has come to be challenged.[5]

During the first century A.D., the Jewish philosopher Philo of Alexandria helped to initiate the integration of the biblical tradition with Greek theism concerning the divine repentance. He held that scriptural texts speaking of the divine repentance were, in fact, forms of pedagogical anthropomorphism. The argument on behalf of this claim is rather direct: if the man of great competence does not change his objectives at the whim of passing events, for all the more

---

4. See Jörg Jeremias, *Die Reue Gottes: Aspekte alttestamentlicher Gottesvorstellung* (Neukirchen-Vluyn: Neukirchener Verlag, 1975), 34–36; Terence E. Fretheim, "The Repentance of God: A Study of Jeremiah 18:7–10," *Hebrew Annual Review* 11 (1987): 81–92; Fretheim, "The Repentance of God: A Key to Evaluating Old Testament God-Talk," *Horizons in Biblical Theology* 10, no. 1 (1988): 47–70; Fretheim, "Suffering God and Sovereign God in Exodus: A Collision of Images," *Horizons in Biblical Theology* 11, no. 1 (1989): 31–56; John T. Willis, "The 'Repentance' of God in the Books of Samuel, Jeremiah, and Jonah," *Horizons in Biblical Theology* 16, no. 1 (1994): 156–75; Yairah Amit, "'The Glory of Israël Does Not Deceive or Change His Mind.' On the Reliability of Narrator and Speakers in Biblical Narrative," *Prooftexts* 12, no. 3 (1992): 201–12.

5. See Clark H. Pinnock et al., *The Openness of God* (Downers Grove, Ill.: Inter-Varsity, 1994); Joseph M. Hallman, "The Emotions of God in the Theology of St. Augustine," *Recherches de Théologie Ancienne et Médiévale* 51 (1984): 5–19.

reason does the immutable and blessed Being not change his intentions and close off his decisions.[6] When the Bible is approached with the conviction—one held both through faith and through reason—that God transcendently exists above history, overseeing all things in advance with absolute sovereignty, pursuing his own designs, must the biblical narratives be dispossessed of their singularity in the symphony of revelation? In my opinion, Augustine's reflection concerning God's repentance provides extensive evidence to the contrary.

To speak of God with the aid of likenesses drawn from human emotions is no mere theological invention. It is one of the ways that the scriptures present God to believers. The use of metaphors to signify this or that aspect of God's action does not represent a form of manipulation, although such usage remains ruled by the scriptures themselves. Such pedagogical accommodation is at once founded on and framed by the dynamics of prophecy, which provides a translation of the divine Word into human words.

When Augustine treats of the divine repentance in a theologically explanatory conceptual register, he draws the rules for such metaphorical expression from revelation itself. Here, the metaphorical accommodation is justified by the voluntary limitations taken on by the divine words in their scriptural expression. However, Augustine's decryption of these matters is also commanded by another conviction: God is omniscient and remains immutable in his counsel. Such affirmations are not extrinsic adjuncts to revelation. They too come forth in a number of biblical witnesses. Thus, Psalm 139 bears eloquent witness to God's omniscience in a concrete manner which is applied to the psalmist himself: "O Lord, you have searched me and known me! You know when I sit down and when I rise up; you discern my thoughts from afar. You search out my path and my lying down, and are acquainted with all my ways. Even before a word is on my tongue, behold, O Lord, you know it altogether" (Ps 139:1–4).

6. See Philo of Alexandria, *Quod Deus sit immutabilis*, Les œuvres de Philon d'Alexandrie 7–8 (Paris: Cerf, 1963), §§20–26 and §§51–69 (2–75 and 89–97).

Augustine does feel the need to justify these fundamental convictions when he discusses the divine repentance, for they belong to the common tradition which is shared by all. Before further pursuing this main theme, we should recall how Augustine conceives of the activity of reason when it is deployed in theology.

In the first pages of his *De Trinitate*, Augustine emphasizes the notorious difficulties involved in theological reflection, the common methodological errors to which it is susceptible, and the value of debating theological matters. He denounces squabbling arguments raised by those who rationally debate in this domain without first founding their thought upon the firmament of faith. Augustine pinpoints three errors frequently committed in rational discourse concerning God.[7] They all involve some form of misuse of a given terminological-conceptual transposition or elevation, a process which corresponds closely enough to what in contemporary methodological language we would call theological analogy. The three possible erroneous missteps can be gathered together as follows:

- To transpose to God what one has observed concerning bodily realities by means of the senses
- To transpose to God what belongs to the nature of the human mind and its effects
- To rise above the created order without having fully mastered the language being applied to God

Augustine believes that the third error is the most deceptive of all, for it leads to the production of seductive statements concerning God which nonetheless have no actual purchase on reality. In order to avoid leading believers into such errors, scripture nourishes and regulates the possibilities involved in the process of elevating human reason to knowledge of God. Such elevation of the human mind to God presupposes a prior humbling, for which scripture's ways of speaking provide an applied grammar. Among the three missteps

---

7. See Augustine, *De Trinitate* I.1, trans. Arthur W. Haddan and W. G. T. Shedd, in NPNF-II, vol. 3 (New York: Charles Scribner's Sons, 1905), 17–18.

mentioned above, the third is purely and simply discarded, whereas the first two are adjusted so that they might be employed aright:

In order, therefore, that the human mind might be purged from falsities of this kind, Holy Scripture, which suits itself to babes [*parvulis congruens*] has not avoided words drawn from any class of things really existing, through which, as by nourishment, our understanding might rise gradually to things divine and transcendent. For, in speaking of God, it has both used words taken from things corporeal, as when it says, "Hide me under the shadow of Your wings" (Ps 17:8); and it has borrowed many things from the spiritual creature, whereby to signify that which indeed is not so, but must needs so be said: as, for instance, "I the Lord your God am a jealous God" (Ex 20:5); and, "I repent that I have made man" (Gn 6:7). But it has drawn no words whatever, whereby to frame either figures of speech or enigmatic sayings, from things which do not exist at all.[8]

Augustine does not reject the process of elevating the mind's thought to God. However, it must be guided, instructed, and healed by the scriptures, for they offer us a language that is adapted to our weaknesses. Hearers are thus led to elevate themselves step by step toward God, not allowing their reason to function all by itself without any determinate reference to the created order or to the scriptures. Likenesses drawn from the bodily or spiritual order—for example, the shadow of a bird's wings or the notions of jealousy and repentance—are comparable to "pedagogical allurements" devised for gradually accommodating "childish" minds to that which exceeds them: "for divine Scripture is wont to frame, as it were, allurements for children [*infantilia oblectamenta*] from the things which are found in the creature; whereby, according to their measure, and as it were by steps, the affections of the weak may be moved to seek those things that are above, and to leave those things that are below."[9] Such pedagogical approximations, which are suitable for convincing those who are beginning upon the ways of faith, as well as for turning away the proud, do however call for further theological reflection and, so to speak, deciphering.

8. Ibid., 1.2 (18).
9. Ibid.

In his work gathering together eighty-three difficult issues, the case of divine repentance recounted in Genesis 6 is treated as representing a particular case of scriptural accommodation. Augustine's explanation here is based on a twofold movement, with the human mind ascending toward God and the scriptures descending toward human minds in their weakness:

On the Scripture: "I am sorry that I have made man" (Gn 6:6).—To raise us from the earthly and human meaning up to the divine and heavenly, the divine Scriptures have [themselves] come down to those words which even the most simple customarily use among themselves. And so those men through whom the Holy Spirit has spoken have not hesitated to employ in those books, as the occasion best demands, names of even those passions which our soul experience and which the man who knows better already understands to be completely foreign to God. For example, because it is very difficult for a man to avenge something without experiencing anger, the authors of Scripture have decided to use the name *wrath* for God's vengeance, although God's vengeance is exercised with absolutely no such emotion. Again, since husbands are wont to protect the chastity of their wives through jealousy, the Scripture writers have used the expression *the jealousy of God* to indicate that providence of God whereby he admonishes the soul and seeks to prevent its corruption and, as it were, its prostitution through following after various other gods.[10]

In the rest of his explanation, the scriptural accommodation involves not only the soul's passions, such as anger, jealousy, and regret, but also includes the parts of the body: hands, feet, ears, eyes, and the face. Quite clearly, these latter realities can be applied only by way of rhetorical metaphors, which are easily transposed into one's own language.[11] Augustine easily reduces each of these bodily likenesses to one or another facet of God's strength or power (*vis*). It is precisely through their unrefined character that bodily

10. Augustine, *Eighty-Three Different Questions*, q. 52, ed. Hermigild Dressler et al., trans. David L. Mosher, Fathers of the Church 70 (Washington, D.C.: The Catholic University of America Press, 2002), 88–89.

11. See the previous chapter of this volume, alongside insights found in the work of Paul Ricoeur, "Metaphor and the Main Problem of Hermeneutics," 95–110; Ricoeur, "The Metaphorical Process as Cognition, Imagination, and Feeling," 143–59.

metaphors prevent educated minds from imagining God as though he were a bodily being.

Now, the risk of confusion is greater when one attributes to God the emotions which we often experience in the disordered state they take on in human affairs. When the notion of anger is attributed to God by the scriptures, it there describes the divine judgment which is exercised without the excesses of human vengeance. Jealousy expresses the exclusivity required in worship of God, just as jealousy is what safeguards conjugal chastity. Such an interpretation of human jealousy is generous, but it does not obscure the fact that jealousy frequently takes on an excessive, unruly character in human activity. In the cases of jealousy and anger alike, only one aspect of their human state can be applied to God. What is suitably attributed to God is not passion inasmuch as it is a violent emotion but, rather, an act or intention to which this or that passion is commonly associated in human experience. The activity of discernment is made explicit in the case of repentance:

Therefore, in accord with this rule, since we are not easily accustomed to changing something [already] begun and to turning to something else, except with regret, and although Divine Providence appears to observers of clear mind to administer all things by an absolutely fixed order, nonetheless, in a manner most suited to insignificant human understanding, those things which begin to be but do not continue as long as it was hoped that they would continue are said to be stopped by a kind of regret on the part of God.[12]

The likeness between divine repentance and human repentance is, at best, only faint. Like a kind of backdrop, Augustine retains the immutability of providence, whose order of execution (or effective application) is not subject to change, even when this seems to be the case when considering affairs from the perspective of human actors or intramundane events. Whereas human beings change their direction when they regret having going down a given path or feel remorse for a given intention, for his part, God is said to repent when

---

12. Augustine, *Eighty-Three Different Questions*, qq. 52, 89.

one of his undertakings is interrupted or reoriented in a different direction, even though, from the perspective of human affairs, it seems that it should continue. When a father sees his son placing his hand too close to a stovetop and tells him, "You are going to burn yourself," if the son draws back to a safe distance from the hot surface, the father's words do not thereby become false or deceptive. The same holds for the divine pronouncements that are concerned with the logic of sin and the consequences that will necessarily follow upon it so long as one does not repent and return to God.

For Augustine, such discussion of repentance comes down to a kind of accommodation made by the scriptures so as to meet the contemporary thought and speech patterns of its hearers. God has not really repented, for he changes neither his will nor his designs. Rather, the events in question or the stated intentions undergo an adjustment which, in man's own case, would be the effect of an act of repentance. The divine repentance is thus received as a metaphor, whose accuracy and pertinence are limited to the effect which human repentance usually produces.

In Book XIV of his masterpiece, *The City of God*, Augustine discusses the divine repentance while setting forth the genealogy of the two cities, along with the unfolding narrative of sin through the course of history. The bishop of Hippo's explanations are consistent with the interpretation defended above in question 52 of his *De diversis quaestionibus*. In order to incorporate the divine repentance alongside the wicked acts of humanity, Augustine grants that God is fully aware, in advance, of the fault, along with its consequences and the lengthy narrative of rehabilitation needed for rectifying it. The divine *consilium* is neither changed nor reoriented by the sinful choices made by mankind. From God's perspective, both the fault and its remedy were known and provided for from all eternity:

But because God foreknew all things and must therefore also have been aware that man would sin. For this reason, we must base every doctrine of the holy city on his foreknowledge and dispensation and not on that which could not have comme to our knowledge because it was not part of

God's dispensation. Man could not possibly upset the divine plan [*consilium*] by his sin, as if he could have compelled God to change what he had decreed [*quod statuerat mutare*], for God through his foreknowledge had anticipated both the coming events, that is, both how bad the man whom he himself had created good would become and what good he himself would use him to effect even so. God, it is true, is said to change his decrees [*statuta mutare*], and hence we read in Scripture the statement in figurative speech that God repented. But such a statement is based on man's expectation or on the prospect implicit in the orderly course of natural causes, not the Almighty's foreknowledge of waht he will do.[13]

The divine decrees can be said to change only from the human perspective, insofar as a given chain of events in fact comes to be interrupted, though, to human eyes, it should have been pursued as it was announced or was in the midst of being performed. The distinction between *consilium* and *statuta* does not involve some real difference on God's side, as though some span of time needed to be filled between a general intention and the decrees whereby his will would be applied. However, it does reflect a real difference involved in how man perceives the exercise of divine providence.

In Book XV, Augustine continues his exposition of the unfolding of the two cities and considers the problems posed by the *historia* found in the first chapters of Genesis in order to thereby prevent these texts from merely being brushed aside as something justifying disbelief. Here, repentance provides a metaphor that is closely connected with that of anger. They are both treated in one and the same vein in terms of *cogitatio* and *recogitatio*:

The anger of God is not an agitation of his mind but a judgment [*iudicium*] imposing punishment upon sin [*poena peccato*]. Moreover, his consideration [*cogitatio*] and reconsideration [*recogitatio*] of any matter are merely the unchangeable design for things that are subject to change. For unlike man, God does not repent anything that he has done, and concerning each and every thing his decision [*sententia*] is as unwavering as his prescience is unerring [*certa*].[14]

13. Augustine, *De civitate Dei* XIV.11, trans. Philip Levine (Cambridge, Mass.: Harvard University Press, 1966), 4:323–25.

14. Ibid., XV.25 (4:563–65). The interconnected sequence of verbs *cogitare, recogitare,*

When the signification of the term "anger" is carefully focused and restricted, it designates God's judgment. This falls within a simple, rhetorical sense of the metaphor in question. In the background, Augustine maintains the normative value of the divine foreknowledge. God does not revise his judgment. In reality, he is neither disconcerted nor turned back by the wickedness of the human heart following upon man's sin. Rather, his disavowal of it is translated into terms of anger and repentance. All of this falls within the way that scripture adapts these realities so that they may be received, in faith, by the recipients of divine revelation:

But if Scripture were not to use such expressions, it would not come home so intimately, as it were, to all mankind, for whom it chooses to take thought. For only in this way can it frighten the proud, arouse the remiss, keep the curious occupied and provide nourishment for the wise; nor would it succeed in doing this if it did it not first incline [*inclinare*] and come down [*descendere*], as it were, to the lowly. When it further announces the annihilation of all animals on the earth and in the air, it is emphasizing the magnitude of the coming disaster, not threatening the destruction to irrational creatures if they too had sinned.[15]

Metaphorical language fulfills a number of pedagogical functions. It mobilizes human passions so that one may speak about God and, in this way, moves those who listen to the narratives recounted in the scriptures, leading them to be engaged by the very vivacity of the divine emotions. If the scriptures did not deign to employ the metaphorical resources of language in this way, they would remain dull and wooden, at least for the common run of men. The excesses involved in metaphorical language, like for example, the great extent of the divine disgust—not only for human beings but, as it were, by way of overflow, for the animals creeping on the earth and those flying in the skies—is expressed by means of hyperbole (Gn 6:7). God is thus depicted with vivacity and realism, like a person who inter-

______

and *paenitere* can be found in the ancient, pre-Vulgate Latin translations of Gn 6:6. See *Vetus Latina. Die Resteder altateinischen Bibel*, vol. 2 (*Genesis*), ed. Bonifatius Fischer (Freiburg i.B.: Herder, 1951), 105.

15. Augustine, *De civitate Dei* XV.25 (4:565).

acts with humans and shares their sentiments. This provides an eloquent indication of God's commitment within the covenant itself, as well as throughout its ongoing history, no matter how tumultuous it might be. Of course, following upon one's initial reflections concerning such passages, pastoral or theological explanations must then prevent unrefined readings of such texts from perduring. Indeed, as is recounted in the *Confessions*, one of the benefits that Augustine drew from listening to Ambrose's preaching in Milan was precisely this kind of awareness that one must move beyond such insufficient understandings of the words of scripture.[16]

St. Augustine's interpretation is marked in particular by his adoption of the divine foreknowledge as a normative doctrinal premise. This theological constraint forces him to be creative and leads him to suggest certain points that are highly relevant in these matters. Repentance is a rhetorical metaphor whose very meaning is, by definition, inadequately proportioned to the reality that it signifies. The reality of human repentance and that of the divine repentance are separated by a yawning gulf, for God has full foreknowledge of the future, including even the free choices made by his creatures. Moreover, his counsel and providence are immutable in their intention and decisions. However, the proportional likeness that does indeed still remain is precious and significant: just as humans alter their own undertakings when they experience regret or repentance, so too God is said to repent when that which he had announced or engaged in does not come to pass as expected but, instead, undergoes some sort of reversal (from the perspective of human actors or observers). Thus, the foundation for the metaphor is the effect of repentance, namely, the reversal in the action, and not repentance precisely as such, which is an intimate change provoked by the regret or affliction involved in one's own conduct.

Bringing this section to a close, let us summarize our findings up to this point. On the level of the expected effects of God's pronouncements or undertakings, repentance signifies a reversal or suspension

16. See Augustine, *Confessiones* V.14.24.

in such actions. However, at another, deeper level, repentance paradoxically bears witness to the perseverance of God's designs, forever accomplishing what he intends and wills. Thus, when the threat of punishment is suspended because it has provoked the conversion of those destined to receive it, God's intention to save man is what is reflected in his repentance. Before developing this intuition through a focused narrative analysis, undertaken alongside Jean-Pierre Sonnet, we first should provide a brief biblical typology of repentance, basing our own reflection on the work of Terence Fretheim.

BIBLICAL REPENTANCE: TYPOLOGY
AND NARRATIVE STRUCTURE

Among the various possible translations for the Hebrew verb *nicham / nacham* when it has God as its subject, Fretheim chooses the reversal of a given direction taken or of a decision that has been made. Such a change is often connected to a lively emotion experienced in the face of how a given situation has developed: sadness, anger, regret, etc. Although it is commonly admitted that we only metaphorically speak of the divine repentance, we still must examine the degree to which this metaphor is, in fact, revelatory.

Fretheim holds that repentance is a "controlling metaphor" for Old Testament discourse concerning God. This principally means that the metaphor, one that is in touch with human experience, has much potential as an instrument of revelation and serves in the organization of other motifs expressed in biblical discourse. At a quick, first glance, we can see that this last aspect is indeed attested to in various works, literary genres, and biblical traditions. With all of this in mind, Fretheim provides a rather elaborate description of the use of *nicham* in the Old Testament. His reflection provides an illuminating typology of the divine repentance and non-repentance, whose essential lineaments can be summarized in abridged fashion as follows:[17]

17. See Fretheim, "The Repentance of God: A Key to Evaluating Old Testament God-Talk," 53–54.

1. Rejection of an act already performed (Gn 6:6–7;
   1 Sm 15:11–35)

2. God does not repent:
   - Concerning certain matters, making a promise (1 Sm 15:29,
     Nm 23:19, Ps 110:4)
   - On certain occasions, rendering a judgment (Jer 4:18, 15:6,
     20:16; Ezek 24:14; Hos 13:14; Zec 8:14)

3. Reversal of what God said he would do or what he has
   already begun to do:
   - General affirmation (Jl 2:13; Jon 4:2)
   - In response (potentially) to prayer / repentance (Ps 90:13,
     106:44–45; Is 57:6?; Jer 18:7–10; 26:3, 13, 19; Jl 2:14;
     Jon 3:9–10)
   - In response to an intercessor (Ex 32:12–14; Am 7:3–6)
   - By God's own initiative, without any apparent human
     mediation (Dt 32:36; 2 Sm 24:16; 1 Chr 21:15; Jer 42:10;
     Jgs 2:18; Ps 135:14?; Hos 11:8)

Fretheim notes that the divine repentance also outstrips the lexical scope of *nicham*. In a number of biblical narratives, God amends his decisions without the use of the specific language of repentance. This is particularly the case in 1 Kings 21:27–29 (toward Ahab), Isaiah 38:1–6, and 2 Kings 20:1–11 (toward Hezekiah), and in 2 Chronicles 12:1–12 (under Rehoboam). Moreover, a motif akin to that of repentance is encountered when God turns back (*shuv*) from his anger.[18] Fretheim suggests that the controlling metaphor of repentance plays its role precisely as a creative resource for interpreting and organizing these various biblical materials and traditions into something like a coherent whole. A reading of what God communicates to his prophet in Jeremiah 18 supports such a claim. We will return to this below.

If the divine repentance is indeed sung of in some psalms (Ps 90:13

---

18. See Dt 13:17, Jos 7:26, 2 Kgs 23:26, Is 5:25, Jer 4:8, Ps 78:38, Ezek 20:22. Fretheim also notes the mediating role in Nm 25:11, Ps 106:23, Jer 18:20.

and 106:45) and proclaimed in certain confessions of faith (Jl 2:12–14; Jon 4:2), it finds particular expression in narratives where such a reversal takes place in the form of an event. Thus, it is quite expedient and, indeed, fruitful to analyze several master narratives involving this theme. Jean-Pierre Sonnet reflectively explored this topic at some length, doing so with no small amount of creativity and inspiration.[19] Through an attentive reading of Genesis 6, Exodus 32, and 1 Samuel 15, this exegete developed a paradigm of the divine "beginnings" which emerge through a kind of double reversal. Here, we will schematically present it as follows: first attempt (creation or election); this is now jeopardized by a grave fault or pervasive evil; this leads to a delayed recovery, by means of a radical purification or new election.

In order to advance our own attempt to decipher the plotlines revealing God's anger, we must integrate the divine repentance into our considerations as providing a decisive moment in this overall interpretive endeavor. Otherwise, our interpretation of this anger will remain a merely notional affair. Therefore, let us first turn our attention to the account of Moses's intercession presented to us in Exodus 32. Following this, we will consider the reflective theorization which can be found in the prophetic body of writings themselves. However, already in Exodus 32, the mutual interactions between anger and repentance enable theological reflection to gain access to novel aspects of God's identity.

---

19. See Jean-Pierre Sonnet, "God's Repentance and 'False Starts' in Biblical History (Genesis 6–9; Exodus 32–34; 1 Samuel 15 and 2 Samuel 7)," in *Congress Volume Ljubljana 2007*, ed. André Lemaire (Leiden: Brill, 2010), 469–94; Sonnet, "Dieu sauve l'histoire comme en sous-main. La rhétorique des amendements divins," in *Raconter Dieu. Entre récit, histoire et théologie*, ed. Christian Dionne and Yvan Mathieu (Brussels: Lessius, 2014), 173–96.

FROM REGRET FOR THE ELECTION TO REPENTING OF THE THREAT ISSUED (EXODUS 32)

After repenting of the fact that he created mankind (Gn 6:6–7), it seems that God repents of the election of the people whom he created from next to nothing: an old and infertile couple. In his dialogue with Moses, God seems rather manipulative. He separates himself from the people whom he himself had called. Indeed, God addresses Moses by speaking of "your people," who denied the very God who freed them through the exodus. Instead of remaining devoted to the God who freed them and to the Law that he had given them, the people voluntarily estranged themselves from him by turning to the golden calf, thus (so to speak) slapping God in the face through their mendacity and infidelity:

And the LORD said to Moses, "Go down; for your people, whom you brought up out of the land of Egypt, have corrupted themselves; they have turned aside quickly out of the way which I commanded them; they have made for themselves a molten calf, and have worshiped it and sacrificed to it, and said, 'These are your gods, O Israel, who brought you up out of the land of Egypt!'" And the LORD said to Moses, "I have seen this people, and behold, it is a stiff-necked people; now therefore let me alone, that my wrath may burn hot against them and I may consume them; but of you I will make a great nation." (Ex 32:7–10)

Here anew, just as God once saw the goodness of what he had created, he now sees his people's sin. Next comes his rather ambivalent request to Moses: "now therefore let me alone, that my wrath may burn hot against them and I may consume them; but of you I will make a great nation" (Ex 32:10). God presents himself as exercising self-control, while being ready, however, to give free rein to his anger. The request addressed to Moses, "let me alone," has two meanings. First, "do not hold me back, for you have the power to do so." Yet, an implicit undertone is also present: "hold me back, or I will bring about some form of woe." God himself places Moses in the position of being a potential intercessor on behalf of the people, who now are faced with God's anger.

At the same time, God presents Moses with an attractive possibility: he would thus become the new head of the chosen people, a second Abraham. The destruction of the chosen people would still save the possibility of a new beginning, a new election. In this way, the divine design would continue along its course. Such a proposal could well be tempting, though it should also raise some concern. If God eliminates his first chosen people from the earth with such ready ease in response to their first grave failure, will he not act this way in the future as well? Does not the new beginning of the election merely postpone the problem to some future date? In any case, Moses resists this divine proposal that he himself become the chosen one. Instead, he chooses to take up God's proposal, implicit in the words, "let me alone," deciding instead to play, here and now, an intercessory role on behalf of the chosen people.

Now, whereas God, in his anger directed against his people, had imputed to Moses the exodus from Egypt, Moses, for his part, reestablishes the true assignment of roles: God is the one who led his people out of Egypt, a fact that was clear to everyone involved, starting with the Egyptians themselves. Hence, were God now to brush aside the people whom he had just saved, he would thereby provide a kind of divine counter-witness against his own activity. Moses reflects the image of God's anger back toward him: to give free rein to such anger would entail a resounding repudiation. This would represent a glaring contradiction on God's own part, ultimately presenting a counter-witness against his own action:

But Moses begged the LORD his God, and said, "O LORD, why does your wrath burn hot against your people, whom you have brought forth out of the land of Egypt with great power and with a mighty hand? Why should the Egyptians say, 'With evil intent he brought them forth, to slay them in the mountains, and to consume them from the face of the earth'? Turn away [*shub*] from your fierce wrath, and repent [*nacham*] of this evil against your people. Remember Abraham, Isaac, and Israel, your servants, to whom you swore by your own self, and said to them, 'I will multiply your descendants as the stars of heaven, and all this land that I have promised I will give to your descendants, and they shall inherit it forever.'" And the LORD repented [*nacham*] of the evil which he thought to do to his people. (Ex 32:11–14)

Moses's argument is unassailable. Taking into account the full perspective of the narrative presented, this is likely the response God had wanted to receive from his prophet when he said to him, "Let me alone." Nonetheless, it is quite remarkable that Moses ultimately addresses God in imperative statements: "turn away … repent …" Whereas God had opened before Moses the doorway to a new election, one centered on himself, Moses recalled the requirements of the already-existing election which already had been subject to a number of reversals for Abraham, Isaac, and Israel. Instead of mentioning Jacob by his birth name, Moses here makes use of the new name given to Jacob, whereby he had become the representative of the chosen people: Israel.

Let us note well that Moses's pleading is indeed unassailable, even for God. If the latter's intention was for Moses to hold him back from giving in to his anger, he could have expected no better service from his prophet. The ultimate outcome suggests that God did not inflexibly wish to harm his people but, rather, simply *said* that he wanted to do so, precisely so that Moses might prevent him from doing so. Moses himself provides God with the justification for his own perseverance. In the overall drama, God changed his position twice, first concerning the election of the people, then in relation to the threat that he would destroy them. Literally speaking, the divine repentance (*nacham*) is connected to the threat that was uttered but not performed.

The rest of the narrative is at odds with the mollifying intercession that Moses presents to God. Indeed, Moses then gives free rein to his own anger, rallying those who are partisans on behalf of the Lord so that they may attack their unfaithful fellow men and women in the camp. Similarly, God promises to undertake a targeted punishment of those who are guilty. Indeed, the text of Exodus clearly states that God struck the people (Ex 32:35). Reading this text with a critical eye, we can assume that two different textual traditions were brought together here, ones that resist being easily reconciled into a single, coherent narrative framework. Hypotheses can be formed and solutions offered by assuming that there are successive layers of writing involved in the received account. As the adjustments to the sacred text have been brought about by way of addition and not elimination, the tension between the beginning and the end of the narrative is tolerable. Nonetheless, we could justify a reading of the narrative as presenting God repenting of his excessive anger without thereby nullifying the justice of a limited punishment. The generation that sinned in the desert will not enter the Promised Land, and even Moses himself will only see it from afar.

By continuing to read Exodus, we can see that God's repentance leads to a significant reshuffling of affairs, indeed, constituting a turning point in the progressive unveiling of God's identity. This is quite clear in God's self-presentation when the covenant is renewed in Exodus 34. Just before this, God and Moses spoke like two friends. Moses begged God to turn back to his people and to walk alongside them, for this represents the only privilege that differentiates them from among the nations (Ex 33). Finally, Moses recarves the two stone tablets on which God himself wishes to rewrite his Law. The renewal of the covenant opens up with two, interconnected stages: God's descent and Moses's invocation. God then declares his identity in words that are similar to those spoken in Exodus 20, when the covenantal Law was given to the people. What is new here is the fact that the divine attributes of judgment and mercy have come to be reversed.[20] In this self-presentation of the divine identity, we find a kind of echo of the conversion that was already brought about in a narrative form through the divine repentance discussed above. Compare Exodus 20:1–6 and 34:5–7 (respectively):

---

20. See Jean-Pierre Sonnet, "Justice et miséricorde. Les attributs de Dieu dans la dynamique narrative du Pentateuque," *Nouvelle Revue Théologique* 138, no. 1 (2016): 3–22.

And God spoke all these words, saying, "I am the LORD your God, who brought you out of the land of Egypt, out of the house of bondage. You shall have no other gods before me. You shall not make for yourself a graven image, or any likeness of anything that is in heaven above, or that is in the earth beneath, or that is in the water under the earth; you shall not bow down to them or serve them for I the LORD your God am a jealous [*qanna*] God, visiting [*paqad*] the iniquity of the fathers upon the children to the third and the fourth generation of those who hate me, but showing mercy [*chesed*] to thousands of those who love me and keep my commandments."

And the LORD descended in the cloud and stood with him there, and proclaimed the name of the LORD. The LORD passed before him, and proclaimed, "The LORD, the LORD, a God merciful [*rachum*] and gracious [*channun*], slow to anger, and abounding in mercy [*chesed*] and faithfulness [*emeth*], keeping merciful love for thousands, forgiving iniquity and transgression and sin, but who will by no means clear the guilty, visiting [*paqad*] the iniquity of the fathers upon the children and the children's children, to the third and the fourth generation."

In what sense does God inspect man and to what degree does he punish faults? In each text, Exodus 20 and 34, time is measured in generations. God takes the fault into consideration for three or four generations, whereas he extends his faithfulness over thousands (i.e., an infinite number) of generations. The mention of three or four generations does not necessarily mean that God inevitably attributes guilt from generation to generation, down to the fourth, to the point of holding even little children guilty of faults they did not themselves commit. This would represent a kind of arbitrary automatism contrary to just retribution. The language of three or four generations indicates an extent of time that falls within the awareness of a single person's lifespan. Therefore, it should be understood, instead, as meaning that the fathers who are at fault are exposed to the possibility that their sin would be reproduced by their own offspring who will know these faults during their own lifetime. Thus, Jean-Pierre Sonnet interprets the three or four generations on the basis of the verb *paqad* which means "to visit, inspect, intervene in favor of, or to punish":

What God inspects is a process: sons, grandsons, and great-grandsons all live in the wake of an "original" wrongdoing. They suffer its consequences … Thus affected by the repercussions of their father's wrongdoing (as well as that of their grandfather and great-grandfather), will the sons go so far as to give this fault new life by themselves committing it in their own turn (see Jer 16:11–12)? In the end, this is what God is concerned with here.[21]

While God does indeed rigorously inspect his people, his show of grace is even greater in its fidelity. In Exodus 34, the affirmation that God is faithful unto thousands of generations is emphasized in two ways. On the one hand, the ordering of the attributes of judgment (*paqad*) and fidelity (*chesed*) is reversed in comparison to Exodus 20. On the other hand, fidelity is preceded by an extended, contextualizing list of related descriptors, thereby being set in relation to the earlier events wherein God made the visceral depths of his mercy prevail over his anger: "A God merciful [*rachum*] and gracious [*channun*], slow to anger, and abounding in mercy [*chesed*] and faithfulness [*emeth*]" (Ex 34:6).

Another element distinguishes the statement of identity expressed in Exodus 34 from that which is found in Exodus 20. After the episode involving the golden calf and God's sovereign repentance, the attributes of judgment and fidelity—in other words, the divine justice and mercy—no longer seem to be conditioned by the human attitudes of hate or love, as was the case in the self-presentation found in Exodus 20. Such an accentuation of the divine sovereignty or freedom is consistent with the divine repentance for which Moses had interceded. Indeed, God made his mercy prevail over his judgment without there being any noteworthy change on the part of his people. We must not look to them to find the determining factor for the divine action. Moreover, the sovereignty of the divine repentance is proclaimed by Moses in his canticle to the Rock of Israel at the end of the Pentateuch in Deuteronomy 32:36.

21. Ibid., 7; reference is made to Vincent Sénéchal, *Rétribution et intercession dans le Deutéronome* (Berlin: W. de Gruyter, 2009), 231.

Thus, in view of the full development of the fundamental plot of Exodus 32, we come to see that anger is not a first-order attribute of the biblical God. Love and grace, as well as patience and mercy, are all first-order dispositions which God has in relation to his chosen people and, indeed, to all of his creatures (Ex 34:5–8). The priority of love and grace is not expressed by way of a hierarchized set of abstract principles but, rather, as the ultimate outcome of the plot presented to us in the scriptural narrative. *A priori*, anger should never have the final, irrevocable word, and the divine repentance bears witness to this fact (Ex 32:14). However, we still must fear that sinners could indeed make their own anger and sanctions definitive when they harden their hearts without the hope of reversal.

The scenario presented in Exodus 32 is not a fixed model for later cases of divine repentance. The body of prophetic writings presents us with other modalities of the divine repentance, revealed through the various ways that humans take up their relationship with God. Thus, the triangulation that exists between God, his people, and his prophets plays out in various ways.

REPENTANCE OF A PREVIOUSLY ANNOUNCED WOE: JEREMIAH, JONAH, JOEL

Up to this point, the divine repentance has played out without itself being explicitly reflected on or explained. In the body of the prophetic works, there will be many more scenarios bearing witness to God's mercy, but here they are accompanied by the first sketches of a theological justification for the divine repentance or non-repentance. This finds a particularly eloquent expression in Jeremiah.

In this prophetic text, the divine repentance is given a precise meaning which is at once clarified by God and experienced by the people of Judah. If the people turn back and listen to the Lord's words, spoken invectively against his people, God will then, in his own turn, repent of the woe that had been proclaimed as a threat to his people. This is clear in the narrative in Jeremiah 26, which presents a biographical account of Jeremiah's preaching in the Temple courtyard (Jer 7:1–15). The Lord's words of warning explicitly aim at leading the people to conversion and, consequently, also aim at his own repentance of the woes that had been announced:

In the beginning of the reign of Jehoi'akim the son of Josi'ah, king of Judah, this word came from the LORD, "Thus says the LORD: Stand in the court of the LORD's house, and speak to all the cities of Judah which come to worship in the house of the LORD all the words that I command you to speak to them; do not hold back a word. It may be they will listen, and every one turn (*shub*) from his evil way, that I may repent [*nacham*] of the evil which I intend to do to them because of their evil doings. You shall say to them, 'Thus says the LORD: If you will not listen to me, to walk in my law which I have set before you, and to heed the words of my servants the prophets whom I send to you urgently, though you have not heeded, then I will make this house like Shiloh, and I will make this city a curse for all the nations of the earth.'" (Jer 26:1–6)

The first reaction by the priests, prophets, and people is to threaten Jeremiah with death. Nonetheless, the authorities do indeed recognize that he spoke in the name of the Lord. This is due to the fact that the elderly recall how the prophet Micah had himself predicted to King Hezekiah that Jerusalem would be destroyed. However, in that case, the king and the people took the Lord's threat to heart, and the Lord thus repented of the woe that he had announced (Jer 26:17–19; Mic 3:12). When the Lord's threat is followed by the people's own amendment, it thus attains the end that it had aimed at, and God therefore has no reason for maintaining it. Thus, he repents of the evil that had been previously announced.

Prior to this, making use of the allegory of the potter and the clay, the Lord had himself revealed to Jeremiah a brief, figurative theology of the divine repentance, thus presenting his prophet with a theory explaining his own praxis. However, this explanation is not given to the people as a whole but, instead, only to the prophet who is thereby introduced into the intimate justification for the divine behavior:

Then the word of the LORD came to me: "O house of Israel, can I not do with you as this potter has done? says the LORD. Behold, like the clay in the potter's hand, so are you in my hand, O house of Israel. If at any time I declare concerning a nation or a kingdom, that I will pluck up and break down and destroy it, and if that nation, concerning which I have spoken, turns [*shub*] from its evil, I will repent [*nacham*] of the evil that I intended to do to it. And if at any time I declare concerning a nation or a kingdom that I will build and plant it, and if it does evil in my sight, not listening to my voice, then I will repent [*nacham*] of the good which I had intended to do to it." (Jer 18:5–10)

The theory thus appears as being more complete than the current practice. God can repent of good and not only of evil. Whereas the prophet is informed about the divine pedagogy, the portion of the prophecy that is immediately intended for the people is limited to the injunction and threat: "Now, therefore, say to the men of Judah and the inhabitants of Jerusalem: 'Thus says the LORD, "Behold, I am shaping evil against you and devising a plan against you. Return (*shub*), every one from his evil way, and amend your ways and your doings"'" (Jer 18:11).

The people do not have access to the motivations for the divine plans. They are simply and directly challenged. This prevents them from seeing the pressing urgency of conversion as being a kind of coercive threat presented to them by God. By contrast, Jeremiah is aware of the code of conduct that God is following as he works to save his people. All of this is in harmony with the way that God joins his mediators and intercessors with his own action: "Surely the Lord GOD does nothing, without revealing his secret to his servants the prophets" (Am 3:7).

What holds true here for Judah or Israel remains no less true when God speaks to the pagans. An analogous kind of triangulation is found in the events involving God, Jonah, and Nineveh, the large pagan city. Here, the narrative tension is even more pronounced, for the prophet Jonah and the pagan king play inverted roles. Instead of acting as an intercessor, the prophet is distressed by the conversion of Nineveh and the divine repentance. Immediately upon the proclamation of the Lord's words by Jonah—"Yet forty days, and Nineveh shall be overthrown" (Jon 3:4)—the inhabitants of the city respond through penitential actions. The king of Nineveh decrees that the people are to fast and pray, thus making explicit the hope that God may repent of misfortune, which nonetheless has been declared as being their certain fate in a mere forty days' time:

Then tidings reached the king of Nineveh, and he arose from his throne, removed his robe, and covered himself with sackcloth, and sat in ashes. And he made proclamation and published through Nineveh, "By the decree of the king and his nobles: Let neither man nor beast, herd nor flock, taste anything; let them not feed, or drink water, but let man and beast be covered with sackcloth, and let them cry mightily to God; yes, let every one turn from his evil way and from the violence which is in his hands. Who knows, God may yet repent [*nacham*] and turn [*shub*] from his fierce anger, so that we perish not?" When God saw what they did, how they turned [*shub*] from their evil way, God repented [*nacham*] of the evil which he had said he would do to them; and he did not do it. (Jon 3:6–10)

The king of Nineveh was correct in his intuitions—indeed, they turn out to be edifying as regards faith, hope, and self-abandonment. By contrast, the prophet still needs time to catch up. The prophet's own proclamation of Nineveh's destruction was formulated in an unconditional manner. It seemed to be unavoidable. Thus, Jonah finds himself to be in an unsettling, if not dangerous, situation, for the prophet who announces events which then fail to be fulfilled risks being likened to a false prophet (Dt 18:21–22). Despite his ill temper at this state of affairs, Jonah does manage to set forth God's attributes accurately. Railing against God's mercy for Nineveh, he nevertheless is forced to integrate mercy and repentance into the characteristic attributes of his God:

But it displeased Jonah exceedingly, and he was angry. And he prayed to the LORD and said, "I pray you, LORD, is not this what I said when I was yet in my country? That is why I made haste to flee to Tar'shish; for I knew that you are a gracious God and merciful, slow to anger, and abounding in mercy, and that you repent [*nacham*] of evil. Therefore now, O LORD, take my life from me, I beg you, for it is better for me to die than to live." And the LORD said, "Do you do well to be angry?" (Jon 4:1–4)

God then presents Jonah with a practical lesson in mercy. While Jonah is preoccupied with the shade provided by his castor bush, God has mercy on Nineveh: "And should not I pity Nineveh, that great city, in which there are more than a hundred and twenty thousand persons who do not know their right hand from their left, and also much cattle" (Jn 4:11). However surly Jonah might be, his experience of the divine repentance leads him to confess mercy and repentance as being first-order divine attributes. Moreover, he also obtains, as a prophet, an explanation for how God acts.

What God was aiming at by threatening to destroy Nineveh was actually something other than the destruction of the city. Nonetheless, the proclamation of the threat fulfilled its function as something intended to spur the people on to conversion. On another level of explanation, we could say that the Nineveh to which it was addressed, the sinful Nineveh, has indeed been destroyed. The threat was not made in vain. As Augustine argues: "What God predicted came to pass: the Nineveh that was wicked was overthrown, and a good Nineveh was built which did not exist before."[22] Some dimension of the threat has indeed been fulfilled—not the material destruction of Nineveh but rather the moral destruction of what Nineveh was at the moment when the divine threat sounded forth in the words conveyed to Jonah. Indirectly, this leads to a new way of understanding the divine repentance. God repented in the sense that he did not do what his threat meant for the Ninevites and for Jonah. However, God did not repent of what he had first foreseen and aimed at: the conversion of Nineveh and the destruction of its sins.

The prophets perfectly integrated the divine repentance into the characteristic traits of God's behavior in relation to sinners. In Joel, a call to repentance, mercy, and repentance are established as being stable features of God's identity. Henceforth, it is a rather settled affair: God repents of announced woes when those to whom they are announced convert in response to his threat:

---

22. Augustine, *De civitate Dei* XXI.24 (455).

"Yet even now," says the LORD, "return to me with all your heart, with fasting, with weeping, and with mourning; and tear your hearts and not your garments." Return [*shub*] to the LORD, your God, for he is gracious and merciful, slow to anger, and abounding in mercy, and repents [*nacham*] of evil. Who knows whether he will not turn and repent [*nacham*], and leave a blessing behind him, a cereal offering and a drink offering for the LORD, your God? (Jl 2:12–14)

In the prophets, the divine repentance does not merely represent a key moment in the particular interactions between God and his people (or other groups) but, even more so, represents a distinctive trait of God such as he is invoked and confessed. This is accompanied by rather developed points of theological elucidation. Repentance has become one of God's stable attributes, having affinity with the priority of God's mercy over his judgment.

THE KEY SCENARIOS BEARING WITNESS TO GOD'S REPENTANCE AND THE MEANINGS OF HIS ANGER

Within the resounding polyphony expressed in various biblical texts, the divine repentance is encountered in various narrative sequences. Here, drawing our focused rereadings to a close, we can schematically represent these sequences as follows:

- Creation ⟶ perversion ⟶ divine rejection / another election ⟶ divine non-repentance (Gn 6; 1 Sm 15)
- Election ⟶ sin ⟶ divine threat ⟶ intercession by the prophet ⟶ divine repentance (Ex 32)
- Election ⟶ sin ⟶ divine threat ⟶ conversion of sinners ⟶ divine repentance (Jer 26; Jon 3)

The motif of divine repentance is connected with the emotions imputed to God or expressed by him: sadness, anger, and pity. When God's repentance is part of a pedagogical threat, such as we find in the text of Jeremiah, God appears relatively serene in comparison to other situations where we find him viscerally upset in his Fatherly love, to the point of turning aside from destructive punishment of any sort, as we see in Hosea 11:8–9.

Let us return to Jean-Pierre Sonnet's intuition, already glimpsed in Augustine, for we now can confirm it. Through the divine repentance, the election comes to be overhauled, revived, transferred, or bifurcated. None of the stages of repentance indicate a definite stopping point or a pure annihilation. Under the modality of repentance, we can discern, paradoxically, a form of divine perseverance: God revives, resumes, adjusts, and renews the covenant in fidelity to his plans. The divine decrees can change in relation to their foreseeable effects and their human meanings, whereas the divine plan is perfectly stable. The divine repentance is compatible with the immutability of his *consilium* and will.[23] Both the divine threat and God's repentance are paradoxically signs of the continuity of his commitment. However, we must bear in mind that even when God repents of a woe that he has announced or anticipated as a threat, this does not always exempt sinners from suffering historical evils which are interpreted as being a punishment that is just or mitigated.[24]

By recognizing the importance of the plot that connects them together, we have striven to do more than merely interpret God's repentance and anger as though they were rhetorical metaphors. In response to the aporetic questions raised in our introduction, we thus have attempted to recognize anger and repentance as being semantic metaphors whose meaning can be qualified through the interplay of the various interactions found in a given poetic framework or narrative construction. It is important that we remember that anger and repentance are not revealed as isolatable concepts within wholly separable sequences of actions. They receive their meaning within spe-

---

23. In addition to the aforementioned distinctions made by Augustine, see their creative reception in Gregory the Great, *Moralia in Job* XVI.37.46 and Aquinas, *SCG* III.96.15. For a discussion of this issue in terms of the effectiveness of the prayer of request, see Emmanuel Durand, "The Gospel of Prayer and Theories of Providence," *The Thomist* 78, no. 4 (2014): 519–36.

24. See Thomas Römer, "Yhwh peut-il changer d'avis? Arbitraire, colère, repentir, compassion divins dans la Bible hébraïque," in his *Colère et repentirs divins*, 313–24, at 323–24.

cific chains of events. Nonetheless, we can make significant strides in the direction of a more generalized theology of the divine anger and repentance. In relation to the plotline having the renewal of the covenant as its ultimate outcome, Exodus 34:6–7 places mercy before judgment in God's self-presentation. Thereafter, in a number of confessions of faith, repentance is duly situated among the attributes related to God's mercy. If divine anger and repentance are indeed metaphors, we can quite fruitfully receive them as semantic metaphors. Their theological scope is not entirely knowable in advance.

Our initial objective was to envision the divine anger with fresh eyes by taking a detour through the biblical narratives that present us with cases of the divine repentance. This journey has turned out to be theologically fruitful. We now can thematically summarize a number of functions of God's anger. They are variously attested to in the biblical narratives where this motif arises:

- Anger reveals and partially anticipates the fatal outcome which unfolds from the constraining logic of sin
- Anger aims at the amendment of sinners so that they may turn away from their wicked ways and return to God
- Anger reveals what the chosen people would be exposed to in the absence of the divine favor and mercy
- Anger manifests the fundamental incompatibility between God and evil, as well as the energy God expends in confronting it, without allowing it to have the last word

If the metaphor of anger is theologically deciphered, it contains a precious intuition which reveals something properly attributable to God: sin is completely intolerable and unbearable to him. God's anger is essentially an active and consistent indignation in the face of evil.[25] He expresses no indulgence for the evils and sins that affect his people or creatures, an attitude that stands in stark contrast to

25. See Abraham J. Heschel, "The Meaning and Mystery of Wrath," in his *The Prophets* (New York: Harper and Row, 1962), 2:59–78; Raymund Schwager, "Der Zorn Gottes. Zur Problematik der Allegorie," *Zeitschrift für katholische Theologie* 105, no. 4 (1983): 406–14.

human beings who often remain ambiguous when faced with such evils. God does not suffer the disfiguration that his sinful creatures inflict upon themselves and, correlatively, upon one another. The complete incompatibility between God and sin comes to be expressed, in metaphorical language, by the excess or disproportion of the divine anger. On the level of human emotions, anger implies a reversal: instead of suffering evil, it enables him to confront it and, if possible, to turn it back. God's anger expresses a form of his victorious confrontation with evil and sin.

Anger is a derivative passion, the antecedents of which are love or sadness. When God is its subject, it is proportioned to the love that he has invested in creation or in the election of his people. God's disappointment is not expressed in the form of bitter sadness but rather in the form of anger. Anger implies the power to turn back and for God's own part, this power becomes salvation. God confronts sinners and closed-off situations. His anger comes to be expressed in the efficaciously performative utterance: "That's enough!"

Finally, the biblical plotlines concerning the divine anger and repentance take the form of divine self-declarations and confessions of faith. Wending through the twisting paths of these storylines, the priority of mercy over anger comes to be revealed in a convincing and credible manner. It was fitting that this would be revealed through events and narrative accounts, for otherwise it would never have been taken seriously, nor believed.

At the beginning of his *Confessions,* Augustine asked himself, "What, then, are You, O my God?" He responds by way of an invocation, reflectively presenting a series of superabundant attributions and mysterious paradoxes, such as "most hidden and most near." Among the paradoxical associations, one sequence incorporates a series of passions: desire, love, jealousy, remorse, and anger. However, from the outset, his manner of enunciating these attributes functions at lofty heights: "You love without frenzy, you are jealous yet secure, you regret [*paenitet*] without sadness [*doles*], you grow angry yet remain tranquil, you alter your works [*opera*] but never your plan [*consilium*]."[26] When St. Augustine's writing takes the form of a direct invocation, he readily makes use of metaphors drawn from human emotions, as do the scriptures. His use of paradox helps to establish an immediate form of equilibrium, without presenting a didactic exposition. The language used by the believer in direct invocations to God is far loftier than the vocabulary used by exegesis or theology. Nonetheless, as we can see, for example, in the fifth book of the *De Trinitate* (where Augustine presents paradoxes similar to those of the *Confessions*, though in a non-doxological, argumentative manner), exegesis and theology help to increase one's clarity regarding the subject of the invocation in question, thus helping to provide greater precision and determination to our language concerning the divine mystery revealed in the plotlines presented to us in scripture.[27]

26. Augustine, *Confessiones* I.4.4 (41). The first five sections of the *Confessions* present a brief theology of invocation in action, questioning the close relations that exist between seeking, understanding, invoking, and praising.

27. See Augustine, *De Trinitate* V.2, where the forms and categories of common experience are ruled out in relation our knowledge of God, after being grasped by our intellect. God is to be considered as "good without quality," "great without quantity," "creator without need," "present without localization," "containing all things without possession," "in all places without being in space," "eternal without time," and so forth.

6

Is the Immutable God Subject to Sorrow?

The sorrow of God is a motif which does not immediately jump to one's eyes when reading the Bible. And yet, from the first pages of Genesis, we very quickly see God revealing that he is afflicted as the adventure of creation begins to run its course. Looking upon the orientation of the first generations following the sin of Adam and Eve, God is, as it were, forced to experience the wickedness which flourishes in human hearts (Gn 6:5–6). As the narrative is presented to us, God seems almost astonished and disconcerted by what he sees. Nonetheless, in the history of Noah and his descendants, we see that God has resources at hand for assuring that his design may be recovered in a realistic manner.

The rhetoric of God's complaints or his sorrow can be found elsewhere in the Bible as well, although such complaints more often come forth from the prophet (e.g., Jer 4:19–21, 8:18, 14:17–18) than from God himself (e.g., Jer 12:7–13). Sometimes, the prophet expresses his own sorrow in solidarity with his people, whereas at other times he speaks in the name of the Lord, expressing in human words what God is, in some manner, living through. However, it remains a striking fact that sorrow is imputed to God much less than are other divine passions or emotions such as anger, joy, love, and so forth.

According to the New Testament, human beings can somehow affect God by resisting the Spirit's inspirations: "And do not grieve the Holy Spirit of God, in whom you were sealed for the day of redemption" (Eph 4:30). By yielding to bitterness, anger, or wickedness, the Christian is said to bring sorrow to the Spirit of God.

In order to understand the full amplitude of God's sorrow, we must widen the vistas of our investigation into this theme, turning our attention toward the way our faith is expressed liturgically. Thus, we understandably find our gaze drawn to liturgy of Good Friday, the celebration of Jesus' passion. Beginning our reflection with a consideration of an ancient liturgical chant, we will thus listen to the *lex orandi*, the authentic testimony of Christian prayer. After grasping its scope and teaching, we will see how the eloquent expression of God's complaints can be reconciled with the *lex credendi*, heeding, in particular, the testimony of the Councils concerning God's immutability. This will require us to describe God's sorrow anew, looking upon it as a specific kind of sorrow, lived entirely for the other and not in the form of oneself being affected by others.

THE ELOQUENT EXPRESSION OF
GOD'S COMPLAINT

The chanting of the reproaches (in Latin, *improperia*) performed during the veneration of the cross during the liturgy of Good Friday in the Roman Rite eloquently expresses God's complaints.[1] The interpretation of this chant is rich, complex, and contentious.[2] According to a variety of interpretive outlooks, the reproaches bear witness to a close connection which exists between God and the

---

1. I would like to thank Patrick Prétot for his advice, which was of great assistance in clarifying certain points involved in this brief, theological reading of the reproaches. For an excellent discussion concerning the liturgy of Good Friday, see Patrick Prétot, *L'adoration de la croix. Triduum pascal* (Paris: Cerf, 2014).

2. See Louis Van Tongeren, "Les Improperia du Vendredi saint au banc des accusés," *Questions liturgiques* 83, no. 4 (2002): 240–56; Michael D. Brocke, "On the Jewish Origin of the Improperia," *Immanuel* 7 (1997): 44–51.

crucified one. However, serious objections have been raised against this chant in Jewish and Lutheran circles, accusing it of being a vector for justifying secular anti-Judaism. The first, direct reference for God's reproaches are the Jewish people. They are inveighed against as though they alone were responsible for the crucifixion and, in the final analysis, guilty of deicide.

Today, this kind of projection of guilt onto the Jewish people is unacceptable for Catholic theology, even though its tradition does indeed bear the marks of anti-Judaism, following in the wake of the Church Fathers (both Greek and Latin). Moreover, an anti-Jewish interpretation of this chant seems far too abstract when we consider the character of its execution in the course of the liturgy. This broader context makes it quite clear that the assembly should understand God's complaints and reproaches as being addressed to the assembly gathered there and not to the Jewish people, as though they were a scapegoat upon whom blame might be projected from a distance.

The chant itself is composed of a refrain along with a response, with two series of couplets. The first series is composed of three stanzas of increasing length, whereas the second series parallels nine brief stanzas having a balanced structure: "I have … You have …" Here, it will suffice to consider the whole that is formed by the first sequence, which is the most ancient and the most developed one. It already contains, in full, the riches that will be taken up in all nine stanzas making up the second series. Moreover, the three first couplets involve three subjects: the One who speaks, the savior, and the people. By contrast, the couplets of the second series adhere to simple back-and-forth between God and his people. See the *Missale Romanum*, issued by Pope Paul VI in 1969:

> O my people, what have I done unto you?
> Or in what way brought you sorrow?
> Answer me!
>
> Because I led you out of the land of Egypt,
> You have prepared a cross for your savior.
> O my people, what have I done unto you?

Or in what way brought sorrow unto you?
Answer me!

Holy God. Holy God.
Holy and Mighty. Holy and Mighty.
Holy and Immortal, have mercy on us.
Holy and Immortal, have mercy on us.

Because I led you through the desert for forty years
and fed you upon manna,
then leading you into a land of plenty,
you have prepared a cross for your savior.

Holy God. Holy God.
Holy and Mighty. Holy and Mighty.
Holy and Immortal, have mercy on us.
Holy and Immortal, have mercy on us.

What more should I have done for you which I did not do?
Indeed, I planted you, my chosen and most beautiful vine,
and you have only great bitterness toward me,
for you have given me vinegar to quench my thirst,
and with a lance you have pierced your savior's side.

Holy God. Holy God.
Holy and Mighty. Holy and Mighty.
Holy and Immortal, have mercy on us.
Holy and Immortal, have mercy on us.

The refrain is addressed to "my people," and the response is addressed to God: "Holy God, Holy and Mighty, Holy and Immortal." This places the assembly in dialogue with God himself, a dialogue which he himself has initiated. The expression "my people" has two possible meanings: in the literal sense, it refers to the chosen people, the immediate beneficiary of the blessings mentioned in the couplets; and typologically, it refers to the Christian assembly performing the chant and responding to God.

Within this liturgical context, it would be preposterous to wish to separate these two meanings. The meaning of the chant involves neither solely the Jewish people in opposition to God, nor the church which would have been substituted for the chosen people.

The Christian assembly is included among the people to whom God addresses his complaints and reproaches. And it is the Christian assembly who uniquely chants *miserere nobis*, not the Jewish people.

A TRIANGULATION OF INTERLOCUTORS

The first three stanzas respectively counterbalance the exodus from Egypt and the cross, the crossing of the desert and the cross, and the election of the people of Israel and the passion, referred to under the two motifs of vinegar and the lance. Depending on the various possible identities of the "savior," the theology involved in the couplets varies in significant ways:

- If the savior is God, he is identified with the initial subject who speaks: God is fully identified with the crucified one
- If the savior is Christ and is identified with the initial subject: Christ is the author of the exodus and the election
- If the savior is Christ but is not identified with the initial subject: God expresses his complaint concerning the crucified

At first glance, the dialogue between the refrain and the response presents itself as being a dialogue between God and his people. However, it could also be a dialogue between Christ and his people. Placed within the context of the liturgical veneration of the cross, the crucified one would thus be confessed as the "Holy God, the Holy and Mighty God, the Immortal God."

It seems impossible to settle exclusively on one of the three interpretive options presented above. They open up the condensed riches of the mystery into the liturgical performance of chant, where emotion and action leave little room for clear, formalized distinctions.

In terms of emotions, those who live the very celebration of Good Friday, where the reproaches are chanted, experience a challenge which is presented to them by God and by Christ. They feel an intimate solidarity between the passion of the crucified one and the complaints of God, as well as a contrasting correlation between the

blessings of the exodus and the punishment exacted upon the crucified one. The chanting of the reproaches enables the members of the
assembly to experience a sorrow that can develop into contrition.

In the liturgical action, this chant accompanies a procession toward the cross, ending with each believer coming forward to kiss either the body of the crucified one or the wood which bears him. The
response to the complaint expressed by the chant is a gesture of veneration and love by those who recognize that they are implicated in
Jesus' passion precisely because of their own sins.

In the dialogue between God and his people, the rhetoric of sorrow is subtle. God (or Christ) challenges the people by the question: "In what way have I brought sorrow unto you?" The question
itself reveals the sorrow felt by him who asks it, and he who initiates
the dialogue stands in a kind of inverted position. If God (or Christ)
poses such a question, he does so because he himself is profoundly sorrowful, to the point of seeking out an answer to the question,
"Why?," which is raised by his sorrow, all the while knowing that no
justification can be offered in response to his inquiry. Indeed, the
only response that the people brings forth is the confession of God's
holiness, the *miserere nobis*, and the kisses that they deposit upon
the cross.

The interplay among the various subjects suggests that God's sorrow is at once revelatory and yet indirect. It is by means of the cross
that God is affected in Christ. The expressive and powerful character
of the complaint cannot ultimately be translated by some unquali-
fied suffering experienced by God, given the subtle triangulation of
subjects implied here. God's sorrow is expressed in a doubly indirect
fashion: he asks his people about their sorrow; God's implicit sorrow
is concerned with how Christ is treated.

Let us bear in mind the intensity of God's complaint and the eloquently expressive character of the sorrow modulated through the
paradoxes of giving and rejection, along with the response directly
addressed to the crucified one through the kissing of the cross.

GOD'S IMMUTABILITY: A DIFFICULT
BUT IRREDUCIBLE TRUTH

In order to shed some light on what is needed for setting forth a theology of God's sorrow, we must reconsider his complaint in light of the divine immutability, using this as a kind of necessary filter for understanding the divine reality we are here reflecting upon. In short, we are here looking to attempt, concerning God's sorrow, what St. Augustine succeeded in doing for the case of the divine repentance. The divine immutability does not intrude here like a principle which would overshadow the eloquently expressive nature of God's complaint. Instead, it represents a necessary criterion for maintaining orthodoxy in our discourse concerning Christ, in whom humanity and divinity are united, without confusion or separation. This divine immutability was confessed by the ancient Councils on a number of occasions.

The Councils on the Immutability
and the Flesh of Christ

The divine immutability is something that is repeatedly affirmed by the church in her declarations concerning God. At the Council of Nicaea, the anathema connected to the symbol of faith rejects the claim that "the Son of God may be created or subject to change and alteration."[3] For the Fathers of Nicaea, the denial of Son's immutability would ultimately lead one to fall into Arius's heresy, making the Son into a superior kind of creature. To hold that the generation of the Son is a kind of becoming goes hand in hand with the rejection of his eternity. On the level of Christological speculation, such an

---

3. Council of Nicaea, "Profession of Faith," in Heinrich Denzinger, *Enchiridion Symbolorum definitionum et declarationum de rebus fidei et morum / Compendium of Creeds, Definitions, and Declarations on Matters of Faith and Morals*, edited by Peter Hünermann, 43rd ed. (San Francisco, Calif.: Ignatius Press, 2012) [hereafter Denzinger], no. 126 (51): "However, those who say: 'There was a time when he was not' and 'Before he was born he was not' and that he was made from nothing or who say that the Son of God may be of a different hypostasis or essence, or may be created or subject to change and alteration, [such persons] the Catholic Church anathematizes."

outlook requires one to make a distinction between the immutability proper to Christ inasmuch as he is the Word and the weaknesses which belonged to him in the flesh that he received from Mary.[4]

A little after the First Council of Constantinople (381), the Council of Rome (382) refused to connect the suffering of the cross directly to God: "Anyone who says that in the Passion of the Cross it is God himself who felt the pain and not the flesh and the soul that Christ, the Son of God, had taken to himself—the form of a servant that he had accepted, as Scripture says [Phil 2:7]—he is mistaken."[5] Here we see, as it were, a dawning articulation of the distinction of Christ's two natures, something necessary for the Christological interpretation of the New Testament[6] and for a correct theological understanding of the cross of the Son of God.

The second letter of Cyril to Nestorius, proclaimed at the Council of Ephesus in 431, explicitly makes recourse to the distinction between the two natures in the one Christ, holding that the Word is impassible and incorruptible by his very nature:

In a similar way we say that he suffered and rose again, not that the Word of God suffered blows or piercing with nails or any other wounds in his own nature (for the divine, being without a body, is incapable of suffering), but because the body which became his own suffered these things, he is said to have suffered them for us. For he was without suffering, while his body suffered. Something similar is true of his dying. For by nature the Word of God is of itself immortal and incorruptible and life and life-giving, but since on the other hand his own body by God's grace, as the apostle says, tasted death for all, the Word is said to have suffered death for us, not as if he himself had experienced death as far as his own nature was concerned (it would be sheer lunacy to say or to think that), but because, as I have just said, his flesh tasted death. So too, when his flesh was raised to life, we refer to this again as his resurrection, not as though he had fallen into corruption—God forbid—but because his body had been raised again.[7]

4. See Athanasius of Alexandria, *Contra arianos* III.29–35.

5. Council of Rome, "Tome of Damasus," in Denzinger, no. 166.

6. See Augustine, *De Trinitate* I.14.

7. Cyril of Alexandria, "Second Letter of Cyril to Nestorius," in *Decrees of the Ecumenical Councils: Nicaea I to Lateran V*, ed. Norman P. Tanner (Washington, D.C.: Georgetown University Press, 1990), 42.

As regards the passion, death, and resurrection of the one Christ, the Word born in the flesh, Cyril makes use of the distinction between the divine nature and his body or flesh. He does not expressly speak of his soul; however, in speaking of Christ's "flesh," he is referring to the whole of his human nature.

In the face of a reinvigorated monophysitism, the introduction to the declaration of Chalcedon responds to those who, following the example of Eutyches, "introduce admixture and mingling and foolishly imagine that there is one nature of the flesh and the Godhead and make the preposterous claim that, because of the commingling, the divinity of the Only-Begotten is subject to suffering." Moreover, the Council "excludes from the assembly of priests those who have the effrontery to say that the Godhead of the Only-Begotten is subject to suffering."[8]

A century later, the interpretation of Chalcedon expressed by Constantinople II (553) will finally enable an orthodox reception of the formula, "One of the Trinity Suffered." The union of the divinity and humanity is brought about in the one hypostasis, allowing the properties of each of the two natures to remain safe and distinct: "Our Lord Jesus Christ is true God, Lord of Glory and one of the Holy Trinity."[9]

Thus, let us summarize the data we have briefly gathered together here. In the Conciliar tradition, immutability represents an indisputable property of the divine nature. The primary objective of these dogmatic declarations is to assure that this property is fully respected in relation to discussions concerning the generation of the Son of God, his incarnation, or his passion, without improperly transferring the becoming or suffering involved therein to the divine nature of the Word or to the Person of the Father. In their affirmations concerning the divine immutability, the Councils' affirmations quite clearly are focused on Christ.

Now, beyond such Christological discernments, the Coun-

<hr>

8. Council of Chalcedon, "Profession of Faith," in Denzinger, no. 300.
9. Second Council of Constantinople, "Canons," in Denzinger, no. 432.

cils also declare that immutability is a characteristic properly belonging to the divine nature, common to the three Persons of the Trinity. We see this in the first canon of the First Lateran Council (649). It is found once again in the profession of faith promulgated by the Fourth Lateran Council (1215), at the Second Council of Lyon (1274), in the decree against the Jacobites at the Council of Florence (1442), and in the first proposition, aimed against pantheism, found in Pius IX's *Syllabus of Errors* (1864). We find immutability being brought up again in the dogmatic constitution *Dei Filius* at the First Vatican Council (1870).[10]

Thus, the affirmation of God's immutability is one of the church's constant teachings, especially witnessed to in the Christological declarations made by the early Ecumenical Councils. This affirmation was needed so that the eternity of the generation of the Word might be affirmed. Likewise, it guaranteed the integrity of the Word in the incarnation and, similarly, enabled one to avoid imputing the human sorrow of the crucified one to God. Consequently, immutability is regularly noted as being one of the key truths of the Christian teaching concerning God. The affirmations of the Conciliar tradition possess a rather precise formal object. They do not betray a reduction of God to an inert and lifeless substance (*ousia*). Nor do they entail that God would be indifferent to his creatures' suffering. Their primary aim is to hold together the properties of Christ's divine nature along with the truth of the economy that he lived out in the flesh.

I believe we can reconcile the immutability and sorrow of God in light of the cross. In order to advance toward such a potential integration, we must begin by first clearing out false notions or distorted representations of the divine immutability.

---

10. See Denzinger, nos. 501, 800–801, 853, 1330, 2901, 3001. The declaration from Lateran IV is taken up by the *Catechism of the Catholic Church* [hereafter CCC], no. 202; available at www.vatican.va.

Four Contemporary Objections against
the Divine Immutability

The classical doctrine of the divine immutability runs into a number of weighty objections today. They are inspired by a variety of concerns, be they Christological, experiential, philosophical, or biblical in nature.

The Christological objection holds that the passion of the Son in the flesh cannot be something utterly foreign to the Father. Jesus' passion cannot be reduced merely to the suffering of his humanity but, rather, is truly the passion of the incarnate Son. In his very person, the Son is the subject of this passion. Now, the Son is always in full communion with the Father, through their constitutive correlation and their unity of will. Therefore, it is unthinkable that the Father would not himself also be co-implicated as a subject in the Son's ordeal and passion. Moreover, one of the perfections of human paternity or maternity is found in the fact that the suffering of one's child is something utterly heart-wrenching for a parent. This is verified in Hosea 11 in the sentiments that God has in relation to his people. How could things be different for God the Father in relation to the suffering experienced by his own incarnate Son?

The experiential objection is founded on the suffering that takes place before God's gaze. When one comes to have a lively and direct awareness of the excess and weight of human suffering—at the level of individual lives, as well as at that of entire generations, indeed, in oppressed classes and spread throughout wholly devastated nations—it is unthinkable that God would remain callously unaffected by the suffering experienced by human beings who are thereby led to the brink of the physical or psychological shattering of their humanity. Now, divine immutability would be the *de facto* equivalent to a kind of ontological callousness, for it exempts God from every form of real alteration. Is such a God still compassionate?

The philosophical objection can be summarized in one line: ontological plenitude is not found in substance but, rather, in the vital process of becoming. The affirmation of the divine immutability is directly correlated to an identification of God with the supreme essence or substance which is perfectly subsistent and autonomous. The fullness of being is thus conceived of as though it were a kind of lifeless stability, neither varying nor growing. It is rather difficult to see how a true, vital fullness could be found in such a God, for life requires the process of becoming, and its fullness presupposes development. Can an immutable God truly be living Being *par excellence*?

The biblical objection emphasizes the fact that Old Testament bears witness to a God whose dispositions are adapted to men and women. Throughout numerous Old Testament passages, it is quite clear that God adjusts himself to the ways that human persons react to his covenant, his word, his mercies, and his threats. On many occasions, beholding an unexpected conversion or even the congenital weakness of the human will, God repents of having intended to punish a given people, village, or individual. We see quite striking examples of this in Genesis 6:6–7, Exodus 32:12 and 14, Jonah 4:2, Joel 2:13, and Jeremiah 26:3. Therefore, it seems quite clear that God is not immutable in his interior dispositions in relation to human beings. He responds in a way that is adjusted to their own instability or conversion. As I have already shown in the chapter on the divine repentance, this objection can be overcome by following St. Augustine's own reflections on this matter.

Without dwelling on them at length, let us here sketch out a brief response to the experiential and philosophical objections raised above.[11] On the one hand, the immutable God is in no way indifferent or callously insensitive to human woes. His very life is permeated with the loftiest and most effective compassion one could feel for them. Such compassion far exceeds the human ability to take on another person's suffering. In reality, this divine compassion is nothing other than a form of effective aid given to the other who is in need

---

11. See Michael J. Dodds, *The Unchanging God of Love: Thomas Aquinas & Contemporary Theology on Divine Immutability* (Washington, D.C.: The Catholic University of America Press, 2008); Serge-Thomas Bonino, *Dieu, "Celui qui est" (De Deo ut uno)* (Paris: Parole et Silence, 2016), 385–93.

or distress.[12] The divine compassion transcends emotion and empathy, though it takes up their positive outcome: engagement and action. God's ontological impassibility is the condition for pure compassion, without him needing to experience the mere affection of his own self before the sufferings undergone by his creatures. On the other hand, God's immutability in no way implies some kind of shortcoming in the vitality that is God's transcendent and eminent life. His immutability is pure act and spiritual life at its loftiest, uncreated degree. God cannot be reduced to a narrow and cramped version of substance, one that is inert and isolated, separated from every kind of vitality and relationship. Such a reduction would ultimately represent a deistic reduction of the divinity. The immutable God is the perfection of life, love, and tender awareness. However, the Christological objection remains in force, and it must be confronted with the definitive, indeed ultimate, gesture expressed in the crucifixion.

GOD'S SORROW IS FOCUSED ON THE FACT THAT HIS CREATURE IS DISFIGURED

Let us now return to God's sorrow, such as it is expressed in the liturgical chanting of the reproaches. The immutability of the divine nature is perfectly compatible with the three possible divisions of the roles expressed therein between God, the savior, and Christ. Indeed, in light of this immutability, God's sorrow takes on the full weight of the redoubtable mystery encountered here. Without undergoing alteration in himself, in his divine nature, God is profoundly grieved by man's deviation from the ways of his salvation, as well as by the disfiguration suffered by the crucified one. What is the astonishing sorrow of God? Let us advance some proposals in order to lay the groundwork for future reflection on these matters.

12. See Augustine, *Confessiones* III.2.2–4. Unlike the emotions that one experiences at the theater, in resonance with the fictive woes of the protagonists on the stage, true compassion is found in effective aid. This is why compassion is befitting to God to the highest degree, even though he is immutable.

Like anger, sorrow is a derivative emotion. In contrast to the mere feeling of sadness or "the blues," the emotion of sorrow is aroused by an object. Our emotions must be refracted through the prism of some fatigue, stifled desire, or deception if we are to be sensitive to this or that potential event that might trigger our sorrow. Fundamentally, in us humans, all of this presupposes the experience of expectation, lived out within time in relation to an object of love or attachment. If God experiences a loftier form of sorrow, its first referent is the love that God has for that which brings him sorrow. The love expressed in creation and election represents God's primary intentionality for everything that he arouses and considers as being a created good. Without this primordial love, nothing determinate would have a unique value in the eyes of God. The divine love bestows the value which belongs to those very things that he calls into existence, for he is the creator of goodness.

Does such an investment of love render God potentially vulnerable to the becoming experienced by his creatures, especially those endowed with the freedom to respond to his love? In the final analysis, the intentionality of God's love for those who can possibly bring him sorrow represents a kind of engagement, in the twofold sense of being an investment and a promise.

Nonetheless, God is unchanging. His vulnerability is an analogical quality. It is a perfection, something surpassing the furthest bounds of our own human sensitivity for others, especially for our beloved ones. God is pure actuality, containing immanently within himself, in the state of eminent perfection, all the various perfections that are scattered out among his creatures. In him, these perfections do not exist in the composite and fragmentary manner that they exist in the created order. Spread out and untied in a thousand and one ways throughout the whole diversity of the created order, these perfections preexist in him as a cohesive and infinite plenitude. This holds for all created perfections, according to the various degrees of being, and, therefore, *a fortiori* likewise holds for human perfections. In this way, the perfections that we identify in ourselves as sensitivity, delicacy, kindness, benevolence, attention, love, and compassion all preexist in God in a unified, superior, and simple manner. Here, in this unified eminence of the Deity, we see the true and full meaning of his superabundant eternal and creative love.[13]

If sensitivity and vulnerability are indeed human perfections, their corresponding realization in God can also be related to his perfection. Sorrow does not disfigure God in himself. He does not fold back upon himself when faced with offense or rejection. God's sorrow is a disappointed, wounded, and offended love. However, here we find an important and significant difference.

When a human being is wounded in his or her own love, two sides can be considered: the humiliation of the offended party and the disfiguration of the offender. In the wounded subject, the feeling of mortification is what most often prevails over the feeling of desolation experienced in the face of the evil that the aggressor simultaneously afflicts upon himself. In certain situations, on account of their profound compassion for their children, human parents are able to almost completely overcome their own pain and experience one that does not somehow redound upon them, a pain that is ecstatic and wholly felt for the other. However, immediately upon being separated from these beloved little ones, these same parents find that they too are burdened with a pain which they experience for themselves. They too are affected in themselves by the errant wanderings and sufferings of the other. They weep not only for the other but also for themselves. The difference between a purely compassionate sorrow for a beloved person and the pain that one feels for oneself when faced with the reality of this person is revealed quite clearly by two contrasting human attitudes. It is a sorrowful fact of human experience that a woman who accompanies her dying child or spouse often experiences pure compassion while she is physically present with this sick person, whereas upon leaving the latter's room and momentarily losing this sensible presence of the other, she is

---

13. Here, we take up as our own the argument found in Origen, *Homilies on Ezekiel* VI.6. Likewise, see chapter 3 in this volume.

submerged by her own pain and weeps for herself. God alone can have endless sorrow lived solely for the other, without turning back to himself or experiencing pain for himself.

In his own sorrows, God is completely filled with sadness for his creatures and not for himself. God's sorrow is more than a passion. It is a pure affection of his loving will, entirely concerned for the other without itself being altered. God's sorrow thus reflects two different aspects of his relation to creatures: principally, the divine love exposed to rejection; by way of consequence, the disfiguration of creatures which accompanies their sin.

GOD'S SORROW HAS A HUMAN COUNTENANCE

In the tears of the incarnate Son of God, we have a human expression for the pure sorrow of God. In himself, God is unchanging, whether as Father, Son, or Spirit. Now, there is a modality of created sorrow which truly is the sorrow of God. However, it is specific to the incarnate Son. According to Christological orthodoxy, the eternal Son of God is the sole subject of all the actions and passions that he performs and takes up through his unique humanity. Thus, his bodily exhaustion, sorrows, and tears, as well as everything suffered upon the cross, are all quite truly the exhaustion, sorrows, and sufferings of the Son of God. He is the unique subject of all of this. Without a doubt, the divine nature is not what suffers, weeps, and is sorrowful. However, no more is it the human nature of the Son that suffers, as though this were all experienced in utter separation from Christ's divinity. Rather, it is the incarnate Son of God who personally suffers in his flesh, in virtue of his human nature in its vulnerability and ability to undergo suffering.[14] Jesus' tears are those of the Son. God wished to weep in the flesh which he shares with us.

The mysterious, yet radiant, truth that God is not disfigured in

---

14. See Bruce D. Marshall, "The Dereliction of Christ and the Impassibility of God," in *Divine Impassibility and the Mystery of Human Suffering*, ed. James F. Keating and Thomas J. White (Grand Rapids, Mich.: Eerdmans, 2009), 246–98.

his sorrow finds an expression in the disfiguration of his own Son in the flesh. During his trial and passion, Christ takes upon himself and incorporates all the disfigurations of the world's sin, which is projected upon him. The holy and innocent one catalyzes the sin of humanity in all of its components: false testimony, repudiation, betrayal, abandonment, derision, cynicism, lynching, violence, etc. That which befalls Jesus in his passion brings into broad daylight the ultimate fruit of sin: disfiguration and death. Thus, the cross is the judgment of sin which there finds its logic to be exhausted. The disfigured face of Jesus reveals, in created terms, the utterly real affection of the unchanging God in the face of the world's evil and sin.

7

God's Power and the Impossible
Who Delineates Them?

From Epicurus to Hume, and from Hume to Hans Jonas, the notion of omnipotence has been periodically called into question, if not dismissed. Contestation or circumvention is found in both theology and philosophy.

From a theological perspective, it might sound convenient to distinguish between God's almightiness, confessed in the Creed, and God's omnipotence, articulated by philosophers. The almighty would disclose the ultimate meaning of his power in the Paschal mystery, whereas omnipotence is subjected to a great variety of definitions. The latter should be abandoned to the arena of philosophers and the stalemated arguments undertaken by logicians.[1] Moreover, as Origen suggested, almightiness proves to be trinitarian,[2] whereas omnipotence is metaphysical. Excellent contemporary theologians orient, intentionally or not, the theology of God's almightiness and sovereignty in this direction.[3] Within Catholic tradition, though,

---

1. See Peter T. Geach, "Omnipotence," *Philosophy* 48, no. 183 (1973): 7–20. For a sharp divide between almightiness and omnipotence, see already Duns Scotus, *Ordinatio* I, d. 42, q. un.

2. See Origen, *Treatise on Principles* I.2.10.

3. See, among the very best ones, Jean-Pierre Batut, *Pantocrator: "Dieu le Père tout-puissant" dans la théologie prénicéenne* (Paris: Institut d'Études Augustiniennes, 2009);

true omnipotence should be thought of in a way which can be integrated in the confession of the almighty. At the same time, the concept of almightiness should not depart from a wisely defined omnipotence.

From a philosophical perspective, one might observe—at least in the continental context—a transfer from omnipotence to what might be called the "omni-possible." From this perspective, the unmastered possibilities of God cannot be submitted to any human concept of power. We literally cannot conceive what God is capable of. God is the only master of the impossible. No conceptually delimited power can hem in the open field of possibilities. Moreover, human reason has no ground nor right to frame or limit the kind of impossibilities God might be *willing* to overcome.[4] Otherwise, God would be constrained by some idolatrous concept of ours. The impossible should in no way limit God, who surpasses our knowledge of limited capacities. Should we engage in this line of postmodern thinking about the unbounded God?

In this chapter, I will attempt to bring omnipotence and almightiness together. Searching for integration and unity in this field relies on the assumption that reason and faith aim at the very same truth who is God and his wisdom, embodied in both the created order and in the Paschal mystery. Instead of fostering a sharp divide of registers or notional contents between almightiness and omnipotence, I will argue that the very same attribute of the one true God might be approached by both philosophers and theologians, relying on their proper and different instances of judgment. The key to this epistemological argument will be provided by Thomas Aquinas's analysis of the possible and the impossible, within a theology which remains mindful of God's power.

Marc Vial, *Pour une théologie de la toute-puissance de Dieu. L'approche d'Eberhard Jüngel* (Paris: Classiques Garnier, 2016); Richard Bauckham, *The Theology of the Book of Revelation* (Cambridge: Cambridge University Press, 1993), 23–65.

4. See Jean-Luc Marion, "L'impossibilité de l'impossible: Dieu," *Archivio di Filosofia* 78, no. 1 (2010): 21–36. Marion does not make any distinction between impossible to nature and impossible *per se*, merging both in the impossible "for us."

There are four common, often-overlapping objections to God's omnipotence. First, omnipotence is arbitrary. If God is omnipotent, his power is infinite, and nothing is compelling within the created order. Anything is possible and the opposite as well, so that a given sequence of events can be replaced at any time by another possible sequence of alternative events. Everything therefore seems to be on hold, without intrinsic value or reliability. The regularity of phenomena, physical laws, ethical norms, and human responsibility are all pending, in the end determined by divine volition.

Second, omnipotence is overwhelming, if not self-contradictory. If God is omnipotent, his power is infinite and leaves no room for other powers. Nothing can stand against God. Ultimately, nothing should exist outside of him because he saturates the whole range of possibilities with his power alone. The idea that God would be, at once, omnipotent and creator would seem to involve a contradiction, insofar as creation implies a real otherness and a proper space of existence.[5]

Third, an omnipotent God would be guilty. If God is truly omnipotent, he is guilty of the woes and evils he tolerates in this world, at least as soon as they exceed the proportion of what his creatures could bear. An omnipotent God ought to curb evils and hold back plagues, while obviously he does not do so and lets human beings face them to the best of their ability. Most of the time, however, they are submerged and dehumanized.[6]

Fourth, the idea that God is powerful might well be a pitiful fantasy and a poor projection, set up by males who themselves dream of being all powerful themselves. While we are often powerless, especially while facing our limitations, woes, and evils, we dream of being all-powerful. However, perversion consists precisely in refusing limitations and want. God then comes into the picture as the maxi-

---

5. See Hans Jonas, "The Concept of God after Auschwitz: A Jewish Voice," *The Journal of Religion* 67, no. 1 (1987): 1–13.

6. See David Hume, *Dialogue concerning Natural Religion*, in *Dialogues concerning Natural Religion and Other Writings*, ed. Dorothy Coleman (Cambridge: Cambridge University Press, 2007), Book X, 97–102.

mized projection of archaic representations of power: male, paternal, creative, sovereign, limitless.[7]

HISTORICALLY FRAMING THE ISSUE
OF UNBOUND POWER

In this chapter, I would like to address the first objection in particular. I will do so by weaving together statements from the Gospels and metaphysical arguments. However, first I would like to refine the fabric of the objection at hand, giving it more precision.

If God's power is understood in such a way that it has no objective limitation because of its infinity, everything could be, or could become, very different. Realities, events, chains, cycles, orders, laws, norms, values … all this is suspended. As long as God wills them to be as they are, they remain. Yet, God could also will another kind of physical world, a different ethical order, or for that matter, a human history quite unlike our own. At any moment, another sequence of events, causes, and effects could replace the usual world that we experience. As a consequence, regularity of phenomena, physical laws, ethical norms, and human responsibility rest on borrowed time. This kind of omnipotence shares a great deal with the infamous *potentia absoluta* of late Scholasticism, the unbound power of God.

Until the late Scholastic period, the distinction between *potentia absoluta* and *potentia ordinata*, unbound power and ordained power, was considered a purely rational experiment. Wisely, Aquinas states that the order inscribed by God in creation never equals the fullness of his wisdom and justice, identical to his very essence in divine simplicity. However ordered the works of God may be, the divine goodness always exceeds the proportion of the created order. This leaves room *theoretically* for other possible orders in the course of things,

---

7. See Charles Hartshorne, *Omnipotence and Other Theological Mistakes* (Albany: State University of New York, 1984), 6–26; Jean Ansaldi, "La toute-puissance du Dieu du théisme dans le champ de la perversion," *Laval Théologique et Philosophique* 47, no. 1 (1991): 3–11; André Wénin, "Au-delà des représentations, Dieu," in *Dieu à l'épreuve de notre cri*, ed. Adolphe Gesché and Paul Scolas (Paris: Cerf, 1999), 25–44.

apart from contradictions.[8] For Aquinas, the distinction between unbound power and ordered power is merely a distinction of reason, not a real one. Ordered power is the only one actually implemented by God according to his benevolent designs. As a rational experiment, though, one might abstract power from other divine attributes. In that case, unbound power extends to everything that ultimately coheres with the notion of being (*ratio entis*), thus excluding only that which is contradictory.

However, Duns Scotus turned the thought experiment into a real distinction.[9] For him, the unbound power of God might, at any time, breach through and make an exception in the usual implementation of his ordinary power, as well as all mediation by secondary causes. This huge difference between Scotus and Aquinas in regard to the divine power stems from a significant epistemological divide which separates the two thinkers. Whereas Aquinas holds that there is a convergence between faith and reason in respect to the very same objects, Scotus states that faith and reason cannot reach the same objects. This deficiency applies to the case of the divine power.[10]

For Scotus, divine omnipotence cannot be demonstrated by reason, for it is an object of faith, attested by the first article of the Creed. Rational demonstrations do not deal with omnipotence as a divine attribute but, rather, with infinite power. This kind of power has been known by philosophers, such as Aristotle, Avicenna, and Averroes. They describe the first cause that moves all things through secondary causes. Infinite power might be rigorously inferred from the secondary causes that metaphysically depend on the first cause. As revealed to faith, the divine omnipotence differs essentially from the infinite power of the first cause because it is not tied to secondary causes. God does not need anything to accomplish what he

8. See Aquinas, *ST* I, q. 25, a. 5; *De potentia*, q. 1, a. 5.

9. See William J. Courtenay, *Capacity and Volition: A History of the Distinction of Absolute and Ordained Power* (Bergamo: P. Lubrina, 1990).

10. Compare Aquinas, *ST* I, q. 25, a. 5, ad 1, and Duns Scotus, *Ordinatio* I, d. 42, q. un. See Olivier Boulnois (ed.), *La puissance et son ombre. De Pierre Lombard et Luther* (Paris: Aubier, 1994), 53–65, 263–67.

wants. He is not subjected to any order of secondary causes he pre-established. At will, God can bypass worldly causes, suspend them, or modify their natural order. Divine omnipotence therefore is the same as the unbounded freedom of God. God should not be limited by any of the laws he has established in creation. Within the overall context of Scotus's thought, this is connected to the assumption that every free agent might, at the very moment it does something specific, do the opposite. Such freedom ultimately is that of God's unbound power, considered here as a kind of alternative manner of operating.

With a slightly different terminology, we have returned to our initial problem. As an object of faith, God's almightiness is drawn from God's mighty deeds in salvation history. It cannot be demonstrated nor qualified by natural reason, whereas omnipotence—as infinite power—should be investigated by or abandoned to philosophers. With this challenge in mind, I would like to move back to the way Christ speaks of power, possibility, and impossibility in the Gospels. Taking into account these statements in a sound theology will require some metaphysical awareness.

GOD'S POWER IN THE NEW TESTAMENT

I am not going to solve any exegetical issue in this chapter, but I would like to make clear that New Testament statements concerning God's power often call for basic metaphysical clarifications and decisions. When these options are not made explicit, they are nevertheless operating within interpretations, though beyond awareness. A very famous illustration has been provided by Bultmann's theology of divine action and miracles. His vision presupposed a clear discontinuity between the field of human affairs, open to God's action, and the field of nature, closed to such action.[11] This disjunction implies two metaphysical assumptions: that nature is a

---

11. See Rudolf Bultmann, "New Testament and Mythology," in *Kerygma and Myth: A Theological Debate*, ed. Hans W. Bartsch (London: SCPK, 1953), 1–44; Ian G. Barbour, *Religion in an Age of Science: The Gifford Lectures 1989–1991* (London: SCM Press, 1990), 254–56.

closed and deterministic system, and that physical, noncontingent causation and God's action are incompatible. Therefore, God cannot act within nature, though he might be involved in the existential self-understanding of human subjects. Unfortunately for Bultmann, at least one of these metaphysical assumptions proves to be wrong. In both Aristotle's *Physics* and *Metaphysics*, causation is increasingly coming to be acknowledged as occurring in a contingent manner. The second assumption should be discussed as well, but it would take too long. Of course, Bultmann's metaphysical assumptions were not his main motives for proposing an existential theory of divine action, but this facet of his argument falls apart once it is made explicit. In a similar way, by the end of this chapter, I would like to provide one key of discernment in respect to unbound readings of Luke 1:35: "Nothing is impossible to God."

God's power is testified or confessed in manifold ways in the New Testament. First, in the Pauline epistles, the overcoming of the usual mundane hierarchy of power and weakness is strongly stated by Paul, who speaks eloquently of the inversion of all worldly powers through the cross. Unexpectedly, God's power has been demonstrated and exalted through the ultimate weakness of Christ. Whereas all human power seemed totally exhausted in the crucified one, he was nevertheless fulfilling the ultimate goal of his mission. This paradoxical event spoke not only of Christ alone, but also, through him, of God's unique way of salvation (1 Cor 1:23–25). The same paradox is at work in Paul's preaching, which is entirely derived from the cross, as well as in his governance of the turbulent community in Corinth (1 Cor 2:2–5; 2 Cor 12:9–10; 13:2–4, 9).

Second, in the Synoptic Gospels, God's power is said to be the unique capacity of his for specific actions, such as forgiving sins (Mk 2:7, Lk 5:21), raising up children for Abraham (Mt 3:9, Lk 3:8), destroying both soul and body (Mt 10:28, Lk 12:5), and miraculously healing the sick (Lk 5:17). Some of these divine actions can be performed through human actions, as the last one is throughout Jesus' ministry.

In contrast, the Gospel of John does not qualify the power that God has of doing so and so. Instead, this Gospel underscores many actions that human beings could never accomplish unless they were helped by God or Christ: perform signs, enter the kingdom, believe in Jesus, receive the Spirit, and, indeed, do anything.[12] In this way, God's gracious power is also indicated through all kinds of incapacities of human beings regarding the supernatural realm.

Third, power (*dunamis*) is employed at times as a proper name or attribute of God. The angel designates the Spirit as "the Power of the Most High" when announcing to Mary Jesus' conception (Lk 1:35). The Virgin praises God as "the Powerful" (*ho dunatos*) in the Magnificat (Lk 1:49). Jesus himself, arguing with the Sadducees about the resurrection of the dead, denounces their inability to know scripture as well as God's power (Mk 12:24, Mt 22:29). During his trial, Jesus responds to the high priest that the Son of Man will be seen sitting at the right hand of "the Power" (Mk 14:62, Mt 22:29). These designations are also numerous in the Book of Revelation, by means either of the attribute *dunamis* or of the title *pantocrator*.[13] Just by paying attention to the semantic field of power in the New Testament, one can acquire some biblical sense of God's ordered power in the economy of salvation, revealing God's identity, his soteriological initiatives and aims, as well as his means: forgiving, healing, performing signs, provoking faith, empowering little ones, and so on.

Fourthly, another mode of attestation of God's power is found in fthe Synoptic Gospels: statements about the possible and the impossible. These retain our attention and call for further scrutiny. The subject for whom something is said to be possible or impossible might be: God; Abba, Father; or those who believe.

Following the Synoptic Gospels (here in the Douay-Rheims ver-

---

12. See Jn 3:2–5; 5:44; 6:44, 65; 7:34–36; 8:21–22, 43; 9:16; 12:39; 13:33, 36–37; 14:17; 15:5; 16:12.

13. *Pantocrator* and *pantrocratoria* express in a definite manner the lordship or sovereignty of God and Christ over creation and history; see Rv 1:8; 4:8; 11:17; 15:3; 16:7, 14; 19:6, 15; 21:22.

sion[14]), we can highlight four statements within dialogues and one prayer.

The angel to Mary at the Annunciation: "And behold thy cousin Elizabeth, she also hath conceived a son in her old age: and this is the sixth month with her that is called barren. Because no word shall be impossible with God." (Lk 1:36–37)

To the father of a possessed boy: "If thou canst believe, all things are possible to him that believeth." (Mk 9:23)

To the disciples unable to help the father: "For, amen I say to you, if you have faith as a grain of mustard seed, you shall say to this mountain: Remove from hence hither, and it shall remove: and nothing shall be impossible to you." (Mt 17:20)

Regarding how hard it is to enter the kingdom of God: "[The disciples] wondered the more, saying among themselves: Who then can be saved? And Jesus looking on them, saith with men it is impossible; but not with God. For all things are possible with God." (Mk 10:26–27; cf. Mt 19:25–26, Lk 18:27)

Jesus praying at Gethsemane: "And when he was gone forward a little, he fell flat on the ground: and he prayed that, if it might be, the hour might pass from him. And he saith: 'Abba, Father, all things are possible to thee: remove this chalice from me; but not what I will, but what thou wilt.'" (Mk 14:35–36; cf. Mt 26:39)

According to the angel, God's word stands as some promise which goes beyond what human beings would consider possible. God's power overcomes the barrenness of the post-menopausal Elizabeth, accomplishing something that is impossible for nature, according to the normal limitations of human procreation.

In Jesus' own words, "everything is possible" or "nothing is impossible," not only to the power of God, but also to whoever believes. It is such a challenge for a father who experienced his son's possession (and/or epilepsy) from childhood to believe without re-

14. In this section, I use this old English translation of a Latin version of the Bible because its Latin original remains very close to the texts Aquinas made use of. Most of the time, Aquinas did not read Lk 1:35 in the same way we usually do in modern translations of the Greek New Testament.

striction that Jesus might free the boy from this affliction. This exceeds the disciples' own ability to sufficiently have the boundless faith needed to intercede efficaciously and drive out the spirit. Still, wholehearted faith would make everything possible when the disciples face insurmountable obstacles with God, relying entirely through faith on God's own might.[15]

Eventually, facing extreme anguish in Gethsemane, Jesus himself expresses directly to God his own confidence in God's saving power. Crying out to God, Christ's words are, nonetheless, marked with a kind of ambivalence. "Everything is possible for you" is highly true, but in this specific setting, it entails an ultimate temptation for Jesus himself: "Take this cup from me." Jesus resists this temptation and opposes his final consent: "Yet not what I will, but what you will."

In this context, Jesus' statements are not theoretically detached. They might have a significant theoretical load, to be unpacked. However, they are always vitally connected to ultimate challenges for human resources and confidence. As we consider the narrative setting of these statements, they are not to be dealt with as unrestricted theoretical propositions. Nevertheless, some metaphysical distinctions prove very useful for interpreting the angel's and Jesus' words with care and seriousness. At the least, such distinctions avoid misreading the Gospel and, in this way, help to strengthen our faith.

REGISTERS AND MEANINGS OF POWER

Dealing with power in the *Scriptum super Sententiae*, Thomas Aquinas starts from the usual meaning of power in common language, most often drawn from the field of human action (ethical or political), then moves to the physical order and, from there, abstracts a metaphysical concept of power. This concept is then enhanced and

---

15. A classical distinction between dogmatic faith and faith as a charism might be helpful here, in line with Cyril of Jerusalem, *Catechetical Lectures* V.10–11. Miracles could not be secured by theological faith; they often depend on a charism of faith, granted to a few believers for the edification of all.

fully developed for theological use.[16] I suggest that we follow a similar path.

In common language, one might distinguish three principal senses of power: impact and influence in the political order; force and intensity within the physical realm; and charisma, or the ability to subjugate others. Charismatic power over others is a very human phenomenon, often abusive and male. God might make use of this occasionally in specific biblical narratives, but these ambiguous traits should not define God's power. Both political and physical power hardly befit God, as they imply some counterforces and resistances. The more extensive political influence becomes, the more independent counterpowers are needed. With greater intensity in a given physical force, an equally intense opposite force is needed in response. Envisaging God's power along these lines would be highly misleading. God would be one more intraworldly power, albeit the highest. If this were so, God would essentially be involved in a power balance with other physical forces or political powers.

These essential limitations of the common concepts of power call for a metaphysical discernment. For the sake of theology, starting from the physical and the political experiences of power, we need to consider power in a much more refined way. We should abstract power from any specific field of action. Such a thought experiment is metaphysical in nature: we have to investigate how and why power is related to being as being, not to being as physical, being as political, being as male, and so on. To perform such an essential reduction of power to its metaphysical lineaments results in a demythologization process. This is much needed to avoid anthropomorphic projections and caricatures of God's power, which lead to rejection, disbelief, and atheism.

Finally, one should remember here that God's act of power as creator has the gift of being (*esse*) as its terminus. Therefore, it is utterly distinct from every intraworldly creature to creature (or human to human) power, and cannot be adequately mirrored by them,

16. See Aquinas, *Sent.* I, d. 42, q. 1, a. 1, resp.

except metaphorically or analogically at great remove and dissimilitude. God's act of power gives being to things. Consequently, far from acting over against the autonomy or flourishing of the creature, it is the foundation of that autonomy and flourishing. This also entails that God is *usually* hidden in his power, as his power enables things to "appear" in their own integrity as gift. This outlook not only provides a kind of demythologization but also enables us to purify intraworldly idolatries concerning power structures which we might take as being absolute.[17]

Commenting on Aristotle's *Metaphysics* V, Thomas Aquinas explicates four meanings of power.[18] Two of them are relevant for our investigation: active power, the principle of moving or changing something or someone else as other; this is the power to act upon something else. The second is passive power, the capacity of being moved or changed by something or someone else as other; this is the power of receiving something else.

Active and passive powers result from a simple analysis of action and passion. For instance, in order to learn a new language, someone uses his or her active power of studying with intensity and assiduity. But this would be beneficial and transformative only because the very same person possesses also the passive power of receiving new sounds, being taught, memorizing, and learning.

The second meaning of power—the passive one—is often forgotten in common language as well as in the day-to-day language of theology in pedagogical and more-popular settings. This leads to tremendous misrepresentations of the relation between God's power and creatures. Prior to standing before God's power with any active power, creatures more radically face God with a passive power.[19] This is not a power to resist passively, but a capacity for

---

17. I thank my friend Thomas Joseph White for having suggested this avenue of thought.

18. See Aquinas, *In Metaphysicorum* V.12, lect. 14, ed. Marietti, nos. 954–60. In Aristotle's *Metaphysics*, this first semantic approach will be eventually completed by the demonstration of the priority of act over potency in XII.8.1049b4.

19. This distinction is totally missing in Jonas, "The Concept of God after

being moved, drawn, called, and so on. Availability to be moved or changed by God is far more radical in every creature than the power to resist or collaborate with God.

THE ACTIVE SUBJECT OF
POWER AND THE LIMITS OF
IMPOSSIBLE OBJECTS

We shall now envisage God's power through two complementary lenses: considering the active subject, God, who exercises power; and focusing on the object to which God's power might apply.[20] Being pure act, God is active power with no mingling of passive power. God does not move from potency to act. He is not changed, for better or worse, according to a passive power. God's active power is pure and primary, perfect and complete. When attributed to God, the notion of power retains only the notion of being the essential principle for acting as God. The common notion of power is pruned of any distant completion by an activity to be achieved.[21] There is no real distinction between God's power and God's activity. The real distinction is found between the created effects of God's activity and the uncreated power of God. We should also notice that God's active power is not granted by anyone else and not received from another. God is his very power, as well as his very essence. Consequently, God's power is not limited by any mode of reception in some subject, as is the case for human power. God's power is infinite in this respect.[22]

Still, there is some limitation of God's active power, which stems from its perfection. As a consequence of God being pure act, any de-

---

Auschwitz," 9. For a Christian dialectical treatment of very similar aporia, see Augustine, *De ordine* II.17.46; Lactantius, *De ira Dei* XIII.20–21 (recalling the argument of Epicurus); Serge-Thomas Bonino, "L'incompréhensible sagesse de Dieu dans l'*Expositio super Iob*," in his *Études Thomasiennes*, 593–624.

20. See Aquinas, *Sent.* I, d. 42, q. 2, a. 2, resp.

21. See Aquinas, *De potentia*, q. 1, a. 1, resp.; *SCG* II.8–10.

22. See Aquinas, *De potentia*, q. 1, a. 2, resp.

fective power should be removed from our thinking of God. In this respect, God cannot sin, for instance, because sin is a defect of the will. In a similar way, God cannot lie, as a lie is a failure in telling the truth; God cannot be tired or forget, and so on.[23]

The objects of God's power might be assessed as possible or impossible according to different frames, scales, or referents. The objective limitation to God's power is set by that which is *per se* impossible. Any concept that equates what is with what is not proposes this kind of radical impossibility. A square circle is impossible *per se*. A man with no soul is similarly self-contradictory. That some past event or some past action would have not occurred is impossible *per se*. The impossible *per se*, being self-contradictory, does not highlight a limitation of God's active power, but entails a simple negation of the very essence of the possible. God cannot do such impossible things—not because of some intrinsic limitation placed upon his power, but rather, because of the absence of any possible object. We shall return to this point below.

We must take into account both the actual perfection of God's power, and its objects (possible or impossible *per se*). This provides a safeguard against the representation of God's power as unlimited. Focusing only on the infinity of God's active power would lead to an excessive or delirious depiction of God's might, one that would ultimately do great damage to true Christian faith.

WHO DELINEATES THE IMPOSSIBLE?

In his *De potentia* (q. 1, a. 3), Thomas Aquinas spells out various senses of the possible and the impossible, with some reference to Aristotle, *Metaphysics* V.12. This analysis unpacks two main categories:

- Possible and impossible in respect to some potency, active or passive

---

23. See Aquinas, *Sent.* I, d. 42, q. 2, a. 2, resp. For a developed and articulated list of many things that the omnipotent God cannot do, see *SCG* II.25.

- Impossible because of some defect of the active power;
  example: for a man to fly like a bird
- Impossible because of some impediment external to the
  power; example: for a man to see through a wall
- Possible or impossible in respect to being, whatever the
  power might be
- Impossible by itself (*per se*), because of some contradiction

Aquinas argues that that which is *per se* impossible, entailing some contradiction, cannot be the object of any action, whatever might be the power in question and whoever might be the agent. The irreducible difference between affirmation and negation is used as the most obvious case depicting at once all contradictions of terms. The assumption is that the principle of noncontradiction between affirmation and negation (regarding the same formal object) is the very first principle of all human discourse and reasoning, without which no rational speech would stand. Further, more particular contradictions can be referred to the paramount one: the mutual exclusion between being and nonbeing.[24] In this way, Aquinas proceeds to a kind of reduction of every contradiction to that which is *per se* impossible.

The two categories of impossibility, spelled out above, can be labeled as (1) that which is impossible to nature—which is twofold, namely, by defect of by hindrance—and (2) that which is *per se* impossible. Relying on this clarification, Aquinas draws proper theological statements, first regarding that which is *per se* impossible:

Those things, then, which are impossible to nature in the first or second way are possible to God: because, since his power is infinite, it is subject to no defect, nor is there any matter that he cannot transform at will, since his power is irresistible. On the other hand those things which involve the third kind of impossibility God cannot do, since he is supreme act and

24. See Aquinas, *De potentia*, q. 1, a. 3, resp.; referring to Aristotle, *Metaphysics* IV.3.1005b18. Some support the view that Aquinas's understanding of the possible is eventually disconnected from any potency; see Kristell Trego, *L'impuissance du possible. Émergence et développement du possible, d'Aristote à l'aube des temps modernes* (Paris: Vrin, 2019), 231–37.

sovereign being: wherefore his action cannot terminate otherwise than principally in being, and secondarily in nonbeing. Consequently he cannot make yes and no to be true at the same time, nor any of those things which involve such an impossibility. Nor is he said to be unable to do these things through lack of power, but through lack of possibility, such things being intrinsically impossible: and this is what is meant by those who say that "God can do it, but it cannot be done."[25]

For Aquinas, "all things are possible to God" does not apply to that which is *per se* impossible, which never meets the sound and very notion of possibility. May we focus on that which is impossible to nature? Should what remains impossible to a specific nature become possible to God? Does this mean that God would then act against the very nature that he has created and set in some definite order? To overcome these aporia, one must acknowledge that every creature has a radical passive power to be moved by God, even beyond all its natural active and passive powers. This radical passive power is labeled "obediential" potency.

Aquinas argues for this deeper level of consideration while responding to an objection drawn from a gloss on Romans 9:24: "if thou were cut out of the wild olive tree, which is natural to thee; and, contrary to nature, were grafted into the good olive tree" (Douay-Rheims). The gloss soundly states that "since God is the author of nature he cannot do what is contrary to nature." Shall we equate what is impossible to nature and what is contrary to nature? Should we conclude that God cannot do what is impossible to nature? Aquinas gets out of this trap by articulating a key distinction:

Augustine's words quoted in the gloss mean, not that God is unable to do otherwise than nature does, since his works are often contrary to the wonted course of nature [*contra consuetum cursum naturae*]; but that whatever he does in things is not contrary to nature, but is nature in them, forasmuch as he is the author and governor of nature [*conditor et ordinator naturae*]. Thus in the physical order we observe that when an inferior body is moved by a higher, the movement is natural to it, although it may not seem in keeping with the movement which it has by reason of its own

---

25. Aquinas, *De potentia*, q. 1, a. 3, resp.

nature: thus the tidal movement of the sea is caused by the moon; and this movement is natural to it as the Commentator observes (*De coelo et mundo*, iii, comm. 20), although water of itself has naturally a downward movement. Thus in all creatures, what God does in them is quasi-natural to them [*omnes creaturae quasi pro naturali habent quod a Deo in eis fit*]. Wherefore we distinguish in them a twofold potentiality: a natural potentiality in respect of their proper operations and movements, and another, which we call obediential, in respect of what is done in them by God.[26]

The example of the tide is easy to grasp. As an effect of gravity, the natural power of water is to flow downward. Nevertheless, as an effect on the moon, the sea periodically moves up and down, contrary to the natural power of water. Such a move of flux and reflux is not really against nature, though, as the moon is a higher (celestial) cause by which water by its very nature can be moved. The availability of the sea to be moved by the moon is analogous to the obediential potency of every creature to be moved by God, beyond its natural power.

Today, one might object to this specific example that both the earth and the moon belong to the same order of causality and both influence the sea thanks to the same law of attraction by gravity. A simpler example could be the skills of a dog. A good one might sniff truffles. This belongs to his natural power. Once the same dog is properly trained by a police dog handler, it might sniff drugs and help identifying criminals. This results from a higher cause, the training by an officer, but the dog has the obediential potency to be elevated to this kind of skills. We could choose another example, like some healing process. An epileptic boy might be healed by the natural virtue of his own body and soul, by the right medication appointed by a good physician, and by the attentive care and affection of his parents and close friends. These are proximate causes of a restored good health. At least in the ancient world, the very same disease might be connected with higher causes or disturbances (like the bad spirit of Mk 9:14–29). In any case, higher causes might be

---

26. Ibid., ad 1; see *Super Epistolam ad Romanos lectura* [hereafter *Sup. Rom.*] 11, 24, ed. Marietti, no. 910.

involved in the healing of the boy, like petitionary prayers and, ultimately, God's very action. These kinds of causes belong to a different order than proximate causes and would operate without competing with the latter. The boy has the natural power of healing himself thanks to the help of proximate causes, but he also has some obediential potency to be healed—God willing—thanks to petitionary prayers, in conjunction with God's saving power.

Consequently, if we take into account the higher causes, that which is impossible for a specific natural active or passive power is not entirely impossible, for two main reasons: first, the active power of God is infinite on the side of God; second, every creature stands in obediential potency toward God. Just by being created, every creature is fully available to God's power; and this is more deeply rooted in this being's creaturely condition than are any of its particular active or passive powers.

May we leave aside that which is *per se* impossible, which is excluded from the very notion of possibility? Who should state what is possible and what is impossible for some power? How can one distinguish what is possible and impossible for a nature? What sort of frame of reference should guide such discernment? I suspect that the Cartesian dormant in many of us would immediately respond: God is the only One to judge the possible and the impossible, as he is the master of the impossible.[27] Aquinas's response to these questions proves astonishing, though in the end, it presents a case of his characteristic way of integrating common-sense reason into Christian theology.

Thomas proposes a double consideration: on the side of those who judge and on the side of what is judged. Dealing with the former, Aquinas summons philosophy and theology as two different wisdoms: "Wisdom is twofold: mundane wisdom called philosophy, which considers the lower causes, causes namely that are themselves

---

27. See Marion, "L'impossibilité de l'impossible: Dieu," 21–36. Regarding the background of this line of thought, see Boulnois (ed.), *La puissance et son ombre*, 40–45, including key references to Ockham, Montaigne, and Descartes.

caused, and bases its judgments on them; and divine wisdom or theology, which considers the higher, that is the divine, causes and judges according to them. Now the higher causes are the divine attributes, such as the wisdom, goodness, will of God, and the like."[28] The example of some disease, provided by Aquinas, is relevant. An illness should be diagnosed according to its proximate causes. This falls to the skills of the physician. Nevertheless, the very same illness might also be assessed by taking into account remote causes, like a disturbing astral conjunction for instance. Discerning such an astral pattern pertains to the skills of the astronomer. In this way, insomnia might be referred to a digestive trouble by the physician and to a full moon by the astronomer. Philosophy and theology relate to one another in a similar way as medicine and astronomy.

Philosophy and theology have their specific frames of reference and scopes. For effects that might stem from both inferior causes and superior causes, both wisdoms can work to discern what is possible and what is impossible according to their specific lenses of investigation. However, effects that could only proceed from superior causes are out of reach for the judgment of philosophy.

Let us now consider what is to be judged. The possible and the impossible should be assessed, first of all, in relation to the proximate causes of phenomena, and not in relation to superior and remote causes thereof. Such an analysis is required as a priority, because effects must be labeled as being possible or impossible in relation of their proximate causes. Otherwise, there would be no common meaning and no basic agreement concerning what is possible and what is impossible. In the same way, Aquinas remarks elsewhere that to discern necessity and contingency in this world should be done by reference to proximate causes.[29]

An initial assessment of the possible and the impossible pertains to philosophy, properly speaking. It requires an etiological investiga-

---

28. Aquinas, *De potentia*, q. 1, a. 4, resp.

29. See Aquinas, *SCG* III.72.2; *ST* I, q. 25, a. 3, ad 4; Guy Jalbert, *Nécessité et contingence chez Saint Thomas et chez ses prédécesseurs* (Ottawa: University Press of Ottawa, 1962), 133–64.

tion of proximate causes, as it is done through a medical diagnosis. In the case of theology, however, two kinds of judgment might be registered concerning these matters.

First of all, theology discloses the involvement of superior causes in the very effectuation of inferior causalities. What is possible for nature does not merely come forth from proximate causes alone. It depends also on higher causes and, first and foremost, on the only and ultimate first cause, who is God as creator of all creatures and governor of all created effects or activities.[30] Secondly, theology might explain how natural limits (in relation to proximate causes) are exceeded, by pointing to the active power of God *and* at the obediential potency of all creatures in relation to God.

Relying on these qualifications of philosophy and theology, Thomas can make a sound argument: "All things are possible to God. Therefore, if we must judge of a thing's possibility or impossibility in reference to him, nothing will be impossible: and this is not fitting [*inconveniens*]. The theologian would say that whatever is not impossible in itself is possible to God; according to Mark ix, 22: *All things are possible to him that believeth*, and Luke i, 37: *No word shall be impossible with God*."[31] The specific assessment provided by theology widens the scope of the possible, going beyond what is impossible to nature. Still, that which is *per se* impossible does not cohere with any notion of the possible, even theologically speaking. In order to decisively settle on a common and understandable language regarding the possible and the impossible, philosophy's own judgment is required. Judging according to God, theology goes far beyond the reach of philosophy, but the theologian cannot deal with the common and proper meanings of the terms "possible" and "impossible," even in Gospel statements, without philosophical judgment on realities involved according to proximate causes. We rightly

---

30. Theology also highlights how secondary causalities interplay in such a way that God's will might be implemented, notwithstanding the usual course of nature or the predictable outcome of events; see Aquinas, *SCG* III.96.8; *ST* II-II, q. 83, a. 2, resp.; also, see already Augustine, *De civitate Dei* X.12.

31. Aquinas, *De potentia*, q. 1, a. 4, s.c. 4 and resp. (translation slightly adjusted).

should hope that, in many matters at hand, philosophical judgment is not so different than the shared discernment provided by common sense and practical sciences.

Eventually, Thomas dismisses three explanations of God's omnipotence which were common in his own time, explanations which focused on secondary aspects of this reality, thereby missing the very notion (*ratio*) of omnipotence:

- Focusing on the cause: God is omnipotent because he has an infinite power
- Focusing on the perfection: God is omnipotent because he cannot endure any defect
- Focusing on the mode of possession: God is omnipotent because he can whatever he wills

Accordingly, Aquinas states that the very *ratio* of omnipotence is to be found in the unique relation of God's power to everything that is truly possible:

God's power, considered in itself, extends to all such objects as do not imply a contradiction. [...] as regards things that imply a contradiction, they are impossible to God as being impossible in themselves. Consequently God's power extends to things that are possible in themselves: and such are the things that do not involve a contradiction. Therefore it is evident that God is called almighty because he can do all things that are possible in themselves.[32]

This sober and minimalist statement proves crucial for a sound theology. God should not be qualified nor aimed at as the One who might overcome every impossibility without any restriction, as some of them are nonsensical, insofar as they entail contradiction. Leaving that which is *per se* impossible out of reach even for God's power does not mean that we, poor human beings, limit God by our own judgment or enclose him in some conceptual idol of our own. Aquinas's sound judgment on God's omnipotence relies on his fundamental confidence that there is some coherence or analogy be-

32. Ibid., a. 7, resp.

tween God the almighty, creator of all that is;) the created order of (actual and potential) beings; and the ability of the created human intellect to discern contradictions and to know God, thanks to his works and his word.

BACK TO THE SCRIPTURES

Let us now turn back to the New Testament. Following Aquinas, the words "all things are possible" and "no word is impossible" presuppose the obediential potency which lies at the depths of every created being, still however excluding that which is *per se* impossible. A sound theology should interpret these statements as meaning *even things impossible to nature are possible to God* and *no word is impossible, except those entailing contradiction.*

That which is impossible for nature is not only possible for God, but also for the one who believes. Why? Because the act of faith connects the believer directly to God's power. That which becomes possible to the one who believes depends radically on God's power, as when a delegate servant implements in a specific matter the power of a king.[33] This is fully articulated in Aquinas's theology of petitionary prayer, as one of the most powerful forms of human cooperation with the implementation of God's will, despite the frailty of petition in terms of worldly efficacy.[34]

Our reading of Aquinas has attempted to bring together the Gospel's statements concerning the possible/impossible and a sound metaphysical discernment, which should respect some objective structure within a coherent network: what is impossible to nature; why God can go beyond it, as creator; and how God can go beyond it without bypassing structural contradictions. We should avoid positing an undetermined sovereignty of God over every kind of impossibility, including contradictions, unless we wish to leap into irrationality rather than faith.

33. See Aquinas, *Lectura super Matthaeum* [hereafter *Sup. Mat.*] XVII, 20, ed. Marietti (1951), no. 1471.

34. See chapter 8 of this volume.

We might even go two steps further. Neither philosophers nor theologians should claim to specify what God could do or should do beyond the order of natural potencies. Nevertheless, some metaphysicians might agree that God is wise, good, all-knowing, and omnipotent, in such a way that these attributes are compatible and co-terminate in God's simplicity of essence. One should keep in mind, though, that in the *De potentia,* Aquinas attributes to theologians—not to philosophers—the ability to judge the possible and the impossible in accord with the divine attributes. Such a statement should be accompanied by the acknowledgment that human beings are not capable of mastering this compatibility by reason in every historical or existential context. Faced with overwhelming evils and woes, many do not see the compatibility of classical divine attributes. They prefer to dismiss omnipotence and/or to hold some postmetaphysical apophaticism. I have still argued that God's ordered power, his *potentia ordinata,* is not a conceptual idol.

Theologians should go further, however, acknowledging that God's ordered power is entailed by Christ's preaching and deeds. Theological knowledge of God's action is not merely conjectural, but instead draws directly from revelation. In many and various ways, the scriptures profess and interpret what God enacted or brought to completion above the mere order of nature. The scriptures are not interested in framing all that God might have hypothetically done. Theology might proceed further thanks to the analogy of faith. The scriptures are first of all fulfilled in Christ's preaching, actions, passions, death, and resurrection. However, they also might be accomplished in the life and ordeals, faith and hopes, self-surrender and holy death of humble believers, who cling to Christ and receive his Spirit, the very same One who inspired scripture. In this way, scripture supports our faith and confidence in the wisdom and power implemented by God through his providence, despite the obscurities of reason and the darkness of faith.

8

The Gospel of Prayer and Theories of Providence

The term "providence" (*pronoeô* or *pronoia*) does not appear in the Gospels, though the image of God underlying this word is revealed there under many facets. In the New Testament, the verb *pronoeô* is used in Romans 12:17; 2 Corinthians 8:21; and 1 Timothy 5:8. The noun *pronoia* is found in Acts 24:2 and Romans 13:14. None of these occurrences carries a specifically theological sense. They simply evoke a human disposition or activity.

And yet, God knows in detail all that matters to humans. He looks after them, and their life has value in his eyes. Persecutions or misfortunes should not confuse the disciples, but rather, invite them to steadfastness and to conversion, for they remain in the hand of God. Faith and trust in God ought to liberate the disciples from concern for riches, for God looks after them and their true treasure is in heaven (cf. Lk 12:4–7, 22–32). However, they must also recognize that the quest for the kingdom entails concern for others, in their needs and in their trials. Instead of interpreting the woes of others by reference to their imagined faults, those who hear about them ought rather to let themselves be challenged and questioned by this kind of news (cf. Lk 10:29–37, 13:1–5). Moreover, through prayer that is persevering, the disciples are assured of being heard by God and can believe that justice will be rendered unto them (cf. Lk 11:5–13, 18:1–8). Finally, and above all, the beneficent and provocative action of Jesus is a very concrete image of the way God meets with human needs, all the while giving priority to the kingdom.

Thus, if we are looking for a theology of providence in the Gospel of Luke (for example), we will not find it there in a literal sense. However, the very concrete teaching of Jesus concerning the disciples' trust in God and concerning the efficacy of petitionary prayer is given weight by an acute perception of God's solicitude at all times.

This leads us to put forward our working hypothesis: the Gospel of trust and prayer is the pedestal of faith on which one can build a theology of providence, with the constant need to evaluate its theoretical progress in the light of the Gospel itself. In dialogue with Thomas Aquinas, we shall test our hypothesis in three stages: how can we arrange the hierarchy and connection of truths involved with the topics of prayer and providence; how can we reconcile the efficacy of petitionary prayer with the immutability of providence; and, finally, is there really a response by providence to petitionary prayer?

HIERARCHY AND CONNECTION OF TRUTHS ABOUT PRAYER AND PROVIDENCE

The theology of petitionary prayer is often conceived, and rightly so, as the litmus test for a preliminary theology of providence. But we intend to show that the connection between prayer and providence is closer and actually cuts both ways. It is not enough to deduce consequences from a theology of providence for an understanding of prayer. The theory of providence should also be worked out in the light of the Gospel teaching on petitionary prayer.

Systematic theology more often than not tries to make some kind of efficacy of petitionary prayer compatible with a preestablished notion of providence. This can be found quite clearly in the study undertaken by the Evangelical theologian, Terrance Tiessen, on the many possible relations between providence and petitionary prayer.[1] Through a typology expounded in ten models, he shows how a given conception of providence determines a particular explanation of the way petitionary prayer operates in relation to God. The discriminating criteria which enable, according to their variations, a schematization of the different models are the following in particular: the kind of internal relation of God to created temporality, the divine knowledge or nonknowledge of possible events that will never actually occur, the element of risk taken or not by God in creating, the compatibility or incompatibility of human freedom with constraining conditions, the nature of the impact of prayer on the outcome of events and, finally, the question of knowing whether or not God changes his mind in response to the prayers of humans. To begin with, Tiessen notes that the biblical data on the subject of petitionary prayer are not consistent among themselves and do not clearly imply a particular line of theology. The fact is that most of the time each theologian finds in the biblical teaching some form of coherence which suits him, refracted through a predetermined doctrinal and conceptual prism.

If we maintain the conviction, however, that the Gospel can and must direct theology, we need to find the means to moderate the unilateral influence of a preliminary conception of providence on the doctrine of prayer, in order firstly to clarify this connection the other way around. The better way forward would, rather, be to ask which theology of providence is required by the Gospel faith in the supernatural efficacy of petitionary prayer.

But let us proceed with caution. Such an inversion cannot be held in a unilateral manner, for the efficacy of petitionary prayer is often misunderstood and easily leads to a caricature of God. Indeed, the answering of prayers risks being spontaneously linked with a pagan understanding of the divine, according to which incantations addressed to the gods have the immediate goal of coaxing their wills and influencing their attitudes toward humans.

It is, therefore, not possible purely and simply to "index" a theory

---

1. See Terrance L. Tiessen, *Providence and Prayer: How Does God Work in the World?* (Downers Grove, Ill.: InterVarsity Press, 2000), 363–64.

of providence on the basis of a supposedly obvious doctrine of the efficacy of requests made to God. One should, rather, recognize the primacy of the Gospel teaching on the subject of trust in God and petitionary prayer, while showing that its proper theological reception demands a refined concept of divine providence in its relation to human affairs.

In order to illustrate the simultaneous difficulty and possibility involved in finding a true connection between providence and petitionary prayer, let us turn to the teaching of Thomas Aquinas in the *Summa theologiae*. He writes about providence and predestination in the *Prima pars* (*ST* I, qq. 22–23), taking up his discussion of prayer in the *Secunda secundae* (II-II, q. 83). A study of these two sections reveals that an appropriate analysis of one of these poles calls for, or presupposes, a correct conception of the other. The potential benefit of prayer does not enter into question 22 on providence, but rather comes at the end of question 23 on predestination. At first sight, the cooperation of prayer with providence is not discussed. However, predestination is a part of providence, insofar as the latter orders rational creatures toward their final and supernatural end (q. 23, a. 1). In a consistent manner, the help of the prayers of the saints *vis-à-vis* the *effect* of predestination is treated as a particular case of the integration of secondary causes into the providential order of God (q. 23, a. 8). Ultimately, prayer, combined with other good and holy actions, is considered by Aquinas as being the most efficacious kind of human cooperation with the eternal plan of God, as the prayers of the saints are, through grace, eminently fit for obtaining, either for themselves or for others, the highest of all goals, namely salvation and eternal life. This presupposes a clarification of the proper efficacy belonging to petitionary requests precisely as human acts, issuing from the practical intellect and underpinned by desire, just like any other secondary causality integrated with providence.

Let us now turn to the section on petitionary prayer,[2] where Aquinas examines whether it is appropriate to pray to God (II-II,

2. See Jean-Pierre Torrell, "L'interprète du désir. La prière chez saint Thomas d'Aquin," *La Vie spirituelle* 752 (2004): 213–23.

q. 83, a. 2). In the first part of his reply, he takes care to discard three errors of the ancients on the subject of providence, for they either undermine the soundness of prayer or mangle the power of its efficacy. Those who held the first error held that human affairs are not regulated by divine providence. It would thus be quite simply futile to pray or to worship God. However, scripture abundantly refutes such an impiety. The supporters of the second error held that everything, including human affairs, happened by necessity, for diverse reasons: the immutability of providence, astrological necessity, or the chain of causes. Again, prayer would be vain and useless. Finally, the originators of the third error rightly admitted that human affairs are governed by providence while respecting their free and contingent character, but they affirmed that the disposition of divine providence was changed by prayers and other cultic practices. At the end of this brief catalogue,[3] Aquinas justifiably considers that he has already corrected these errors in question 22 on providence. He can therefore deliver, in the second part of his reply, an account of how to include the proper efficacy of prayer in the effective completion of the providential disposition of God. We shall return to this later.

For the present discussion, the essential point lies in the conclusion which St. Thomas draws. Putting aside those three errors, it clearly expresses the criteria which any sound explanation of the usefulness of prayer must meet: "And so one must account for the utility of prayer in such a way as neither to impose necessity on human affairs subject to divine providence, nor to imply that the divine disposition is changeable."[4]

Conversely, the three errors draw attention to three truths which

---

3. See Aquinas, *SCG* III.96.9; *Super librum Dionysii De divinis nominibus*, chap. 3, nos. 241–42; *Compendium* II.6; *Sup. Mat.* 6:9, no. 584; Augustine, *De civitate Dei* V.8; Serge-Thomas Bonino, "Providence et causes secondes. L'exemple de la prière," in *Saint Thomas d'Aquin*, ed. Thierry-Dominique Humbrecht (Paris: Cerf, 2010), 493–519, at 500–511; Lawrence Dewan, "St. Thomas and the Ontology of Prayer," *Divus Thomas* 77, nos. 3–4 (1974): 392–402.

4. Aquinas, *ST* II-II, q. 83, a. 2, resp. [§1 *in fine*]: "Et ideo oportet sic inducere orationis utilitatem ut neque rebus humanis, divinae providentiae subiectis, necessitatem imponamus; neque etiam divinam dispositionem mutabilem aestimemus."

any theology of prayer must take into account: the submission of human realities to providence, the contingency of those things for which one prays, and the immutability of the providential disposition by which God orders every event to the ultimate end. The specifications of a theology of petitionary prayer thus appear to depend on a speculative refutation of common mistakes regarding providence.

In order to account for the close bonds between providence and prayer, we should therefore distinguish several levels of assertion and intelligibility. The noun "providence" (*pronoia* or *pronoeô*) does not appear in the Synoptic Gospels. On the other hand, the Gospel teaching insists in an expressive manner that the disciples must each and every day depend on the will of God, that they must trust God in their most concrete needs, and that perseverant prayer, directed first and foremost toward the things of the kingdom, has a supernatural efficacy. Thus takes shape the Gospel teaching on filial trust and petitionary prayer, inseparably connected to the benevolence and paternal watchfulness of God, ever solicitous for our subsistence and salvation. At that level, filial trust, petitionary prayer, and salvific providence are intimately interwoven in the unique teaching of the Gospel faith.

Next, as regards theological elaboration and verification, a theory of providence requires, in order to be complete, the integration of the prayers of the saints involved in the obtaining of the ultimate end willed by God for human beings. And, reciprocally, an explanation of the efficacy of petitionary prayer presupposes a speculative adjustment of the conceptions available regarding providence. The doctrinal connection has repercussions in terms of explanatory theories. For Aquinas, the inclusion of prayer consummates the theology of providence, and a correct conception of providence is required for a sound theology of prayer.

From the Gospel and Thomistic theology, the ideal sequence would seem to be the following: (1) the Gospel teaching given by Christ himself on the subject of trust and prayer; (2) the correctness of a speculative theology of providence, obtained by adding metaphysical judgment; and (3) the correctness of an explanatory theology of the efficacy of petitionary prayer, purified from all pagan notions. Thus, the consideration of prayer frames the theology of providence as a doctrinal pedestal on the one hand and, on the other, as a locus of theological verification.

THE EFFICACY OF PETITIONARY PRAYER AND THE IMMUTABILITY OF PROVIDENCE

Having addressed the specifications of Aquinas for a theology of prayer in harmony with a sound conception of providence, let us now consider his explanation of the *modus operandi* of petitionary prayer, given the disposition and providential action of God. Aquinas's *tour de force* consists in situating the help of prayer as a particular and outstanding case of the inclusion of human action within divine providence.

Divine providence disposes not only what effects shall take place, but also from what causes and in what order these effects shall proceed. Now among other causes human acts are the causes of certain effects. Wherefore it must be that men do certain actions. Not that thereby they may change the Divine disposition, but that by those actions they may achieve certain effects according to the order of the Divine disposition: and the same is to be said of natural causes. And so is it with regard to prayer. For we pray not that we may change the Divine disposition, but that we may impetrate that which God has disposed to be fulfilled by our prayers in other words "that by asking, men may deserve to receive what Almighty God from eternity has disposed to give," as Gregory says (*Dial.* i, 8).[5]

In relation to providence, prayer is comparable to human acts. Indeed, it truly is a human act, raised up and supernaturalized by grace. As a general rule, God integrates the proper activity of secondary causes into his providential plan and government. Among such causes, man is capable of acting effectively and freely. Thus he

---

5. Aquinas, *ST* II-II, q. 83, a. 2, resp. [§2]; see Augustine, *De civitate Dei* X.12.

may, for example, bring aid to a sick friend and employ all appropriate human means to restore him to health. But God alone is the master of life and death, of health and sickness. The effect of healing thus proceeds conjointly, with both human causality (of friendship and medical practice) and divine causality being involved, not through a division of effects but entirely from one and from the other.[6] When God wills and arranges the healing of a sick person, because this will help him or his friends grasp an ultimate end, more often than not this healing is accomplished effectively by the application of human care.

The same is true of prayer, a human contribution analogous to medical care. When God mediates the accomplishing of his will through the help of our prayers, the effect of providence also becomes fully the effect of prayer. It is not the case that only one part of the fulfillment is due to prayer, while God for his part accomplishes all that he wills. Rather, the effect willed by God is not only entirely caused by him, as first cause, but also entirely caused by prayer, as secondary cause. In reality, prayer is not merely fulfilled by a crowning which would be quite extrinsic to it. No, it fully cooperates in its own causality with the fulfillment of providence. All this, however, requires some elucidation concerning how prayer exercises its causality.

From the anthropological point of view, Aquinas specifies that petitionary prayer is an act of the practical intellect, whose role is to be in charge of action or make requests. At first sight, this seems disconcerting, inasmuch as petition is always the expression of a desire, which comes from the appetitive power. But such an expression proceeds for its part from the practical intellect, which can guide desire, even though the intensity of desire underpins the petition.[7]

To explain the connection of prayer with the practical intellect, Thomas argues in the following way: the function of the practical in-

---

6. See Aquinas, *SCG* III.70.8.

7. See Aquinas, *ST* II-II, q. 83, a. 1, ad 1–2; *Sent.* IV, q. 4, a. 1, qla. 1, resp.: "oratio est actus rationis, applicantis desiderium voluntatis ad eum qui non sunt sub potestate nostra sed supra nos, scilicet Deum."

tellect is not only to apprehend the real but also to cause action.[8] Now, a causal power can operate in two ways: perfectly, when the effect is totally subject to the power of the cause; and imperfectly, when the effect is not totally subject to that power.

When applied to the practical intellect, this distinction is expressed by two kinds of act: on the one hand, to command (*imperare*) in order to accomplish whatever depends directly on oneself or on one's subordinates; on the other hand, to ask (*petere* or *deprecari*) that a thing might be done by another who is equal or superior to oneself. This description of an anthropological possibility, when elevated by grace, coincides with petitionary prayer addressed to God. In this way, prayer retains all the attributes of human action, while simultaneously unfolding a supernatural activity.

When it corresponds to God's salvific will, prayer accomplishes the supernatural effect of providence, because petition is eternally integrated by God as a human mediation adapted to a properly divine effect. Most of the time, we pray to obtain something beyond our power and depending exclusively on the divine power. However, prayer thus has a role to play precisely as the ultimate human cooperation by which we can hope to contribute to the work of God and facilitate its fulfillment.

Without modifying the divine dispositions in any way, the prayers of human beings have been granted by God the singular power of cooperating with the fulfillment of his salvific will and his providential plan, especially when all other human means are exhausted. In the Thomistic view, to say that prayer is useless is as absurd as to judge that medical care is useless for a restoration to health that is willed by God. In the *Summa contra Gentiles*, Aquinas eloquently expresses the same conviction with reference to daily acts, which no one could believe should be suspended in order to permit God to accomplish the effects of his providence:

The cause of some things that are done by God is prayers and holy desires. But we showed above that divine providence does not exclude other caus-

8. Aquinas, *ST* II-II, q. 83, a. 1, resp.

es; rather, it orders them so that the order which providence has determined within itself may be imposed on things. And thus, secondary causes are not incompatible with providence; instead, they carry out the effect of providence. In this way, then, prayers are efficacious before God, yet they do not destroy the immutable order of divine providence, because this individual request that is granted to a certain petitioner falls under the order of divine providence. So, it is the same thing to say that we should not pray in order to obtain something from God, because the order of his providence is immutable, as to say that we should not walk in order to get to a place, or eat in order to be nourished; all of which are clearly absurd.[9]

It is very clear that to fulfill one's everyday duties, one must use one's legs and consume food; these daily tasks are included in God's providential order. Thus, for instance, a mother will take care of her little children in a thousand and one ways, deploying all her energies in conformity with the divine disposition. In the same way, going to the hospital to spend a moment with a sick friend represents a response to the providential order that friendly support is favorable to the recovery of health, all the while supposing that I actually make the effort to find transportation there. So, Aquinas wants to convince us that the mediation of prayer in the fulfillment of God's work is just as necessary, useful, and concrete as the use of our legs. Without the help of our prayers in God's work, these would not be fulfilled, at least as being our work also.

Like any other contingent secondary cause, our prayer can be deficient. Does this mean the effect of providence would be cancelled out as a result? It is very likely that, if we fail individually in the real cooperation that our prayer might bring to God's work, he would mobilize support from someone else, to co-opt him in turn for the fulfillment of his plan by grace. In this way, the purpose of providence will always be accomplished, while the loss incurred by deficiency applies above all to the one who was lacking, thus depriving himself of the grace of helping with God's work.

9. Aquinas, *SCG* III.96.8, trans. Vernon J. Bourke (New York: Image Books, 1956), 1:62.

DOES PROVIDENCE GIVE A REPLY
TO PETITIONARY PRAYER?

One of the principal contemporary objections to an eternal incorporation of prayer into an immutable providence consists in repudiating the lack of "responsiveness" in God in the granting of prayers. The critique comes from the devotees of process theology (or open theism), as well as from the Molinists.[10] For the process theologians, God would adjust his will in accordance with human actions and would thus respond effectively to prayers. This supposes that God is himself "eternal" in a temporality superior to our own, which is proper to him, in order to follow step-by-step the rhythm of our liberty. In the Molinist framework, on the other hand, God does not change and his eternity is not "temporalized," but he possesses an eternal and complete knowledge of all the potential consequences of all the possible contingencies and choices. In this way, God would eternally possess in himself all the potential response to all our possible trajectories.

Insisting in various ways on the accommodation (either temporally or eternally) of God to human actions (be they real or potential), these thinkers claim that they express an original and coherent advance regarding the "responsive" dimension of providence. Such a property of providence is attractive to a believer's mind because it seems to be in close conformity with biblical teaching. Indeed, in many biblical passages, God's action accommodates itself to human attitudes, especially infidelity, hardening of heart, or conversion. What's more, the God of the Bible willingly responds to the intercessory prayer of his servants, prophets, and ministers, as well as to the requests of the humblest people. A simple and trusting reading of the Bible easily allows one to believe that God replies in a thousand and one ways to the prayers of the saints and that he actually regulates his action according to human choices, good or bad.

10. See Tiessen, *Providence and Prayer*, 52–70 (Process), 71–118 (Openness), 153–77 (Molinist); Pinnock et al., *The Openness of God*; Thomas P. Flint, *Divine Providence: The Molinist Account* (New York: Cornell University Press, 1998), 41–46.

It is appropriate, then, to examine how Aquinas deals with this aspect of the biblical witness and whether he gives way to a certain "responsive" dimension to providence. Let us return to the *Summa contra Gentiles*, to the passage immediately following the argument discussed above. The integration of prayer into the immutable order of providence leads Aquinas to refute two typical errors on the subject of prayer, already encountered earlier.[11]

First of all, for different reasons, the Epicureans and the Stoics considered human prayers to be futile and fruitless, for the first group removed human affairs from providence, while the second thought that everything subject to providence happened necessarily. These two positions are strongly refuted by the teaching of Aquinas on the subject of providence insofar as he has demonstrated the extension of providence to everything that exists, without exception, the inclusion not only of necessary causalities but also contingent causalities in the order of providence, and finally the incorporation of prayers in the eternal plan of providence.

In connection with our examination of the "responsive" dimension of providence, the refutation of the second error is more decisive. In effect, it concerns the pagan conviction holding that prayers can change the providential disposition of God. Following Nemesius, Thomas imputes this error to the Egyptians who thought they could change destiny by all sorts of practices, fumigations, and incantations. Before demolishing this error, Aquinas acknowledges that many biblical passages appear to move in this direction. He quotes three particularly eloquent ones from the prophets: Isaiah 38:1–5, Jeremiah 18:7–8, and Joel 2:13–14. Each time, it does seem that God is changing his mind, or at least shows himself ready to do so, in response to prayer and penitence on the part of those who, he had decided, would shortly meet their doom.

But Aquinas refuses such an interpretation, judging it to be superficial and inappropriate, for two reasons: one speculative,

11. See Aquinas, *SCG* III.96.9. See Nemesius of Emesa [confused with Gregory of Nyssa], *De natura hominis*, chaps. 34–36, trans. Burgundio of Pisa, ed. G. Verbeke and J. R. Moncho (Leiden: Brill, 1975), 133.

the other biblical. In line with the conclusions of the two preceding books of the *Summa contra Gentiles*, Thomas firstly recalls that the will of God does not change and that God himself is not dependent on what happens to creatures in time. These clarifications only have argumentative value in relation to relevant, antecedent metaphysico-theological demonstrations.[12] They rest upon the exclusion of all mutability in the divine substance and of all potentiality in the divine will, as well as upon the asymmetry of relations between God and his creatures.

Nevertheless, Aquinas does not limit himself to arguments of this first kind. The inappropriate interpretation is also rejected by the authority of the scriptures themselves, where it is repeatedly affirmed that God is not like man: he does not go back on his word and he does not repent of his will, according to Numbers 23:19, 1 Samuel 15:29, and Malachi 3:6. Evidently, Thomas considers that these few demonstrations of God's perseverance in his plan and the immutability of the divine will are normative for a correct hermeneutic of those passages, which are admittedly more numerous, in which God appears to change his dispositions or to go back on his word. These figures of speech therefore reveal themselves to be metaphorical and must be interpreted as such. It is clear that the prevailing of one biblical register over another stems from the convergence of the nonmetaphorical declarations on the immutability of the divine will with the metaphysico-theological discernment established antecedently. To put it another way, in contemporary language, a canonical reading of the scriptures under the analogy of faith finds itself oriented here in a given direction by a theological conviction which falls within the analogy of being.

Here, some methodological reservations must be expressed. Our preliminary analyses of the texts invoked call for a different hermeneutics than the one practiced by Aquinas. According to the fine-tuning of our exegetical method, it is not fitting to overrule one verse by another, when they are extracted from different literary

12. See Aquinas, *SCG* I.82.7, 83.2–3, II.12.5.

units. Theological accounts of divine repentance go beyond a simple rhetorical metaphor. Among them, 1 Samuel 15 mobilizes two contrasting registers of affirmations: "I repent" and "God does not repent." I have reflected on this more closely in chapter 4.

Having thus put aside in principle the false opinion of swaying the providential disposition of God by prayers, Aquinas nevertheless returns to this problem in a more thorough way, in order to clarify the grain of truth contained in the errors of the Egyptians and the Stoics. This leads him first to posit the distinction between the universal order and a particular order, which enables him to situate the immutability of providence at its proper level:

Now, if a person carefully considers these statements, he will find that every error that occurs on these points arises from the fact that thought is not given to the difference between universal and particular order. For, since all effects are mutually ordered, in the sense that they come together in one cause, it must be that, the more universal the cause is, the more general is the order. Hence, the order stemming from the universal cause which is God must embrace all things. So, nothing prevents some particular order from being changed, either by prayer, or by some other means [*nihil igitur prohibet aliquem particularem ordinem vel per orationem, vel per aliquem alium modum immutari*], for there is something outside that order which could change it.[13]

Under the universal order, related to the first cause, fall all the particular orders, where particular chains of causation occur between secondary causes and their proper effects. A particular chain can be prevented, short-circuited, accelerated, or overtaken by the interference of another secondary cause. But, whatever the case may be, this latter remains subject to the influence of the first cause and to the universal order to which it is relative. Insofar as prayer is a human action, supernaturalized and integrated into the universal order just like other secondary causes (as Thomas taught in the passages considered above), it can certainly receive from God an efficacy that overrules other secondary causes and suspends their

13. Aquinas, *SCG* III.96.14 (trans. Bourke, 1:64).

expected natural fulfillment. In this case, however, the efficacy of prayer and its supernatural effect always belong to the universal order established by God, as they are integrated from all eternity into the immutable disposition of his providence.

In light of this argument, Thomas explains the error of the Egyptians by stating that they believed that prayers could modify destiny relative to the influence exercised by the stars on human affairs, an influence which, in reality, depends upon a particular order. Conversely, fascinated by the universal order, the Stoics supported the immutability of the order instituted by God and consequently esteemed prayers to be futile, without perceiving their potential effect on the causal chains of lesser particular orders, which are also always included in the universal order. In response to the Stoics, Aquinas rightly recalls that the prayer of humans belongs to the vast field of secondary causes:

For, when [the Stoics] say that, whether prayers are offered or not, in any case the same effect in things follows from the universal order of things, they clearly isolate from that universal order the wishes of those who pray. For, if these prayers be included under that order, then certain effects will result by divine ordination by means of these prayers, just as they do by means of other causes. So, it will be the same thing to exclude the effect of prayer as to exclude the effect of all other causes. Because, if the immutability of the divine order does not take away their effects from other causes, neither does it remove the efficacy of prayers. Therefore, prayers retain their power; not that they can change the order of eternal control, but rather as they themselves exist under such order.[14]

Let us remind ourselves of the example given above by Aquinas: to deny the efficacy of prayer under the pretext that the universal order of providence is immutable would be as absurd as to refuse to eat or to use one's legs. It is evident that these human activities are willed and disposed by God as allowing the fulfillment of his will. Antecedently, the comparison presupposes the anthropological analysis of prayer, as such an analysis enables us to grasp wholly its character as a human act and, from this perspective, as secondary

14. Ibid. (trans. Bourke, 1:65); see Augustine, *De civitate Dei* V.8–9.

cause. Far from the pagan fumigations and incantations, prayer is efficacious because it is a human act to which God, in the order of his providence, connects certain natural and supernatural effects.

Having thus established the efficacy of prayers in this or that particular causal order, Aquinas can finally shed new light on the biblical verses where God appears to repent:

But nothing prevents some particular order, due to an inferior cause, from being changed through the efficacy of prayers, under the operation of God Who transcends [*supergreditur*] all causes, and thus is not confined under the necessity of any order of cause; on the contrary, all the necessity of the order of an inferior cause is confined under him [*continetur sub ipso*] as being brought into being by him [*quasi ab eo institutus*]. So, insofar as something in the order of inferior causes established by God is changed through [the prayers of pious people], God is said *to turn* or *to repent*; not in the sense that his eternal disposition is changed, but that some effect of his is changed. Hence, Gregory says that "God does not change his plan [*consilium*], though at times he may change his judgment [*sententia*]", not, I say, the judgment which expresses his eternal disposition, but the judgment which expresses the order of inferior causes, in accord with which Hezekiah was to have died, or a certain people were to have been punished for their sins. Now, such a change of judgment is called God's *repentance*, using a metaphorical way of speaking, in the sense that God is disposed like one who repents, for whom it is proper to change what he had been doing. In the same way, he is also said, metaphorically, *to become angry*, in the sense that, by punishing, he produces the same effect as an angry person.[15]

First of all, let us note that Aquinas probably quotes Gregory the Great from memory, using a striking but shortened formula, at the risk of becoming ambiguous. God's will cannot be divided between an immutable intention and a mutable implementation of his decrees. Gregory's text does make use of the distinction between *consilium* and *sententia*, but it does not simply say that the *sententia* changes. He says that it seems to be changing externally. Gregory is thus faithful to the explanations already given by Augustine about repentance. Here is Gregory's source text, as we have it today:

15. Aquinas, *SCG* III.96.15 (trans. Bourke, 1:65–66).

And with regard to his immutability, Job immediately adds, not without accuracy: "And no one can divert his purpose [*cogitatio*]." For if he is immutable in his nature, he is also immutable in his will. Indeed, his purpose, no one diverts him, because no one has the strength to resist his secret judgments. Indeed, some may have given the impression that they had diverted, by their supplications, a purpose of God, but his deep purpose had been that they had the power to divert a sentence of the master [*sententia*] by begging him, and what they received from him was to plead a cause before him. Job can therefore say: "And no one will be able to divert his thoughts," because, once fixed, his judgments cannot be changed. Hence the Scripture saying: "He has established his commandments and they will not pass away" (Ps 148:6). And again: "Heaven and earth will pass away, but my words will not pass away" (Mk 13:31). And again: "For my thoughts are not your thoughts and my ways are not your ways" (Is 55:8). Thus, at the moment when his sentence externally seems to change, internally his counsel does not change [*cum ergo exterius mutari uidetur sententia, interius consilium non mutatur*], because, in all things, what is established within him in immutability is established within him what is outside is accomplished in mutability.[16]

Although the quotation is simplified, the explanation provided by Aquinas is consistent with Gregory's thought.

God never repents, properly speaking, because he does not change his will; however, he can declare through the mediation of his prophets that death of the sinner is near, following this or that particular order of causality, even though he wills for the latter a different outcome, following the primacy of his will and the universal order of his providence. When his grace instigates, against all expectation, the repentance of the sinner, God then accomplishes the plan of his will and the effect of his providence. To our eyes, God appears to have repented, for the prophet initially had access only to his word regarding a matter of fact and a foreseeable *dénouement*, whereas his ultimate will yet remained veiled to him.[17]

Through the secondary efficacy of the prayers of the saints, what

16. Gregory the Great, *Moralia in Job* XVI.37.46 (Paris: Cerf, 1975), 209–11; Augustine, *De Genesi ad litteram* VI.17.28; *De civitate Dei* IX.5, XIV.11, XV.25, XVII.7.

17. See Aquinas, *ST* I, q. 19, a. 7, ad 2; q. 83, a. 3, ad 2; II-II, q. 171, a. 6, ad 2; *Sent.* IV, d. 45, q. 2, a. 2, qla. 2, ad 1; *De veritate*, q. 6, a. 4, ad 1; *Sup. Psalmos* 32, no. 10; 50, no. 6.

is sometimes found to be modified by God is not the plan of his will nor the order of his providence, but rather this or that such causal chain circumscribed in the lower order. If one considers this particular order alone, according to the most common field of human observation, one can hold that God modifies it by allowing another influence to prevail. In so doing, he does not however change his providence. Rather, he accomplishes its supernatural effect through the secondary efficacy which he accords to the prayers of the saints.

Thus, for example, the causal chain of a terminal illness can be impeded by the efficacy of our prayers, inasmuch as God, willing the healing of so-and-so, achieves this in connection with our supplications. From our temporal perspective, fixed on this or that particular causal order, we can thus say that God "responds" to our prayers when he answers them and accomplishes the requested healing effect. Nevertheless, in a Thomistic perspective, it is more fitting to say rather that our prayers "respond" on this occasion to the universal order of his providence, according to which it eternally disposes that the unexpected healing of this or that person be obtained, in time, by the secondary efficacy of our ardent prayers. In this case, God does not answer our prayers in the sense of conforming himself to them, but he does, in reality, involve us in the implementation of his salvific will, thereby mobilizing the efficacy of our prayers to accomplish its own effect of salvation. Let us not imagine that the providence of God precedes our prayers in a temporal way. Eternal and simple, providence is always "contemporaneous" with our prayers.

Let us finally return to the proper efficacy of prayer as secondary causality. What is it? It seems difficult to conceive of the efficacy of prayer as a measurable efficacy, in the manner of other causalities in the physical world. Most often, these have a perceptible impact, in the way of a motion or a making. The proper efficacy of petitionary prayer, as an entirely separate secondary cause, could however be of two kinds.

On the one hand, it is a request articulated, at greater or lesser length, by a human soul to God. As such, prayer introduces something effective on our part. We establish the act of addressing our-selves to God and we ask of him something more or less defined. This certainly produces new dispositions in us, as Augustine read-ily emphasized.[18] Beyond the material or immediate object of the request, prolonged prayer effects an interior transformation in the person praying: it deepens his desire and adapts it to the will of God.

Moreover, the influence of prayer can take effect, when God wills it, upon this or that particular order which otherwise might easily prevail. Here, two possibilities can be envisaged. First, God alone directly makes some causal chains prevail in the world in or-der to remove another non-desired causal chain. In this way, God himself gives in an extrinsic way all his efficacy to prayer without its prevailing on its own, even though one must always attribute their common effect to God as much as to the one praying, according to a complete causal synergy. Second, prayer possesses its own spir-itual efficacy which is not of the material order yet has a physical impact. The effectiveness of prayer could thus be compared to the "miracle" of a spiritual freedom altogether unexpected, whenever it prevails here or there over all the conditions and constraints which would seem to preclude its emergence; or again, it could be com-pared to the influence of angelic creatures upon the physical and hu-man world. The effectiveness of prayer would then signify a real pri-macy of the invisible over the visible, a primacy which is very often overlooked or neglected.

THE PRIORITY OF GRACE

The Thomistic theology of prayer is fitted, not only to his theory of providence, but also to the essentially Christian doctrine of the pri-ority of grace over all human cooperation in the fulfillment of the works of God. Accordingly, it is not God who answers our prayers,

---

18. See Augustine, *Letter* 130 *to Proba*, §§17–18 (PL 33:500–501); Gérald Antoni, *La prière chez saint Augustin: D'une philosophie du langage à la théologie du Verbe* (Paris: Vrin, 1997).

but rather these prayers which answer to his call. The prayers of the faithful are indeed integrated from all eternity into the providential order of God, by reason of the primeval gratuity of his will of grace, according to which he associates human beings as free subjects with the temporal effecting of his plan. Thus, to conceive the efficacy of petitionary prayer in this way amounts to conferring upon it the highest efficacy there can be, proportioned by grace to the proper effects of the divine will itself. From this perspective, the theology of prayer remains subject to the need to respect absolutely the eternity of God and the priority of his grace. In the final analysis, this is the very heart of the doctrinal challenge of harmonizing the efficacy of petitionary prayer with the immutability of salvific providence.

9

Divine Action, Providence, and the Three Main Articles of the Creed

In this chapter, I intend to present God's commitment in the world and in history in a "phenomenological" manner. Divine action and providence are most often considered from a metaphysical or hermeneutical perspective. Metaphysics builds up a theory of providence and/or divine action on the basis of certain common features of created beings, such as structures and order, causalities, necessity and contingency, physical models, and so forth.[1] Hermeneutics focuses on the ways that providence and/or divine action might be discerned and interpreted by individual human subjects, relying on their experiences, expectations, and faith.[2] Thus, for the metaphysician, providence is thought of as a preordered fine-tuning of the whole creation in relation to its ultimate end, whereas the hermeneutician looks on the divine action as something to be discerned

---

1. Among the very best ones, see Michael J. Dodds, *Unlocking Divine Action: Contemporary Science & Thomas Aquinas* (Washington, D.C.: The Catholic University of America Press, 2012); Ignacio Silva, "Revisiting Aquinas on Providence and Rising to the Challenge of Divine Action in Nature," *Journal of Religion* 94, no. 3 (2014): 277–91; "Providence, Contingency, and the Perfection of the Universe," *Philosophy, Theology and the Sciences* 2, no. 2 (2015): 137–57.

2. See the seminal proposal of Bultmann, "New Testament and Mythology."

180

and confessed through individual narratives, as we find in St. Augustine's *Confessions*. In this chapter, I would like to consider a possible "middle path" between metaphysics and hermeneutics by exploring a "phenomenological" way of addressing providence. Phenomenology intends to perceive phenomena in their self-manifestation. I propose to apply this kind of approach to human action, as the best analogy for providence, and to the Creed, as the best short testimony to effective providence in this fallen world.

First, I explain why one might privilege the motif of God's action as being the most integral such motif, compared to causality, event, and meaning. In a second step, I spell out Christian faith in providence inasmuch as the latter is applied in this world, broken and sinful, according to the three main articles of the Creed. The premise of this theological reflection is the following: God is sovereign in the world and in history, on the ground of both creation and resurrection. The testimonies of creation and the resurrection are solid; nevertheless, God's sovereignty awaits eschatological actualization and manifestation. The challenge of conceiving God's sovereignty in an opaque world and in a shattered history remains, but the confession of faith nonetheless proves the best starting point and guideline.

INTERPRETIVE OPTIONS: CAUSALITY, ACTION, EVENT, MEANING?

In order to think theologically about the commitment, involvement, or presence of the God of revelation in this world, one of the main challenges is to adopt categories that are not too restrictive or reductive in relation to God's sovereignty. He reveals himself and hides, speaks and acts, calls and warns, makes himself present to groups and individuals as he wills, according to his design. Theology draws from faith a constellation of testimonies rendered to God's saving action in the history of his people. Choosing categories, whether carefully considered or not, and handling them more or less accurately, have consequences for how a given theology honors or disfigures testimonies of faith.

Resources of Causality

Causality is one of the ancient resources of theological thinking. This notion is analogical. It is modulated in various but coherent ways. The four ancient causalities (formal, efficient, material, final) answer fundamental questions of human intelligence before that which is unknown: What is it? Where does it come from? What is it made of? For what purpose does it exist? In addition to these four causes, there is a variant of the formal cause, namely the exemplar cause, which provides the answer to the question: On what model is this done or made? Whatever the critics of metaphysics may say, these causalities remain operative in contemporary philosophical thought and scientific research.[3] Even final causality, which is often rejected as being anthropomorphic and projective, is relevant in accounting for certain physical or biological phenomena that are difficult to explain otherwise.[4]

Causality is very useful for analyzing certain human phenomena without being satisfied with an indefinite description of surface symptoms. For example, the 2008 stock market crash becomes partly intelligible if banking parameters and economic sequences are analyzed in terms of causalities. Such a causal reduction of this phenomenon is certainly not commensurate with the roots and human consequences of the crisis, but it makes it possible to understand certain mechanisms of the phenomenon in order to imagine new regulatory systems that might provide better protection for companies and households.

The use of causality delivers some intelligibility concerning God's actions toward his creatures, such as electing, creating, governing, justifying, saving, resurrecting, etc. Facing the testimonies

---

3. See Dodds, *Unlocking Divine Action*, 153. The author shows the deep affinities that exist between the four classical causalities and new formalizations of causality: top-bottom, whole-part, bottom-up, by attraction, etc.

4. See Karl Popper, *A World of Propensities* (Bristol: Thoemmes, 1990); Robert J. Russell (ed.), *Scientific Perspectives on Divine Action: Twenty Years of Challenge and Progress* (Vatican City / Berkeley, Calif.: Vatican Observatory / CTNS, 2008).

of faith by which such divine acts are attested, the cardinal questions of a causal search enable us to identify, with respect and rectitude, some degree of human intelligibility concerning the divine action: What is it? Where does it come from? Out of what does it proceed? On what does it operate? In view of what does it accomplish?

Thus, according to the grand biblical narrative, when God elects, he assigns to a person or a people a specific mission. This type of calling is the result of God's free initiative. The convocation is addressed to interlocutors who do not possess sufficient qualities or plans adjusted to God's design beforehand. The election is not given to the elected representative primarily because of his or her personal achievement, but rather is bestowed with a view to an outcome that goes far beyond him or her while including him or her. Such a qualification of divine election, however rudimentary it may be, is based on causal analysis.

The presupposition of such an approach is that there is an analogy and coherence between the fundamental questions of human intelligence, the structures of human and physical reality within our reach, and a true—albeit limited—intelligibility in what God himself accomplishes with his creatures in the logic of the covenant. Analyzing God's involvement with his creatures provides considerable intelligibility, but the abstract part of such an approach is always likely to take away from God his own spiritual physiognomy as a personal subject engaged in a covenant with his people and with his creation.

The Irreducible Singularity of Action

When we conduct a causal analysis to advance in the understanding of any of the acts of the biblical God, we assume the paradigm of action as appropriate to apprehend those phenomena in which God might be involved as a personal subject. It is only natural that this should be so, for action is the analogical notion by which we intuitively grasp most human activities that have meaning and completeness, as opposed to work and transformative activities that tend toward a material outcome or result. Awakening, engaging, conversing, loving, playing, reading, are all common human actions that include a form of intrinsic completion, having pleasure or joy as the sign of such consummation.

The choice of the notion of action to qualify the commitments of the biblical God in history gives credit to an intuition rather than analytical unpacking. It even seems that action somehow resists causal decomposition. Surely, it is always relevant to grasp an action by questioning its nature, object, purpose, motivations, impact, etc. For example, God promises descendants to Abraham so that the latter might become the vector of the election and a blessing to future generations. This act can be duly analyzed and formalized as a specific promise. Still, stating the properties of a singular act always reduces the originality of the action as perceived in person or through the words of testimony. Indeed, the essence of action, in its full sense, is to be surprising and new, so that it reveals unexpected and intriguing aspects of the subject that engages in such activity.[5]

To consider the involvement of the biblical God in history under the paradigm of action directs theology toward a perception of the divine author who is revealed in a surprising way each time through the uniqueness of his actions. The work we must do in order to move forward in this direction does not consist in analyzing God's commitments by means of causal decomposition, however enlightening this exercise may be. Rather, it is advisable to let oneself be guided by the particularities of each biblical narrative or testimony, in order to perceive the part of revelation that is quite specific to this or that instance of revelation.

For example, in Genesis 12, God's first words to Abram spring forth from nowhere and manifest a singular authority on the part of the one who speaks. The sovereign command to leave all familiar ties for an unknown destination is coupled with grandiose promises that only God can responsibly make to someone. It remains theo-

---

5. See Hannah Arendt, *The Human Condition* (Chicago: University of Chicago Press, 1958), 175–81.

logically relevant to categorize this expression of God in terms of vocation or promise. However, something irreducible remains here in the uniqueness of the one who speaks and in the singularity of his elective action. This is left to the intuition of the listener or reader who is a witness to the unprecedented authority of this primordial call.

The main asset of the action paradigm is to highlight the revelation of God's singularity as a personal subject through his involvement in his actions and words. The limit of such an approach lies above all in the anthropomorphisms attached to human patterns of action, starting with the presupposition of a way out of inaction.

The Unmastered Nature of the Event

Even if the difference between God and creation can be honored in this way, thinking of God's commitment to his creatures as an action is grounded on an analogy whose first field of experience is ethical: God is considered as the superior and ultimate agent based on the defining elements of human action. This does not in itself lead to a competition between divine and human action, but the analogy of action is partial, as is any theological similitude.

Another possibility might be to consider God's involvement in history by using the paradigm of the nature of events. What happens as an event goes beyond the limited scope of action. An event cannot be attributed to a single agent or even to a few key players. An event is not simply a historical fact or circumstance. In a full sense, it is characterized by novelty. It happens in an unexpected way. It could not be projected or deduced from the usual framework of causalities, actors, and circumstances. An event is a milestone because it comes out of the predictable and surprises everyone. It changes the course of history and forces contemporaries to reconfigure their worldview.[6]

An event radically alters those involved in it or witnessing it.

---

6. See Claude Romano, *L'événement et le monde* (Paris: Presses Universitaires de France, 1998), 35–77.

This can be verified at the level of an individual, a family, a people, or a nation. For example, the unexpected or hasty death of a loved one forces the bereaved spouse to learn how to live differently. The announcement of a fatal disease completely changes the existential conditions and the perception of time for the person involved. On a larger scale, a revolution or war often forces people and individuals to alter their usual behavior and design new types of human relationships. Those who experience such an event are summoned by what happens. Some are even commissioned as witnesses as they rush to find the words to translate the unseen past and transmit to their children the memory of the event. Some Holocaust survivors thus felt compelled to write down their experiences in order to put into words something which had hitherto been unthinkable.

An authentic event is not some manageable affair. It triggers off a new story, that of a gradual appropriation by witnesses. The grand narrative of salvation history is marked by such events, accessible through a chain of witnesses and transformative effects. An event-paradigm is well suited to the qualification of God's vivid implications in the history of his people.

One limitation of the event-paradigm is that an event is most often woven together with interactions so complex that it is not attributable to anyone in its own right as a singular agent. This approach therefore tends to portray God as an unknowable author upstream of the facticity of the events in which he is involved. A risk associated with this paradigm is that it can lead us to systematically conceive of God's commitment in terms of discontinuity and objective evidence. However, the Judeo-Christian tradition confesses a God who is also involved in the most ordinary and quotidian details of life, as is evidenced by the Law of God and the contemplation of the wise. Despite the hidden character of God's presence in everyday realities, we also confess that he is committed, present, and sovereign in the non-events of the long journey of his people and every believer.

Extra Meanings That Rise
from Immanence?

For fear of understanding the relationship of God with human history in far too extrinsic a manner, too easily assimilated to the paradigms of causality, action, and event, some contemporary theologians seek to situate the divine fully within the immanence of human subjectivity.[7] In full truth, neither causality, nor action, nor an events-paradigm necessarily lead us to detract from human realities, so as then to aggrandize God with this element, would thus be removed from our domain of being and experience.[8] None of these paradigms require a partitioning of causalities or a separation of effects, setting the divine on one side and the human on the other. God's radical difference from the causalities of the world, human actions, and historical events makes his involvement perfectly compatible with the full consistency of the systems of creation. Without associating extrinsicism with the three avenues of exploration mentioned so far, let us give fair consideration to the fourth approach proposed as an alternative.

God is made present and revealed in the abundance of meaning and the flowering of grace that rise from human existence without coming to it from the outside. To discern God's involvement as an extra life or an epiphany of grace thus involves a kind of turning of our gaze. To discern and interpret the fullness of human existence empowered by God, we must have the double depth of vision that faith offers. The word of God plays a vital revelatory role here, offering interpretive keys that enable us to relate to God the multiple experiences of transcendence that rise from immanence.

It is undeniable that certain human experiences, beginning with those that involve a labor of conversion that has been engaged in for a long time, manifest that God is actively present in the depths of

7. See Robert Mager, "Un enchantement de l'histoire?," in *Dieu agit-il dans l'histoire?*, ed. Robert Mager (Montreal: Fides, 2006), 47–74.

8. See Bernard of Clairvaux, *De gratia et libero arbitrio* XIV.47; Aquinas, *SCG* III.70.8.

human existence, with its desires, its shortcomings, its rhythms, its complexities, etc. St. Augustine's long journey of conversion, leading up to the eighth book of the *Confessions*, is a good example of this long labor of grace in immanence. Nevertheless, through his rereading of faith, Augustine relates each step of the process to various modalities of God's action. Through the gaze of faith, he even discerns God's mark in the sorrows, disappointments, illusions, and disgusts of his sinful existence, wherein God was ever at work.[9] Here, the sinner's human experience in no way impedes the sovereignty of the creator, the holy, immanent, and transcendent God.

Under the guise of opposing extrinsicism, God should not be locked into a false alternative between immanence and transcendence. God's transcendence has nothing to do with the exteriority of a god merely endowed with hypertrophied worldly attributes, as is the case in Deism. Because of his true transcendence, God is present within the innermost part of the human being and makes his voice heard even in the wanderings and infernos of the sinner.

Moreover, limiting God's involvement to extra meanings discernible by faith in the density of human existence leaves out of sight everything that remains hidden away in seeming nonsense. As Qohelet expresses it, the test of human beings is their ability to embrace the cycles of life without being able to penetrate its meaning: "I have seen the business that God has given to the sons of men to be busy with. He has made everything beautiful in its time; also he has put eternity into man's mind man, yet so that he cannot find out what God has done from the beginning to the end" (Eccl 3:10–11). The difference between meaning and nonsense is related to our experiences, our perceptions, and our more or less theological penetration. Let us think of the ultimate experience of nonsense: the lynching of the innocent One. At the foot of Jesus' cross, human nonsense almost completely blurred the possibility of meaning. Only Mary and a disciple saw a Paschal sense in this chiaroscuro of a terribly tried and tested faith.

9. See Emmanuel Durand, *Évangile et providence. Une théologie de l'action de Dieu* (Paris: Cerf, 2014), 91–129.

Yes, the extra meanings and dazzling grace that rise from the depths of the human being probably bear witness to God's presence within human immanence. The tree will be judged by its fruits. It is essential to recognize that God can act not only in objectivity but also in interiority or subjectivity. It is even reasonable to think that he does so by coordinating both of these kinds of activity. Nevertheless, God's involvement in such experiences can be honored in terms of causality, action, or event without artificial exteriority or preclusion of his immanence in the depths of our being.

FIRST ASSESSMENT

To my eyes, the motive for God's action remains the conceptual pivot of a theology of God's commitment in the world and in history. The semantics of action are in line with the current language of faith. The divine action orients its beneficiaries and witnesses toward its utterly unique author. It includes a dimension of personal revelation, something that loses something if it is conceptualized merely in terms of being an event.

Certainly, like any theological concept, the notion of God's action requires adjustments and corrections. We must avoid conceiving divine action as an exit from inaction, passivity, or rest. "My Father is working still, and I am working" (Jn 5:17), Jesus replied to the Jewish authorities in a controversy on the Sabbath. It is not appropriate to conceive God's action exclusively in terms of discontinuity and rupture with the usual course of intramundane phenomena and human affairs.

Through faith and reason, three possible registers of God's action can be schematized. Let us remember that the divine activity does not add external layers to intraworldly happenings and human decisions. Because of its difference and transcendence, divine action suffuses both necessary and contingent processes. Thus, for example, at the very moment when a professor is teaching a theology course on God, God himself can personally speak in the intimate depths of one of his or her students. The professor does not need to be silent in order for God to be able to speak. God can pass through certain words spoken by the teacher, although it is also possible that the connection between these human words and the divine word to the intimate depths of a listener be accidental. God speaks without competing with the teacher.

Thus, we can consider three registers of activity:

- At any moment of created time, God acts by means of conservation, accompaniment, orientation, amplification, attraction, etc. However, some of God's actions contrast with the natural course of things and human possibilities.
- At certain times in human history, as the scriptures testify, God acts through mighty deeds of salvation and events of speech, which trigger new phases in the lives of his people, nations, servants, friends, etc.
- On the temporal scale of singular human lives, God also acts by inspiring grace, converting one's gaze, bringing about intimate growth, etc.

These three registers are not mutually exclusive. Christian faith confesses that God acts in at least these three ways.

God's action is most often discreet because of its very transcendence. On occasion, it can be acknowledged under the influence of a kind of supernatural coefficient, but recognizing it still requires a willingness to believe. There are always pharaohs who are capable of denying any exodus. For God's commitment to be perceived in the external traces of his activity, he must also act within the intimate depths of certain observers, who thereby become witnesses in the fullest sense, with God opening their minds and hearts to what they see. Otherwise, it is always easier to look without understanding and to deny the invisible, which nevertheless sends forth visible signals of its presence and activity.

CONCEIVING PROVIDENCE AS
A CONFESSION OF FAITH

It is fruitful, I think, to conceive of providence on the basis of the characterization of God as pure act and creator of all beings. Aquinas developed this path in a powerful way in the third book of his *Summa contra Gentiles*. However, in an era when metaphysics has become inconceivable for most of our contemporaries, it is also necessary and, indeed, opportune that we offer alternative paths of access to these mysteries. In his own time, marked as it was by empiricism, John Henry Newman argued that it was always possible to consider history and worldly sequences indefinitely with a simple vision of immanence.[10] Such logic often saturates the immediate need for explanation. According to a Humean understanding of causality, we do not need to seek out some kind of transcendence beyond the multiple states prior to any given phenomenon. The religious man is free to believe in a transcendent and benevolent God, but inferring a first cause no longer meets the necessary requirements of contemporary thought. Undoubtedly, such a rejection of metaphysical inquiry is questionable and, indeed, open to legitimate criticism, but it no longer suffices that we lock ourselves, digging in our heels as metaphysicians who speak a tongue that resounds with a foreign philosophical tone. For the sake of making the word of God intelligible, we must also attempt to provide other possible paths of accesses to the theology of providence and God's action.

Sketching a theology of providence in the form of a confession of faith is very appropriate for another reason, not only drawn from our current, generally antimetaphysical milieu but also from a structural dimension. Christians are summoned by the Gospel to believe

---

10. John Henry Newman, "Milman's View of Christianity," in his *Essays Critical and Historical* II (London: Longmans, 1897), 196–97. A similar debate took place in France; see Guillaume Cuchet, "Comment Dieu est-il acteur de l'histoire? Le débat Broglie-Guéranger sur le 'naturalisme historique,'" *RSPT* 96, no. 1 (2012): 33–55.

in providence while facing a world shaken by evil.[11] The real problem lies quite deep. The common condition of sinners, structures of sin, historical woes, and the entanglement born of personal sins all blur the human ability to decipher creation as being a work of God, conceived and sustained, directed and governed by him. The disproportionate nature of evil remains the most commonly shared justification for unbelief. In such a context, adhering to providence and discerning its traces in this world partly disfigured by evil, is, most often and to begin with, part of an approach grounded firmly in faith and hope. Thinking of providence becomes a spiritual exercise based on the Creed shared by the various Christian confessions. It is from this perspective that I would like to state the essence of Christian faith in divine providence. We can ground it on three key propositions related to three articles in the Creed.

Providence as Divine Sovereignty

Belief in providence presupposes that we confess God the Father "Almighty," not thereby meaning a kind of theoretical omnipotence, postulated by reason's own projections, but in the sense of the *Pantocratoria* spoken of by the Ante-Nicean Fathers: the sovereignty of God.[12] God "bears all things" and "contains all things" through his word in his benevolent designs in creation and in our filial adoption through grace. God leads each creature to its own end and to its ultimate end according to a benevolent design of elevation, care, and fulfillment. For spiritual creatures, the orientation of the created becoming is properly filial. He is "almighty" through his "maintenance" of and solicitude for every creature.

Confessing providence as God's sovereignty today implies a serious clarification, because the asymmetry of the relationship between God and human beings tends to disappear, and even to be reversed, in some contemporary theologies. One observes a strange transfer of sovereignty from God to human beings. Throughout contempo-

---

11. See chapter 8 of this volume.
12. See Origen, *Treatise on Principles* I.2.10; Batut, *Pantocrator*.

rary discussions concerning providence, human autonomy and freedom stand forth like inviolable premises deserving a central place in this domain of theology. One of modernity's positive conceptual acquisitions is to have revealed human freedom's potentials, doing so through a multifaceted process of emancipation and empowerment.[13] This holds true in the interconnected domains of religion, knowledge, and action. In contemporary thought, human autonomy represents a common foundation for reflection, something ultimately shared by those who hold some form of atheist humanism as well as by the defenders of Christian theism.[14] Therefore, it is not surprising that contemporary debates surrounding the topic of providence adopt these premises. Nonetheless, it is fitting that we take a moment to question them. I will do so at the level of lived existence, not that of principles.

The reign of autonomy and freedom sometimes so saturates contemporary thought that it partially conceals certain commonly experienced realities: in birth and death, man is dependent, and human action struggles to attain true freedom. Perhaps our fascination with autonomy in fact reveals how much it falls short in the midst of the circumstances of real life. Rather than being an exercise of absolute autonomy, human maturity involves in taking up and accommodating the dependencies—whether familial, affective, institutional, or economic—which press upon us without our own choosing. Human actions wend their way through an entire network of circumstances, conditions, and positive or negative solidarities, including structures of sin. If autonomy and freedom are essential properties of man considered in his positive capabilities, we must acknowledge the fact that we stand in need of a kind of apprenticeship, requiring support, community, patience, and great clarity of mind if we are to realize this autonomy and freedom in the midst of the real conditions besetting our life and action. Freedom often is actualized

13. See Dilthey, *Weltanschauung und Analyse*, 246–83.

14. See Paul Clavier, "Le jeune Sartre et le vieux Sertillanges: le chassé-croisé de la création," *RSPT* 96, no. 3 (2012): 493–511.

in the nooks and crannies of life's realities, indeed, sometimes even emerging like a kind of miracle springing forth from unsuspected resources in the human person faced with adversity, deprivation, and oppression.

Now, having nuanced these points, let us willingly admit that autonomy and freedom should be integrated into any sound theology of providence, for they are inalienable properties of man, considered in his positive capabilities, along with his historicity, bodily nature, social existence, morality, and so forth. Here, however, we face a disconcerting reversal which deserves serious reflection. Whereas for centuries it seemed evident to believers that the divine will could hold evil human wills in check, contemporary thought insists, so to speak, on the opposite power relationship: man must be able to foil God's will. This seems to be a point of capital importance for a number of contemporary theologians, who wish to respect the freedom which God has bestowed upon human beings. However, God curiously seems to be deprived of an analogous power—it is said that he cannot hold human wills in check. The impulse animating this conviction is the human observation that he has not, in fact, held them in check, neither in the past nor in the present, in the midst of the earthly hells of human history. This is no mean argument.

Allow me to raise two questions here. First, have we taken the time to describe the criteria that should rule the discernment of God's action or inaction toward wicked human wills? According to what criteriology can we affirm that God does or does not act at a given moment of history, in this or that evil occurrence? In the absence of a kind of tacitly presupposed interventionist model of God's activity, whose principal criterion would be the experience of observable discontinuity in a supposedly predictable world, the task of establishing parameters for identifying God's action is not at all an easy task. In another work, I have attempted to propose such a criteriology, presenting a spectrum spanning from rather objective modalities found in God's action (vestiges, effects, gestures, works, and institutions) to partially subjective modalities (meaning, grace, inspiration, persuasion, revelation, and conversion). At the intersection of these two registers, we find the actions, words, presences, and events in which faith discerns that God acts.[15]

For example, is it appropriate to conclude that God did not hold the wicked wills of Jesus of Nazareth's persecutors in check simply because he did not intervene in order to stop his trial and execution? However, we are quite justified in thinking that God is opposed to the wicked and proud in a way that differs from what we find in the power struggles of men.[16] This remains disconcerting, difficult, and even revolting when judged according to human standards, including those of believers. However, I still think that we should maintain that God also has the power—though, one that is different, for it is divine—to hold free, human wills in check. This need not lead us to deny the scandal that we experience, even as believers, when we are presented with mob violence against the innocent, as well as with man's dehumanization of his fellow men.

Second, if man can hold the divine will in check, whereas God supposedly could not hold human wills in check, do we not find ourselves thereby tacitly asserting that man is God and God a creature? If we envision the relationship between God and man along such lines, thinking of possible or impossible interpersonal defeats, do we not thereby run the risk of reducing their relationship to one more intraworldly power relation? It is indeed possible that God would thus surreptitiously become another intraworldly actor, po-

15. See Durand, *Évangile et providence*, 61–89; Hans Jonas, "Is Faith Still Possible? Memories of Rudolf Bultmann and Reflections on the Philosophical Aspects of His Work," in *Mortality and Morality: A Search for the Good after Auschwitz*, ed. Lawrence Vogel (Evanston, Ill.: Northwestern University Press, 1996), 144–64.

16. Here, we are in agreement with a quite astute thesis: "God's almightiness does not lead to any neutralization or annihilation of powers which are contrary to God's creative purpose, but consists in depriving them of the power to impede it conclusively." See Marc Vial, "God's Almightiness and the Limits of Theological Discourse," *Modern Theology* 34, no. 3 (2018): 443–56, at 447. In its developed and masterly form, see Vial, *Pour une théologie de la toute-puissance de Dieu*. This work opens with a deconstruction of Jonas, "The Concept of God." This deconstruction is undertaken in order to resituate the Christian theology of the divine "omnipotence" on a different terrain than that of theodicy.

tentially rivaling his creatures and, consequently, would no longer be God. Thus, we would *de facto* lose God in the process of rethinking providence in relation to human freedom.

We face another major problem in contemporary theology of providence: is there a divine self-determination to allow God to be determined by his free creatures? The concept of self-limitation is ubiquitously found all throughout contemporary literature about God, often inspired by Karl Barth's intuitions, as they were conveyed and systematized by Eberhard Jüngel.[17] God, *in himself*, is infinite by his very essence, but he has determined to become God *for us*. Creation, the election of the chosen people, the covenant, and the incarnation, all consequently imply a self-limitation by God.[18] This outlook is not utterly novel. The concept of such a divine self-limitation represents an interesting and updated form of the themes of *kenosis* and *katabasis* which did in fact play an important role in the Church Fathers' own thought.

In contrast with some of his predecessors, Barth was careful in how he interpreted the notion of *kenosis*, being clear that he thought of it as a kind of unveiling of given divine attributes and not as the disappearance or suspension of these traits. Let us consider an important extract from his *Kirchliche Dogmatik* IV, where the theologian from Basel maintains that the divine essence remains immutable in the incarnation: "God is always God even in his humiliation. The divine being does not suffer any change, any diminution, any transformation into something else, any admixture with something else, let alone any cessation. The deity of Christ is the one unaltered because unalterable deity of God. Any subtraction or weakening of it would at once throw doubt upon the atonement made in him."[19]

One condition for the true efficacy of reconciliation by Christ

---

17. See the seminal work of Eberhard Jüngel, *God's Being Is in Becoming: The Trinitarian Being of God in the Theology of Karl Barth*, trans. John Webster (Edinburgh: T and T Clark, 2001).

18. On the relevance played by the concept of self-limitation in a related domain of issues, see Vial, *Pour une théologie de la toute-puissance de Dieu*, 22–29.

19. Karl Barth, *Church Dogmatics* IV.1, §59.1, ed. and trans. Geoffrey W. Bromiley and Thomas F. Torrance (London: T and T Clark, 2004), 179–80.

through the Paschal sequence (the passion, resurrection, and Pentecost) is that "God is always God even in his humiliation." Nonetheless, Barth rejects every projection of "God" as being nothing more than a mere idol, simply being freed from the limitations befalling man's essence:

We may believe that God can and must only be absolute in contrast to all that is relative, exalted in contrast to all that is lowly, active in contrast to all suffering, inviolable in contrast to all temptation, transcendent in contrast to all immanence, and therefore divine in contrast to everything human, in short that he can and must be only the "Wholly Other." But such beliefs are shown to be quite untenable, and corrupt and pagan, by the fact that God does in fact be and do this in Jesus Christ. We cannot make them the standard by which to measure what God can or cannot do, or the basis of the judgment that in doing this he brings himself into self-contradiction. By doing this God proves to us that he can do it, that to do it is within his nature.[20]

Hence, the divine essence, whose immutability is preserved through the incarnation, is the divine essence which was revealed in scripture and not an essence that is philosophically postulated after the manner of a kind of grotesque inversion.

In light of all this, let us return to the relationship existing between providence and creatures. Is an immutable providence of itself a grotesque caricature? Does it contradict the freedom which God bestows upon certain creatures? Must we purely and simply rid ourselves of providence's immutability in order to assure that created freedom receives the full respect owed to it? Just as we find that faith's correct response to the incarnation is to maintain the paradox we experience in thinking about the relationship between the Son's divine essence and the humanity of the crucified One, so too would it not be more just in the matter facing us now to retain the paradox existing between these two great powers (i.e., providence and created freedom) without being too quick to cry out concerning their supposed contradiction?

20. Ibid., 186. In the background, see Ludwig Feuerbach, *The Essence of Christianity*, trans. George Eliot (Amherst, N.Y.: Prometheus Books, 1989).

If God determined himself in his nature to allow himself to be determined by his free creatures, I cannot see how God would not thereby be reduced to a kind of superior creature, negotiating with the consents and refusals offered by his creaturely partners. As is attested in the granting of prayers of request, God quite obviously "can give to the requests of [his] creature a place in his will."[21] Clearly, according to the story presented to us in the Bible, he does so. However, in my opinion, this is different from a determination to allow oneself to be determined by another person. Such a relational schema is perfectly suitable for partners in a covenant established between beings of the same nature. For example, by sealing their union, spouses determine that they will each be codetermined (rather than simply determined) by each other, as well as by the children who may one day be born, along with their own freedoms. In these scenarios, it is part of our very human condition that we bind ourselves by making promises, even though the other person's freedom is unpredictable in the mid-range.[22] This may well have some similarity with God's relationship with man; however, we ultimately must admit that God and man do not share the same nature.

One thing that distinguishes the mutual covenant between human spouses from the covenant existing between God and humanity is quite precisely the absence or presence of sovereignty in the covenantal structure itself. Despite all the various existential and historical asymmetries that may exist between the spouses, we recognize that they are by rights equal and fully codetermined in this covenant. By its very nature, the relationship between God and humanity is asymmetrical, precisely on account of the infinite distance separating their natures. God is sovereign, and humanity is not. This quite clearly comes to the fore in the biblical passages where the metaphors of marriage or of parentage are used for signifying the relation-

---

21. Karl Barth, *Church Dogmatics* III.4, §53.3 (London: T and T Clark, 2004), 109; cited by Jean-Baptiste Lecuit, "L'épreuve de la providence," *Recherches de Science Religieuse* 106, no. 2 (2018): 255–74, at 264.

22. See Arendt, *The Human Condition*, 243–47.

ship involved in the covenant between God and his people, in particular in Hosea 1–3 and 11. Here, God's sovereignty does not take the form of "domination," but rather represents a primacy of initiative, an utterly unheard-of endurance, a kind of surplus in compassion, and a power that can recreate the beloved.[23]

Undoubtedly, through the incarnation, the Son of God exposed himself in his humanity to the possibility of being codetermined by worldly phenomena and agents, but—as we will soon see—it is precisely within this worldly scene that we come to glimpse God's creative and utterly astounding sovereignty. To maintain God in his rightful place in the theologies of providence, it is crucial that we confess that he alone is sovereign in relation to creation and history, with an ineffable and obscure sovereignty, one which is properly divine. Through faith, this lordship distanced from more or less rational caricatures taking the form of control, rivalry, oppression, competition, withdrawal, and the many other patterns of human power relations.

In the wake of the Ante-Nicean Fathers, Christians confess that God forever exercises his providence as Father, that is, by the mediation of the unique and beloved Son, who works with him in creation, reconciliation, and recapitulation. God's sovereignty will be fully established and revealed only at the end of history, through the eschatological fulfillment of history. In the hardships and trials of the present time, God's sovereignty most often remains opaque to a merely natural outlook. Nonetheless, the way that God's sovereignty is accomplished is really anticipated and unveiled by Christ's Paschal mystery. To continue to think of providence as a confession of faith, it is absolutely necessary that we move from the first article of the Creed to the second.

Providence as a Paschal Mystery

To believe in providence in this world, which has been overthrown and disfigured by evil, presupposes that we profess the incarnation,

---

23. See chapter 4 of this volume.

God's definitive historical engagement with his creatures, as well as the Pasch of the Son, the *kenosis* and restoration of the righteous One. The concrete exercise of providence follows no other path than that which the Son himself traveled among men.

Let us consider for a moment the way that creation is "readable" as containing in itself something like a divine message. In theory, creation should lead people to recognize God and give glory to him for the gift of creation. But human intelligence often stops at a fascination with immanence (Wis 13:1–8). Moreover, pushed to a certain threshold of truth, recognition of the creator requires a change in lifestyle (Rom 1:18–25). The testimony of creation is thus difficult to receive in all of its truth. The visible should lead to the invisible, but it can also easily veil over it for those who are satisfied with a superficial gaze or do not want to penetrate beyond the veil. The veiling can become blurred when sin gets involved. The visible, the tangible, the fashionable, the domesticated, the useful; all of these thus risk capturing our eyes and our appetites entirely. The creature becomes an idol, an object of lust and a pretext for alienation; the creature's path back to God is thus hindered.

If one moves from creation to human history, the darkness increases. By its very nature, history is much less legible than creation. It speaks more of human beings than of God. It requires even more faith and hope to believe and eventually discern the hand of God in history than in creation. Certain segments of history, be they personal or collective, can be revisited with the eyes of faith. To establish such discernment in the present, it is necessary to have, to a certain degree, the charism of prophecy. It is the hallmark of prophecy that it illuminates with divine light the complexity of an ongoing history. But the darkness of history is not simply natural. No, indeed, it is multiplied by the weight of sin in human actions and the events that result from them. Human enterprises with the highest ideals are blurred and sometimes ruined by acts, failures, and abuses which cannot be explained by reason alone. Revolutions based on legitimate aspirations for freedom give rise to fratricidal clashes and corrupt regimes. Nothing evades suffering an inconceivable amount of waste, through the interference of narrowness, fragility, and human error.[24]

In this world, providence is not the subject of a peaceful rational inference. To regain its solid foundation in the testimony of the created order, we must transcend the blurring caused by disorder and sin. Admittedly, disorder presupposes order. The suffering experienced in the presence of waste, chaos, and disfigurement is made possible and enhanced by a perception of the order, beauty, and good that should prevail. But this reasoning, however solid and sane it may be, does not exempt human intelligence from experiencing a profound trial of faith when faced with evils that blur the legibility of creation and obscure the meaning of human narratives in history. This is why providence is not only a truth of reason but also an article of faith.[25]

How are we to penetrate the veil of the visible? How can we overcome the darkness of sin? We must elevate our eyes and convert our gaze. The believing mind must consent to the Paschal form of the exercise of divine sovereignty in this world. Scripture invites us to this new view. God's sovereignty is exercised in a mysterious way, through delays, failures, purifications, and unsuspected resources. Three types of passages give the measure and profile of how God exercises his sovereignty. He is not only the one who calls into existence what did not exist, but also is the one who calls his creatures from death to life, from sin to grace. God is the only one who has this creative power of overcoming or reversing: from nothing to being, from death to life, from hostility to friendship. Creation, resurrection, and justification all reveal how God is sovereign in his action and providence. The testimony of the resurrection is accessible to faith alone, but it is of great value in corroborating the testimony of creation and that of God's friends.

24. See Emmanuel Durand, "Note sur la théologie de l'histoire," *RSPT* 98, no. 2 (2014): 353–79; Henri-Irénée Marrou, *L'ambivalence du temps de l'histoire chez saint Augustin* (Paris: Vrin, 1950); Marrou, *Théologie de l'histoire* (Paris: Seuil, 1968).

25. Regarding two fundamental articles of faith, including providence, see Aquinas, *ST* II-II, q. 1, a. 7, resp.

God accomplishes his designs and joins his creatures anew even when they remain, to the eyes of men, in a state of utter collapse and abandonment. For as long as this age lasts, the paradoxical fate of the righteous One remains the paradigm for God's ways: even within persecutions and under the blows of sin, God's power is committed to the righteous who, when judged in accord with this world's criteria, are nonetheless reduced to weakness. Thus, they become small, shimmering rays of Paschal light, even in the midst of this world's darkness.[26] Through the human freedom of the Son who, utterly stripped of all he has and appearing to be defeated, definitively overcomes sin, God's sovereignty attains, within our own history, the anticipated form of his final victory.

Providence as a Synergy between Spirit and Church

In order to believe in providence so that we might cooperate with it and resist evil, we must first confess the synergy which exists between the Spirit and human beings of good will. The Spirit of Christ the Lord is powerfully at work in this world, with the same power found in the Paschal mystery, able to overthrow this world's evils. The action of the Spirit is all the more discernible to the degree that men and women are open to his inspirations and to his bold summons within the world's stage.

Thus, in Acts 5:32 and 15:28, we see that believers can legitimately consider the Spirit as being the intimate partner of their ecclesial and missionary "we / us."[27] As the principal actor each time that the Apostles came to cross new frontiers, especially those that had become walls of contempt (8:17, 10:44), the Spirit led Christ's disciples onward, even if this meant that he had to close off certain all-too-human paths in order to open up ones that were even more audacious.

26. For a lengthier discussion of this theme, see Durand, *Évangile et providence*, 295–331.

27. See Daniel Marguerat, "L'œuvre de l'Esprit," in *La première histoire du christianisme. Les Actes des Apôtres* (Paris / Geneva: Cerf / Labor et Fides, 1999), 149–74.

The Book of Revelation confers a specific role on the Spirit and the church, with a kind of divine synergy, in the ultimate completion of God's plan. From the very beginning of the book, God presents himself as sovereign with regard to a vast conflict taking place both in heaven and in history, illuminated from above by revelations and visions. God's sovereignty is immediately affirmed by a temporal declination of the Tetragrammaton. Compared to Isaiah's antecedents (Is 41:4, 44:6, 48:12), this new formula of divine self-presentation is characterized by an eschatological emphasis through the use of the verb "to come" instead of the verb "to be," in the future tense: "'I am the Alpha and the Omega,' says the Lord God, who is and who was and who is to come, the Almighty [*Pantocrator*]" (Rv 1:8).

The great opening vision of Revelation 4–5 reveals that God's sovereignty is already acknowledged in heaven and that the sacrificed Lamb plays a decisive role in the extension of worship to all creatures.[28] The challenge of our current history seems to be the full extension and universal recognition of divine sovereignty, both on earth and in heaven. They are acquired, but the fighting is not over, both in heaven and on earth.

The book's final vision, opening out onto a new heaven and a new earth, also receives the seal of the sovereign God: "It is done! I am the Alpha and the Omega, the beginning and the end" (Rv 21:6). However, it is Christ's responsibility to mediate the full extension and universal recognition of God's sovereignty. In this function, Christ shares God's prerogatives: "I am the Alpha and the Omega, the first and the last, beginning and the end" (Rv 22:13).

With one voice, the Spirit and the church also have roles to play in ultimate fulfillment through an urgent call: "The Spirit and the Bride say, 'Come'" (Rv 22:17). The answer comes from Christ himself. It is he himself who finally proclaims: "Surely, I am coming soon." And this outstanding promise receives the whole amen of the church: "Amen. Come, Lord Jesus!" (Rv 22:20). The ultimate outcome thus involves God and Christ, the Spirit and the church.

28. See Bauckham, *The Theology of the Book of Revelation*, 54–65.

These last two actors play their own part in an intertwined synergy. The Spirit guides, sustains, and animates the church's urgent call and amen, even as time passes along its course.

BACK TO INVOCATION

In order to bring about the reconciliation of divine providence and created freedom in a satisfactory manner, does the renunciation of God's immutability—in terms of self-determination and self-limitation to be determined by creatures—really provide a fitting solution to the problem facing us? I have argued in favor of a different perspective that does not move in this direction. To suppress one of these divine attributes like a kind of troublesome fact would only offer a pure and simple suspension of the mystery, not a resolution to the aporias thus raised.

In the background of such projects which seek to unburden themselves of these mysterious aporias, we sometimes discover a hidden and erroneous conception of theology. Theology is not a kind of ultimate arbiter, resolving various rational problems arising between incompatible data posed by the mysteries of the faith.[29] If this were indeed theology's objective, one might well be justified in redefining the initial conditions, eliminating given inconvenient parameters from the point of departure of such reflection so that thought might be freed from needing to reach some kind of reconciliation which is unthinkable for pure reason. Such a quest is legitimate in scientific experiments or in thought experiments, over which we ourselves are the masters. However, in a confessional theology, one's premises are received from Christological revelation in the twofold form in which it is made present to us: the witness of scripture and the ecclesial transmission of faith. Theologians do not have complete and utter freedom in defining their premises. Nonetheless, they must forever maintain an outlook of critical vigilance,

---

29. This argument was developed in a masterly fashion, against a deceptive transfer of the world's suffering to God, by Weinandy in *Does God Suffer?*

for human groups also hand on confusions between the faith's own truth and various associated representations which sometimes come from other sources like false forms of evidence, especially ones pertaining to anthropology and cosmology. The reception and transmission of faith require us to ceaselessly purify our cultural representations.

When Christian theology approaches mysteries like that of providence, it finds that its principal task is to avoid false representations and to overcome apparent contradictions so that our faith in God may be freer and purer, without tampering with the mystery he has revealed.[30] Invocation, paradox, and integration are the hallmarks of a sound *theologia viatorum* in relation to God's sovereignty.

---

30. Basing his observation on the Fathers' practice in trinitarian matters, this is how the purpose of theology is described by Aquinas in *De potentia*, q. 9, a. 4, resp.; see also *SCG* I.9.3.

10

How Should the Universality of God's Saving Will Be Understood?

How can one accurately hold the New Testament affirmation of a universal salvific will without falling prey to *a priori* restrictions or hasty conclusions? The divine will to save all human beings does not enter into Catholic theology as the conclusion of a demonstration, but rather as a premise of faith coming from revelation. Despite the evidence and sobriety of its New Testament affirmation, it has been subjected to all kinds of restrictions or extrapolations. It is nevertheless part of the fundamental convictions of the Catholic faith. It has therefore been possible to state it particularly clearly in several documents of the Second Vatican Council.[1]

The most obvious scriptural basis for a universal salvific will is undoubtedly found in 1 Timothy. The recommendation of a daring prayer on behalf of all men and women is justified by a strictly theological conviction: the divine salvific will extends itself to all persons, without any prior restriction.

---

1. See especially Vatican Council II, *Sacrosanctum Concilium*, no. 5; *Lumen Gentium*, nos. 1, 3, 13, 16; *Nostra Aetate*, no. 1; *Dei Verbum*, no. 14; *Ad Gentes*, nos. 2–4, 7; *Gaudium et Spes*, no. 22.

First of all, then, I urge that supplications, prayers, intercessions, and thanksgiving be made for all men, for kings and all who are in high positions, that we may lead a quiet and peaceable life, godly and respectful in every way. This is good, and it is acceptable in the sight of God our Savior, who desires all men to be saved and to come to the knowledge of the truth. For there is one God, and there is one mediator, between God and men, the man Christ Jesus, who gave himself as a ransom [*antilutron*] for all, the testimony to which was given at the proper time. For this I was appointed a preacher and apostle (I am telling the truth, I am not lying), a teacher of the Gentiles in faith and truth. (1 Tm 2:1–7)[2]

Following the sequence of statements, the oneness of God is considered to be the ultimate foundation for the universality of salvation and the oneness of the mediator. Such a statement, one of great theological density, is enshrined within a pastoral exhortation. The author is primarily concerned with prayer in the Christian assembly to which he writes. Prayer must indeed be addressed to God for all men, including kings and authorities.

The pivotal point in this pericope leads from God the savior to Christ Jesus. Within salvation history, the best evidence of the amplitude of the salvific will is found in the Paschal event through which the man Jesus delivered himself for all, following the same extension and universality as God's salvific will. The life and offering of Christ Jesus for all, up to the point of death, is thus presented as being the best expression and the only mediation, in human history, of God's universal salvific will. Through his own ministry, the Apostle in turn transmits to all, especially through his preaching to the nations, the unique testimony to the divine offer of salvation for all, a testimony given once and for all by Christ Jesus.

Concerning the universality of salvation, it is important to remain both bold and sober on the dividing line drawn by 1 Timothy 2:1–7. In order to ensure an optimal balance, in accord with theological tradition, I will first present two opposite but symmetrical lines. The contemporary line is universalist, while the Augustini-

---

2. See Michel Gourgues, *Les deux lettres à Timothée. La Lettre à Tite* (Paris: Cerf, 2009), 97–106.

an line is restrictive. For various reasons, Karl Barth, Hans Urs von Balthasar, and Karl Rahner incline toward a soteriological optimism that includes all. By contrast, the Augustinian tradition has modulated a restrictive interpretation of God's saving will. Thomism traces a third path, undoubtedly more balanced, but always subject to adjustments, as Jacques Maritain and Charles Journet have already suggested. In the end, we will see that these various currents, despite their speculative divergences and potential excesses, all in practice refer to a (fourth) common theological attitude: praying and hoping for all, relying on the objective offer of salvation given through Christ Jesus. The orientation toward a common hope does not relativize doctrinal and speculative divergences. These are not insignificant and they certainly have an impact on the accuracy of one's hope. But the prospect of shared hope can enable us to continue an intellectual dialogue on a firm confessional foundation.

FASCINATION, THEORETICAL
UNCERTAINTY, AND HOPE FOR
UNIVERSAL SALVATION

Several contemporary theologians of great stature have variously taken up proposals, inspired by Origen, concerning an eschatological salvation without any remnant, effectively universalistic in character and involving punishments which are only temporary. They have indeed supported and argued for an optimistic vision of the final outcome of the divine plan, maintaining a more or less dialectical relationship of fascination with the ancient and unsettled hypothesis concerning a final reconciliation encompassing all fallen creatures.[3] Apophaticism being today in good standing in relation to eschatology's ultimate outcome, most theologians nevertheless

---

3. On the ancient modulations of *apocatastasis*, see Augustine, *De civitate Dei* XXI.17–22; Ilaria L. E. Ramelli, "Christian Soteriology and Christian Platonism," *Vigiliae Christianae* 61, no. 3 (2007): 313–56; Morwenna Ludlow, "Universalism in the History of Christianity," in *Universal Salvation? The Current Debate*, ed. Robin A. Parry and Christopher H. Partridge (Carlisle: Paternoster Press, 2003), 191–218.

show seriousness and restraint in the extent and ambition of their positions concerning these matters: they limit their attention to the ultimate fate of human beings and do not claim to reach definitive statements. In this first section, I will benevolently present the arguments of these authors, though I do not commit myself to following them.

The Victory of Christ, according to Karl Barth

The tendency toward a complete and definitive eschatological universalism is most pronounced in Karl Barth, as he found a strong support for it at the heart of Reformed soteriology.[4] Indeed, the objective explanation for the effectiveness of salvation, in the form of a penal substitution of the innocent Christ for the punishment of sinners, directs soteriology in the direction of an ultimate eschatological outcome involving no loss.[5] The judgment of sin in its entirety has already been pronounced once and for all through the event of the cross, so that the eschatological judgment seems to have been fully settled in advance. If the cross of Jesus already fulfills the decree of the most decisive judgment, God is left with only an overabundance of mercy toward all sinners. Once they face God, sinners can always be included in the holiness and judgment of the crucified One.

The eschatological consequences of such soteriology are reinforced by the Barthian doctrine of divine election, according to which all humanity is primarily elected in Jesus Christ. The eternal act of election concerns Christ Jesus in his concrete, historical, and Paschal form. It is through the one election of Jesus Christ that God elects all human beings. Through his primordial election, God there-

4. See Karl Barth, *Church Dogmatics* II.1, §30.2 (London: T and T Clark, 2004), 393–406.

5. I have argued elsewhere why "penal substitution" seems to me to be false and distorting; see Emmanuel Durand, *L'Offre universelle du salut en Christ* (Paris: Cerf, 2012), 321–60. In the rest of his work, Karl Barth values the objective destruction of sin on the cross more than the transfers of substitution.

fore predestined all of them positively for salvation, which was acquired and revealed by the crucified One: "In the election of Jesus Christ which is the eternal will of God, God has ascribed to man the former, election, salvation and life; and to himself he has ascribed the latter, reprobation, perdition and death."[6] As God's only chosen One was reproved on the cross, there taking the place of all sinners deserving divine condemnation, it is no longer conceivable that even one of them would be definitively lost: "If we would know what it was that God elected for himself when he elected fellowship with man, then we can answer only that he elected our rejection. He made it his own. He bore it and suffered it with all its more bitter consequences."[7] In Jesus Christ, the first subject of God's eternal election, God substituted himself for reprobate and lost humanity. "God takes to himself the torment that that which is inexcusable must inevitably carry with it.... Rejection cannot again become the portion or affair of man."[8] In this way, one has access to human beings' negative destination toward loss and condemnation only in the concrete form in which God took it upon himself and overcame it in Jesus Christ.[9] Nevertheless, God is never bound by his eternal election as though by a *decretum absolutum*; he remains sovereignly free throughout the extension of his action.

Therefore, the assurance or logical constraint of *apocatastasis* will be formally rejected by Barth, although his radical thesis concerning the primordial election of all humanity in the concrete person of Jesus Christ and concerning the final judgment of the crucified leads to unavoidable implications for universal salvation. Certainly, sinful persons never cease to be restless, living as people who are subject to the imminent threat of condemnation; however, they also come up against the limits that are imposed on their illusions by the truth of Jesus Christ. The sinner's provocations and bravado cannot have the

---

6. Barth, *Church Dogmatics* II.2, §33.2, 163.
7. Ibid., 164.
8. Ibid., 167.
9. Ibid., 173–74.

last word before God.[10] In the final explanations given on this subject, Barth does not reject a universal reconciliation accomplished by Christus Victor, but he clearly resists any "metaphysical" drift which would consist in replacing Christ's effective victory with a theoretical principle or a general law such as *apocatastasis*. Although man can in no way claim that all men and women will ultimately be delivered, having no theoretical assurance that the last form of the divine work coincides with universal reconciliation, he is nevertheless allowed "to hope and pray cautiously, yet distinctly, that, in spite of everything which may seem quite conclusively to proclaim the opposite, his compassion should not fail, and that, as in accordance with his mercy which is 'new every morning' he 'will not cast [mankind] off forever'" (Lam 3:22–31).[11] As for the concrete form of the eschaton, the last word belongs entirely to God and the only human attitude that can correspond to it and anticipate it is total hope, grounded on faith in Jesus Christ, crucified and risen.

To Hope for All, according to
Hans Urs von Balthasar

Hans Urs von Balthasar reproaches Karl Barth for having held, in an overly systematic manner, that penal substitution has definitively settled the divine judgment on the cross. Although he stands apart from any speculative eschatology exclusively oriented toward universal reconciliation, Balthasar is himself magnetized by the attraction of a completely positive eschatological outcome. Following several mystical saints, especially women,[12] he perceived the unbearable nature of the loss of only one of our brothers and the im-

---

10. See Barth, *Church Dogmatics* IV.3, §70.3, esp. 473–78; Tom Greggs, "'Jesus is victor.' Passing the Impasse of Barth on Universalism," *Scottish Journal of Theology* 60, no. 2 (2007): 196–212.

11. Barth, *Church Dogmatics* IV.3, §70.3, 478.

12. See Raymond of Capua, *Vie de sainte Catherine de Sienne* (Paris: Lethielleux, 1903), 481; Teresa of Avila, *Autobiography*, chap. 32, §6. However, the influence of Adrienne von Speyr, omnipresent in the last volume of the *Theodramatik*, has more weight than the above-mentioned writings.

possibility for the blessed to rejoice definitively in the absence of some of loved ones, even though they were called by God to the same beatitude. Among the saints, those who received some revelatory imagery of hell did not resign themselves to it, but rather intensified their intercession and compassion for sinners.[13] Without being normative or conclusive by themselves, such spiritual insights call for and stimulate theological hope for the benefit of all. The hope of a universally realized salvation does not come under the competence of theological reflection, but instead comes from a spiritual requirement flowing from the most lucid insights befitting the lived experience of the Christian life.[14]

Such a theological option of unlimited hope, however, requires some strictly theological reinforcement. Leaving open the possibility that our human condition as wayfarers (*viatores*) may be prolonged until death, if not beyond death, Balthasar suggests that God has the infinite reserves of patience and love needed for overcoming one by one all the resistances of the most hardened human being, without at any time abusing his or her created freedom.[15] At the time of eschatological judgment, faced with the extent of a fully unfolded human life, God would know how to find in each person the tiniest act of love likely to offer a sufficient grip to his infinite mercy. Eschatological salvation would ultimately consist in definitively separating sin from the sinner and casting all sins into hell, along with

---

13. St. Dominic went far in this direction, according to a testimony from the *Bologna Trial of Canonization*, Witness no. 11 in *Saint Dominique de l'Ordre des frères Prêcheurs. Témoignages écrits*, ed. Nicole Bériou and Bernard Hodel (Paris: Cerf, 2019), 708: "He said that [Dominic] was such a champion of souls that he extended his charity and compassion not only to the faithful, but also to the unbelievers, the gentiles and the damned in hell, that he cried much for them and was very impetuous, for himself in preaching, as well as for others in sending them as preachers, to the point that he wished to go preach to the nations."

14. See Hans Urs von Balthasar, *Dare We Hope That "All Men Be Saved?" With A Short Discussion of Hell*, trans. David Kipp and Lothar Krauth (San Francisco, Calif.: Ignatius Press, 2014); Balthasar, *Epilogue*, trans. Edward T. Oakes (San Francisco, Calif.: Ignatius Press, 2004), 122–23.

15. See Hans Urs von Balthasar, *Theo-Drama* V: *The Last Act*, trans. Graham Harrison (San Francisco, Calif.: Ignatius Press, 1998): 312–13.

the unrecoverable ruins of our shattered history.[16] However, such a metaphor remains difficult to accept, because it is accompanied by a strange "substantification" of sin, which would then retain an existence independent of the subjects it affects. More radically, in dependence on Origen, Balthasar ultimately emphasizes the inevitably finite nature of human evil, because of its ultimately unsustainable opposition to the transcendental freedom of the creature positively oriented toward God.[17]

As bold as they may be, the eschatological approximations thus developed by Balthasar remain deliberately symbolic and incomplete.[18] Although the theologian cannot speculate on the utterly mysterious enigma of the eschaton, the hope of a completely positive outcome to salvation history finally seems to be required by any Christian life inhabited by charity for all, while the potential damnation of someone other than oneself ultimately seems incongruous, even unacceptable.

The Inescapable Orientation toward God, according to Karl Rahner

According to a mindset and approach radically different from the paths taken by Barth or Balthasar, the anthropology and Christology developed by Karl Rahner quite clearly direct his eschatology toward the divine possibility of an effectively universal salvation, even if it remains impossible to anticipate the eschaton with a definite configuration. The Rahnerian option in favor of a positive universalism, discreet and highly apophatic in character, can be decoded according to various related registers: hermeneutics, Christology, anthropology, and theology.

From a hermeneutical perspective, Rahner argues that, among the eschatological affirmations of the New Testament, the evangelical parables of the Last Judgment do not have the function of trans-

16. See ibid., 296.
17. See ibid., 300–304.
18. See ibid., 314–16.

porting us in advance to the last day. This would be an exorbitant privilege, incompatible with the temporal exercise of our freedom of decision before God in faith. Rather, the pictorial descriptions of the judgment must be received as presenting a completely hidden eschatological future as something impressed salvifically upon our present lives, a future to which we nevertheless are decisively related, insofar as it sketches a promise or a threat to our earthly existence.[19] While it would be naive, even Gnostic, to receive the apocalyptic depictions as being anticipated testimonies of an already certain and ultimate bipolar outcome, they must be received as prophetic invectives that urge human beings to convert today, placing before them, through adapted representations, the pathways trod by their freedom and the outcomes of their choices. The hermeneutical argument presented here would, however, benefit from being qualified, because a totally unrealistic questioning of human freedoms, as to the ultimate outcomes of the present choices, would be ineffective, false, and manipulative.

From a Christological perspective, the incarnation embodies God's irrevocable commitment for the salvation of the world in the form of the hypostatic union and calls for a definitive victory of grace. Unlike Barth and Balthasar, Rahner relates the full extent of salvation to the fundamental mystery of the incarnation. Jesus brings salvation into history in an absolute manner. He "signifies the beginning of the absolute self-communication of God which is moving towards its goal, that beginning which indicates that this self-communication for everyone has taken place irrevocably and has been victoriously inaugurated."[20] In the one Christ, God's absolute self-gift, in truth and grace, is effectively offered to all human beings. As God's maximum union with mankind, Christ not only

---

19. See Karl Rahner, "The Hermeneutics of Eschatological Assertions," in *Theological Investigations* IV, trans. Kevin Smyth (London: Darton, Longman and Todd, 1974), 323–46; Rahner, *Foundations of Christian Faith*, trans. William V. Dych (New York: Seabury Press, 1978), 102–4.

20. Rahner, *Foundations of Christian Faith*, 193; see Rahner, "The Hermeneutics of Eschatological Assertions," 335.

inaugurates the fullness of grace, objectively revealed and communicated in history, but also completes by way of final causality all the salvific motions at work in human hearts, at every point of space and time. Also, wherever the Spirit makes possible the inner acceptance of the offer of salvation, he always acts in dependence on the incarnate Word.[21] The salvific event accomplished by the incarnation is the critical pivot of the whole history of creation, as Christ makes it turn entirely into an irrevocable economy of salvation and effectively draws it toward a victorious achievement of grace.

If the objective communication of salvation is indeed addressed to every human being, he or she remains free to accept or refuse it through the mediations of his or her concrete existence, whether explicitly religious or not, such as love for neighbors, the search for truth, the ordeal of finitude, tireless hope, abandonment to the unknown, and finally, confrontation with death. Redemption can only be received freely. However, according to Rahner's anthropology, a negative response comes only against the backdrop of a positive and inevitable orientation toward God. Certainly, we must maintain the existential possibility that human beings could stand in absolute opposition to God. More radically, one has to recognize the criterion of the definitive nature of finite acts resulting from human freedom. Indeed, in full anthropological honesty, only good acts are likely to acquire a fully definitive value, because they alone adequately actualize the transcendental orientation of created freedom toward the good, while evil actions remain irremediably limited, incomplete, and contradictory.[22] In these conditions, it seems almost impossible, from an anthropological perspective, to persist definitively in a state of contradiction and hatred toward God.

On a strictly theological level, a final argument drawn from the

21. See Karl Rahner, *Foundations of Christian Faith*, 318.

22. See ibid., 97–102, 443–44; Rahner, "The Hermeneutics of Eschatological Assertions," 338–40; Rahner, "Immanent and Transcendent Consummation of the World," in *Theological Investigations* X, trans. David Bourke (London: Darton, Longman and Todd, 1973), 273–89.

Augustinian vein intervenes to relativize the autonomy of created freedom before God. Apart from the anthropological weakness of a "no" opposed to God, always related to a more radical positive orientation toward God grounding the very possibility of any negation, God's sovereignty cannot be neutralized by the opposition of any created freedom. God always grounds human freedom in a sovereign way, whether it is exercised for good or evil, without ever destroying it. Moreover, this freedom is our own only to the extent that God sustains it. So, while we must always maintain the possibility of a human refusal that claims to be definitive, the last word of human freedom always depends on God's sovereign will.[23] These various reasons tend to orient the theology of Rahner toward a globally—if not entirely—positive vision of final eschatology, although this conclusion is never theoretically stated and remains cautiously pending.[24]

FIRST ASSESSMENT

Allow us to undertake a first discernment. These multiple approximations about universal salvation undoubtedly remain within the uncertain range of theological opinions and are never presented in a peremptory manner. Not everyone has followed this theological thrust.[25] In a moderate manner, one can affirm that the overall outcome of salvation history can only be positive, insofar as God has committed himself without reserve, while individual cases escape any anticipated discernment or rational projection. Indeed, many wayfarers have not yet traveled the entirety of their own path, and the recapitulation of human history remains impossible before its end truly arrives.

23. See Karl Rahner, *Foundations of Christian Faith*, 125–27; Rahner, "The One Christ and the Universality of Salvation," in his *Theological Investigations* XVI, trans. David Morland (London: Darton, Longman and Todd, 1979), 199–224.

24. See Morwenna Ludlow, *Universal Salvation: Eschatology in the Thought of Gregory of Nyssa and Karl Rahner* (Oxford: Oxford University Press, 2000), 142–43, 185–86.

25. See Joseph Ratzinger, *Eschatology: Death and Eternal Life*, trans. Michael Waldstein (Washington, D.C.: The Catholic University of America Press, 2007), 215–18.

Beyond all the *pro* and *contra* arguments that could be brought forward, the aforementioned theologians' fascination with *apocatastasis* clashes with an unambiguous *De fide* magisterial discernment. Indeed, the thesis was clearly rejected by the ninth of the anathemas against Origen, issued by the Council of Constantinople, in 543: "If anyone says or holds that the punishment of the demons and of impious men [*asebôn anthrôpôn*] is temporary and that it will have an end at some time, that is to say, there will be a complete restoration [*apokatastasis*] of the demons and of impious men, let him be anathema."[26] Let us leave it at that, while acknowledging that this anathema is not the same as a formal statement that some are indeed damned. Still, hell must be maintained as a real possibility of created freedom in relation to God.[27] In addition to the data drawn from the New Testament and Christian antiquity, the balanced clarifications of the *Catechism of the Catholic Church* are to be taken into account.[28]

According to a canonical reading of the scriptures, New Testament texts that refer to universal recapitulation or reconciliation do not by themselves imply a positive affirmation of the actual salvation of all creatures or all human beings. Rather, they express the eschatological aim of a submission of all things to the sovereignty of God and Christ Jesus, without necessarily having the concrete form of such submission being entirely happy and peaceful.[29] Moreover, the many New Testament texts that present a final outcome involving the division of the good from the wicked cannot be jejunely brushed aside or explained away.[30]

---

26. Denzinger, no. 411.

27. See Bernard Sesboüé, "L'enfer est-il éternel?," *Recherches de Science Religieuse* 87, no. 2 (1999): 189–206.

28. See *CCC*, nos. 1034–37.

29. See 1 Cor 15:24–28; Rom 5:18–19; Eph 1:10; Col 1:20; Phil 2:10–11; Jn 12:32, 17:2.

30. See Durand, *L'Offre universelle du salut en Christ*, 368–71.

RESTRICTIVE INTERPRETATIONS
OF THE SALVIFIC WILL, IN LATE AUGUSTINE
AND BEYOND

The central statement of 1 Timothy 2:4, "[God] desires all men to be saved," has been subject to a long and winding history in Western theology. Therefore, in contrast to contemporary sensitivity, a restrictive interpretative option must be considered. It was developed by Augustine on the fringes of his struggle against Semi-Pelagianism, then perpetuated in the West by radical Augustinism. The underlying aporia of this highly speculative debate is the challenge involved in reconciling the effective universality of God's saving will with the possibility of its defeat by some. Would God really want the salvation of those who would definitely refuse to be saved by grace?

As the Pelagian crisis progressed, in order to restrict the possibilities of the human will in the fallen state and to exalt the gratuitousness of grace, Augustine gradually restricted the scope of the offer of salvation, finally holding that God's saving will was universal insofar as it applied to all the predestined within all human categories, but not simply to all existing individuals.[31] Otherwise, through its free rejection of God's grace, the human will would have the immense possibility of thwarting and definitively frustrating the divine will. This seems at first sight unacceptable because of the sovereignty of the divine will over any particular created will. It would therefore seem better to argue that if a person freely and definitively refused to be saved, God simply did not want him or her to be saved. Ultimately, the Augustinian restriction applies *a priori* to the divine willing of salvation.

In this outlook, the universality of original sin prevails over the

---

31. See Augustine, *De correptione et gratia* XIV.44; Alexander Y. Hwang, "Augustine's Interpretations of 1 Tim. 2:4 in the Context of His Developing Views of Grace," *Studia Patristica* 43 (2006): 137–42. We have set forth elsewhere the virtues of Augustine's theology from the perspective of creation as a call; see Emmanuel Durand, *L'Être humain, divin appel. Anthropologie et création* (Paris: Cerf, 2016), 101–26. This criticism, which is limited in scope, in no way disqualifies these achievements.

extension of grace. Native guilt, contracted by all people and confirmed by most of them, justifies the inevitable loss of the majority, while the gratuitousness of grace seems all the more magnified because it is conferred only on a few. On the one hand, the gratuity of divine grace and mercy would burst forth only in the predestined to whom they are granted; on the other hand, divine justice would be honored at the expense of sinners, not predestined for salvation and rightly condemned under the weight of original sin.[32]

However, Augustine must be rendered justice on a point that is part of the spiritual and practical attitude of a Christian when faced with such an abyss: "Not knowing who is among the predestined, and who is not, we must have such an affection of charity that we want all to be saved."[33] A universal hope is thus conditioned not only by a lack of certitude but also by the amplitude of charity.

Augustine's theory had a strong influence on the later Western tradition, despite serious resistance and some alternatives. The Augustinian restriction of the saving will is sometimes accommodated by Aquinas when he recalls, for example, that justification, mercy, and confession do indeed apply to all categories of humans but not to all individuals in particular.[34] However, the Augustinian option was perpetuated in a privileged way outside the Thomist tradition.

The restriction of the salvific will durably marked out several currents in the Reformation, which *a priori* limit the possibility for some to be saved. While he gradually limited the universal salvific will, Augustine did order it to eternal salvation. He will be faithfully followed on these two points by John Calvin.[35] However, Martin Luther argues that the salvation referred to by 1 Timothy 2:4 is only to lead a calm and peaceful life here on earth. From this perspective,

---

32. See Augustine, *De correptione et gratia* VI.9, VII.12–16, IX.25; *De praedestinatione sanctorum* VI.11; *De civitate Dei* XXI.12.

33. Augustine, *De correptione et gratia* XV.46, Bibliothèque Augustinienne 24 (Paris: Institut d'Études Augustiniennes, 1962), 375: "Nescientes enim quis pertineat ad praedestinatorum numerum, quis non pertineat, sic affici debemus charistatis affect, ut omnes velimus salvos fieri."

34. See Aquinas, *Sup. Rom.* 5:18, no. 443; 11:32, no. 932; 14:11, no. 1111.

35. See Calvin, *Institutes of the Christian Religion*, III.24.16.

the salvific will is universal only insofar as it is related to temporal salvation. With regard to eternal salvation, the saving will becomes pre-selective and does not address every human being.[36]

The staunchest Augustinians will finally postulate a symmetrical double predestination, not only to salvation but also to damnation. This is particularly the case for Gottschalk in the ninth century, Calvin in the sixteenth, and the Jansenists in the seventeenth. On several occasions, the Catholic Magisterium has opposed radical Augustinism in order to safeguard three fundamental truths of the doctrine of faith: God's innocence in the face of evil freely committed by human beings, the possibility offered to every being to effectively accept salvation, and the truly universal significance of Christ's death. Indeed, according to the New Testament revelation, his blood was shed for all human beings without exception, and not only for a small (or even a large) number of predestined people.[37]

The Augustinian tradition finally seems to call for a theological choice of major importance. Either, with the late Augustine, we must restrict *a priori* the amplitude of the divine will in relation to the intended salvation of all human beings, thus guaranteeing the infallible success of the divine will and grace above any human response, be it positive or negative; or the possibility of a (relative) defeat of the

36. See Lowell C. Green, "Universal Salvation (I Timothy 2:4) according to the Lutheran Reformers," *Lutheran Quarterly* 9, no. 3 (1995), 281–300; Green, "Luther's Understanding of the Freedom of God and the Salvation of Man: His Interpretation of 1 Timothy 2:4," *Archiv für Reformationsgeschichte* 87 (1996): 57–73. Melanchthon differs here from Luther, applying the salvific will to eternal salvation and valuing the weight of the human will that can potentially hinder salvation.

37. See Synod of Arles (473), Denzinger, nos. 330–42; Synod of Quierzy (583), Denzinger, nos. 621–24; Synod of Valence (855), Denzinger, nos. 625–33; Council of Trent, sixth session (1547), Decree on Justification, Denzinger, nos. 1523, 1556; Innocent X, Constitution *Cum occasione* (1653) against errors of Cornelius Jansen, Denzinger, no. 2005; Clement XI, Constitution *Unigenitus Dei Filius* (1713) against Jansenistic errors of Pasquier Quesnel, Denzinger, nos. 2400–2502 (esp. propositions 1–32); *CCC*, nos. 604–5. See also the Letter of Cardinal Arinze (2006), in *Notitiae* 499–500 (2008): 132–33. The choice to exclude the translation of the *pro multis* by "for all" in the words of Eucharistic consecration in certain vernacular languages should not lead us to forget the affirmation of Vatican Council II, *Ad Gentes*, §3: "Filius hominis non venit ut sibi ministraretur, sed ut ipse ministraret et daret animam suam redemptionem pro multis, id est pro omnibus."

divine will of salvation by some must be left open, by means of a just and wise divine permission, without however restricting *a priori* the universality of the salvific will.

THE UNIVERSALITY OF THE SAVING WILL: THREE PROPOSALS

Apart from the Augustinian tradition, the Thomistic path deals with the possible refusal of the salvific offer through the distinction between God's antecedent will and his consequent will. This resolution, coming to Aquinas from the Greek tradition, is largely accepted, but it might be possible to avoid it if one takes into account, more simply, the "relative" character of the divine will of salvation in its application *ad extra*. Let us first specify this potential adjustment, before discussing, in addition, two elements drawn from responses to the Augustinian problem, suggested by Jacques Maritain and Charles Journet.

Behold the Salvific Will in Its Source

Thomas Aquinas does not *a priori* restrict God's saving will. He develops the distinction, received from John Damascene, between the anterior will to save all human beings, which *a priori* is not entirely realized, and the consequent willing of salvation, which is effective and takes into account circumstances and human response.[38] Indeed, God's will is not really bifurcated here as regards its eternal source, because the formal *ratio* for the divine will remains unique and simple—namely the divine goodness to be communicated. The divine will is only duplicated as to its saving effect (aborted or accomplished) on the creature's side, according to the creature's particular conditions.

38. See John Damascene, *De fide orthodoxa* 43, §§10–12, ed. Eligius M. Buyteart (New York: Franciscan Institute of St. Bonaventure, 1955), 160; Aquinas, *Sent.* I, d. 46, q. 1, a. 1; d. 47, q. 1, a. 1; *Sent.* IV, d. 45, q. 3, a. 3; *De veritate*, q. 6, a. 2, ad 2; q. 23, a. 2; q. 28, a. 3, ad 15; *ST* I, q. 19, a. 6, ad 1; q. 23, a. 4, ad 3; *Super Primam epistolam ad Timotheum lectura* 2:4, no. 62.

Would it be possible to think of such an adjustment without the conceptual duplication of the salvific will, with the related risk of rendering the so-called antecedent will (in other words, the universal salvific will) vain and theoretical? This seems conceivable if we acknowledge that the divine will is always exercised in a "relative" way (in the sense of a necessity relating to a primordial gift) when it concerns created realities.[39] The universality of God's saving will does not impose any absolute necessity on God or on human beings. Indeed, the divine will is driven by the necessity of nature only to its own object, namely the divine goodness itself. Certainly, God also wills all things created through the one eternal act by which he wills his own goodness, but the necessity of his relationship to himself does not imply necessity in his relationship to realities other than himself.[40] No created reality is necessary for him, even if the ones he leads to existence are befitting in light of his wisdom and the free radiance of his goodness. According to the coherence of his benevolent design, these created realities call for other divine initiatives and other divine effects. Everything that God actually does for the sake of his creatures follows a *relative* necessity on the presupposition of their actual existence as intended by God and their intrinsic orientation toward the ultimate end that he assigns them.

The universal salvific will falls within such a relative necessity; in other words, it is a matter of gratuitous fittingness.[41] At the most radical depth of his will (as far as we may analyze it, although it is simple), God wills the eschatological salvation of all human beings because this intention is befitting in light of his goodness; nonethe-

---

39. The distinction between the antecedent will and the consequent will is absent from *SCG* (even when *SCG* III.159.2 integrates 1 Tm 2, 4); here what prevails is the qualification of the salvific will by its relative necessity (*ex suppositione*), distinct from any absolute necessity (by nature). See Michał Paluch, "The Salvific Will according to Aquinas: An Inspiration for Contemporary Theology?" in *Religion and Religions*, nos. 1–2 (2016): 181–83; Paluch, *La profondeur de l'amour divin. Évolution de la doctrine de la prédestination dans l'œuvre de Thomas d'Aquin* (Paris: Vrin, 2004), 274–90; Paluch, "Note sur la distinction entre les nécessités chez Thomas d'Aquin," *Archives d'histoire doctrinale et littéraire du Moyen Âge* [hereafter *AHDLMA*] 70, no. 1 (2003): 219–31.

40. See Aquinas, *SCG* I.80–81.

41. See ibid., I.82.8–9.

less, it is not necessary for him. In its eternal emergence, the salvific will coincides with God's benevolent design, which justifies the divine initiative of creation. However, the salvation of all creatures is not a necessary property of the creative act. The universal salvific will unfolds the primordial intention according to which God orders and governs all his creation: for the free radiance of his goodness in creatures called to the eternal sharing in the divine bliss.

In its circumstantial application to all human beings, the salvific will does not follow an absolute necessity, but a relative necessity: it aims at salvation for each person in particular in a way relating to the constitution of its created nature and its proper mode of activity. All this process aims at the best participation of divine goodness by each person. The salvific will thus pursues its primordial intention not as an absolute necessity but by a fittingness coherent with some potentialities in the free creature. As a general rule, the divine will does not remove contingency from created things and does not impose an absolute necessity on them. Once they are constituted, the natural orientation of each creature toward its own end is necessary; however, it may be missed due to multiple contingencies.[42] With regard to creation, God wants not only this or that thing to occur, but also that it may happen as it should: sometimes in a necessary way and, most often, in a contingent way.

With regard to the salvation of all human beings, God therefore wills it to be realized eternally—not in any indiscriminate manner whatsoever, but rather in accordance with their capacity for free response and in accordance with the covenantal design that governs all his creation. God wills not only that all people be saved, but that they be saved in a manner that magnifies both their created freedom and the radiance of the divine goodness. The universal salvific will could therefore encounter, in some people, a definitive obstacle that God does not intend to overcome.[43] It would therefore be wrong to

42. See ibid., I.85.

43. On metaphysical-theological aporia regarding the relationship between the sovereign will of God and the free self-determination of creatures, see Serge-Thomas Bonino, "Contemporary Thomism through the Prism of the Theology of Predestination," in

invoke the claim that grace is invincible, thus enabling one to conclude with Augustine that wherever grace is not victorious, it has not really been given in such a way as to be effective.[44]

In order to avoid forcing an undue restriction upon the universal amplitude of the salvific will, two complementary clarifications, proposed by Jacques Maritain and Charles Journet, are quite illuminative. They are concerned with the theological concept of divine election. First, the divine election of some does not have a necessary correlation with the disapproval of others. Secondly, the primordial election, concerned with eschatological salvation, is distinct from "economic" elections, which temporarily privilege some for the ultimate benefit of all.

The Asymmetry between Election and Reprobation

Following Jacques Maritain, we should be careful not to conceive of the disapproval of some by God as though it were a necessary counterpart to the divine election of a few others.[45] Such an alternative may be appropriate for most human selections, themselves often quite arbitrary, but it does not exhaust the highest degrees of human love. With regard to their children, some mothers attest, for example, that preferential love for each one is possible in the form of a personalized multiplication of one's preferences, without removing from other children the unique preference given to one of them. By contrast, the novel *Sophie's Choice* by William Styron unpacks the incurable drama of a mother forced to choose which of her two children will live. When one speaks analogously of divine election, the notion of a personalized preference without parallel exclusion must be brought to its maximum acuity, as God's gift in creation is

---

Thomism and Predestination: Principles and Disputations, ed. Steven A. Long (Ave Maria, Fla.: Sapientia Press, 2016), 29–50.

44. See Augustine, *De correptione et gratia* XII.38; *De praedestinatione sanctorum* VIII.13.

45. See Jacques Maritain, *Dieu et la permission du mal* (Paris: DDB, 1963), esp. 100–105; Jean-Hervé Nicolas, "La volonté salvifique de Dieu contrariée par le péché," *Revue thomiste* 92, no. 1 (1992): 177–96, esp. 186–93.

the singular existence and original goodness of each person. One cannot transpose into God the disenchantment, disappointment, and oblivion that most often remain the counterpart of human preference.

Divine choice cannot therefore be considered as an *a priori* selection, motivated by a kind of discretionary love. In return for the divine election of some people, some sinners would then be left to their own devices for no other reason than the fact that they were not freely elected to salvation. The Augustinian justification for such divine selection, whether by the weight of the original sin or by the aesthetic suitability of a contrasting totality, was not satisfactory and could not withstand the test of time. Indeed, for sinners who have remained outside divine mercy, a lateral reintegration into the divine plan under the order of divine justice through their condemnation would only safeguard a secondary accomplishment of the divine project. The sad revelation of divine justice in the mode of damnation is in no way proportionate to God's benevolent design, which positively directs his spiritual creatures toward the attainment of and participation in the divine goodness itself.[46] If eventual damned people remained subject to divine justice and thus indirectly served the paradoxical radiance of the glory of God, they would nevertheless have caused a failure in relation to God's primordial salvific design.

Admittedly, strictly speaking (and, indeed, by its very literal meaning), divine grace is never owed to anyone. It is all the less so as a result of original sin, which affects all humanity in its fallen condition. However, is the mere fact of having contracted that sin of nature enough to be condemned in full justice? Catholic tradition has clearly maintained that the penalty of original sin is to be deprived of the vision of God. However, this does not equate to reprobation.[47]

---

46. See Jean-Miguel Garrigues, "Miséricorde et justice dans le dessein divin sur les créatures spirituelles selon S. Thomas," *Nova et Vetera* 79, no. 4 (2004): 9–18; Garrigues, "La persévérance de Dieu dans son dessein universel de grâce," *Nova et Vetera* 77, no. 4 (2002): 35–59.

47. See the letter of Innocent III to Humbert, archbishop of Arles, *Maiores Ecclesiæ*

The free creature always keeps the first initiative to commit a fault and thus commands, by its possible stubbornness in this way, a possible reprobation.[48] By allowing this, God would then only sanction the definitive refusal of his love and forgiveness, precisely because of his respect for all created freedom. God cannot decree reprobation without reason, purely *a priori*, prior by nature to the faults actually committed and the definitive hardening of his free creature.

In the end, God's election to salvation must be universal in scope, for only such an aim justifies the creation of each of them, according to a primary design of grace. Indeed, no human creature would come into existence, even after the Fall, if he or she were not previously elected for the sharing of divine life through divine filiation. In biblical revelation, the threat that any sinner would have his or her name removed or erased from the book of life presupposes that all human beings originally had their name written in it, according to the universal call to salvation addressed to every creature promised to share in divine life.[49]

Because the primordial election is universal, at the root of any creative initiative, it is essential that the salvific will addressed to fallen people be just as universal. How can one conceive, in fact, that God would revise his primordial design downward as a result of the Fall, as though the latter could modify the amplitude of his eternal intention in a way that would be proportionate to the overabundance of divine goodness? Following the primordial election which assigns a supernatural purpose to all men and women, God tirelessly offers to each and every one, through the course of every human life and up to each person's last free act, the grace to be able to reject evil and to be saved by divine mercy. It is inconceivable that God would quietly leave some in their misery after they have fallen, even if they

---

causas, in Denzinger, no. 78: "Poena originalis peccati est carentia visionis Dei, actualis vero poena peccati est gehennae perpetuae cruciatus."

48. Aquinas, *Sup. Rom.* 9:13, nos. 762, 764; 9:17, no. 781; 9:23, no. 795; see Augustine, *De correptione et gratia*, VI.9, XI.31.

49. See Rv 3:5, 20:15, 21:26; Ex 32:32–33; Dn 12:1; Ps 69:28; Lk 10:20.

have thus ratified the guilt inherited from original sin.[50] Such passivity would be a terrible disavowal of God's superabundant goodness, which nonetheless is the foundation for a primordial mercy found at the root of all divine works.[51]

Economic "Reprobation" and Eschatological Reprobation

Having acknowledged the asymmetry between election and disapproval, let us make another decisive adjustment regarding the modulations of reprobation, drawing on a suggestion made by Charles Journet. Let us start from the universality of the primordial election of all human beings for eschatological bliss, an election which justifies both the creative initiative and the universality of the salvific will. This election calls for a distinction between, on the one hand, the definitive reprobation by which God may respond to a free creature's perseverance in evil and, on the other hand, a kind of temporary "reprobation" by which God favors this or that human person as a mediating vector of his designs, to the exclusion of another, for the benefit of the universal offer of his grace.[52]

However, one should be aware of the ambiguity of the term "reprobation" in both cases. Literally speaking, God does not eschatolog-

50. Considering that it does not lead to any breach of divine justice and enhances in contrast the radiance of God's mercy for others, Aquinas seems, following Augustine, to be satisfied with such a hypothesis; see Aquinas, *Sup. Rom.* 9:15, no. 773; 9:18, no. 784; 9:20–22, nos. 790–92.

51. See Aquinas, *ST* I, q. 21, a. 4, resp.

52. See Charles Journet, "Predestination," in *The Meaning of Grace*, trans. Arthur V. Littledale (New York: Scepter, 1996), esp. 54–56. To the consequent will, John Damascene links two different possibilities of divine concession or divine abandonment: one is "economic and educational for salvation," while the other leads to "final perdition"; see John Damascene, *De fide orthodoxa* 43, §§7 and 11, ed. Eligius M. Buyteart, 159–60. While he appropriates the distinction between antecedent will and consequent will, Aquinas does not take up—at least to our knowledge—the other distinction concerning divine concession. He negotiates the problem differently using another traditional distinction, namely, that between divine *consilium* and divine *sententia*. Thus, for example, in relation to Paul's condition before his conversion, see Aquinas, *De veritate*, q. 6, a. 6, ad 2, s.c.: "Paul has never been reproved according to a disposition of the divine counsel, which is immutable, but only according to a disposition of the divine sentence which is taken from inferior causes, which sometimes change."

ically condemn those who are not rewarded with a shining mission in the large economy of salvation. The ordinary system of dispensation of grace even suggests that each of the chosen ones actually has a specific mission for the service of all, however discreet it may be, with a mysterious reflection on the whole body of the redeemed.

The primordial election, aiming at eschatological salvation, is concerned *a priori* with all human beings, and God does not abandon any of his creatures until their ultimate free act. However, in the course of salvation history, elections directly related to the economy of salvation as such mobilize some individuals through preferential choices, while they temporarily leave others aside, without however depriving the latter of any personalized blessing on their own path of struggle and salvation. Thus, Seth, Abraham, Isaac, Jacob, Noah, Moses, and David were favored with exceptional blessings or revelations so as to be the vectors of divine grace for the advantage of all, whereas Cain, Lot, Ishmael, Esau, and Saul were not chosen or retained as the privileged channels of divine blessings for the sake of all. In biblical history, this applies not only to individuals, but also to certain peoples. Thus, Israel was created and elected by God in a very unique way in order to be the light of the nations. Nevertheless, such elections related directly to the economy of salvation as such also apply, though in a more punctual manner, to other nations temporarily chosen by God to accomplish his design.[53]

Intermediary elections, in which a servant of God or a chosen people is set apart and blessed in order to bring grace to the largest number of people, are selective, certainly, but only on a temporary basis. On the other hand, the primordial election regarding the offer of eschatological salvation applies effectively to all people, members of various nations, notwithstanding their freedom to oppose the divine call through hardened pride, to the point perhaps—though no one knows for sure—of clearly and definitively refusing mercy, however abundantly and readily it may be offered to them. The logical couplet of election and reprobation might therefore be only valid

53. See Am 9:7; Is 5:26–29, 19:21–25.

with certainty within the history of salvation, without the economic "reprobation" of an individual engaging his or her eschatological destination. On the other hand, with regard to the ultimate end, the primordial election of all creatures called to salvation does not of itself entail any symmetrical reprobation.[54]

A THEOLOGICAL ATTITUDE GROUNDED IN THE OBJECTIVE OFFER OF CHRIST JESUS

Whatever may be the theological opinions concerning the best way to understand the modality of the divine will's exercise and the actual outcome of the salvific offer, the cultural contrast between contemporary sensibility and the dominant voices of past centuries is rather striking, at least in the West. Our ancestors were far less optimistic than present generations concerning the number of those saved.[55] For Augustine, only a few elected people would be separated from the mass on the way to perdition. The damnation of the greatest number of people used to appear (wrongly) as a sure affair, while the damnation of a few now seems (rightly?) a very improbable outcome.

Such a development is not by itself normative, but it is significant. One could argue that the positive expectation of eschatological bliss has not intensified in a way proportional to the demythologization of eschatological representations and the obliteration of the fear of hell.[56] This is unfortunately true, but despite the swinging of the pendulum, leading to a new eschatological optimism replacing Au-

54. In accordance with Eph 1:4, Aquinas conceives divine election as a selective one; see *SCG* III.163; *ST* I, q. 23, a. 4; *Super Epistolam ad Ephesios lectura* [hereafter *Sup. Eph.*] 1:4, no. 8; *Sup. Rom.* 9:11, no. 759. When defining the election of one person as a selective preference by which another is symmetrically left out, Aquinas does not consider the distinction between election regarding the ultimate end and economic election; see *Sup. Rom.* 9:13, no. 763.

55. See Guillaume Cuchet, "Une révolution théologique oubliée: Le triomphe de la thèse du grand nombre des élus dans le discours catholique du XIXe siècle," *Revue d'histoire du XIXe siècle* 41, no. 2 (2010): 131–48.

56. See Richard Schenk, "The Epoché of Factical Damnation. On the Costs of Bracketing Out the Likelihood of Final Loss," *Logos* 1, no. 3 (1997): 122–54.

gustinian pessimism, it is remarkable that the theological outlook inspired by these various theological currents remains fundamentally the same: given the irreducible uncertainty of the ultimate eschatological outcome and the singular creativity of divine mercy, we have a duty, through charity, to hope for all.

Apart from speculative restrictions, Christians should maintain that the salvific will is indeed universal, that is, qualified and equipped to reach, in fact, every person as an offer, whatever the acceptance or refusal proper to each of them may be. We receive as a principle the affirmation that the universal salvific will is a divine one that engages the concrete means suited to an offer which is effectively addressed to all and to each one. We are not justified in concluding that the salvific will should be restricted in order to thereby support a theoretical infallibility of grace, as though the human refusal of grace should never be able to definitively thwart it. Reconciling the sovereignty of the divine will with the possibility of human refusal is a real theoretical difficulty, but its treatment should not interfere from the outset with the principal affirmation of a universal salvific will which is strong and persevering.

The pivotal verse of 1 Timothy 2:1–7 establishes a strong connection between the universal salvific will and the oneness of God: in order to ground the extension of God's design, the Apostle refers to God's oneness. This presupposes that the universal extension of the divine will proceeds from a single design for all, itself rooted in God's own oneness. The main idea seems to be the following: because God is fundamentally One, the origin and end of all created things, he does not exercise his salvific solicitude in a limited and restrictive way, but rather in a way that is universal and superabundant. This does not imply that God's ways are constant and uniform, but rather that they all converge toward one unceasingly pursued goal, reaching at all individuals and include them into salvation. By his saving will and concern, the One God embraces the totality of his creation in one and the same unified and ordered plan, whatever may be the economic modulations and intermediate delays involved therein. As a principle, the oneness of God requires both the oneness and universality of his salvific design. If any human creature comes from him, it would be totally unfitting for some to be *a priori* cast aside, even after the Fall.

In 1 Timothy 2:1–7, between God's saving will for all and the realization, in Christ Jesus, of salvation for all, the divine unity intervenes not only to justify the amplitude of the divine will, but also to ground the oneness of the man Jesus in his saving mediation. The unicity of the mediator is thus an extension of the unicity of God, which ultimately justifies his universal salvific will. The uniqueness of the universal mediator testifies, in the course of history, to the unique origin of salvation and the universality of its offer. According to Christian revelation, Jesus Christ is both the point of convergence and the point of diffraction for salvation, offered to all human beings by the One God.

PART 2

Analogy, Trinity, and
Christ the Savior

11

·

The Interplay of Effects
of Nature and of Grace in
Knowing God

Aquinas is well known for having carefully distinguished two modalities in our knowledge of God: that which proceeds from the natural capacities of human reason and that which proceeds from Christian revelation. Before him, it was common for thinkers to mingle these two registers of discussion together. After him, the tendency would be to separate them.[1] Merely from a historical perspective, Thomas's solution could therefore be described as representing a point of equilibrium or a turning point. Thus, we find ourselves faced with the question of knowing whether such an outlook can still have a kind of paradigmatic value for a contemporary theological epistemology. In this study, we intend to describe the resources available in our knowledge of God according to Thomas's account of these matters and to assess the conjoint application of the divine effects of nature and of grace in his theology.

We will begin by describing the overall goal of Thomas's theology, doing so by spelling out its explicit ends. Then I will set forth the

---

1. Gilles Emery, "Trinité et unité de Dieu dans la scolastique. XIIe-XIVe siècle," in *Le christianisme est-il un monothéisme?*, ed. Gilles Emery and Pierre Gisel (Geneva: Labor et Fides, 2001), 195–220.

justification, functions, and extent of our knowledge of God through his effects of nature and of grace. This will lead us to specify the correspondence between God's identity and this twofold approach as well as the dispositions required in the theologian attempting to undertake it. Finally, we will conclude our discussion by briefly reflecting on the epistemological restructurings adopted by contemporary theology.

THE HIERARCHY AND COORDINATION OF THE ENDS OF THEOLOGY

Aquinas assigns a twofold task to theology using two words: the contemplative *manifestare* and the defensive *solvare*. First and foremost, the theologian must manifest the truths of faith in their unity by, for example, attempting to illuminate one article of the Creed by another.[2] However, it is also fitting for the theologian to respond to adversaries of the faith by resolving, to the degree that this is possible, their objections or at least by showing that their arguments do not have probative force.

In the conference addressed to the participants attending the annual Thomist gathering at Le Saulchoir in Paris in 2003, Gilles Emery emphasized an interesting interrelationship between these two tasks. Seeking to characterize "the goal of St. Thomas Aquinas's Trinitarian theology," the well-known theologian emphasized the "guideposts" of Thomas's intention in theological reflection. This intention is particularly clear in the trinitarian questions in the *De potentia*, where Thomas explains that, faced with objections coming from heretics, the "Holy Fathers" merely wished "to grasp enough of the truth of the matter so that they could exclude errors."[3]

---

2. See Aquinas, *ST* I, q. 1, a. 8, sol.: "*Sacra doctrina* does not argue in order to prove its principles, namely, the articles of faith. Rather, on the basis of them it proceeds to something to be shown, as the Apostle does in 1 Cor 15:12 arguing from the resurrection of Christ in order to prove the common resurrection [of believers]."

3. Aquinas, *De potentia*, q. 9, a. 5, resp.; see also *SCG* I.3.3.

Such a delimitation of Thomas's explanatory goal by way of this defensive aim is useful for recalling the modesty, sobriety, and precaution required as theology treats of the mysteries of the faith. Nonetheless, we must bear in mind the hierarchy of ends introduced by Thomas in his *Exposition* of Boethius's *De Trinitate*: "[Boethius] makes allusion to the principal end [of theology], which is interior, namely, the perception of the divine truth, and explains its secondary end, namely the judgment of the wise man."[4] Here, the defensive goal is quite obviously included in the judgment of the wise man, who has the office of resolving difficulties and discerning errors.

We must not interpret Thomas's words in the *De potentia* describing the trinitarian reflection of the "Holy Fathers," himself drawing inspiration from their theological methods, as fixing a pre-set, invariable ceiling for theological *scrutatio*. Rather, let us say that they constitute a warning or recollection of our inability to grasp what God is in himself. Nonetheless, it remains the case that the horizon of Thomas's theology is not limited to its defensive office, as we see in the hierarchy of ends noted above in his comments in his *Super Boetium De Trinitate*. Despite the inadequacy and infirmity of our knowledge of God, it has contemplative resources, ones that are indirect though quite fruitful. We will emphasize them in the pages that follow.

TO KNOW GOD THROUGH HIS EFFECTS OF NATURE AND OF GRACE

Having taken into account our inability, as wayfarers, to know God as he is in himself and proceeding in the wake of an established tradition, Thomas highlights a roundabout path that we can travel in knowing God: we can approach him through his effects or opera-

---

4. Aquinas, *Super Boetium De Trinitate*, exp. proh.: "insinuans finem principalem, qui est interior, scilicet perceptio divine veritatis, et explicans finem secundarium, scilicet judicium sapientis." Already, see *Super Boetium De Trinitate*, prol.: "The end of this work is the manifestation the hidden [truths] of the faith to the degree that this is possible in this life" (*finis huius operis est ut occulta fidei manifestentur quantum in via possibile est*).

tions. Indeed, "God is not made known to us as he is in his nature. However, he makes himself known to us through his operations or effects, and from these we can name him."[5] Such knowledge of God is not limited solely to the reasoning that passes from effect to cause. Rather, it is broken down into three modalities, which Thomas takes over from Dionysius: "On the basis of the divine effects, we cannot know the Divine Nature according to what it is in Itself such that we might have quidditative knowledge of it. Rather, we know it by way of eminence, causality, and negation."[6] Elsewhere, completely ruling out the possibility of having natural knowledge of the Trinity, Thomas, on this occasion, specifies the way that the threefold methodology functions: "By natural reason we can know about God only what is perceived about him on the basis of a relation of effects to him, like the [truths] that designate his causality and eminence over [the realities he has] caused and that remove from him the imperfect conditions of those effects."[7] If it is indeed true that *in statu viae* God will never be known except on the basis of his effects, such knowledge nonetheless must be sought out in a diversified and adapted manner, depending on what one wishes to consider concerning God.

Fortunately, the effects or operations that can serve as the point of departure for our knowledge of God, in fact, belong to two orders: "Although we cannot know him quidditatively, nonetheless, in speaking of those things which are considered about God in *sacra doctrina*, in place of a definition, we can make use of his effects, whether they be of nature or of grace."[8] However, we must still show precisely what these effects of nature or grace are.

5. Aquinas, *ST* I, q. 13, a. 8, resp.

6. Ibid., ad 2. Likewise, see *Sent. I*, d. 3, q. 1, *divisio* of the first part of the text (reference is made here to Dionysius, *De divinis nominibus* VII.8) and also a. 3, resp. On the replacing of *remotio* by *negation*, see Ysabel de Andia, "Remotio-Negatio. L'évolution du vocabulaire de Saint Thomas touchant la voie négative," *AHDLMA* 68, no. 1 (2001): 45–71.

7. Aquinas, *Super Boetium De Trinitate*, q. 1, a. 4, resp.

8. Aquinas, *ST* I, q. 1, a. 7, ad 1. On the many meanings of the expression *sacra doctrina*, which encompasses the many ways of listening to revelation, including theology, see Jean-Pierre Torrell, "Le savoir théologique chez Saint Thomas d'Aquin," *Revue thomiste* 96, no. 3 (1996): 355–96.

We find an illuminating comparison of these two registers at the end of the question on the *quomodo* of our knowledge of God. Thomas there examines: "Whether beyond the knowledge we have through natural reason there is some knowledge of God through grace in the present life."[9] The body of the response states that we have more perfect knowledge of God through grace than what we have through natural reason, both on the side of our capacity for knowing—for "the natural light of our intellect is strengthened by the infusion of grace"[10]—and likewise on the side of the *phantasmata* provided by God. Indeed, the light of revelation is accompanied by prophetic images or by sensible realities, like the dove or the voice from on high at Christ's baptism. Therefore, on both sides (i.e., the *lumen* and the *phantasmata*), it is indeed true that "human knowledge is aided by the revelation of grace."[11]

In response to the objection stating that we are united to God only through natural reason, all the while not knowing what he is (*quid est*), Thomas expresses a supplementary remark that adds precision on this point:

Although through the revelation of grace in this life we do not know what God is and thus are united to him, as it were, as to something unknown,[12] nonetheless, *we know him more fully inasmuch as we are presented with his effects in greater number and excellence* and to the degree that, on the basis of divine revelation, we attribute to him something that is not attained by natural reason, such as [the fact] that God is three and one.[13]

---

9. Aquinas, *ST* I, q. 12, prol.

10. Ibid., a. 13, resp.

11. Ibid.

12. See Dionysius, *Theologia mystica* I.3; see Aquinas, *Sent.* I, d. 8, q. 1, ad 2–4.

13. Emphasis added. Aquinas, *ST* I, q. 12, a. 13, ad 1: "licet per revelationem gratiae in hac vita non cognoscamus de Deo quid est, et sic ei quasi ignoto coniungamur; tamen plenius ipsum cognoscimus, inquantum plures et excellentiores effectus eius nobis demonstrantur; et inquantum ei aliqua attribuimus ex revelatione divina, ad quae ratio naturalis non pertingit, ut Deum esse trinum et unum." Likewise, see *ST* II-II, q. 2, a. 3, ad 3: "Faith perceives the invisible properties of God in a more elevated manner and with a greater extension than does natural reason proceeding from creatures to God" (*invisibilia Dei altiori modo, quantum ad plura, percipit fides quam ratio naturalis ex creaturis in Deum procedens*).

In line with this text, we can say that the effects of nature are divine effects within the range of our natural reason, whereas the effects of grace are given through supernatural revelation or alongside it.

This distinction is taken from the *specification* of the two orders of knowledge. On the basis of the effects of nature, known in creation, the human intellect is able to know God within the framework and limits of natural reason. On the basis of the effects of grace, transmitted through revelation, the believing intellect can develop a Christian theology of the mysteries of God. Nonetheless, *in exercito*, the theology of the Christian mysteries also mobilizes that which by rights falls to natural knowledge of God, and in turn, the latter's own objects are illuminated by a superior light.[14]

Therefore, basing ourselves on the distinction between effects of nature and those of grace, we must not be too hasty in drawing the conclusion that knowledge of the divine attributes proceeds solely on the basis of the effects of nature, whereas theology of the mysteries draws its knowledge exclusively from the effects of grace. Indeed, effects of nature and of grace are drawn together in concert in these two orders of knowledge, at least if they are considered in their full development in exercise. Thus, for example, the revelation of the Trinity enables us to understand the divine knowledge and love more fully, or again, the revelation of creation enables us to form a more complete account of the divine causality. Reciprocally, the natural image of God in man's spiritual life is conducive to articulating a kind of *intellectus fidei* of the trinitarian life of God. We will return below to this theme concerning the interaction of these two orders of knowledge.

14. On the distinction between *specification* and *exercise*, expressly applied by Aquinas to the relations between the intellect and the will, see Aquinas, *De malo*, q. 6, resp. The reflection surrounding the question of Christian philosophy and the possible support that it could draw from theology led Jacques Maritain (in dialogue with Charles Journet) to emphasize the interaction between philosophy and theology on the level of exercise. This perspective was taken up by John Paul II in *Fides et Ratio*, par. 73. On this subject, see Jean-Miguel Garrigues, "La philosophie et la théologie dans l'exercice interactif de leurs sagesses chez S. Thomas et chez Jacques Maritain," *Bulletin de littérature ecclésiastique* 105, no. 3 (2004): 255–74. In particular, see the explanations given on the subject of *ST* II-II, q. 1, a. 8, ad 1.

Therefore, according to Thomas, knowledge of God through his effects of nature and of grace does not imply a kind of disjunctive opposition between, on the one hand, a strictly philosophical knowledge of God on the basis of his effects of nature and, on the other, a Christian theology of God through his revealed effects of grace. Rather, Thomas's theology, within the framework of *sacra doctrina*, calls for a complete theology which treats not only of the Christian mysteries but also, under their illumination, the naturally-knowable divine attributes, undertaking their activity through the concerted activity of reason and faith, each performing their work on the divine effects of nature and of grace.

This is why Thomas's subtreatise *De Deo Uno* could not be reduced to a kind of simple exposition of natural theology, something which Thomas himself expressly noted: "The theology which pertains to *sacra doctrina* differs generically from the theology which is a part of philosophy."[15] In contrast with what we see too often in the Thomist tradition, Thomas never wrote a "natural theology," properly speaking, in a philosophical sense. Instead, he effectively integrated into his Christian theology the potential acquisitions that could be drawn from a natural knowledge of God. We will return to this point below.

THE CONTRIBUTION OF EFFECTS OF NATURE: PRAEAMBULA AND LIKENESSES

The necessity of *praeambula fidei* and the use of created likenesses in Christian theology provide an important illustration for how the understanding of the faith, while indeed principally proceeding from supernatural revelation and "effects of grace," nonetheless also mobilizes "effects of nature" in service of knowledge of God in his mysteries. Let us not have a knee-jerk reaction against the idea that faith could have *praeambula*. If the latter are indeed *de iure* accessible to us through natural reason, *de facto* we see that revelation com-

15. Aquinas, *ST* I, q. 1, a. 1, ad 2.

municates them to us through a kind of objective superabundance. In relation to faith, these *praeambula* enjoy the same finality that nature has in relation to grace.[16]

In the article of the *Super Boetium de Trinitate* where he examines the use of philosophical sciences in Christian theology, Aquinas conjointly treats of the *praeambula fidei* as well as likenesses of the realities of faith. To his eyes, the two are constitutive elements of a full and complete theology of the Christian mysteries:

The gifts of grace are added to nature in such a way that grace does not destroy nature but, rather, perfects it … Now, in imperfect [realities,] we find a kind of imitation of perfect ones, and in those things that are known by natural reason there are certain likenesses of those things which are handed on through faith. However, just as sacred doctrine is founded on the light of faith, so too philosophy is founded on the natural light of reason. Whence, it is impossible that those [truths] that fall to philosophy would be contrary to those which are of faith. Rather, they fall short of them. Nonetheless, they contain certain likenesses of them, as well as certain preambles to them, just as nature is a preamble to grace.[17]

For St. Thomas, the *lumen naturale rationis* and the *lumen fidei* never enter into dialectical opposition with each other, but rather maintain a relationship of finality, according to the relationship that exists between the imperfect and the perfect. Even if the truths acquired by natural reason remain below the level of the truths of faith, they can be of service in understanding the mysteries of faith by providing faith with either *praeambula* or likenesses. This is how Thomas describes and illustrates each of these resources a little later on in the same text:

Therefore, in *sacra doctrina*, we can use philosophy in three ways. *First,* we can use it for demonstrating those things that are *praeambula fidei*, which must be known in faith, such as those [truths] that can be proven about God by natural reasons (such as the fact that God exists, that God is one, and other such things, as well as those things proven about creatures in philosophy). *Second,* it can be used in order to indicate through certain

---

16. See ibid., q. 2, a. 2, ad 1.

17. Aquinas, *Super Boetium De Trinitate,* q. 2, a. 3, resp.

likenesses those [truths] that are of faith, as St. Augustine, in his *De Trinitate*, uses many likenesses drawn from philosophical teachings so that he may manifest the nature of the Trinity. *Third*, philosophy can also be used in order to resist those [propositions] that are declared against the faith, either by showing that they are false or by showing that they are not necessary.[18]

Thomas does not fully develop the role that he wishes to accord to the *praeambula fidei*. Only by considering his own practice of theology and the order that we can find therein can we respond to this question. In his theological activity, we discern two functions assigned to *praeambula*: that of being a *conditio sine qua non* and that of being a criterion of critical verification. Thus, for example, the theologian must begin by recognizing that God is true and good in order to understand how he could be knowledge and love. This is what then enables us to envision the trinitarian life as a kind of generation by way of intellection and a procession by way of love. However, once the theologian gets this far in his reflection, the critical effect of the other divine attributes (in particular the divine perfection and simplicity) prevents him from reifying his first analysis and even requires him to give it stability through recourse to other perspectives concerning the given consideration. For example, we can see Thomas performing this sort of activity when he completes the trinitarian model of *processio* by combining it with that of *relatio*, then pushing the latter to its limits by defining it, in a paradoxical manner, as a *relatio ut subsistens*.[19]

The *praeambula fidei* are only "elementary" affirmations concerning God, but nonetheless they help us to situate what we could call rational delimitations for an accurate reception of revelation and for an understanding of the mysteries and divine paradoxes that does not involve us in absurdities. Under the critical regulation of the *praeambula fidei*, it then falls to created *likenesses* to enrich the expression of the enunciations of the faith. We can find Thomas using

18. Ibid.
19. See Aquinas, *ST* I, qq. 27–29.

such likenesses throughout his theology. However, his privileged reference in this matter turns his readers' attention to the paradigmatic example of the trinitarian theology of the *imago Dei* found in Augustine's *De Trinitate*. By having recourse to such created likenesses, Augustine and Thomas do not desire to produce imaginative representations of the divine realities but, instead, seek to *signify* and *designate* in a roundabout way,[20] in a way that is as spiritual as possible and submitted to the obscurity of faith, these divine mysteries which transcend all of our formulations and representations, beginning with those received from revelation itself.[21] Even if Aquinas places his accent upon the technical precision with which likenesses will be "shaped" and "adjusted" in light of what they must designate, he nonetheless intends to give this procedure the contemplative scope of a kind of "spiritual exercise":

Therefore, in order to know truths of faith, which can be perfectly known only by those who see the divine essence, human reason has the task of gathering together certain likenesses [*verisimilitudines*] of them; however, these likenesses do not suffice for these truths to be fully embraced in a quasi-demonstrative way or as understood in themselves. Nonetheless, it is useful for the human mind *to exercise itself* in these forms of reasoning, however weak they may be, so long as it does not have the pretense of understanding or demonstrating what is known. For the greatest of joy is experienced in being able to observe something concerning the loftiest realities, even if our glance upon them is brief and weak.[22]

---

20. In this regard, the perspectival shift in Augustine, *De Trinitate* VIII.14 and IX.2 (a shift noted in XV.10) is very significant, for Augustine explains the strategic detour through the image of God as being necessary because of the too-luminous character of the mystery (which he originally sought to approach directly).

21. See Aquinas, *Sent.* III, d. 24, a. 2, sol. 3: "The [truths] of faith are not proposed to our intellect in themselves but, rather, through certain words that do not suffice for expressing them and through certain likenesses that do not fully represent them [*quibusdam similitudinibus ab eorum repraesentatione deficientibus*]. This is why they are said to be known 'in a mirror and an enigma.'" Likewise see *Sent.* III, d. 14, a. 1, resp. 3; *ST* I, q. 27, a. 1, resp.

22. Aquinas, *SCG* I.8. See Gilles Emery, "Trinitarian Theology as Spiritual Exercise in Augustine and Aquinas," in *Aquinas the Augustinian*, ed. Michael Dauphinais (Washington, D.C.: The Catholic University of America Press, 2007), 1–40.

It is clear that for Thomas the use of created likenesses in the theology of the mysteries thus corresponds to the principal end of theology, namely the internal perception of the divine truth which itself demands that it be rendered more manifest to our own eyes.

The proper role falling to created likenesses in the theology of the mysteries requires a clarification concerning Thomas's use of analogy inasmuch as this method remains one of his well-furnished theological techniques. We must note that the function and scope of analogy is different in the attributions made in the *De Deo Uno* and in the theology of the mysteries. Whereas for the determination of the divine attributes a proportionate *notion* (*ratio*) leads—by way of causality, negation, and eminence—to a proper attribution, in the theology of the mysteries, at least two likenesses fulfill their "indicative" function in a kind of reciprocal modification. Thus, in the attribution of goodness to God, the entire *ratio* of good is proportionally preserved. (This is traditionally emphasized by specifying that analogy is "proper.") However, in the attribution of generation to God, a more complex discernment must be undertaken between what can and cannot be applied to the divine being. Thus, to correct the exteriority of the Son implied by the notion of generation as drawn from its realization in humanity, Thomas completes this first likeness by that of intellectual conception, which however itself lacks the unity of substance proper to generation.[23]

Jacques Maritain distinguished "superanalogy" from the "analogy" by which the knowledge in question comes to us respectively from revelation or from natural reason.[24] Here, we find ourselves touching on the same distinction, though according to another parameter of the attribution of the terms: is analogical knowledge adequate to its object through the use of a proportionally transposed *ratio* or, rather, is it adjusted to its object through the interplay of two

---

23. See Aquinas, *ST* I, q. 34, a. 2, ad 3.

24. See Jacques Maritain, "Réflexions sur le savoir théologique," *Approches sans entraves*, in his *Œuvres complètes*, vol. XIII (Fribourg / Paris: Éd. Universitaires / Saint-Paul, 1993), 832. Also see Charles Journet, *L'Église sainte mais non sans pécheurs* (Paris: Parole et Silence, 1999), 125–31.

likenesses that mutually purify each other? The second case seems to describe the theology of the Christian mysteries (the Trinity, the incarnation, the redemption, grace, the sacraments, and so forth).

**WHAT ARE THE EFFECTS
OF GRACE AT THE ROOT OF A
CHRISTIAN THEOLOGY?**

In reading *Summa theologiae* I, q. 12, a. 13, we already noted that, among the effects of grace that enter into *sacra doctrina*, thus sustaining our knowledge of God, we must count supernatural sensible manifestations (e.g., certain prophetic visions or the dove and voice that were present at Christ's baptism). This indication is confirmed and brought to its completion when Thomas discusses the visible mission of the Holy Spirit. Here, Aquinas takes up for his own part an extract drawn from Augustine's *De Trinitate*, where the latter associates the dove at the baptism with the tongues of fire at Pentecost and likewise recalls theophanic manifestations in Old Testament: the flames of the burning bush, the column leading the people in the desert, and the lightning and thunder accompanying the giving of the Law.[25] Thus, the notion of "effects of grace" refers to the manifold register of more or less direct sensible manifestations of God in salvation history. From the perspective of the divine economy of revelation, the most proper manifestations of God's inner mystery will certainly be delivered with the visible missions of the Word and the Spirit.

To make clear the fittingness of the visible mission of the Spirit, Thomas makes use of common noetic foundations for explaining the paths traveled by our knowledge of God, beginning its ventures on the basis of visible experience:

God provides for everything according to the mode of each thing. Now, man's connatural mode [of activity] is that he be led by the hand [*manud-*

---

25. See Augustine, *De Trinitate* II.6.11. This is cited in particular by Aquinas in *ST* I, q. 43, a. 7, ad 2.

ucatur] from visible realities to invisible ones … and thus, it was necessary that God manifest invisible things to man through visible ones. Therefore, just as God made himself, as well as the eternal processions of the persons, known to men through visible creatures according to certain indications, so too it was fitting that through the visible [missions] the invisible missions of the divine persons would be manifested according to certain visible creatures.[26]

The first term of the comparison here seems at once to embrace effects of nature and those of grace—though distinct from those of visible missions of the Son and the Spirit, properly speaking—as it is at once concerned with the manifestation of God (without distinction) and that of his eternal processions. Doubtlessly, Thomas is here thinking not only about the vestiges of creation and about the image of the Trinity but also about the theophanies of the Old Testament such as, for example, the apparition that came to Abraham at the Terebinth of Mamre mentioned (at the end of ad 6) in the same article.

From this overall perspective, we can easily understand how it is that Christ's humanity plays an eminent role among these "effects of grace" making possible our knowledge of God in his mysteries. In fact, for Thomas, Jesus' concrete human nature and his own proper activity are the counterparts of the Spirit's own sensible manifestations, notwithstanding the important difference constituted by the hypostatic union.[27] This perspective sketched out by the question on the divine missions leads Thomas to develop this theological theme considerably. Nonetheless, his Christology does still furnish some important additional clarifications.

Thus, in an argument from authority given in response to the question of knowing whether it was fitting for God to become incarnate, Thomas affirms: "It seems utterly befitting that the invisible reality of God would be made manifest to us through visible things. Indeed, this is why the world was made, as is obvious in the Apostle's

26. Aquinas, *ST* I, q. 43, a. 7, resp.
27. See ibid., ad 1.

words to the Romans [1:20]: 'The Invisible things of God are clearly seen through created things.'"[28] Given the question thus posed, Thomas here means to apply this point of illumination in the first place to the created humanity of Christ. The *sed contra* continues with a citation from John Damascene explaining how, through the mystery of the incarnation, "We are at once shown God's goodness, wisdom, justice, power, and might."[29] This complementary remark is particularly interesting, for it shows that the incarnation enables us to have fuller knowledge of the divine attributes which are by rights enrolled among the *praeambula fidei* or the truths about God that are accessible to natural reason. In this same vein, Thomas himself elsewhere emphasizes how explicit knowledge of the Trinity reverberates back on our appreciation of creation, to the degree that the procession of creatures proves to be freely caused by the procession of the divine Persons.[30]

A little later on, while evaluating the necessity of the incarnation for the restoration of mankind, Thomas responds to the objection stating that the incarnation would be an obstacle to the reverence owed to God: "By assuming flesh, God did not diminish his majesty. Consequently, we cannot say that the motive for our reverence for God is thereby diminished. Rather, this reverence grows through this increase in our knowledge of him. However, inasmuch as he wished to draw close to us through the assumption of the flesh, he *drew* us toward greater knowledge of himself."[31] Now, the assumption of our flesh not only leads us to recognize God in his incarnate Word next to whom the Father and the Son reveal themselves—especially at the baptism and the transfiguration—but, moreover, the assumption of our human spirit by the divine Word also comes to re-

---

28. See Aquinas, *ST* III, q. 1, a. 1, s.c.

29. See John Damascene, *De fide orthodoxa* 45, ed. Eligius M. Buyteart, 168.

30. See Aquinas, *ST* I, q. 32, a. 1, ad 3. On the relation between the procession of creatures and the procession of divine Persons, see in particular Gilles Emery, *La Trinité créatrice. Trinité et création dans les commentaires aux "Sentences" de Thomas d'Aquin et de ses précurseurs Albert le Grand et Bonaventure* (Paris: Vrin, 1995).

31. Aquinas, *ST* III, q. 1, a. 2, ad 3.

store and perfect our own capacity for knowing God.[32] The decisive idea holding that the incarnation itself thus makes our knowledge of God grow—indeed, by way of attraction, which presupposes the action of grace—will undergo exquisite developments in Thomas's theology of the mysteries of the life of Christ.[33]

Along with Christ's humanity, we most certainly must count the sacraments of the church and the tradition of the scriptures among the effects of grace that lead us to God: "Those things that pertain to Christ's humanity and to the sacraments of the Church, or to whatsoever creatures, fall under faith inasmuch as we are ordered to God through them. Thus, we assent to them on account of the divine truth. And likewise, we must say the same of all those things that are handed on in Sacred Scripture."[34] To the unity coming from the principle of revelation (i.e., God) and from the formal object of faith (i.e., the divine truth), there corresponds here the single end of the entire divine economy: God himself, the principle of the many effects of nature and of grace by which he draws us to himself, our end and our beatitude.

Indeed, the mutual contribution of the effects of nature and of grace in *sacra doctrina* reveals the personal unity of God as the principle of creation and as the end of the economy of grace. The real identity of God should not be split apart into two faces that are alien to each other, as though we were to reach the principle of creation on the natural level and the principle of revelation and the end of the economy of grace on the supernatural level. In Christian theology, to affirm that "God is the principle of all things" does not pertain only to the potential acquisitions coming from a simply natural knowledge of God. This proposition must be understood in accord with the relationship of finality between creatures' own going-forth from God and their return to him—the second movement being entirely taken up by grace.

32. See Aquinas, *ST* I, q. 5, a. 4, ad 1 and 2.

33. See Jean-Pierre Torrell, *Le Christ en ses mystères. La vie et l'œuvre de Jésus selon saint Thomas d'Aquin* (Paris: Desclée, 1999).

34. Aquinas, *ST* II-II, q. 1, a. 1, ad 1–2.

Revelation is not accidental in relation to our return to God, and therefore no more is it accidental in relation to creation. Indeed, God reveals himself though his supernatural governance of his creatures and thus offers us the intelligibility we need in order to enter freely into the God's reign over all things, cooperating in his program of divinization. Revelation is addressed to our intellect supernaturalized by faith at the very heart of a regime which constitutes an economy of grace for our free will. This economy aims at bringing about our own personal access to beatitude, which consists in taking joy in God himself. All the intermediate realities of the economy of salvation must be considered not as simple speculative objects annexed to faith, but rather as inseparable mediations offered to our practical quest for beatitude.

Thus, it is fitting to emphasize the fact that the knowledge of God through the "effects of grace" that we have brought to light up to this point only becomes effective if grace itself is at work in the person who is seeking to know God. Also, our consideration of the sensible and external effects of grace connected to the divine missions must be connected to the interior effects of grace (whether actual or sanctifying) produced in the soul through the divine missions—all the more so as the visible missions are teleologically ordered to the invisible missions which are effectively proposed to men through those visible missions. Indeed, supernatural knowledge of God is finalized by the filial adoption[35] that is realized in us through the invisible missions of the Word and the Spirit with the aim of uniting us to the Father.[36]

Therefore, the knowledge of God that we have through his effects of grace is not only an intellectual affair. Beyond merely rational knowledge, it normally presupposes the process of a living faith and a positive openness to sanctification. Certainly, Thomas distinguishes three wisdoms: philosophical wisdom, theological wisdom, and mystical wisdom. The second is acquired and makes its progress

---

35. See Aquinas, *De potentia*, q. 9, a. 9, resp.; *ST* I, q. 33, a. 3, resp.
36. See Aquinas, *Sent.* I, d. 14, q. 2, a. 2, resp.; d. 15, q. 4, a. 1, resp.

through study, whereas the third is given freely by the Holy Spirit so as to make us "suffer divine things" and to allow ourselves to be enflamed by God himself.[37] Nonetheless, let us not forget that at the root of theological wisdom there must be a kind of disposition to allow ourselves to be called, led, and drawn to the knowledge of God through the effects of grace in salvation history—from the theophanies of the Old Testament up to the concrete humanity of Jesus and the multiform outpouring of the Spirit at Pentecost. This disposition is nothing other than the grace of believing, hoping, and loving, or at least a motion teleologically finalized by living faith.[38]

HOLDING TOGETHER
PREAMBULA FIDEI AND
ANALOGIA FIDEI

Theological epistemology underwent profound upheavals during the twentieth century, at once being affected by criticisms coming from philosophy as well as from the increasing strength of historical critical exegesis, followed by that of hermeneutics. Thus, two important displacements were produced within contemporary theology. On the one hand, the natural knowledge of God and of the *praeambula fidei* were profoundly placed into question, settling the issue either through a pure and simple rejection (as is found in the work of Karl Barth)[39] or through a complete recasting of it into a kind of precomprehension of God—understood as a "provisional anticipation" (as found in the work of Wolfhart Pannenberg).[40] On the other hand, there was the downgrading of created likenesses through a recentering upon the revealing role played

---

37. See Aquinas, *ST* I, q. 1, a. 6, ad 3; q. 43, a. 5, ad 2–3; II-II, q. 45, a. 2, resp.

38. See Aquinas, *ST* II-II, q. 2, a. 9, sol.; I-II, q. 111, a. 2; q. 113, a. 3, a. 4; II-II, q. 2, a. 1, ad 3; q. 4, a. 1, resp. and ad 2; a. 2, ad 1; q. 6, a. 1, resp. and ad 3. The Council of Orange called this motion to belief the *affectus credulitatis*; see Denzinger, no. 375.

39. For an ecumenical assessment, see Thomas Joseph White (ed.), *The Analogy of Being: Invention of the Antichrist or the Wisdom of God?* (Grand Rapids, Mich.: Eerdmans, 2011).

40. See Pannenberg, *Systematic Theology*, 1:73–107.

by Christ's humanity (as is found in the work of Eberhard Jüngel, among others).[41]

Nonetheless, it is only with great difficulty that one can allow the preparatory and critical functions of the *praeambula fidei* to remain vacant in Christian theology. Already in Aquinas, the acquisitions of a philosophical theology were taken up by Christian theology as part of *sacra doctrina* so that the *De Deo Uno* accomplishes such an integration without ever developing a natural theology free from the superior light of revelation. Therefore, the illumination of the *praeambula fidei* in the form of a *De Deo Uno* does not necessarily derogate the primacy of revelation and of the *analogia fidei* but quite obviously fulfills indispensable functions in a Christian theology that does not wish to degenerate into a form of mythology and that refuses to allow itself to become an anthropomorphic projection.

If we compare the contemporary emphases with those of Aquinas's epistemology, in addition to the debates concerning the theological integration of potential acquisitions taken over from natural knowledge of God, we must ask about the recentering on Christ's humanity which, in its revealing role, tends to replace the use of created likenesses. It is appropriate to question the implications of a Christocentric centering of revelation: does it sufficiently leave room for the trinitarian finality of God's design? If we deny that likenesses—above all, the human spirit, made in the image of God—have the power of serving revelation by way of analogy, do we not thus declare a kind of arbitrary muting of the trinitarian origin of creation, thereby running the risk of forgetting its trinitarian value by overvaluing a kind of Christological finality?

Nonetheless, we are indeed created to participate in the trinitarian communion and not to fulfill our human aspirations for sublima-

---

41. The most important and insightful criticism of Aquinas's theology is that of Eberhard Jüngel, *God as the Mystery of the World*, esp. 250–81 and 343–51. Nonetheless, the posterity of the Barthian intuition concerning Christ's humanity as the only *vestigium trinitatis* is considerable. Above all, see Barth, *Church Dogmatics* I.1, §8.3, 334; Balthasar, *Theo-Drama* III, 220–29. As an important background text, also read Balthasar, *Karl Barth: Darstellung und Deutung Seiner Theologie* (Cologne: J. Hegner, 1951).

tion, under the influence of a kind of final and exemplary causality coming from the hypostatic union. The goal of divinization does justice to Christ's mediation of salvation history and of the redemption, such that the hypostatic union is not an ontological perfection for which we would have been created. Rather, for God, it is the means for communicating to us the adoptive grace lost through sin and, for us, is our intermediate end, as God wishes to save us by incorporating us into Christ in his Paschal mystery.[42]

42. See François Daguet, *Théologie du dessein divin chez Thomas d'Aquin: Finis omnium Ecclesia* (Paris: Vrin, 2003), esp. 191–239 on the "motive for the Incarnation."

12

─────────·─────────

From Conceptual Rectitude to Truthful Speech *vis-à-vis* God

One of the practical difficulties facing systematic theologians today is an utter eruption in forms of rationality, often presented as being alternative options that can be indifferently used by the theologian. The historical succession of various forms of rationality—metaphysical, critical, phenomenological, hermeneutic, communication, narrative, analytic, and so forth—can lead one to think that the theologian must resign himself or herself to being devoted to one particular current of thought or to accept eclecticism as the only acceptable outlook. Nonetheless, theology cannot completely pledge unflinching loyalty to a particular philosophical school, for the faith that it must render account of transcends the various divisions of human rationality and by rights is addressed to all men. Therefore, can we still today delineate an integral conception of truth in dogmatic theology? Formulated in this way, the question is doubtlessly overly ambitious in its scope. Nonetheless, it delineates an important horizon for the theologian's epistemological reflection.

We have no pretense of here sketching out a prolegomenon to any future theology. Such an undertaking would be an empty and sterilizing enterprise. Every attempt to define the activity of theological reflection must be preceded by a lengthy, effective practice of theology, which only can come to reflect on itself late into its own work—and even then, doing so briefly. The initial guidelines laid out in this domain forever remain provisional, and we must take care to avoid announcing principles and judging their eventual outcomes without undertaking the effort of deploying and effectively exploring them. More often than not, such an effort requires an adjustment of the rules enunciated at the start, if not a true revision of them. Thus, these pages are written as a provisional study of these matters.

What are the decisive parameters of the truth of our statements concerning God? This will be the question guiding us at the beginning of our study. Note that it is limited to statements which are directly concerned with God himself. Obviously, this does not constitute the whole of theology—far from it. However, let us admit that this conceptual register is also most certainly not an innocuous domain of theological language. The "parameters" studied here are diverse. They include at once the foundations, criteria, protocols, and interlocutors engaged in theological statements.

LINDBECK'S *STATUS QUAESTIONIS*

In order to situate more precisely the overall problem which contextualizes this question, let us consider a classification which highlights three decisive parameters that are key reference points for doctrinal truth. In his 1984 work *The Nature of Doctrine: Religion and Theology in a Postliberal Age*, George Lindbeck took up anew the discussion regarding how truth in religious and doctrinal matters should be posed.[1] He believed that the decisive truth parameters vary along the lines of three different models:

- In the propositional model, which was classically that of
  the Western theological tradition and has been taken up
  anew, though in a renegotiated form by contemporary

---

1. See George A. Lindbeck, *The Nature of Doctrine: Religion and Theology in a Postliberal* (Louisville, Ky.: Westminster John Knox Press, 2009).

analytic currents of thought, the criterion of truth would be the objectivity of the reality aimed at, as well as the internal coherence of an ensemble of statements.

- In the liberal model, issuing from nineteenth-century Protestant theology and fostered in Catholic thought in a mitigated form by certain thinkers holding a kind of hermeneutic theology, the principal truth criterion is drawn from the intimate experience of the believing subject. This perspective presupposes that our fundamental religious experience is universal and can be translated into the various doctrinal expressions that maintain a symbolic relationship with a transcendent religious experience. Various beliefs are the projection of a common experience onto various cultural screens, so to speak. Nonetheless, in the end, they remain convertible, given their common anthropological roots.

- In the post-liberal model, doctrinal truth is relative to a system of cultural-linguistic coordinates, and its relevance is above all practical. The criterion of theological truth lays in its relationship with the religious practices at the heart of a delimited confessional community. A statement is true so long as it succeeds in inspiring and ruling the religious life and doctrinal convictions of an ecclesial community which is relatively homogeneous and placed in a particular situation. This practical perspective is unfortunately accompanied by a form of cultivated agnosticism regarding the divine reality aimed at by the doctrinal enunciation.[2]

In the current study, my intention is to argue that the propositional model, judiciously qualified, can integrate into itself the truth that can be found in the other two models, namely the intimate dispositions of the believing subject and the reference to the practices of a community of faith. More positively stated, the propositional outlook can benefit by recognizing the parameters put forward by

---

2. See ibid., 52–53.

the other two models. This task of integration, which must of course be undertaken with discernment, falls to the offices fulfilled by theology as a sapiential discipline. In order to arrive at an "integral" conception of theological truth, we must measure the distance which exists between correctly signifying something about God and attaining God by the mediation of a correctly acquired signification. This will shed light on the notable difference that exists between understanding something and adhering to it. The philosophical atheist can indeed understand the Christian theologian's words without, for all that, intimately adhering to what the latter believes.

This distinction, which has its foundation in Aristotle's philosophical analyses, proves to be useful in theology, for however correct theological statements may be from a formal perspective, they do not lend themselves to any kind of usage whatsoever. They exceed the register of a minimal (although necessary) knowledge and free themselves from being idle chatter, at last reaching their true destination only when the apprentice theologian integrates his knowledge into the theological life of faith and charity.

Christian theology is the discursive elaboration of our human knowledge concerning God, founded on revelation and developed in accord with our capacities. Even more than other objects of knowledge, it is important to know God precisely as he gives himself to be known. Indeed, the internal constitution of an object determines the right method for knowing what pertains to it. I do not here mean "object" in the Heideggerian sense, as something that would be domesticated and mastered by the intellect which posits, measures, and manipulates it. Rather, I simply wish to mark out the priority of the terminus of knowledge over the act of knowledge. When it is a question of knowing God such as he reveals himself, the priority of the object is even more demanding than it is in any other discipline, for God reveals himself as Lord, having a sovereignty that must rule our relation to him, including in our knowledge of him.

What does God offer us in order that we may know him precisely as he gives himself to us? His communication to us is not presented by way of pure intuitions, direct significations, and immediate experiences. Rather, he speaks in human language through the words of scripture.[3] In order to know him in accord with his self-revelation, we have at our disposal an ensemble of origin tales, histories, prescriptive texts, prophetic oracles, the maxims of Wisdom literature, evangelical parables and discourses, narratives telling us of interpersonal encounters, letters to the churches, and so forth. These words are associated with actions, signs, situations, events, and salvific realities. However, note that God already has revealed himself partially in his creative work, thus meaning that we can know him on the basis of the created world, of which we are a part. Nonetheless, the knowledge coming from revelation is superior and integral in comparison to this "revelation" in creation, for the former takes advantage of that part of revelation that is inscribed in the created order.

God reveals himself to us through the intermediary of human words, and thus we are invited to theologize in words, discursively, making use of discourse which is constructed in accord with the rules of human language. The first theologies we can encounter are themselves found within the Bible itself, especially in the various works of the New Testament. They take on a number of genres: narrative, discursive, liturgical, and so forth. However, systematic theology preferably will develop itself in a discursive and argumentative form, for it seeks to explain the objective coherence of what is presented as a matter to be believed in, preached, and contemplated.

The principal source of theology is the word of God, attested to in the Christian Bible and ecclesial preaching. Now, this divine word is embedded within a human form of speech. Therefore, I will discuss the question of theological truth inasmuch as it is, at first glance, the truth of a language, that is, of theological propositions formed out of a subject, a verb, predicates, and complementary verbal components. The path that we will follow requires us to know how God can be attained and not only signified. Therefore, we have chosen to limit our consideration to statements concerned with God himself.

3. See Vatican Council II, *Dei Verbum*, no. 13.

DISTINGUISHING THE RECTITUDE
OF MEANING FROM THE TRUTH
OF A STATEMENT

Following Aristotle, Thomas distinguishes three operations in human intellection: the grasping of what a thing is, judgment which composes (or divides) attributes with a subject, and finally, reasoning which sets forth from an already-known statement in order to acquire new certitude regarding a point that heretofore was unknown.[4] Apprehension is ordered to judgment, and reasoning arrives at a judgment, an enunciable conviction. Thus, according to our complex manner of knowing, judgment constitutes the ultimate terminus of our activity in the discursive register: in the conclusion that it reaches, discursive syllogizing ultimately discerns what is (or is not) truly attributed to a subject.

Following Aristotle, signification, which is more fundamental than judgment, is not of itself submitted to truth or falsity.[5] The intelligibility of a reality (i.e., what it is) is indivisible in reality and is grasped through an act of simple understanding. Its apprehension is either successful or unsuccessful, for one cannot have a half-grasp of that which is simple.

The outcome of apprehension is probably never as clean and clear as Aristotle presents it as being, for it often requires no small preliminary labor. Phenomenology is of use here in its sharpening of our intellectual "perception" by reducing the parasitical notions that blur the intellect's ability to receive the intelligibility of things themselves. This is the benefit drawn from its work of "reduction" to pre-predicative evidences. From Aristotle's perspective, these evidences fall to simple understanding, but the discernment of their truth requires a new act wherein confirmation can be found for the correlation between the reality aimed at and the understanding acquired.

---

4. See Aquinas, *Expositio libri Peri Hermeneias* (Rome: Commissio Leonina, 1989), I, prol.

5. See Aristotle, *Peri Hermeneias*, 1–4.

Thus, the simple understanding of indivisible realities falls short of the opposition between truth and falsity.[6] Indeed, for the intellect, truth resides in the conformity of the acquired meaning with the reality aimed at.[7] Now, judgment has the office of establishing this relationship, and the act of judgment is translated into language in the form of a declarative statement. This is why a statement, not its isolated parts (the noun or the verb), is what is true or false.

Only affirmative or negative declarative propositions that are sufficiently determinate can be true or false.[8] Statements can, of course, take on other forms. Aristotle mentions prayers (i.e., optative statements) and vows. Thomas also notes deprecative, imperative, interrogative, and vocative sentences.[9] Nonetheless, truth is involved and discernible only in declarative statements, for example, in the following: "Man is a mammal," "Pascal always eats breakfast," and "God is the sole Lord of every creature." By rights, such statements are susceptible to verification or falsification.

Before considering more closely the truth or falsity of a complex statement concerning God, we should first examine the element of signification involved in applying a term to God himself, as well as the conditions required for such a term to be applied correctly to him. Indeed, he is not accessible to our simple understanding. Therefore, we must ask whether we have proper significations at our disposal for designating him. The theological application of the analogy of the divine names corresponds precisely to this problem.[10]

The first article of the *Summa theologiae*'s discussion of the divine names carefully sets forth the correlation between words, significations, and things. In his *respondeo*, Thomas refers directly to Aristotle's *Peri Hermeneias*: "Words [*voces*] are signs of concepts [*intellec-*

---

6. See Aquinas, *In I Peri Herm.*, lect. 2, no. 20, which follows Boethius. Also see *In Metaphysicorum*, IX, lect. 11, ed. Marietti, nos. 10–12.

7. See Aquinas, *In I Peri Herm.*, lect. 3, ed. Marietti, no. 31; lect. 7, no. 84. Also, see *De veritate*, q. 1, a. 1; *ST* I, q. 16, a. 2.

8. See Aquinas, *In I Peri. Herm.*, prol.

9. See ibid., lect. 7, ed. Marietti, no. 85.

10. See the remarkable analysis in Rudi te Velde, *Aquinas on God: The 'Divine Science' of the "Summa theologiae"* (Burlington, Vt.: Ashgate, 2006), 95–121.

tus], which themselves are likenesses of realities [*res*]. Thus, it is clear that words are related to the realities that are signified through the mediation of what is conceived by the intellect [*mediante conceptione intellectus*]."[11] This triangulation established among words, concepts, and realities is a matter of great philosophical and theological importance. Certainly, speaking in terms of the genesis of our knowledge of things, the structure of language is an indispensable condition for the emergence of thought. Without a sign, it would probably be impossible to distinguish an idea from a confused heap of impressions and emotions.[12] Nonetheless, once we have sufficiently learned a language and have come to the point when reflection is possible, in the order of perfection, thought is prior to the language which expresses it. Ever enmeshed in our use of language, it is all too easy for us to forget the conceptual mediation existing between words and things. The word does indeed aim at the *res*, but this is only possible through the mediation of a conception. In his commentary on the *Peri Hermeneias*, Thomas explains this fact in the following manner:

It cannot be the case that [words] signify the things themselves, as is clear from their manner of signifying, for the word "man" signifies human nature in abstraction from singulars. Whence, it cannot be the case that it would immediately signify a singular man ... However, because, according to Aristotle's thought on this matter, [human nature] does not subsist in reality as such but exists [with such unity] only in the intellect, Aristotle found it necessary to say that words immediately signify intellectual conceptions and then things through them.[13]

Therefore, our words do not directly grasp onto things, for otherwise they would have a kind of magical efficacy. Their ability to designate things themselves is modulated by the mode of signification to which they are connected. This does not, of course, mean that our words would be reduced to simple labels pasted onto our con-

---

11. See *ST* I, q. 13, a. 1, resp.

12. See in particular Ferdinand de Saussure, *Cours de linguistique générale* (Paris: Payot, 1971), 155. Before him, however, see Augustine, *De Trinitate* XIV.5.7.

13. Aquinas, *In I Peri Herm.*, lect. 2, ed. Marietti, no. 15.

ceptions: through the concept, they aim at signified realities in an effective manner.

Analysis of our language is not limited to a kind of conceptual grammar which would simply suffice as a thematic presentation of our rules for communicating. Moreover, when a word is used or misunderstood, to change it without considering the underlying concepts runs the risk of missing some aspect of the very reality that we are aiming at. Before replacing a term, we must undertake a profound examination of the complete signification that it bears, for that signification mediates its relationship with the signified reality.

In the wake of philosophy's linguistic turn, we risk emptying language of its access to a reality lying outside of itself precisely by analyzing it in a purely functional manner. Thus, our statements would be related to the speaker and to the hearer, not to a reality that is directly aimed at. Above all, language plays the role of establishing a common rule between these two subjects.

From this perspective, the statements of faith would be a grammar of our beliefs and our practices, without however reaching the truth of the mystery aimed at in itself. This is the opinion held by Lindbeck, who thinks that doctrinal statements communicate no information concerning the mystery aimed at through it, but rather only communicate information concerning the language and practices of the human tribe under consideration. Here, he touches on an important point regarding the practical dimension of language; however, he refuses to allow language to have access to a reality that stands outside of human action. By preserving the objective scope of the semantic triangle, we can avoid this pitfall and maintain the contemplative or doxological aim of theological language.

When our words designate not only concrete individuals or particular objects, the *res significata* cannot always be identified with a concrete, determinate, and observable reality. The term "dog" is not limited to only signifying my neighbor's dog. Thus, the reality signified is any dog worthy of the name "dog." Likewise, for more abstract terms like "life" or "goodness," the *res significata* is not the life of this or that thing, plant life, human life, or God's life. Rather, what is signified is the life that is found in all of these occurrences, every time that I make use of this word and its signification to designate the reality of life.

Language's opening onto the *res significata* through the intermediacy of our conceptions enables us to anticipate now how we are able to name God in himself, despite the imperfection of the conceptions that we apply to him. The limitations of our knowledge of God do not do away with the correlation between the names that we give him and God thus aimed at and signified through those names. Although we still do not know his essence, the divine names nonetheless signify God in himself, in his substance.[14] We will return to this point below.

AFFIRMATIVE NAMES IMPERFECTLY SIGNIFY THE DIVINE BEING

We utilize a host of names in speaking about God, invoking him under various titles: the Lord, the Most High, the eternal One, the all-powerful One, he who is, the merciful One, and so forth.[15] As temporal beings, we must have recourse to a number of denominations and predicates designating the various aspects of God such as we know him through faith and reason. If this were not the case, we would already exist in the state of eschatological fullness, and would completely (albeit not comprehensively) know God in his essence under a single name. "If we could understand his essence such as it is and apply a proper name to it, we would express it by means of a single name. Indeed, this is what is promised in the last chapter of Zachariah to those who will see him: 'On that day the LORD will be one and his name one.'"[16] Therefore, we must accept the complexity of our human language as well as the plurality of the di-

---

14. See Te Velde, *Aquinas on God*, 100–101.
15. See Dt 32:4, Ex 34:6.
16. Aquinas, *SCG* I.31.4.

vine names, understand their aim, qualify their diversity, and ensure their complementarity. Nonetheless, how can this language signify and aim at something determinate on the side of God?

Let us reflect more closely on how our manner of knowing things provides a foundation for the way that we name God. According to the semantic triangle, we can name realities to the degree that we know them. Therefore, the modality under which we can name God depends on the way that we know him:

As we showed above [in *ST* I, q.12], we cannot see God through his essence during this life. Rather, we know him on the basis of [our knowledge of] creatures as being related to their principle, as well as through the mode of excellence and negation [*remotio*]. Consequently, we can name him on the basis of [our knowledge of] creatures, though not in such a manner that the name signifying him would express the Divine Essence such as it is [*secundum quod est*].[17]

The naming of God will always be indirect, for it is based on our knowledge of creatures, that is, on our knowledge of his created effects. Given that the names that we apply to God are drawn from material creatures, our manner of signifying remains stamped with the character of this creaturely origin. Thus, the distinction between forms and subjects which we find in the realities with which we are familiar leads us to use concrete and abstract terms when we speak of God, even though there is no distinction between the abstract and the concrete in God. Nonetheless, from our own perspective, this double naming expresses various aspects of God.[18] Our inability to name God in a simple manner manifests our inability to know him in his essence. Our practice of doubling terms in our language nonetheless represents an ingenious response to this difficulty: we are indeed able to name God by combining various aspects which, in us, most often are separate from each other, like simplicity and perfection. This reflects the discursive character of our knowledge of God through theological reasoning.

17. *ST* I, q. 13, a. 1, resp.
18. See *ST* I, q. 13, a. 1, ad 2.

Certain names are applied to God by way of negation. This is the case, in particular, for qualifications like "infinite," "immutable," and so forth. Other names are drawn from God's relation to creatures. Thus, we call him "omnipotent," "creator," or "Lord." The former names "in no way signify his substance but, rather, signify something that he is not [*remotio* alicuius *ab ipso*] or his relation to something else."[19] However, there are indeed names that we say of God in an absolute and affirmative manner (*absolute et affirmative*) such as "good," "true," "wise," "loving," "holy," "unique," "living," "one and triune," "communion," and so forth.

Certain theologians have always likened the latter kinds of names to the first two categories. For some (e.g., Maimonides), these names would signify a negation even though they have an affirmative form: to say, "God is living," would mean that he does not lack life. For others (e.g., Dionysius), it would only mean a causal relation: to say, "God is good" would simply mean that he is the cause of the goodness of his creatures. These explanations are not totally false, but they are, nonetheless, insufficient. Thomas makes this clear from three perspectives. (1) These opinions do not explain why certain names are applied to God and not others: must we say that God is a body, given that he is the cause of bodies? (2) These opinions suggest that the names applied to God always belong to him in a secondary manner in relation to what he creates. (3) Those who speak about God do think that this is what they are saying: when they say that he is living, they do not thereby mean to express a simple negation or something that belongs to him only because he is a cause. This is why we need a different explanation for the use of these absolute and affirmative names:

Terms of this kind do indeed signify the divine substance and are predicated substantially of God, though they fall short in their capacity to represent him [*deficiunt a repraesentatione ipsius*]. This clearly must be so, for names signify God in accord with the way that our intellect knows him. Now, since our intellect knows God on the basis of [our knowledge of]

---

19. *ST* I, q. 13, a. 2.

creatures, it thus knows him inasmuch as creatures represent him. However, we showed above that God embraces within himself all the perfections of creatures, as it were, simply and in a universally perfect manner. Whence, to the degree that any creature represents him and is like unto him, it likewise has some perfection. However, this does not mean that it would represent him as something of the same species or genus but, rather, as a transcendent [*excellens*] principle, whose form is only imperfectly found in his effects. Nonetheless, they retain some kind of resemblance to him, just as the forms of inferior bodies represent the sun's power. Thus, the aforementioned names signify the divine substance, though imperfectly, just as creatures represent it imperfectly.[20]

We know God positively on the basis of the likenesses of his perfections that can be found in creatures. Our concepts' manner of signifying (*modus significandi*) thus remains very imperfect, for creatures present us with only a very imperfect likeness of their author.[21] We must be clear-eyed about the gap that exists between the way our significations are acquired and their openness to the universal and to God. Having recognized the inadequacy of our manner of signifying, we can nonetheless say that the divine reality is itself signified affirmatively and not only in a negative or causal manner.

When we apply positive names to God, we aim, through the way of eminence, at the uncreated perfection of which created perfections are only distant likenesses:

Therefore, when we say, "God is good," we do not mean, "God is the cause of goodness," or "God is not evil," but rather, that what we call goodness in creatures first exists in God, though indeed in a loftier manner. Whence, it does not follow that God is good because he causes goodness but, rather, on the contrary, because he is good, he pours fourth goodness into things, according to the words of St. Augustine, "Because he is good, we exist."[22]

Therefore, eminence is what founds the causality involved here and not causality which measures the affirmative naming of God.

The names that we are considering here are applied to God in

20. *ST* I, q. 13, a. 2, resp.
21. See *ST* I, q. 13, a. 2, ad 2.
22. *ST* I, q. 13, a. 2, resp.

their proper sense. To understand this point, we must distinguish between the signification itself and the manner of signifying (*modus significandi*). We know God on the basis of the created perfections that have their source in him, and we know that they preexist in him in a super-eminent manner. Nonetheless, our intellect grasps these perfections as they exist in creatures. Moreover,

> in the names that we attribute to God, we must consider two things, namely, the very perfections signified (such as goodness, life, and other such things), and their manner of signifying. Therefore, with regard to what names of this kind signify, they properly do belong to God, indeed, doing so in a more proper sense than they do to creatures, being said of him by way of priority [*per prius*]. However, as regards their manner of signifying, they are not properly said of God, for they have a manner of signifying that is suited to creatures.[23]

If we can distinguish between the imperfect manner of signifying attached to our concepts and their own proper signification, they do indeed bear upon God himself. If we cannot discern the difference between their signification and their manner of signifying, we will be forced to use names whose signification remains metaphorical, for such a signification would be entirely enclosed within the material world of creation which surrounds us.[24]

Our ability to perform the necessary discernment between the *modus significandi* and the signification itself proves to be absolutely decisive for the rectitude of our theological discourse. Without this, we could never successfully distinguish between metaphors and analogies, between poetic language and rational discourse. Thus, we would be forced to accept a structural anthropomorphism in theological language, all the while invoking the very logic of the incarnation in order to justify it. On the other hand, without this key distinction, we risk disqualifying all of our knowledge of God on account of its inevitably imperfect character.

Are the multiple affirmative names that we use for God syn-

---

23. *ST* I, q. 13, a. 3, resp.
24. See *ST* I, q. 13, a. 3, ad 1 and ad 3.

onyms? In this case, our speech about God would be an empty verbal accumulation. Once we admit that absolute names signify the divine substance, though in an imperfect manner, we must recognize that they signify with different meanings. Indeed, we will always need to bear in mind our human manner of knowing God, both in the names that we give him or in those that he reveals to us:

The formal notion [*ratio*] which the name signifies is what the intellect conceives concerning the reality signified through the name. Now, when our intellect knows God on the basis of its knowledge of creatures, it forms for such knowledge of God conceptions proportioned to the perfections which creatures receive from God. These perfections preexist in God in a united and simple manner, whereas they are received in creatures in a divided and multiplied manner. Therefore, just as one, simple principle corresponds to the various perfections of creatures, with that principle being represented in various and manifold ways through the various perfection of creatures, so too something one and entirely simple corresponds to our intellect's various and multiple concepts, with that one, simple thing being grasped imperfectly by means of these concepts. And therefore, although they signify one reality, the names attributed to God are not synonyms, even though they do indeed signify him in accord with multiple and various formal characters [*rationibus*].[25]

The diversity of our conceptions and denominations for God is not something purely subjective on our part. It arises from the fact that his simple and unique perfection is reflected with a real diversity in the creatures he has created. The diversity of creation provides the foundation for the diversity of the names that we apply to God. It is always one and the same God who is aimed at with these names, though this aim is oriented by the various formal characters [*raisons diverses*] drawn from the consideration of creatures who participate in the divine perfection in various ways. This need not shatter our discourse or reduce it to tautological assertions. Rather, it should lead to a multifaceted form of discourse that always seeks to have its notions converge toward this unity in God.

In Aquinas's own works, analogy is more so a practice used by

25. *ST* I, q. 13, a. 4, resp.

the Angelic Doctor rather than a theory which he explicitly elaborated. In our common use of language, we readily make use of analogy. However, this practice possesses metaphysical foundations which must be clarified. On the level of language, analogy lies between univocity and equivocity. Univocity connects two different realities by using a single term (and notion) for both of them, as is the case, for example, in generic univocity: the term "boat" as applied to a canoe and to a motor-driven recreational water vessel. Equivocity connects two identical terms without any relationship on the level of signification, for example, "pound" as describing an action of one's hand on a hard surface and "pound" as a unit of weight. Nothing can be attributed to God in a univocal fashion, for God does not produce effects that are equal to himself.

The multiplicity and diversity of the created perfections coming from him found the various formal characters: wisdom, goodness, power, essence, existence, etc. While they are indeed distinct from one another when they are applied to us, they are not really distinct when they are applied to God. Thus, "when the word 'wise' is said of man, it in some way circumscribes and embraces the reality that it signifies [*quodammodo circumscribit et comprehendit rem significatam*]. However, this is not the case when it is said of God, for then it leaves behind the signified reality as being unembraced, exceeding the name's signification [*relinquit rem significatam ut incomprehensam, et excedentem nominis significationem*]."[26]

Therefore, analogy is not a kind of domestication of God, enabling us to objectify him so that we might enclose him within our created horizons. It does not represent a rational domination of what God means, so to speak.[27] And yet, for all that, we can indeed signify God, for the act of signifying implies an intellectual gaze that is open to that which is universal. The names at once attributed to us

26. *ST* I, q. 13, a. 5, resp.

27. In the strict sense, ontotheology presupposes the univocity of the concept of being, as a kind of response to the desire to have a flawless certitude in our knowledge of God. It is after Thomas's own day, with thinkers like Henry of Ghent and John Duns Scotus, that this path was followed. See Olivier Boulnois, *Être et représentation*, 223–91.

and to God are not attributed in a univocal manner, but instead have different significations. However, does this mean that they are purely equivocal? Assuredly not, for otherwise we could have no knowledge of God in human language. This is refuted merely by the fact of a divine revelation made in human words which are not deprived of the significations that they draw from our field of experience. Thus, we have this middle solution: analogy, the proportion of one term to another or of many terms to another.

Therefore, we must say that names of this sort are said of God and creatures by way of analogy, that is, through a kind of proportion. Now, this happens in names in two ways. On the one hand, many things may have a proportion to one thing, just as health is said of medicine and urine inasmuch as both have a relationship and proportion to the health of an animal, which is caused by the former and has the latter as a sign of the fact that the animal is healthy. On the other hand, analogy can occur because one thing has a proportion to another, as health is said of medicine and an animal, inasmuch as medicine is a cause of the health that is in the animal.

Medicine is called healthy because it causes the health of the animal, whereas urine is a sign of the state of the animal's health. Therefore, a direct relationship does not exist between urine and the medicine. Nonetheless, they are both relative to the animal's health. This common reference explains the analogy between the healthy medicine and the healthy urine, even though medicine and urine are not both contained within the same genus of realities. Thus, analogy constitutes a mode of predication by means of which the limits of one genus are exceeded so that a predicate may be applied outside of its original genus.[28] Let us see how such a linguistic practice is applied to the divine names:

It is in the latter fashion that certain things are said of God and creatures analogically, and not by way of pure equivocation or univocation, for we can only name God on the basis of our knowledge of creatures, as we said above. Thus, whatever is said of God and creatures is said inasmuch as there is a kind of ordering of creatures to God, as to their principle and

---

28. See Rudi te Velde, *Aquinas on God*, 111.

cause, in whom all the perfections of things preexist in an excellent manner. And this mode of community is a kind of middle between pure equivocation and simple univocation, for in things that are said equivocally there is neither a single formal character [*ratio*] as happens in univocation, nor totally diverse formal characters, as happens in univocation. Rather, in analogical predication, there is a name that is said in many ways, signifying various proportions to some one thing, just as health signifies being a sign of an animal's health when it is said of urine and signifies being a cause of it when it is said of medicine.[29]

Theologically, the analogy between the divine names and the predicates drawn from creatures takes place following several characteristics brought to light as regards the example of health. (1) God is named in an indirect manner on the basis of our knowledge of creatures to the degree that creatures are referred to him as to their unique, ultimate cause. (2) Nonetheless, God and creatures do not enter into a common genus. When a term is applied to God, it is used outside of the genus whence it draws its original signification.[30] Moreover, God and creatures are not related to each other as though they belonged to two different genera. God exceeds every genus as the transcendent principle of all genera.[31]

The analogy of the divine names drawn from creatures fundamentally stems from the creative causality, by which all the created perfections that are scattered throughout all the various genera preexist by way of eminence in God who possesses them in a simple manner: "Thus, whatever is said of God and creatures is said inasmuch as there is a kind of ordering of creatures to God, as to their principle and cause, in whom all the perfections of things preexist in an excellent manner."[32] Between God and creatures, the analogy of predicates is not exercised through a reference to a third term, like that existing between healthy medicine and healthy urine, both of which are related to the animal's health. No third term exists to

---

29. *ST* I, q. 13, a. 5, resp.
30. See Rudi te Velde, *Aquinas on God*, 112.
31. See *ST* I, q. 4, a. 3, ad 2.
32. *ST* I, q. 13, a. 5, resp.

which God and creatures could be related in some indirect way, for God transcends all genera. Here, analogy is established directly from one term to the other, like the analogical relationship of healthy medicine to the health of the animal, that is, in this particular case, from the cause to that which comes from that cause.[33]

In order to describe the kind of likeness implied in the analogy between the divine names and the predicates drawn from creatures, we must refer to *Summa theologiae* I, q. 4, concerning the divine perfection, where Thomas examines the likeness between creatures and God. As every agent exercises its own, proper activity through its form, it communicates a likeness of its form to its effects. When the effect is of the same species as the cause, the likeness is greatest, as when man begets man. In this case, we speak of the exercise of univocal causality. If the effect enters into the same genus as the cause, without however partaking in its species, the likeness will be less perfect, as when the sun confers light and heat to plants. Finally, it can happen that the cause and the effect do not enter into any common genus, and this is precisely the case for the likeness between God and creatures in the case of creative causality:

Therefore, if there is an agent that is not contained in a genus, the likeness of the effect to the agent's form will be even more distant, and it will not participate in the likeness of that form according to the same specific or generic formal character but, rather, will do so according to a kind of analogy, just as existence itself is common to all things. Thus, all created things that come from God, inasmuch as they are beings, are rendered like unto him as to the first and universal principle of all existence.[34]

The likeness between God and creatures is not a formal likeness, on the level of essence, but rather is a likeness as regards *esse*—not that existence would be a kind of genus embracing God and the creature as a common term but, rather, analogically, inasmuch as a God is the ultimate and universal principle of every created being. It is not

33. See Rudi te Velde, *Aquinas on God*, 113. Also see Gottlieb Söhngen, "La sagesse de la théologie par la voie de la science," in *Mysterium salutis. Dogmatique de l'histoire du salut* (Paris: Cerf, 1969), 4:159–250, at 197.

34. *ST* I, q. 4, a. 3, resp.

through their essence or their particular, limited mode of existence (*esse*) that creatures have some degree of likeness to God but, rather, from the perspective of their concrete *esse*, which depends upon God for its actuality.

The various perfections found in created beings are perfections of existence so much so that existence indicates their analogical unity and their common reference to their unique origin in God. The perfection of existence is comprehensive, for it is the actuality of all the various perfections spread out throughout diverse creatures. The analogy of divine names is thus founded on the analogy of existence (*esse*).[35]

INTEGRAL TRUTH IN RELATION TO GOD

Let us now attempt to shift this epistemological scaffolding somewhat toward a more comprehensive, "integral," conception of theological truth. Through the use of analogy, we have at our disposal possible means for signifying God in a correct manner, not that we would comprehend him, utterly understanding every aspect of him, but by indeed signifying him from a given, specific perspective. Let us return to the relationship between apprehension and judgment. The act of judgment has the office of establishing the relationship of a predicate to a subject in order to gauge its adequation to reality. Moreover, it is proper to judgment (and to the statement that it expresses) to be true or false. When it is a question of knowing God, we cannot remain within the acquisition of an analogical signification but must go on to use judgments and statements, indeed relating such judgments to one another through causal reasoning so as to establish the full structure of the analogy by which he is known.

---

35. See Aquinas, *De Potentia*, q. 7, a. 2, ad 9; *ST* I, q. 4, a. 1, ad 3; Rudi te Velde, *Aquinas on God*, 115–18. Concerning the way that the *actus significandi* exceeds the *ratio concepta*, as well as the objective foundation of analogical knowledge of God, see the diachronic study (issued in 1952) in Edward Schillebeeckx, "The Non-Conceptual Intellectual Dimension in Our Knowledge of God according to Aquinas," in *The Collected Works of Edward Schillebeeckx*, vol. II: *Revelation and Theology* (London: Bloomsbury, 2014), 207–38.

In this way, we can speak of God, and our interlocutors can discern and debate about the truth or falsity of what we think.

The act of signifying God by means of a given name (a subject or predicate) does not constitute the satisfying terminus of our knowledge of God. To invoke him under a simple name falls to prayer, not to theological discourse. If we possess the capacity for signifying God, this is naturally in view of truly aiming at him and, indeed, reaching him. Now, we can signify him in a correct yet "insignificant" manner without the knowing subject being engaged in the names and statements that he wields. One's phrases can quite certainly remain objectively true, but the act of signifying has no ontological bearing, for the reality in question is neither intentionally aimed at nor really reached. Indeed, the intentionality of the aim in knowledge presupposes an application of the intellect, that is, an act of the will.

According to the theology of grace and its virtues, the acts of the life of the theological virtues are intrinsically characterized by the fact that they receive God himself as the intentional object of our knowledge and love. Already, the act of faith does not terminate in this or that creedal statement but, rather, in the divine reality itself.[36] Faith, hope, and charity have God himself, in his mystery, as their principal object.[37] In this sense, they are analogous to virtues, for in him they attain the *ultimate* measure of our acts.[38] From three complementary and ordered perspectives, the acts of our life in the theological virtues truly attain God himself: "However, faith and hope indeed attain God inasmuch as knowledge of the truth or the attainment of the good comes to us from him, whereas charity attains God himself so that we may take rest in him, not so that something may come to us from him. And therefore, charity is more excellent than faith and hope."[39]

Therefore, to signify God in a way that truly takes him as the in-

36. See *ST* II-II, q. 1, a. 2, ad 2.
37. See *ST* II-II, q. 17, a. 4, resp.; q. 23, a. 3, resp.
38. See *ST* II-II, q. 17, a. 1, resp.
39. *ST* II-II, q. 23, a. 6, resp.

tentional object of knowledge presupposes faith. Without faith, our words, statements, and reflections can only have our own conceptions and idea of God as their object, without really aiming at the reality at stake, that is, God. An atheist can very well understand everything that the Christian expresses concerning his knowledge of God, but he does not adhere to that which he considers. The act of adherence is a different act from that of signifying. Charity is presupposed for us to signify God in a way that does not merely aim at him but also attains him at whom one aims through the intentionality of knowing.[40] We can manipulate our conceptions of God or be aware of things regarding him without loving him. However, we cannot truly know him—in the fullest sense of the term—without loving him.[41] In these conditions, *our ability to signify God does not reach its goal without grace.*

We can verify this conviction very easily. We can signify God without either aiming at him or attaining him. This is why we are able to discuss and debate at length about him without ever really being concerned with him. This is the difference between chatting about God and speaking of God. In the first scenario, the formal rectitude of our significations and statements is not inscribed within the truth of a judgment that at once involves the knowing subject and the known object.

Thus, the integral truth of a theological statement should take into account the intimate dispositions of the person who speaks. In this way, we can partially make room for the parameter that is privileged by the liberal model of theological language, not on the level of a radical and common experience at the foundation of every true expression, but rather on the level of the profound interior dispositions of the subject in relation to the reality signified by a theological statement. For example, the affirmation that "the Lord God is the only

40. See *ST* I, q. 12, a. 7, ad 1.

41. On the contrary, when the blessed know God in the beatific vision, they cannot hate him. See *ST* II-II, q. 34, a. 1, resp.; *Sup. Rom.* 8:7, ed. Marietti, no. 622; Jean-Yves Lacoste, "The Knowledge and Love of God: Beyond 'Faith and Reason,'" in *The Appearing of God*, 68–90.

Lord" takes on its integral truth only when it remains accompanied by the existential translation of it that immediately follows in Deuteronomy: "You shall love the LORD your God with all your heart, and with all your soul, and with all your might" (Dt 6:5). These two biblical formulas must not be separated. Conceived in this way, the truth reaches God in a true manner only if it is confirmed by an ethical disposition and, let us also note, a communal practice (here, the exclusive adoration within a living tradition).

Indeed, we cannot describe the ethical dispositions of the subject of theological discourse without likewise emphasizing the need that he be engaged in relation to the signified reality through some form of effective practice. This connection is suggested by the very text of Deuteronomy 6:5, which joins the heart and soul to the power, ethical disposition, and intimate choice of self-engagement with God. In this way, we also are able to retrieve the parameter privileged by the post-liberal model, namely, the need for a practical confessional engagement with God. The practice determined at the heart of a local community is assuredly one of the criteria of the truth of one's words pronounced concerning God. For the Catholic theologian, inclusion within a local community is the same as belonging to the universal church and implies his or her inclusion in the activity of the tradition of the divine word in all of its dimensions. And yet, for all that, the truth of statements concerning God cannot be primarily evaluated in function of its sway over the real practices of the members of the community. The validity of a theological statement is not discernible through a simple juridical hermeneutic, as would be, for example, the relevance of a jurisprudential decision.

Thus, we have passed from the objective truth of the statement to the broader conditions for its integral truth: the intimate dispositions of the subject and communal practice. These are not the immediate and primary parameters of theological truth, but they nonetheless remain very important. However, they play different roles for him who speaks and for him who hears. The statement, "There is only one God," will remain true in all circumstances for the hearer of a theological discourse, for this statement is conformed to the divine reality. God remains uniquely one, whatever our dispositions in relation to him may happen to be and whatever we may think or do. Nonetheless, for the person who pronounces such a claim, the achievement of the truth—and not a mere acquisition of the signification at play in the statement—presupposes a true theological engagement, for it is a question of God himself. "He who says, 'I know him,' but disobeys his commandments is a liar, and the truth is not in him" (1 Jn 2:4). In theological matters, the true judgment that aims at God and indeed attains him will always be a judgment of living faith, which takes up the signification regarding the divine reality expressing it with its full meaning and force. Such a judgment will only reach its terminus if it ultimately comes from the wisdom that is conferred by God himself, a gift which disposes the heart and of itself calls for a practical living of the divine life of grace.[42]

Whatever may be the importance accorded to the integral truth of our words in relation to God, we cannot renounce the fundamental conception of theological truth assured by the propositional model. Indeed, in preaching and teaching, all of the true statements in which the orator is not himself truly engaged from the perspective of the life of the theological virtues, through his own relationship to God attested to by the practice of this love for his neighbor, can indeed be of use for those who hear him, but they remain ineffectual for him who speaks, even to the point of risking his own condemnation. He may chat on and on about him with his empty rhetoric, but the conformity of his statements to God can always be grasped profitably by those who, through and by the significations thus acquired, truly do discover and reach God.

Therefore, we must maintain an important distinction between this integral truth of theological statements and their essential, objective truth. Indeed, statements can be recognized and held as being objectively true even when he who pronounces them is obviously disconnected from the truth to which these statements refer. This

---

42. See *ST* II-II, q. 45, a. 3, ad 1.

distinction is critically important and must be maintained, for it enables the hearer to receive the truth of a speech all the while discerning that the dispositions or practice of the speaker are unfortunately inadequate to the truth that he proclaims. Absolutely speaking, it is desirable that truth be proclaimed by a true witness, but this is not always the case. Nonetheless, the truth still remains audible and discernible. Therefore, we must guard against completely shifting the center of gravity of theological truth toward authenticity, practice, personal witness, or holiness as the essential criterion of the truth of theological statements.[43] However, he who makes a theological statement should seriously be concerned about his relationship to what he says.

THE PARAMETERS NEEDED FOR AN
INTEGRAL TRUTH IN THEOLOGY

We now are well-situated to present a brief recapitulation of the parameters of the integral truth of a discursive theology that uses statements regarding God. This sketch gathered together the stages through which we have passed, beginning with the fundamental point at hand. It has attempted to honor our initial project of integrating the decisive parameters which are often considered in a disconnected manner, if not in a way that sees them as being mutually exclusive. Finally, let us note, however, that we should explore the variables that need to be introduced when we discuss not only statements concerning God but also ones concerning the other truths of the faith, such as Christ's humanity, the grace conferred upon man, the sacraments, and so forth. Indeed, in these cases, the reality to be attained is at once closer to our experience and more complex, something reflected in the fact that in their cases, we find ourselves forced to multiply the analogies that we employ in our theological

---

43. Here, let us note Aquinas's comments in *ST* I, q. 16, a. 4, ad 3, regarding the non-equivalence of, on the one hand, the virtue of truth, the truth of life and the truth of justice, and, on the other hand, *veritas communis*.

discourse. Be that as it may, let us here simply (and provisionally) reformulate the principal foundations and parameters of the truth of statements concerned with God himself:

- Upon God's initiative, the adoption of human speech by divine revelation, attested to by biblical speech.
- The orientation of the intellect toward being, which founds the dynamic of the semantic triangle.
- Our ability, on account of the creation of the world by God, to produce analogical significations which pass beyond created limitations without, for all that, overcoming our inability to represent the divine reality.
- The requirement that our statements concerning God must have coherence and must be able to be integrated into the full ensemble of our faith's affirmations. This responds to a true need expressed by reason and likewise reflects the organic character of the truths of faith.
- The faith and charity of the speaker and/or of the hearer enable them to aim at and attain God through the significations that we have at our disposal.
- The verification of the effective sway of statements related to God through the ethical dispositions and concrete practice that they demand. This implies membership in a confessional community—inserted into the universal church in Catholicism—and inclusion within a determinate practice (one that is liturgical, charitable, etc.).
- The eschatological orientation of theological discourse, whose complexity will, in the end, be brought back to unity in the beatific vision. This enables us to accept the imperfection and complexity of our knowledge of God and to maintain an authentic hope for the believer's understanding.

13

The Practice of
Trinitarian Theology as
Wayfaring Pilgrims

Trinitarian theology must bear witness to the fact that it remains a theology of wayfaring pilgrims (*theologia viatorum*).[1] It is well aware of its infirmities. Aiming at the loftiest of all realities, discursive thought knows quite well that it is infinitely surpassed by them and therefore maintains a kind of measure in its pretenses. This state of affairs holds true not only in trinitarian theology but is also found in other domains of Christian theology, particularly in eschatology. The immediate difficulty is foundationally the same in all such cases: how are we to speak about that which has not yet been completely unveiled to human knowledge, well aware too that vision itself will not deliver a complete comprehension of the divine mysteries?

It is well known that Thomas holds that *sacra doctrina*, which is articulated in theology in particular, is a science that is at once

1. Aquinas does not use this suggestive expression. It is particularly esteemed in the Protestant tradition as an expression emphasizing the incomplete character of every theology here below while we are *viatores*, in the state of being on the way. See Richard A. Muller, *Dictionary of Latin and Greek Theological Terms Drawn Principally from Protestant Scholastic Theology* (Grand Rapids, Mich.: Baker Academic, 2006), 304.

speculative (i.e., contemplative) and practical. It is primarily speculative[2] for it is concerned with the loftiest truths, the divine truths
revealed by God about himself.[3] However, it also has a "practical"
aspect to the degree that it is likewise concerned with the acts and
means needed for arriving at eternal beatitude, which itself principally consists in knowing God fully.[4] As it elaborates the loftiest
form of judgment (*judicare*) and discerns the order of all things to
their ultimate end (*ordinare*), *sacra doctrina* is wisdom in the highest
degree.[5] Thus, theological science involves the exercise of a sapiential manner of knowing.

In order to describe trinitarian theology as being a theology of
wayfaring pilgrims, we must ask about the relationship between trinitarian theology and eschatological beatitude. However, it is fitting
that we begin by illuminating an objective correlation which exists
between divine beatitude and the mystery of the Trinity. Our theological hypothesis is as follows: the mystery of the Trinity is the unfolding of what is enclosed within God's beatitude; moreover, the
theological gaze at the trinitarian mystery is itself a movement toward the divine beatitude.

Therefore, we find ourselves faced with a relatively technical
question: when reading the *Summa theologiae*, how should we interpret the inconspicuous progression from the final question on
God's essence, dedicated to the divine beatitude (q. 26), to the first

2. In Aquinas, the term "speculative" (in reference to Aristotle) is essentially the
same as "contemplative" (in reference to Christian sources). See Servais T. Pinckaers,
"Recherche sur la signification véritable du terme 'spéculatif,'" *Nouvelle Revue Théologique*
81, no. 7 (1959): 673–95, esp. 690–94.

3. The closing words of the very first prologue in the *Summa theologiae* eloquently manifest the limitations involved in the discursive side of the speculative enterprise:
"With trust in divine assistance, we will strive to set forth briefly and clearly those things
that pertain to sacred doctrine, to the degree that the material will allow us to do so [*secundum quod materia patietur*]."

4. See *ST* I, q. 1, a. 4, resp.; a. 5, resp.

5. See *ST* I, q. 1, a. 6, resp. and ad 3. To describe the functions of wisdom, Thomas
weaves together three sources (namely, Aristotle, Augustine, and Paul) and combines
theoretical activity with ethical ordering. See Bernard Montagnes, "Les deux fonctions
de la sagesse: ordonner et juger," *RSPT* 53, no. 4 (1969): 675–86.

question on the Trinity, dedicated to the two trinitarian processions (q. 27)? In order to better negotiate this delicate passage from God's essential beatitude to the Trinity of the divine Persons, we must analyze the conflict between Thomas Aquinas (d. 1274) and Richard of St. Victor (d. 1173) regarding the status of the "reasons" utilized in trinitarian theology. A precise textual study bears witness to the fact that Thomas increasingly distanced himself from Richard's argument whereby the Victorine theologian deduced the Trinity from the divine beatitude (the latter being conceived of as a perfect felicity in the possession of the divine goodness).

For Richard, God's beatitude and felicity demand that the mutual love of the Father and the Son be opened up to a third friend (*condilectus*), the Holy Spirit.[6] Before formally evaluating such an argument, let us try to find the fulcrum points in questions 26 and 27 of Aquinas's *Summa theologiae* so that we may thus be able to envision another possible way of articulating the relationship between the God's essential beatitude and the Trinity.

FROM ESSENTIAL BEATITUDE TO THE TRINITY OF PERSONS: WHAT ARTICULATION?

Before designating our ultimate happiness (i.e., our integral contemplative activity super-elevated through the vision of God and union with him), the term "beatitude" expresses a characteristic of God's very own being.[7] In the *Summa theologiae*, the subtreatise on God considered in his essential perfections is brought to its con-

---

6. See Richard of St. Victor, *De Trinitate*, ed. Gaston Salet, SC 63 (Paris: Cerf, 1999), II.116 and III.3, 12, 17 (138–41 and 170–73, 194–97, 207). Also, see Bonaventure's own use of this argument in *Sent.* I, d. 2, a. un., q. 2, arg. 1. The thesis holding that "there is no joyful possession of a good without the presence of a companion" is drawn from Seneca, *Epistulae ad Lucilium* I.6.4. For a study of the sources and the genesis of Richard's trinitarian theology, see Pierluigi Cappiapuoti, "Deus existentia amoris," in *Teologia delle carità et teologia della Trinità negli scritti di Riccardo di San Vittore* (✝ 1173) (Turnhout: Brepols, 1998).

7. See *ST* I, q. 26, a. 3, resp. Here Aquinas distinguishes the object of the act from the act itself.

clusion with a discussion of his beatitude, which is identical with God's essence and life.[8] The fact that this is how Thomas concludes his discussion of God's essential attributes calls for thorough reflection on our part.

Must we conceive of the singular continuity between the divine beatitude (q. 26) and the Trinity (q. 27) as being something quasi-fortuitous, to the degree that question 26 is primarily connected to the subtreatise on the divine essence, which comes to a close with this very discussion of beatitude? Or, rather, must we think, by contrast, that the ultimate consideration concerning God's sovereign beatitude in himself constitutes the best possible point of connection between the subtreatise concerned with the divine essence and that which is concerned with the distinction of the Persons in God? Interpreting this adjacency of God's essential beatitude and the Trinity is so delicate a matter that we here find ourselves caught between a Scylla and Charybdis, being tempted either to hold that the adjacency is a case of pure juxtaposition or to fancy that a deduction is performed at this point of connection.

Aquinas's theological epistemology requires us to immediately cast aside any fanciful desire to deduce the Trinity on the basis of this or that attribute of the divine essence. More precisely, Thomas did not give in to the logical force of so-called necessary reasons enabling such a deduction. Indeed, through the course of his career, he critiqued, with increasing clarity, Richard of St. Victor's way of speaking about such necessary reasons, which Aquinas also found in a developed form in Bonaventure's writing. Likewise, Aquinas explicitly refutes the Ricardian thesis holding that the divine unity would require the trinitarian plurality on account of the perfection of the divine beatitude.[9] We will consider his criticism in a moment.

However, once we have identified Aquinas's epistemological pre-

---

8. Already, see *SCG* I.100–102 (the final three chapters).

9. See *ST* I, q. 32, a. 1, ad 2, which responds to Richard of St. Victor, *De Trinitate* I.1–4.

caution, it remains appropriate to ask about the relationship between the affirmation of the divine beatitude and trinitarian faith which enables us to understand something new about it, not in virtue of any kind of necessity whatsoever but, rather, according to a fulfillment by way of a kind of non-necessitated expansion. It is possible to show that our initial understanding of the divine beatitude does not come away unscathed by its adjacency with the first question of the treatise on the Trinity dedicated to the *processiones* in God.

As a kind of reflective experiment, I propose to illuminate this connection by making use of two key notions, namely, *sufficientia* which defines beatitude (from the very beginning of q. 26) and *fecunditas* which provides a summary of the two processions (at the end of q. 27). At the end of his study of the divine essence, Aquinas explains beatitude by way of analogy with the sufficiency (*sufficientia*) which accompanies the perfect knowledge that God has of himself in his own proper goodness.[10] Consequently, the blessed will find in God the *sufficientia* of all goods.[11]

Thomas forms this analogy based on the notion of *sufficientia* from two conjoined sources, one philosophical and the other drawn from the Gospels.[12] In one and the same *sed contra* in his commentary on the fourth book of the *Sentences*, he refers to the *Nicomachean Ethics* on the one hand, "Felicity or beatitude is the good wherein *sufficientia* [*autarkeia*] is found *per se*,"[13] and to the words of the fourth Gospel on the other, "Lord, show us the Father, and this will be enough [*sufficit*] for us."[14]

---

10. See *ST* I, q. 26, a. 1, resp.; also see a. 4, resp.

11. See *ST* I-II, q. 4, a. 8, ad 2.

12. See Aquinas, *Sent.* IV, d. 49, q. 1, a. 1b, s.c. 4, citing the two phrases referred to below.

13. See Aristotle, *Nicomachean Ethics* I.5.1097b6–21 and X.7.1177a27–b1. See Aquinas, *In I Ethic.* I.9, ed. Leonine 47.1:32–33. On the vision of God's *sufficientia* in relation to all human desires, see *SCG* III.63.

14. Jn 14:8. In his scriptural commentary on John's Gospel, Aquinas comments on the words "this will be enough for us" in the following manner: "To see the Father is the end [*finis*] of all our desires and actions, so that nothing more would be needed" (*Sup. Io.* 14:8, no. 1883). This does not mean that there would be "more" to be seen in the Father than in the Word. Indeed, the same "sufficiency" (*sufficientia*) is encountered in

At the beginning of the *Ethics*, Aristotle shows that the highest good not only is something that is chosen for its own sake but also is something that brings self-sufficient goodness along with itself. This *autarkeia* is not limited to the needs of one man by himself, leading a solitary life, but rather, must be extended to his familial circle and to that of his fellow citizens. At the end of the *Ethics*, this characteristic trait of happiness holds true in its loftiest manifestation in the contemplative activity of *theoria*,[15] even if it also needs to be provided for on the level of economic and political activity.[16]

Thomas transposes to God the contemplative dimension of *autarkeia*.[17] In order to articulate how he understands the divine *sufficientia*, it is helpful to refer to the *Summa contra Gentiles*, where Thomas establishes that joy (*gaudium*) and pleasure (*delectatio*) find their loftiest realization in God: "Joy and delight are a kind of resting by the will in its willed object. Now, God, who is his own principal willed object, is most supremely at rest in himself as containing complete sufficiency [*sufficientiam*] in himself. Therefore, through his will, God rejoices in himself and delights in himself."[18] God thus experiences the full enjoyment of his own essential goodness through perfect self-knowledge as well as through his will's complete taking of rest in himself.

This point is illuminated anew in light of the trinitarian faith

---

knowledge of the Father and in that of the Father (see *Sup. Io.*, 14:9, no. 1889; Augustine, *De Trinitate* I.8.17). Therefore, the explanation of the *sufficientia* here calls for a trinitarian focus.

15. See Aristotle, *Nicomachean Ethics* X.7.1177a27–b1.

16. In particular, see Aristotle, *Politics* I.2.1253a2 and III.9.1280b32.

17. It might seem that this bold use of terminology bears witness to an excess of confidence being placed in Aristotle's philosophy by Thomas. We can wonder whether it is "advisable" today to envision beatitude in this way before making its trinitarian dimension explicit. This is not a merely theoretical question, for it possesses an important ecumenical dimension, given that the Aristotelian way of proceeding clashes with the way that Orthodox and Protestant theologians think about these matters.

18. *SCG* I.90.4. The final section on the divine beatitude refers in particular to this chapter on the divine joy and delight. See *SCG* I.100.5, 102.3, 102.9. For the distinction between *gaudium* (affective union) and *delectatio* (effective union), see *SCG* I.90.7. For a discussion of God's rest as being *sufficientia* in himself, see this discussion as it is already formulated in *Sent.* II, d. 15, q. 3, a. 2, resp.

when we come to envision the *processio* of the Word in the depths of the divine knowledge so that we may then also recognize that it is accompanied by the *processio* of the Spirit as love—something that is justified by the progression of articles found in question 27.[19] In this unique, perfect Word and in this unique, perfect love, we find a complete manifestation of the sovereign fecundity (*fecunditas*) of God in himself.[20] The divine plenitude and fecundity come forth and reveal themselves in their fullness in the two eternal acts of the Father, namely the generation of the Son and the procession of the Spirit, as Aquinas maintains in the final response (ad 3) in question 27.[21] Indeed, here we see the explicitly trinitarian dimension of God's perfect *sufficientia* in his knowledge and possession of his own goodness.

The progressive shift from *sufficientia* to *fecundias* is not subject to a necessary reasoning process from one to the other, but instead is brought about by what we might call a "logic of non-necessitated expansion." The theologian who considers the divine essence cannot remain there with the *sufficientia*, as though it constitutes the last word of the treatise on God, and yet, for all that, the *fecunditas* cannot be deduced from the *sufficientia*. While the former deploys the latter's effective content and manifests its trinitarian configuration, the *fecunditas* nonetheless remains a separate affair, for it falls within revelation's superior illumination. The *sufficientia* is the

---

19. See *ST* I, q. 27, aa. 1, 3.

20. See ibid., a. 5, ad 3. According to the *Index Thomisticus*, there are about seventy occurrences of *fecunditas* (or *foecunditas*) in Thomas's authentic works. The use of the term in trinitarian contexts is not frequent. With the exception of the important ending to q. 27, it is almost exclusively encountered in his commentary on Dionysius's *De divinis nominibus*. This motif plays a much more important role in Bonaventure of Bagnoregio, to whom Thomas implicitly responds in the response to the third objection above. On this topic, see Emmanuel Durand, "L'innascibilité et les relations du Père, sous le signe de sa primauté, dans la théologie trinitaire de Bonaventure," *Revue thomiste* 106, no. 4 (2006): 531–63; Durand, "Le Père en sa relation constitutive au Fils, selon saint Thomas d'Aquin," *Revue thomiste* 107, no. 1 (2007): 47–72.

21. On the importance of this affirmation, see Emmanuel Perrier, *La fécondite en Dieu. La puissance notionnelle dans la Trinité selon saint Thomas d'Aquin* (Paris: Parole et Silence, 2009).

ontological-ethical index of the divine beatitude, whereas the *fecunditas* unveils the twofold deployment of the divine life's plenitude, to which we have access through the revelation of the Trinity.

Of itself, *sufficientia* does not call for fecundity as a necessary development of its conceptual content. However, once God's fecundity is posited through our understanding of the trinitarian faith, we can establish a mutual interrelationship between the two notions. By itself, *sufficientia* would present us with the deformed image of a God who indeed is contemplative but who likewise is solitary and cut off from the world. However, fecundity by itself and without *sufficientia* could not protect itself against a deviant utilization of emanationist schemata, like that found at the root of Arianism or in the erroneous doctrine holding that creation was necessary.

Elsewhere, Thomas explains that God's joy consists in the very love that the Father makes rest upon his Son, who in his own generation receives the entire essential goodness of God.[22] The Spirit comes forth from this love of the Father for the Son, and he returns to the Father through the Son in the mutual love through which the latter responds to the Father.[23] Thus, the one God's beatitude and *sufficientia* are not those of a solitary God but, rather, are the beatitude and *sufficientia* of the triune God. Therefore, theological understanding of the divine beatitude receives a kind of elaborative unfolding which is brims with meaning in light of its close proximity with the first question of the treatise on the Trinity. The passage from beatitude to the Trinity is accompanied by a particularly interesting kind of reillumination of the former by the latter.

In order to understand this correlation more fully, it is now useful to deepen our consideration of the epistemological dimension of the problem. We will see how Richard of St. Victor conceived of the necessary sequence leading from God's perfect beatitude to the trin-

22. See *Sup. Mat.* 3:17, ed. Marietti, nos. 998–99; 17:5, nos. 1435–36. Also, see *De potentia*, q. 10, a. 4, ad 18.

23. See *De potentia*, q. 10, a. 4, ad 10. On the procession of Spirit as love, see Emmanuel Durand, *La Périchorèse des personnes divines. Immanence mutuelle, réciprocité et communion* (Paris: Cerf, 2005), 217–64.

itarian distinction of persons, as well as why Thomas critiqued the Ricardian position on this matter with increasing resolve.

THE EPISTEMOLOGICAL
CONFLICT BETWEEN AQUINAS AND
RICHARD OF ST. VICTOR

Throughout his works, Thomas refers to Richard of St. Victor when determining, on the one hand, how it is that something that we know can also be held on faith,[24] and on the other hand, whether the Trinity is accessible to natural knowledge.[25] Each time, Aquinas cites (or suggests in a relatively precise manner) a delimited extract from the first book of Richard's *De Trinitate* wherein the Victorine theologian expresses himself in this way: "In fact, I am absolutely convinced that in order to explain any of the realities whose existence is necessary, there are plenty of arguments which are not only plausible but even ones that are necessary, even though they may remain hidden from our perspicacity for the time being."[26] Before examining the way Aquinas uses this passage, let us begin by briefly situating it within Richard's theological project.

The Logic of Richard's
Necessary Reasons, as He Himself
Explains It

The prologue of the Richard of St. Victor's *De Trinitate* concludes, "Let us not consider the notion of things of eternity—which we re-

---

24. See *Sent.* III, d. 24, q. 1, a. 2, qla., arg. 3 and resp. 2, ad 3; *De veritate*, q. 14, a. 9, arg. 1 and ad 1.

25. See *Sent.* I, d. 3, q. 1, a. 4, arg. 3 and ad 3; *Super Boetium De Trinitate*, pt. 1, q. 1, a. 4, arg. 7; *ST* I, q. 32, a. 1, arg. 2.

26. Richard of St. Victor, *De Trinitate* I.4, SC 63, 71: "Credo namque sine dubio ad quorum libet explanationem quae necesse esse, non modo probabilia, imo etiam necessaria argumenta non deesse, quamvis illa interim contingat nostram industriam latere." English translation taken from Richard of St. Victor, *On the Trinity*, trans. Ruben Angelici (Eugene, Ore.: Cascade, 2011), 75 (slightly modified)

ceive only by faith—alone to be sufficient, if we do not also learn that notion which our intellect can offer, since we are not yet able to receive knowledge from direct experience."[27] The first chapter of the first book establishes the method to be followed in order to acquire a fuller understanding of the truths of faith. We must not give up too quickly when faced with a common impression: "Actually, some of these truths we are required to believe appear to be not just *above* reason, but rather *contrary to* human reason, if they are not deeply and thoroughly investigated, or rather if they are not made manifest by divine revelation."[28] The final nuance is quite instructive: the rational investigation remains submitted to the illuminative power of divine revelation. Indeed, the task of overcoming the apparent contradictions between faith and reason would first of all belong to the domain of what revelation is capable of doing.

However, quite inappropriately, it is most often the case that one cheaply relies on faith and authority without mobilizing reasoning or rational argumentation. Rather than counseling such facile reliance upon faith, Richard holds that faith's surety actually enables us to acquire an increased understanding of the truths of faith. The ways to be followed in such an enterprise are clarified in the third and fourth chapters of the first book of his *De Trinitate*. To know these truths, we must first of all "enter through faith" (*per fidem intrare*), so that we can then "progress day by day in the understanding of these truths that we hold by faith."[29] Such an acquisition anticipates the contemplative joys of eternal life.

However, Richard makes an important distinction between the truths of faith which are concerned with eternal realities and truths of faith relative to what God does in time (in particular, the mysteries of redemption). Only the former truths can be attained through necessary reasons, whereas the others are simply proven in a factual manner by experience without being able to be reached at the con-

27. Richard of St. Victor, *De Trinitate*, prol. (*in fine*) (69, slightly modified).
28. Ibid., I.1 (73, slightly modified).
29. Ibid., I.3 (75).

clusion of an *a priori* chain of reasoning. The *De Trinitate* is only concerned with truths of faith related to eternal realities:

Therefore, as much as the Lord will allow us, our intention in this work will be to adduce not only plausible reasons to support that which we believe, but rather, necessary ones and to corroborate the teaching of our faith by the clarification and explanation of the truth. In fact, I am absolutely convinced that in order to explain any of the realities whose existence is necessary, there are plenty of arguments which are not only plausible but even ones that are necessary [*Credo namque sine dubio ad quorum libet explanationem quae necesse est esse, non modo probabilia, imo etiam necessaria argumenta non deesse*], even though they may remain hidden from our perspicacity for the time being. Everything that has received its existence in time, by the good pleasure of the Creator, is capable of existing or not existing: therefore, and for this reason, its existence is not really arrived at through reasoning but, instead, is proven through experience. However, eternal realities necessarily must exist: just as they have always existed, certainly they will also always exist. Indeed, they remain constantly what they are and cannot be something else, nor can they exist in another manner. However, it seems completely impossible that things that are necessary would lack a necessary reason. However, it is not within any soul's capability to bring these reasons to light from the profound and mysterious bosom of nature, making them common knowledge after having pulled them up, so to speak, from the inmost recesses of wisdom.[30]

That which is absolutely necessary must not lack necessary reasons for itself.[31] Presupposing the surety of faith, these reasons are to be sought out in created nature, which offers hidden resources for arriving at eternal truths. Therefore, we now see the theological epistemology developed by Richard in the first pages of his *De Trinitate*. Let us remember that the quest for "necessary reasons" does not arise from a vein of pure rationalism in his thought but, instead, presupposes a vigorous and sure faith, which moreover has the last

---

30. Ibid., I.4 (75–76, slightly modified).

31. On Richard's direct sources (primarily Anselm of Canterbury and Hugh of St. Victor), see the complementary note by Gaston Salet in SC 63 (Paris: Cerf, 1999), 465–68. In this note, the final citation of Aquinas is not representative of the latter's complete evaluation of the Ricardian thesis. See note 40 below.

word when it is a question of overcoming a possible contradiction between faith and reason.

Aquinas's Criticism of Necessary Reasons Drawn from God's Beatitude

Let us now consider how Aquinas uses and interprets the principal affirmation of Richard's project (underlined in the selection cited above). We must first note that the Ricardian enunciation is only ever found in the series of objections which Aquinas opposes to himself in order to elaborate his own, proper responses. This manifests the substantial reticence that he feels in relation to the Victorine theologian's thesis.

Let us begin by studying a text in which Thomas responds to the question of knowing whether the Trinity can be known on the basis of natural knowledge. From its first occurrence in his *Commentary on the Sentences*, Aquinas refuses to say that the Ricardian affirmation can be understood *universaliter*. An objection musters the Victorine's affirmation in support of the idea that we can naturally know the Trinity, and Aquinas responds to it in the following manner:

If Richard's dictum is understood in a universal manner, meaning that every truth could be proven by reason, it is expressly false, for first principles, which are self-evident, are not proven. However, if certain things are known in themselves, though they are hidden from us, they are proven by those that are more known from our perspective. Now, the effects of the principles are what are more known from our perspective. However, the Trinity of persons cannot be proven on the basis [of our knowledge] of created effects, as we have already said. And therefore, it remains the case that they cannot be proven in any way, and all the reasons invoked are accommodations [made for our minds] rather than reasons arriving at a necessary conclusion. Indeed, were it the case, *per impossibile*, that there no longer was a distinction of persons in God, the highest goodness, beatitude, and charity would still remain in him.[32]

---

32. Aquinas, *Sent.* I, d. 3, q. 1, a. 4, ad 3.

Here, Aquinas simultaneously counters Richard as regards the logical validity of his project and as regards his applications [of such necessary reasons] based on divine goodness, beatitude, and charity. Contrary to what Richard holds, necessary realities do not refer us to necessary reasons which would be accessible to us. Instead, such first principles are imposed upon us without being able to be the object of an *a priori* demonstration. According to the epistemology that Aquinas draws from Aristotle,[33] principles cannot be the object of a scientific demonstration but instead fall under a simple intuitive grasp exercised by the intellect in its knowing of a *per se nota* enunciation, an "induction" comparable to the passage from the particular to the universal.

After undergoing a significant reworking, this general Aristotelian schema underlies Thomas's conception of *sacra doctrina* as being our knowledge of God articulated on the basis of principles received from divine revelation and gathered together in the articles of faith. Theology does not possess evidential knowledge of its principles, but instead receives them from faith, whose own affirmation of these truths is based upon the authority of God who reveals himself. The theological development of such knowledge forms a science subordinated to the knowledge that God has of himself and that which the blessed have of him.[34]

Having set aside every possibility of there being an *a priori* demonstration of such truths, Thomas observes that we must also exclude the possibility of an *a posteriori* demonstration in the case of the Trinity, as he showed in the response. Thus, the general thrust of the solution was to emphasize that "natural reason knows God only on the basis of creatures." Now, "everything that is affirmed about God in relation to creatures is related to the essence and not to the persons."[35] Therefore, natural knowledge can only arrive at knowl-

---

33. See Aristotle, *Posterior Analytics* II.19.99b15–18; in *The Complete Works of Aristotle*, ed. and trans. Jonathan Barnes (Princeton, N.J.: Princeton University Press, 1995), 1:165–66.

34. See *ST* I, q. 1, aa. 1–2. Also, see *Super Boetium De Trinitate*, q. 2, a. 2, resp.

35. Aquinas, *Sent.* I, d. 3, q. 1, a. 4, resp.

edge of the attributes of the divine essence and not at knowledge of the Trinity of persons. If it touches upon the Persons, this is only done in an indirect manner through the process of appropriation, by means of which essential attributes such as power, wisdom, and goodness are attributed to one person in particular.[36]

Let us now consider two texts wherein Thomas asks whether faith can be concerned with something that is an object of knowledge. In his treatise on faith in the third book of the *Sentences*, he rejects the idea it can *per se* be concerned with something that is known, even if it in fact is the case that revelation also offers man truths that are accessible to reason.[37] Using an analogy based on the dependence of an inferior, subalternating science upon a superior, subalternating one, Thomas here expressly recalls that faith receives its principles from the divine authority without being able to prove them, for God alone knows their proper reasons. Consequently, "Richard's point [concerning the reasons for faith] must be understood as indicating a proof that is not completely probative in nature but, instead, is persuasive in some way."[38] Note that Thomas here retains the persuasive value of such arguments. He will come to renounce this position later in his career.

In the parallel textual *locus* found in the *De veritate*, Thomas concedes to Richard that the truths of faith, inasmuch as they are known, have necessary reasons, even though they remain hidden from us. This is why "the reasons for the objects of faith are unknown to us, though they are known by God and the blessed, who see them in vision, not in faith."[39] In this way, Aquinas saves Rich-

---

36. However, do not forget that appropriation constitutes an accommodation that is not only legitimate but, indeed, is quite welcome, for it is founded on a true affinity (*convenientia*) existing between the *common* [attribute] which is known and the *proper* [one] aimed at by means of the process of appropriation. See *ST* I, q. 45, a. 6, ad 3. Also, see what Aquinas writes already in *Sent.* I, d. 31, q. 1, a. 2, resp.

37. See Aquinas, *Sent.* III, d. 24, q. 1, a. 2, sol. 2.

38. Ibid., ad 3: "verbum Richardi intelligendum est de probatione non sufficienti, sed aliquo modo persuadenti."

39. Aquinas, *De veritate*, q. 14, a. 9, ad 1: "unde rationes credibilium sunt ignotae nobis, sed notae deo et beatis qui de his non fidem sed visionem habent."

ard's affirmation by reinterpreting its final restrictive clause: the necessary reasons "remain hidden from our perspicacity for the time being," in the sense that they will be unveiled before our sight only in the beatific vision of God. For his part, Richard understood this period of delay as existing between the common apprehension of the truths of faith and the achievements gained through extensive theological investigations.[40]

At last we come to the question of the *Summa theologiae* where Aquinas examines anew whether natural reason can arrive at knowledge of the Trinity (*ST* I, q. 32). Thomas's central argument remains the same as the one that he developed early in his career in the *Commentary on the Sentences*. Here again, the key phrase from Richard appears in advance in an objection,[41] illustrated by three arguments frequently advanced in order to prove the Trinity of Persons: first, the infinity of divine goodness is communicated infinitely in the procession of the Persons; second, joyful possession of goods does not take place without being shared in common; and third, the Trinity of Persons can be manifested on the basis of our knowledge of the procession of the word and of love in our spirit—the last is precisely the Augustinian path that Aquinas himself followed.

Thomas's response to the objection makes an important distinction between two types of reasons: "sufficient reasons" and "reasons of fittingness." The latter do not prove the primary datum (*radix*) in a sufficient manner, but once this datum is posited, such arguments show that the resulting effects "are fitting" (*congruere*) in relation to it.[42] The first kind of reasons enable us to prove in particular that

40. Therefore, even though it may be tempting, it is not legitimate to cite the text from *De veritate* as bearing witness to the idea that Thomas approves of the Ricardian doctrine of necessary reasons. Nonetheless, this is what Gaston Salet does in his supplementary note concerning the "necessary" reasons in SC 63:468. Moreover, as we will soon show below, ultimately, in the *Summa theologiae*, Aquinas goes so far as to deny even their persuasive value.

41. See *ST* I, q. 32, a. 1, ad 2.

42. At first sight, it can seem disconcerting to speak about "reasons of fittingness" in this way in trinitarian theology, for the Thomist tradition particularly made frequent use of this (multiform) type of reasoning in theology concerned with the divine economy, in particular in Christology. Nonetheless, the use of arguments from "fittingness" (which

God is one, whereas it falls to the second kind to "manifest" the Trinity, for once the latter has been posited, these reasons are "fitting" in relation to it. Thus, we see the non-probative character of each of the three reasons advanced in the objection:

God's infinite goodness is also manifested in the production of creatures, for to produce from nothing is an act of infinite power. Indeed, if God communicates himself in his infinite goodness, it does not necessarily follow that something infinite would proceed from God, but rather that it would receive the Divine Goodness according to its own mode.—Similarly, too, when it is said that there cannot be any joyful possession of a given good without it being shared in fellowship, this holds only when perfect goodness is not found in a person and hence needs the good of another person joined together with him so that he may have the full goodness of joy.—Finally, the likeness with our intellect does not prove something about God in a sufficient manner on account of the fact that the [formal character of the] intellect is not found univocally in God and in us. Hence, Augustine says (*In Ioan.* 6:64) that we arrive at knowledge through faith and not vice-versa.[43]

In Thomas's opinion, the first two arguments are not suitable for manifesting our faith in the Trinity, for they can easily be overturned and, consequently, expose this faith to contempt—a risk that he explicitly decries in the body of his response. The third argument, drawn from Augustine, concerning the likeness of the word and of love does, however, have a role to play in its rightful place as providing a suitable manifestation of the trinitarian faith.

Therefore, we must recognize that Thomas ultimately strips the so-called necessary reasons even of their persuasive value, something that he had accorded to them earlier in his career in his *Commentary on the Sentences*. Such a use of these arguments would risk being disastrous for the faith, for first of all, these reasons cannot

---

Aquinas synonymously calls "congruence") is a decisive element of Aquinas's epistemology in trinitarian theology. See Emery, "Trinitarian Theology as Spiritual Exercise," 1–40; Gilbert Narcisse, *Les raisons de Dieu. Argument de convenance et Esthétique théologique selon saint Thomas d'Aquin et Hans Urs von Balthasar* (Fribourg: Éditions universitaires, 1997), 50–51.

43. *ST* I, q. 32, a. 1, ad 2.

have a logically rigorous probative force, and moreover they can even enable the nonbeliever to arrive at a conclusion opposed to faith in the Trinity. To respect Richard's intention, we must however recall that the Victorine theologian never thought that the reasons that he advanced could be used without some faith-derived premise.

As a result of this epistemological clarification, we understand what motivated Thomas's resistance to anything appearing to be a deduction of the Trinity on the basis of the divine beatitude. Therefore, we cannot envision the connection that he formed between the section of the treatise on God devoted to the divine essence (qq. 2–26) and the section devoted to the distinction of the divine Persons (qq. 27–43) as being a necessary passage or some kind of deduction from the divine unity in the direction of the Trinity. If, as we showed at the beginning of our study, beatitude in fact receives a kind of non-necessitated expansion in intelligibility from question 27 concerning the two trinitarian processions, beatitude does not of itself demand that it be unfolded in a trinitarian fashion, contrary to what Richard argues.

Now, going beyond the theological interpretation of the adjacency of questions 26 and 27, we must broaden our gaze over the whole *Summa theologiae* in order to perceive how beatitude plays an astounding role as a guiding principle for the *expositio fidei*. This will confirm that Aquinas's discursive theology, as speculative as it may be, can be considered as being the model for a theology of wayfaring pilgrims. This is eloquently clear even in the organic distribution of the material contained in this theology.

THE PURSUIT OF

BEATITUDE STRUCTURES THE *SUMMA*'S

THEOLOGICAL EXPOSITION

The attraction of the divine beatitude does not only function as the teleological lodestar for the entire economy of our knowledge of God, of which theology is an integral part, but it also leaves its mark upon the formal structure of a complete theological exposition.[44] In fact, we find ourselves faced with the orientation toward the divine beatitude at decisive points of articulation of the *intellectus fidei* proposed by Aquinas in his masterpiece.

Let us briefly look at the prologues of the *Summa theologiae*, for they offer us a view of the overall architecture of the work as it unfolds into its various parts. This enables us to recognize that theology is here conceived and exposited from a perspective that guided by the economy of salvation. Indeed, the entire unfolding of the *Summa theologiae* reveals itself as being commanded by a sure perception of the internal logic of God's benevolent plan.

Thus, let us remember that the structure of the *Summa* as a whole is dynamic, for "God is the principle and end of all things, especially of the rational creature." Thus, in sequence, it will discuss:

- God: the divine essence, the distinction of the divine persons, and the procession of creatures
- The rational creature's movement toward God on the basis of his condition as being made in God's image.
- Christ, who as man is the way leading us to beatitude in God[45]

At the threshold of the *Secunda pars* (concerning man's movement toward God), Thomas emphasizes that everything in this part will be explained in relation to the end and that "the ultimate end of human life is beatitude."[46] Finally, at the threshold of the *Tertia pars*, he recalls that Christ "is revealed to us as being the way of truth by which we can arrive at the beatitude of immortal life through the resurrection."[47] Thus, the proposed itinerary forms a circuit which

---

44. For a rich contribution on this subject, undertaken from the perspective of moral theology, see Dalmazio Mongillo, "Les béatitudes et la béatitude. Le dynamisme de la *Somme de théologie* de Thomas d'Aquin. Une lecture de la Ia-IIae, q. 69," *RSPT* 78, no. 3 (1994): 373–88.

45. See *ST* I, q. 2, prol.

46. See *ST* II, prol.

47. See *ST* III, prol.

joins back to its principle inasmuch as the beatitude communicated to man by Christ the savior consists in man's glorious participation in the divine beatitude itself.

According to the *intellectus fidei* which emerges from the *Summa*'s structure, God's plan principally consists in granting bodily and spiritual creatures a new ultimate end, namely, the divine beatitude itself, participated in through the resurrection and eternal life. The finality pursued by God through all of his gracious initiatives remains the communication of his own life and the sharing of his own beatitude. Thus, God offers himself to his creatures in a supernatural way as their true *bonum beatificans*.[48]

Everything done by God is conducted in view of such beatitude, including the adequate remedies and responses for man's sin. Christ does not intervene in salvation history like an ontological marvel with a kind of self-sufficient value, finalizing creation. Nor does he intervene like a superman who through his mere existence would wipe out all the failures and detours of human history. Rather, he is the one who raises us from sin and, in his person, reopens the way toward God the Father and to his beatitude, which is shared with man.[49]

TRINITARIAN THEOLOGY AS AN INTELLECTUAL DOXOLOGY

Having now come to perceive the epistemological choices brought to bear when we interpret the relationship between the divine beatitude and the mystery of the Trinity, it is fitting to briefly take stock of what we have achieved in this brief study, as well as of the distinctive traits of trinitarian theology as a theology of wayfaring pilgrims. Thus, we can formulate several theses:

---

48. See *ST* I, q. 60, a. 5, ad 4.

49. See Luc Devillers, "Le sein du Père. La finale du prologue de Jean," *Revue biblique* 112, no. 1 (2005): 63–79.

- Trinitarian theology cannot proceed by way of "necessary reasons," but instead develops the use of "reasons of fittingness" in view of more fully perceiving and manifesting the truths that we know by faith.
- The aim of the divine beatitude orients the entire development of trinitarian theology and places its stamp upon the key articulation points of an organic exposition of the faith.
- Nonetheless, the trinitarian mystery cannot be deduced through a simple analysis of the divine beatitude as the ultimate attribute of the divine essence.
- Trinitarian theology reveals the real content of the divine beatitude, namely the twofold, intradivine fecundity, as well as the mutual relations through which the plenitude proper to the living and triune God eternally unfolds.

The contemplative aim of trinitarian theology determines how its concepts and arguments should be properly deployed. Even though a treatise on the Trinity does indeed require instruction in the grammar of trinitarian language or conceptual formulations, it cannot be simply reduced to this. It must be conceived as being a sapiential exercise in purifying our representations of the triune God, having as its end a better contemplative perception of the revealed truth as well the acquisition of the ability to eliminate potential errors regarding the Trinity.[50]

In the life of faith, the practice of trinitarian theology by us wayfaring pilgrims represents a speculative moment organically connected to contemplation of God in the Christian life, and it contributes to triangulating [*objectiver*] the ultimate end which is presupposed by Christian prudence as it orients the believing subject's activity.

Thus, trinitarian theology is truly a theology *in via*, at once contemplative and practical. Its perceptions are weak, but with a serene patience, it accommodates the human mind to a consideration of the

---

50. See Emery, "Trinitarian Theology as Spiritual Exercise," 1–40.

loftiest of all realities. Its speculative task, accomplished by the modest ways of "fittingness," nonetheless constitutes an eminent domain in which the believing subject's dignity is exercised. Indeed, the clear distinction which Thomas establishes between faith and reason finds a corollary in the proper dignity of created reason in its ability to actively receive the gift of revelation. Its orientation toward full vision of God is impressed within it by faith, hope, and charity, which are presupposed for any theological undertaking and can take possession of the labor that it requires. In this way, trinitarian theology leads, at least at certain moments of its unfolding, to a form of intellectual doxology, at once arduous and joyful, as well as animated by an authentic intellectual hope.

14

Should the Cross
Be the Sole Revelation
of the Trinity?

The question formulated in the title of this chapter justifies, to my mind, major reworkings of trinitarian theology from the contemporary period. More precisely, such a question could conduct a debate, from a distance, between Hans Urs von Balthasar and Thomas Aquinas. Over and above the centuries, it would be possible to bring them face to face concerning their different ways of conceiving, for example, person and mission, the fruitfulness of the Father, the role of the Spirit, etc.

I prefer, however, to note a more radical divergence on the epistemological plane, with respect to the foundation of a trinitarian analogy, and then to illuminate the trinitarian function of the mysteries of Jesus, which preoccupied each theologian in his own time. Aquinas and Balthasar are indeed two great theologians who undertook an integral theological rereading of the life of Jesus. Here I do not propose to undertake a textual exegesis of Aquinas as a response critical of "troubling" or "doubtful" innovations in Balthasar. In concert with St. Augustine, I will begin by sketching out the issue at hand. Next, I will charitably read and interpret the thought of Balthasar concerning this matter, yielding some benefits and raising a fundamental problem. Finally, I will close by drawing an insight from Aquinas in order to make a forward-looking proposal.

THE MOMENTS OF TRINITARIAN WITNESS, ACCORDING TO AUGUSTINE OF HIPPO

To clarify the unity and aim of my overall proposal, centered on the mode of trinitarian revelation and manifestation, let us begin by gathering the logic of the rule of trinitarian faith handed on by Augustine. Let us briefly recall several points. At the beginning of his treatise *De Trinitate*, Augustine declares his intention to defend the substantial or essential unity of the Father, the Son, and the Spirit. In the first books, he tries to respond to the Arian objections in opposition to the unity and equality of the three Persons.

To begin, he recalls and reformulates the rule of trinitarian faith such as he has received it through the Fathers and his other predecessors.[1] It possesses an elaborate and instructive theological structure that I render as follows:

- The unicity of God: one single substance, indivisible, whence one single God.
- The distinction of the three Persons through the incommunicable properties of each: the Father alone begets; the Son alone is begotten; the Spirit alone belongs to both the Father and the Son.
- The differentiated action or manifestation proper to each in the New Testament: the birth of the Son, his crucifixion, burial, resurrection, and ascension; the manifestation of the Spirit at the baptism and at Pentecost; the manifestation of the Father at the baptism, the transfiguration, and the announcement of glory.
- The inseparability of the three Persons in their differentiated but conjoined action-manifestation.

---

1. See Augustine, *De Trinitate* I.7.

According to the structure of the rule of faith handed on by Augustine, the distinction of the three Persons does not depend on their differentiated manifestation, but rather on the eternal acts and properties enunciated above. Nevertheless, their eternal distinction is attested by certain events in the history of salvation. Augustine assembles the following events under this or that facet: birth, baptism, transfiguration, announcement of glory, crucifixion, burial, resurrection, ascension, and Pentecost.

In virtue of the inseparability of the three Persons, each of these scenes could no doubt be studied as an integral trinitarian unveiling,[2] but Augustine suggests here that what is proper to each is attested in a determinate, concrete way in this or that event. This or that revelatory facet of the mysteries of Christ in reality pertains to the singular mode of presence or action of one of the three. There is no moment *par excellence* for the trinitarian manifestation, even less an exclusive moment. None of the events mentioned appear to loom brightly over the others. For Augustine, the sequence of public trinitarian attestation extends from Christ's birth to Pentecost. It thus practically embraces the whole of the trajectory of Christ Jesus such as it is recounted in the four Gospels and then in the Acts of the Apostles.

Through the remainder of the first four books in *De Trinitate*, Augustine shows that the theophanies of the Old Testament do not afford sure access to the distinction of the three Persons. It is only through the incarnation and Pentecost that the Son and the Spirit are identifiable as sent by the Father. The economy of trinitarian revelation thus stretches between the two beacons of the incarnation of the Son and the Pentecost of the Spirit.

Augustine's rule of faith is a common foundation that makes it possible to frame our background question: how is God the Trinity engaged in the mysteries of Jesus? The mysteries here are understood in the broad sense of salvific events related to the incarnation, life, and Passover of Christ Jesus.

2. See ibid., IV.30.

Such an inquiry makes it possible to situate and honor the contribution of several contemporary trinitarian theologies. In my opinion, there has not been a radical reshaping of triadology since Basil of Caesarea or Augustine of Hippo. If we step across a few centuries for a moment to consider contemporary trinitarian theologies, leapfrogging Bonaventure and Aquinas, and then Luther and Calvin, one of the main concerns of recent theologians has been to take a fresh look at a strong link between the eternal Trinity and the economy of salvation. Let us now interrogate the theology of Balthasar regarding the deployment of the relationship between the Trinity and the cross.

THE CROSS, THE PROPER PLACE OF TRINITARIAN REVELATION IN BALTHASAR

In *Theo-Drama IV: The Action*, Balthasar states that the doctrine of the Trinity can only be developed by beginning with the cross. The cross will then be understood to include the resurrection, though it will designate, above all, the abandonment lived in fidelity to Calvary.[3] In *Mysterium Paschale*, Balthasar stated more clearly that the revelation of the Spirit ultimately shines forth in the resurrection. This led him to conclude that, while being prepared by the opposition of wills during the agony and the abandonment by the Father on the cross, the revelation of the Trinity is properly accomplished by the resurrection.[4] Comparatively, in the *Theo-Drama*, the trinitarian exposition seems almost exclusively centered around the moment of Calvary. Indeed, Balthasar judges that there, "for the first time," the "distance" between the Father and the Son is made manifest in the dereliction of Jesus. The terms chosen are decisive: the theologian seeks the "first" explicit trinitarian epiphany, and he traces it to when Father and Son are presented under the mode of dis-

---

3. See Balthasar, *Theo-Drama* IV, 317–32.

4. See Balthasar, "Mysterium Paschale," in *Mysterium Salutis. Grundriss Heilsgeschichtlicher Dogmatik. Das Christusereignis* III.2, ed. Johannes Feiner and Magnus Löhrer (Einsiedeln: Benziger Verlag, 1969), 269–81.

tance. Two questions arise: Why such a focus on the cross? Why such an attraction to "distance"?

**FROM THE IMPASSE OF THE IMAGE
TO THE LAW OF GIFT**

Balthasar is disappointed by the Scholastic and modern avatars of the Augustinian analogy (mind, knowledge, love; memory, intellect, will, etc.). This image has led to the formalism of a Trinity conceived according to the cleavage of the human mind: the begetting of the Son by way of intellectual operation, and the procession of the Spirit by way of a voluntary impulse. Aquinas and his epigones were thus caught in the snare of the *mens* (mind). The moderns have only accentuated the projection of solipsism onto God. They have rethought the Trinity by the yardstick of the absolute subject who takes possession of himself according to a simple divine self-mediation. This amounts to plunging deeper into the same rut that ensnared Scholastic thinkers.

At the beginning of his article entitled "Der Heilige Geist als Liebe" (The Holy Spirit as Love), Balthasar emphasizes the thinness (or weakness) of the scriptural foundations of the Augustinian analogy, according to which the Son is begotten by way of knowledge, while the Spirit proceeds by way of love.[5] In Johannine literature, love is the love of the Father for the world and for the Son, manifested to the world by the sending and the offering of the Son, while the Spirit has rather a function of teaching and discernment. In Pauline literature, the appropriation of love to the Spirit is not applied in a clear and unequivocal way. The Spirit is often associated with the power (*dunamis*) of God. He also makes it possible to confess and recognize the Lord.

The Augustinian analogy thus seems to be a gratuitous theolog-

---

5. See Hans Urs von Balthasar, "Der Heilige Geist als Liebe," in his *Skizzen zur Theologie III: Spiritus Creator* (Einsiedeln: Johannes Verlag, 1967), 106–22. My attention was drawn to this text by Vincent Holzer, *Hans Urs von Balthasar* (Paris: Cerf, 2012), 136–39.

ical fabrication. There is nothing normative about it; however, it is substituted for New Testament revelation by governing the Western representation of the Trinity. For Balthasar, the trinitarian unfolding is explained entirely by the ecstatic and fecund love of the Father. This seems more in conformity with the New Testament, where love runs through the whole trinitarian economy without, however, being appropriated to the Spirit.

To reconnect with the New Testament economy of trinitarian revelation is to recognize that the Father's love is at the beginning of all trinitarian fructification. Love is the heart of the Trinity and, like absolute love, it is the eternal gift of self. The Father is identical to this gift. He does not lose himself, he does not reserve himself. He is gift as dispossession of self to extreme abandonment. In a word, paternal love is eternally primordial *kenosis* (*Urkenosis*).

The only support mentioned by Balthasar for treating the Father's "self-exteriorization" as *kenosis* is the idiosyncratic thought of Sergei Bulgakov. Surprisingly, Balthasar does not seek to found such an intuition on the New Testament. It must be recognized that the assertion of a primordial *kenosis* of the Father ultimately comes from the way in which the theologian conceives the intrinsic logic of extreme love in the act of giving: excess or plenitude, abandonment or *kenosis*, and envelopment.[6] It belongs in some way to the internal law of love given to pass through self-abandonment. Applicable to us, it would also be applicable in the highest degree to the Trinity, starting with the Father.

6. On the law of gift or extreme love, see Pascal Ide, *Une Théologie de l'Amour. L'amour, centre de la* Trilogie *de Hans Urs von Balthasar* (Brussels: Lessius, 2012); Ide, *Une Théo-logique du Don. Le don dans la "Trilogie" de Hans Urs von Balthasar* (Leuven: Peeters, 2013); Michele M. Schumacher, *A Trinitarian Anthropology: Adrienne von Speyr and Hans Urs von Balthasar in Dialogue with Thomas Aquinas* (Washington, D.C.: The Catholic University of America Press, 2014).

THE SALVIFIC FUNCTION
OF AN INFINITE DISTANCE
ETERNALLY OVERCOME

Thus the begetting of the Son by the Father implies a paternal abandonment. For Balthasar, it is the establishment of an "infinite distance" in the sense that the Son is "infinitely other" than the Father. Why speak here of otherness in terms of distance? This is fully illuminated by the salvific function attributed to the eternal distance between the Father and the Son. If the distance between the Son and the Father is the greatest of all, it eternally includes every possible separation of God from free creatures. The infinite distance between the Father and the Son is eternally maintained in openness and communion through the Spirit. It is, so to speak, eternally overcome in God himself. This is precisely what is made manifest on Calvary: the Son abandoned by the Father, on account of being identified with sin as separation from God, is nevertheless maintained in fidelity and communion with the Father through the Spirit. The event of the cross is thus the temporal epiphany of the eternal trinitarian event. In *The Glory of the Lord: The New Covenant*, with respect to the Paschal glorification of the obedient Christ, Balthasar already referred to the Spirit as "the agent of the reciprocal immanence of the love between Christ and the Father," or even as "the personal identity of the personal difference in the divinity."[7]

The cross reveals therefore that the Trinity envelops the world. The whole drama of created freedoms in conflict with God is eternally included and embraced in the internal drama of the trinitarian life, where the infinite distance is always already overcome in love. In other words, the reconciliation of all possible separations from God, sinners though they be, is already acquired in its eternal foun-

---

7. See Hans Urs von Balthasar, *Herrlichkeit*, III.2: *Neuer Bund* (Einsiedeln: Johannes Verlag, 1969), 243: "als dem Wirker des gegenseitigen In-eins der Liebe zwischen Christus und dem Vater," "als der personalen Identität der personalen Differenz in der Gottheit."

dation. Such a trinitarian conception of reconciliation is the main justification for the daring language of absolute and infinite distance between the Father and the Son.[8] It is at the cross that such a distance is found to be revealed on the world stage.

Undoubtedly, Balthasar takes some methodological precautions. He does not mean to confuse God with mutable, intramundane events, nor to project an eternal suffering onto God. On several occasions, he asserts that it is necessary first to exclude all suffering from God, and then lay the foundation in him, the condition of possibility, for the drama of the world. A moment of negative theology must thus precede the affirmation of an eternal foundation. The whole history of freedom and covenant is made possible by the primordial otherness-distance of the Father and the Son, the foundation of the otherness-distance of creatures, consumed on the cross. To the question, "Why is the cross the proper place of the trinitarian unveiling in Hans Urs von Balthasar?," I ultimately answer: so that every separation from God through created freedom might be reconcilable in God the Trinity, where infinite distance is eternally reconciled.[9]

COMPETING ANALOGIES AND
SCRIPTURAL FOUNDATIONS

Balthasar's option for the cross as the quintessential place for trinitarian epiphany can be questioned (rather than challenged) on several points: the relationship between concepts and metaphors; the supposition of an archetypal eternal drama of the cross; the theological status of an immanent law of love; and the scriptural foundation of an eternal *kenosis* proper to each divine Person. Such points of discussion have in common that they ultimately involve

8. This is confirmed by Balthasar in *Theo-Drama* V, 95.

9. As a counterpoint, Martin Bieler has brought to my awareness the dependence of Balthasar on Ferdinand Ulrich regarding another logic: "separation" (*Trennung*) as a condition for a relation of the recipient of a gift to the giver. See Ferdinand Ulrich, *Leben in der Einheit von Leben und Tod*, in *Schriften* II, ed. Martin Bieler and Stefan Oster (Freiburg i.B.: Johannes Verlag, 1999), 71–72.

theologico-epistemological presuppositions. In other words, they come under the subject of knowing how this or that theology can account for its way of progressing in knowledge and making intellectual decisions. I will treat the last two points together.

Balthasar has distanced himself from the Augustinian analogy. That is legitimate and well-founded. He is right to underscore the difficulty of rigorously anchoring such an analogy in the New Testament. Given the almost autonomous development of the Augustinian *analogon* in medieval Scholasticism, there was cause for concern. To safeguard the right function of the triads mind-knowledge-love or memory-intellect-will in the Western tradition, it is however useful to issue two reminders, which do not erase the real problem. In Augustine, triads are first and foremost mere likenesses illustrating how three figures can at the same time be consubstantial and relative, distinct and inseparable. The use of these illustrations is not first of all oriented toward the identification of each term with one of the three Persons.[10] Similarly, in Aquinas, the reprise of the Augustinian likeness has a precise and limited function: beginning with the natural sequence between knowledge and love, to conceive a real order and a relation of origin between the Spirit and the Son, so as to envision theologically their real distinction.[11] In other words, neither in Augustine nor in Thomas is the Augustinian analogy supposed to acquire a descriptive function of the immanent life of the Trinity. This, however, leaves the whole objection concerning the lack of a scriptural foundation for the analogy.

It is true that to envision the whole trinitarian unfolding, both economic and immanent, in terms of love seems more in conformity with the New Testament (at the very least with the Johannine literature). Balthasar is probably right to want to reimagine the Trinity as love. One must be aware, however, that he himself creates a Balthasarian *analogon*, competing with the Augustinian *analogon* and exposed to the same risk.

10. See Augustine, *De Trinitate* IV.30, IX.4–8.
11. See Aquinas, *ST* I, q. 27, a. 3, ad 3.

We could call it the law of extreme love that gives itself: pleni-tude or excess, abandonment or *kenosis*, and envelopment. It is thus that Balthasar gives an account of the Father's love, before showing that the Son and the Spirit live in turn, in an original way, their own abandonment or *kenosis*. In this way, the trinitarian Person is fun-damentally conceived as a being in kenotic relation. Yes, it is quite possible that extreme human love almost always involves this kind of relation. However, is it a fitting analogy for approaching the love inside the life of the Trinity?

Thus, we see here the question of scriptural foundation. The Johannine literature clearly expresses that the love of the Father is manifested by the Son and that it is extended in the fraternal life of the disciples, inhabited by the Spirit of truth (see 1 Jn 4). The con-ceptual transition from such an economy of manifested love to an understanding of the immanent life of the Trinity in terms of love (and what is more, as kenotic love) is not immediately obvious. That amounts to a free creation comparable to that of the Augustinian *analogon*.

The main criterion for receiving or not receiving a kenotic the-ology of the immanent Trinity should be, in my view, the quality of its scriptural foundation. In this regard, it is instructive to reread the section entitled "Kenosis" in *The Glory of the Lord: The New Cove-nant*. The problem raised is as follows. The identification of Christ with the condition of sin supposes a prior divine decision that per-tains to the preexistent Son. To show that an "abandonment of the *forma Dei*" is possible, Balthasar rules out a first explanation based on the power that the divine nature would have to render itself pow-erless, because he favors another explanatory path, directly based on the interpersonal relations in God the Trinity.[12] Immediately, Balthasar refers to Bulgakov's intuition that the foundation of every-thing is "the selflessness [*Selbstlosigkeit*] of the divine persons, as of

12. See Hans Urs von Balthasar, *The Glory of the Lord* VII: *Theology: The New Cov-enant*, trans. Brian McNeil (San Francisco, Calif.: Ignatius Press, 1989), 211–28; Sergei Bulgakov, *The Lamb of God*, trans. Boris Jakim (Grand Rapids, Mich.: Eerdmans, 2008).

pure relations in the love within the Godhead." This is translated as creative *kenosis*, at the risk of created freedom, carried to its climax by the *kenosis* of the cross. And so returns the trinitarian epiphany already exposited: "the Spirit … uniting them now only in the expressive form of the separation [*Trennung*]."[13]

The cross is thus silhouetted in the creative *kenosis* itself. However, Balthasar immediately challenges the idea that the *kenosis* of God would merely be the amplification of some intramundane law. It is indeed necessary to safeguard the non-necessity of the *kenosis* of God in the economy of salvation. It is only because God has actually lowered himself that we can recognize that such an economy in fact corresponds to his own essence, that is, to the immanent life of the Trinity where the Persons are in a kenotic relationship.

God can seek out and save the created freedom that wrecks itself into nothingness because he is already, in the person of the Son, "the emptiness of love's absolute obedience for the unconditional command."[14] The humanity of Jesus, however, is not from its origin identified with the suffering of the cross. It is led there through a true human life of full availability, although its entire existence be determined by the *kenosis* of God, attested in Philippians 2:7 and Romans 8:3 (by allusion).

Thus, the sole scriptural foundation for the "*kenosis* of God" is found at the outcome of theological reasoning, once the being-in-relation of the divine Persons has been qualified as kenotic by recourse to other references. This poses two serious questions: Is the Balthasarian *analogon* of extreme love as a kenotic relationship theologically valuable by itself, in an autonomous fashion? And does the *kenosis* of Philippians 2:7 found not only a *kenosis* of the Son in view of the cross, but also a *kenosis* of the Father, the Son, and the Spirit in the immanent life of the Trinity? I will leave the first question to qualified interpreters of Balthasar. I will only try to shed light on the second question, which to my eyes seems even more decisive.

13. Balthasar, *The Glory of the Lord* VII, 214.
14. Ibid., 216.

THE BACKGROUND DECISION BETWEEN
TWO TYPES OF CHRISTOLOGIES

There are two basic options in Christology. I call them the Chalcedonian paradigm and the ascending path.[15] The Chalcedonian paradigm holds the unity of the subject Christ and the duality of natures in the form of a paradox. The human nature and the divine nature of Christ are not in a direct relationship of transparency or correspondence. They are incommensurable and are united by the one subject of subsistence and operation who is the Son of God in history. The divine nature is the proper nature of the Son, while the human nature is really appropriated to him as being assumed. In such a perspective, the conditions and properties of Christ in his humanity maintain a paradoxical relationship to the properties of his divinity: impassible, he is nevertheless passible; eternal, he is nevertheless mortal; omnipotent, he is nevertheless reduced to impotence; etc. Impassibility is not revealed in passibility. There are two distinct sources of knowledge that are combined by way of paradox in Christology: on one hand, a biblico-metaphysical doctrine of the names and attributes of God,[16] and on the other hand, the teaching of the whole economy of the Son in the flesh.

Such a paradigm was overthrown by Martin Luther, based on his reflection on the Eucharist. The divinity of the Son is not recognized or predefined from any other source than his flesh. Only the abased humanity of the Son gives access to the proper content of his divinity. This is not in conformity with a divine essence knowable in advance. Through the economy of the Son in the flesh, what is proper to his divinity is unveiled or reflected in transparency. The divinity of the Son is abasement, obedience, consent, etc. In this

15. For a development of the genesis and the consequences of these two options, see Emmanuel Durand, *L'Offre universelle du salut en Christ*, 213–39.

16. See Janet M. Soskice, "Athens and Jerusalem, Alexandria and Edessa: Is There a Metaphysics of Scripture?," *International Journal of Systematic Theology* 8 (2006): 149–62; see also Matthew Levering, *Scripture and Metaphysics: Aquinas and the Renewal of Trinitarian Theology* (Oxford: Blackwell, 2004), 23–74, 110–43.

way, the humanity and divinity of Christ no longer maintain an indirect and paradoxical relationship. They are in a relation of correspondence and fittingness. Initiated by Luther,[17] such a Christology of correspondence was brilliantly implemented by Karl Barth in paragraph 59 of his *Church Dogmatics* IV/1, dealing with the kenotic obedience of the Son of God.

As we have seen, Balthasar does not really seek to found his conception of the kenotic being of each of the three divine Persons, beginning with the Father, on the *kenosis* of the Son of God, attested by Philippians 2:7. To rise from the kenotic state of Christ in the flesh to the kenotic being of God is then an implementation of the ascending path such as I have qualified it. The kenotic obedience of Christ is the direct revelation of his kenotic being as Son in the bosom of the immanent Trinity. Such an assertion is possible, but going any further is not justified. Even in the logic of the ascending path, the *kenosis* of Philippians 2:7 does not allow us to affirm that the Father himself is the abandonment of self in his singular manner of being a person. It is divinity such as it is possessed and exercised by the Son that is revealed in the abased humanity of Jesus, and not the divinity or the being-a-person of just any of the three divine Persons. In my view, the *Urkenosis* of the Father remains completely unfounded on the scriptural level.

Having confronted the Augustinian *analogon* and the Balthasarian *analogon*, some conclusions can be formulated:

- On a scriptural level, the Balthasarian *analogon* is no better founded than the Augustinian *analogon*.
- These are in reality two competing speculative developments. Their validity is rather to be sought in their reception and their fruitfulness.
- The fruitfulness of the Augustinian *analogon* is widely demonstrated, notably by its capacity to found a real participation of human beings in the trinitarian life.

17. See Martin Luther, *Disputatio Heidelbergae habita*, props. 19–22, in *Weimarer Ausgabe* I (Weimar: Böhlau, 1883), 354.

- The reception of the Balthasarian *analogon* is still in progress, as the debate attests.

Up to this point, I have argued especially with Balthasar. Can we, drawing support from Aquinas, provide a different treatment of the initial question concerning proper places of trinitarian attestation, also posing to ourselves the question of the nature of such an attestation: Is it a manifestation or an inference? If it is a manifestation, is it for both the senses and the mind? Under what objective and subjective conditions?

THE TRINITARIAN FUNCTION OF THE MYSTERIES OF JESUS: REVELATION OR MANIFESTATION?

Let us then return to our initial question. We were trying to determine the proper places of trinitarian attestation in the mysteries of Jesus. The vocabulary of the attestation here remains relatively indeterminate, while suggesting a preliminary knowledge of the Trinity. Augustine includes in the economy of trinitarian revelation all the manifestations proper to one of the three, situated between birth and Pentecost. For his part, Balthasar places the emphasis on the cross, then resurrection as the trinitarian revelation of the distance between the Father and the Son carried in the Spirit of communion.

Additional light can be drawn from the treatise on the life of Jesus by Aquinas (*ST* III, qq. 27–59). When he treats of this or that mystery, Aquinas willingly points out the personal implication of the Spirit, the Son, or the Father. In the mysteries of the childhood, the Spirit is often invoked as an actor. It is with respect to the birth and the baptism that Aquinas tackles in the most direct way an economy of manifestation. It is striking that he then speaks of manifestation (*manifestare, manifestatio*) and not of revelation (*revelare, revelatio*).[18]

18. See Etienne Vetö, *Du Christ à la Trinité. Penser les Mystères du Christ après Thomas d'Aquin et Balthasar* (Paris: Cerf, 2012), 98–104. Vetö considers Aquinas's opting for mere manifestation as a limitation of his system. A close study of Aquinas's works would

Concerning the manifestation of Christ by his birth, Aquinas distinguishes three kinds of manifestations, when he considers the role of the angels and the star.[19] As a general rule, the manifestation occurs through the mediations closest to the addressees. For the righteous, the truth is taught from within through the inspiration of the Spirit of prophecy, without manifestation by sensible sign, as was the case with Anna and Simeon. For the pagans, sensible signs are, by contrast, required and adapted to their own conditions, like the star intended for the Magi, whom Aquinas thinks were astronomers. For the Jews, finally, the angels are regular messengers to whom they were accustomed, including for the eminent gift of the Law.

In the strict sense, revelation refers to the interior teaching of salvific truth to be believed brought about by the inspiration of the Holy Spirit. Manifestation requires observers to rise from signs to the truth, while revelation offers the divine truth to the adherence of living faith through the interior action of the Spirit. In the natural order, a sign can maintain proportion to the truth it manifests. In the supernatural order, such a proportion could not exist.[20] The signs become effective only when they encounter in the witnesses an interior perception in faith of the truth manifested by the signs. In this way, the economy of manifestation by signs is relative to an economy of interior revelation by the Spirit.

In the trinitarian economy, this translates as follows. The mysteries of Jesus are privileged places for a trinitarian manifestation in the proper sense, especially in the time of his childhood and baptism. But such a manifestation presupposes an adherence in faith to God the Trinity, made possible through an interior inspiration by the Holy Spirit. Now, such an interior event of inspiration and recog-

---

nevertheless show that revelation and manifestation are not sharply divided and indeed sometimes overlap.

19. See Aquinas, *ST* III, q. 36, a. 5, co., with Jean-Pierre Torrell, *Encyclopédie Jésus le Christ chez saint Thomas d'Aquin* (Paris: Cerf: 2008), 609n69.

20. See Aquinas, *ST* III, q. 39, a. 8, ad 2, concerning the difference in nature between the voice and the Father, the humanity and the Son, and the dove and the Spirit, although these are manifestations proper to each of the three.

nition is precisely what we call a trinitarian revelation in the proper sense. In this respect, our own epistemic conditions in general differ from those of Jesus' own contemporaries, for they had to be driven from his manifold manifestation—mainly, the words and deeds he performed in his humanity—to the internal revelation of his identity, whereas we are usually led from the interior revelation—mediated by being initiated into the rule of faith—to the contemplation of the Lord's manifestations.

From this perspective, it is not appropriate to rummage through the mysteries of Jesus to look for the perfect moment where the Trinity would reveal itself for the first time in a clear and unmistakable way. Rather, we must recognize that all the mysteries of Jesus are marked by a trinitarian manifestation for the one who benefits from the trinitarian revelation. Through Christian initiation and the tradition of the rule of faith, revelation is, from our perspective, prior to the economy of manifestation. It is because believers receive the interior inspiration of the Spirit (the *lumen fidei,* and possibly the *lumen propheticum*) and the tradition of trinitarian faith that the successive events of the life of Jesus become for them a trinitarian manifestation adjusted to revelation. In my view, the trinitarian rule of faith handed on by Augustine illustrates such a link between trinitarian revelation and trinitarian manifestation.

AN INVERSION OF THE RELATIONSHIP BETWEEN LIGHT AND FORM OR FIGURE

Compared to the theology of faith and prophecy established by Aquinas, Balthasar has consciously inverted the relationship between *lumen* and *species*, light and form. This is very clear and recurrent in *The Glory of the Lord: Seeing the Form.* In Aquinas, the *lumen* (of faith or prophecy) is the power of supernatural illumination without which no form or figure can become revelation. The proper angle of revelation always comes from a new *lumen* bestowed by the Holy Spirit in the intimacy of the human intellect thus elevated. In Balthasar, the *lumen* is deliberately rendered relative to the objective evidence of the figure (the *Gestalt* taking over from the *species*). In favor of his theological aesthetics, the Swiss theologian knows perfectly well that he is inverting the order of priority formerly established by Aquinas between *lumen* and *species*.[21] There is an epistemological coherence proper to Balthasar's theological project. It underlies the project's progressive focusing of trinitarian revelation on objective evidence of the trinitarian drama of the cross.

According to the theology of faith and prophecy of Aquinas, it would be futile to seek to identify the first moment of trinitarian revelation. There is always an anteriority of trinitarian faith, a response to the interior revelation by the Spirit, to the trinitarian epiphany really attested in the life and Passover of Jesus. For us wayfaring pilgrims, it is not yet a question of seeing God the Trinity, but of believing in him and, consequently, of contemplating him in rich signs in the life and Passover of Jesus. From his birth to Pentecost, we recognize that Jesus is the center of a trinitarian epiphany precisely because his very identity is relational. He unceasingly presented himself to human beings as the one sent by the Father and as the herald of the Spirit, whom he finally poured out.

21. See Hans Urs von Balthasar, *The Glory of the Lord* I: *Seeing the Form*, trans. Erasmo Leiva-Merikakis (San Francisco, Calif.: Ignatius Press, 1982), 118–19, 151, 177–78. Balthasar knows all the more what he is doing, given that he commented in detail on Thomas Aquinas's treatise on prophecy; see Hans Urs von Balthasar, "Kommentar," in Aquinas, *Besondere Gnadengabe und die zwei meschlichen Lebens* (Heidelberg: Die deutsche Thomas-Ausgabe, 1954), 250–472.

15

Paternal Theocentrism

The Eschatological Finality of
God the Father

Contemporary theologies are divided into two broad camps, embracing either Christocentrism or theocentrism as their primarily structural motif. The objective centrality of the Paschal event usually leads orthodox theologies toward Christocentrism of one form or another. Christ Jesus is, at once, the fullness of revelation as well as the unique mediation of salvation. Thus, the principal hierarchical and organic structure of the mysteries of faith would find its central reference point in the mystery of Christ the savior.

By contrast, contemporary promoters of theocentrism are more often than not pluralist, for they relativize, in one way or another, the universality of the incarnate Christ's unique mediation in order to refer to a God who is "greater" and, on the whole, unknown. This admittedly schematic contemporary opposition between Christocentrism and theocentrism distorts the structural balance of the Christian faith. Christ Jesus is indeed at the center of the whole economy of salvation. However, God the Father is both the origin of the mission of the Son, as well as this mission's ultimate end. In contrast to the polarized state of contemporary theologies, medieval Western writers offer critical resources for getting beyond these unnecessary impasses. For the thinkers of that era, theocentrism was envisioned as a quest to find the most fitting way to articulate what defines the divine Fatherhood in relation to the Person of the Son: is the Father fundamentally approached in terms of his primacy of order in the Trinity or precisely in terms of his relatedness to the Son? Christocentrism was more or less accentuated depending upon the given author in question. Nonetheless, across the board, Christ was understood in relation to the Father. In the following pages, I wish to promote a "paternal theocentrism" having an eschatological orientation.

This theological treatment of the mystery of God the Father will begin with a consideration of the real but partial revelation of the Father in the economy of salvation. The chapter then proceeds to a reflection on two ways of knowing the Father: by way of negation and of analogy. The divine paternity is then contrasted analogically with all human parenthood; finally, the essay centers on the relational character of the paternity of the Father, his primacy in respect to his relational identity, and then focuses on the use of his relational primacy for a treatment of concepts that are central to trinitarian theology: inner-divine fecundity, *perichoresis*, and the eschatological primacy of the Father.

THE INDIRECT REVELATION OF THE FATHER

A systematic consideration of the Person of the Father presupposes the concrete form that the trinitarian epiphany takes on in the history of salvation. The Trinity is revealed through the relation of Jesus Christ to the Father who sends him and through the outpouring of the Holy Spirit. The mystery of the Father as such is inseparable from an eschatological orientation toward him that animates the entire mission of Christ as well as that of his disciples. Divine revelation does not offer its recipients an immediate perception of the Father, but instead places them face to face with Christ, the mediator and plenitude of revelation. The Father remains in some real sense transcendent to the mission of the Son. Through him, the Father truly makes himself known even while remaining radically hidden on account of his primacy. There is no other visage of the Father than the face of Christ. The unique pathway to the knowledge of the Father, then, is Jesus himself, the exegete and the way. He constantly designates the Father as both his own origin and as his ultimate destination. He comes forth from him, and he is going toward him (see Jn 13:1, 14:12, 16:28).

The ultimacy of the Father in divine revelation prohibits the disciples from remaining fixed exclusively on Christ. Christ's departure to be with the Father is an integral part of his mission in relation to us. In theological terms, one could say that the irreducibly Christocentric character of revelation is likewise ordered toward a paternal teleology. If Christ is truly the central and decisive figure of the entire historical economy of revelation, he nevertheless is not its ultimate end. Because of his divine nature, wholly received from the Father, Christ shares with the Father in being the final end of all things; however, in virtue of his relation of origin, he also always designates the Father as his ultimate source. Christ cannot retain his disciples uniquely for himself, then, because he has the mission, in accord with his origin, to send them ultimately to the Father. Through Christ and the Spirit, we have at last an access to the Father.

The person of the Father is not easily accessible to our theological consideration. As Christ says in Matthew 11:25–27, the Father is "hidden from the wise and learned," and the Son is the one who reveals the Father to whomever he wills, especially to the "little ones" of faith. Nevertheless, theological investigation can build upon an inquiry we find in the New Testament itself, where the Apostles, through listening to Christ and living alongside him, asked about the deepest identity of the one who sent him. To Philip who requests, "Show us the Father and we will be satisfied," Jesus responds, "He who has seen me has seen the Father ... Do you not believe that I am in the Father and the Father in me?" (Jn 14:8–10). The words, gestures, and works of Christ in his earthly life are all ultimately founded in and indicative of the mutual reciprocity between Jesus and the

Father. Jesus' preaching and ministry intentionally provokes a kind of Christian searching for the Father, and simultaneously makes this search possible for the first time. Conjointly, Christ firmly condemns forms of false paternalism that would impede a true recognition and acceptance of the one who sent him.[1] The New Testament claims that there is something fundamental at stake in whether or not we come to truly know the Father. Consequently, theology has a contribution to make to this process, to the extent that it seeks to acquire an integral understanding of the mystery of God within faith.

How is God to be understood as Father? The error of Arius and Eunomius was to respond too shortsightedly to this question. One cannot invoke a magic formula in order to treat such a question, such as the term "unbegotten." In order to avoid facile and misleading solutions, it is helpful to reformulate the question in a negative fashion: How is God the Father not to be understood? The negative formulation better respects the limits of our knowledge of God. It also better emphasizes the requirement that we purify our images and reformulate our ordinary concepts when speaking of God. In order to formulate a systematic set of propositions about the Person of the Father, we should begin by identifying the most effective ways to access theological reflection concerning who he is. Our principal resources can be found in the way of negation and of analogy, though which we can come to envisage the properties of the Father.

THE NEGATIVE WAY: THE INCOMPREHENSIBLE FATHER

The first characteristic of the Father is divine incomprehensibility. Contemporary theology resensitized itself to the apophatic dimensions of trinitarian theology in the twentieth century. Karl Barth emphasized this characteristic trait of the first Person of the Trinity, even while developing a robust theology of divine paternity.[2]

---

1. See Jn 4:12; 6:31; 7:22; 8:39, 44; Lk 2:48–29; Mt 23:9.
2. Barth, *Church Dogmatics*, I.1, §10, 384–98.

Even when he takes the initiative to reveal himself freely, God the Father always remains in some sense truly hidden, and this important twofold truth reaches its summit in the divine economy in the resurrection of Christ. Simultaneously, however, the relation of the Father to the eternal Son is revealed in the economy as the intradivine presupposition that stands behind the paternal relation of God toward creatures. The title "Father" does not pertain to the first Person most properly speaking except by virtue of his eternal paternity, while paternity with regard to creatures is attributed to him simply by appropriation. Likewise, our new birth by grace also finds its primal foundation in the paternity of God with respect to the eternal Son. In developing these themes, Barth limits himself almost exclusively to a theology of the works of the Father (*ad extra*); he does not develop any real theological proposals about the Father in himself, in the heart of trinitarian life. Outside of two or three allusions, the properties of the first person are not treated. We can nonetheless identify two ideas that are accentuated by Barth: incomprehensibility and paternity (with the latter as defined intrinsically in relation to the eternal Sonship). Both of these ideas should be retained in contemporary theology as determinate properties for a theology of God the Father.

The theological affirmation of the incomprehensibility of the Father calls for a clarification. Strictly speaking, it is not a property of the first Person alone. Rather, a common attribute (i.e., one that remains attributable to each of the Persons of the Trinity) is appropriated to one of the three in a particular way. In effect, if the eternal Son was not just as incomprehensible as his Father, if he did not remain always in himself invisible with the Father,[3] he would not be the perfect image and revelation of the Father. The Holy Spirit also partakes naturally of this characteristic of the deity. However, the Father is incomprehensible in a primary and unoriginate fashion; the common incomprehensibility of the three Persons finds its origin in the personal primacy of the Father, for he communicates to the Son

---

3. See Augustine, *De Trinitate* II.5.9; Aquinas, *Sup. Io.* 1:18, ed. Marietti, no. 220.

and the Spirit his own incomprehensible nature. As such, incomprehensibility designates one dimension of the exclusive property of the Father as the first divine hypostasis. The appropriation of the incomprehensibility of the divine nature to the Father is therefore not insignificant.

Such an approach to the Person of the Father through the medium of divine incomprehensibility involves a theological *via negativa*. It emphasizes the final inadequacy of our images and our concepts with regard to the first divine Person. In Christian theology, such negative reflection always presupposes for its warrant a more fundamental positive knowledge of God, derived from the events of revelation. To affirm that God the Father is utterly incomprehensible requires in effect that one has previously recognized him as "Father," through an economy of divine initiatives of grace, and finally through the revelation of his paternity in relation to his only-begotten Son. Basically, then, in order to construct a theology of the Father that is truly Christian, the "negative way" must always be articulated with care in reference to the economic revelation of God.

THE ANALOGICAL WAY: THE GIFTS
OF THE FATHER

Once we have recognized that that the Father is incomprehensible, it is fitting to try to understand the Person of the Father based upon his free and uncompelled initiatives in the divine economy: the design of filial adoption, election, the call to sanctification, creation, redemption, the incarnation of the Word, the resurrection of Christ, the outpouring of the Holy Spirit, reconciliation, the recapitulation of all things in Christ, and so on. All of these "effects" of God refer us back to their origin, to a limitless plenitude, to a source that is superabundant. Such a source is implicitly indicated in the hymn in Ephesians 1:3–14, where "the Father of our Lord Jesus Christ" is invoked and blessed in thanksgiving for all the gifts that he has bestowed upon us through his Christological election and the recapitulation of creatures in Christ. The Father is at the origin of every grace. Likewise, all of the free divine actions of creative giving and of salvation lead back in particular to his personal mystery. Spontaneously, "it is due to the benefits we receive that we come to know the benefactor; in effect, it is in taking into account that which occurs to us that we know imperfectly by analogy the nature of the benefactor."[4] Knowledge of the person of the Father arises, therefore, from the economy in which the Word and the Holy Spirit are like the two "hands" of the Father, through whom he acts to our benefit.

This process of ascending from the good gifts to the divine benefactor, as well as from the works to the Person, bears within it a real limitation. It inevitably proceeds by appropriation, that is, by attributing a common trinitarian operation to one of the Persons in a particular way. Appropriation is a conceptual accommodation that is not only legitimate but most welcome. It is a practice found in the scriptures themselves which helps a true affinity (*convenientia*) to become manifest between what is *commonly* known of the three Persons and what is *proper* to one person that we are seeking to know better.[5] Appropriation is based, at once, upon the limits and the true resources involved in the knowledge of God made possible for us through revelation. Its usefulness is real, but remains limited and merits being completed by way of other approaches, notably by an analogical reflection on the trinitarian properties of the Persons, and by the regulative reflection of a robust negative theology.

Thus, the only rigorously proper knowledge of the Father which we can have is developed either in a *negative* fashion or in a *relative* fashion. On the one hand, the first Person is the only origin without origin, the only principle without principle; on the other hand, the Father is only Father in virtue of his relation to the Son. Here we find the two essential ways toward the knowledge of the Father in himself: the negative way (centered upon his incomprehensibil-

---

4. Gregory of Nyssa, *Oratio catechetica* XV, SC 453:217.
5. See Aquinas, *ST* I, q. 45, a. 6, ad 3.

ity and his absence of origin) and the economic way (centered on the relational character of his paternity). The economic way gives rise to an analogical reflection on the eternal relations of the Father and the Son.

In the Old Testament, the images of paternity are rather rare and are usually employed in an "ascendant" fashion: the text employs human images of fatherhood and motherhood to signify the dispositions and pedagogy of God with respect to his creatures. In light of the complete revelation given in Jesus Christ, however, the revelation of divine fatherhood takes on another dimension that is analogical in the proper sense and that is more clearly transcendent (pertaining to the immanent life of God as such). From this point onward, even while presupposing this ascent from creatures to their God, analogy functions also in a descending way: the paternity of God with respect to Jesus as his eternal Son is the transcendent source of all human paternity and maternity. Here, we are no longer limited to understanding what is greater by comparison with what is lesser (God seen in light of creatures) but now also understand what is lesser by comparison with what is greater (creatures seen in light of God). This is why Paul can address the Ephesians in the following way: "I bow my knees before the Father, whom every family [*patria*] in heaven and on earth is named" (Eph 3:14).

When the analogical concept of paternity is employed in view of a transcendent signification in God, its use must be qualified negatively. In the Old Testament, the dissimilarity that is established between human and divine paternity is also accompanied by a multitude of complementary images, and these express other modes of human love and other human sentiments: the love of a mother toward her child, the passion of a young bridegroom for his betrothed, the care of a winegrower for his vine, but also the sense of disappointment, distress, anger, and so forth. In the New Testament, the multiplicity of images remains, but that of the paternity of God is affirmed in a more decisive and recurrent manner, based on the very words of Jesus concerning his mission, and his "coming forth" from and "being sent" by the Father. The theological sense of the preeminence of intradivine fatherhood must be preserved, then, by the use of a strong negative theology, as the dissimilitude between natural human fatherhood and the eternal fatherhood of God with regard to his only-begotten Son is much greater than the dissimilitude between human fatherhood and the fatherhood of God with regard to his creatures.

DIVINE PATERNITY AND HUMAN PATERNITY/MATERNITY

In an effort to deepen our sense of the relation between analogy and negative theology in speaking of the Father, we can profitably compare and contrast the personal Fatherhood of God with regard to the Son with human fatherhood and motherhood. In the context of the Arian crisis, the Church Fathers had to emphasize the difference between human generation and divine generation in order to steer clear of inappropriate projections onto the divine. They saw that the latter could, in the end, lead to an exclusion of the very notion of an eternal generation of divine life. While Origen had already interpreted the notions of emanation and generation in a sufficiently spiritual sense, Athanasius of Alexandria expressed in a thematic way the absolutely unique character of the generation and paternity that are in God.

"For God is not like man" [see Nm 23:19, Jdt 8:16]: For the Father is not from a father and therefore does not beget someone who will in turn himself become a father. The Son does not come forth as an effusion of the Father and is not begotten of a father who was himself begotten. Therefore, neither is he begotten so as to beget. The result of this is that only in the deity is the Father truly father in the proper sense and the Son truly son. For in them and only in them is the Father ever Father, and the Son ever Son.[6]

6. Athanasius of Alexandria, *Contra arianos* I.21.9 (Paris: Cerf, 2019), 171.

Thus generation, paternity, and filiation are all present in God in modes that are absolutely unique and preeminent. This implies that it is not possible to speak of God in terms that correlate directly with what we ordinarily see and experience in a cyclical fashion: a son who becomes a father once he in turn reaches biological maturity. The relations between generation and paternity, and between paternity and filiation, must become the object of a new consideration and of a reconfiguration of concepts, once we apply such terms theologically to God. Thus, in what way should we fittingly conceptualize, in God, the relationship between the Persons, the act of generation, and the entirely relational character of the divine paternity?

Thomas Aquinas articulates a theological contemplation of the eternal generation of the Son based upon a comparison with degrees of immanence that one encounters in created realities. He adduces various forms of perfect activity that remain distinct in human experience can be said analogically to converge in the eternal generation of the Son. Thus, although conception, birth, and eventual manifest, personal presence (*adesse*) represent three different moments in the event of human birth, their mutual perfections are "superimposed" or simultaneously identical in the eternal nativity of the Son.[7] The Son simultaneously is *conceived* in the bosom of the Father, *begotten* as one who is distinct from the Father, and manifestly *personally present to* or "returning" toward the Father. We may employ a diverse palette of images to describe how a child comes into the world: he is begotten by his father and conceived by his mother, who also gives birth to him; we can also ascribe birth directly to him as a subject: he is born. These different terms are employed by the genealogies and birth narratives of the New Testament as well as in conventional modern speech. They designate both the diverse moments involved the process, as well as the various agents involved who take part in human generation. Analogically, then, these multiple words can be used in convergent fashion to denote the simple, unique, and eternal act which constitutes divine generation.

7. See Aquinas, *SCG* IV.11 (*in fine*).

When we ascribe to divine paternity various actions and moments that are found distinctly in the process of human maternity, we thus come to see one difference between God's paternity and the human couple. In addition, in human reproduction, the child receives the human nature of the father and mother (common to each of them) but not their individual personhood (proper to each of them). Therefore, the child has a limited degree of personal resemblance to either of the parents. Rather, the parents experience in the child a new being who has the same nature as they do while also, however, being very different, to the extent that the child develops in his or her own personality. In God, there is no duality of sexes, but there is also no real distinction between nature and Person, such that the Son is—in all that he is (Person and nature)—generated from the *Person* of the Father. The likeness between the divine Persons, therefore, is infinitely greater than that which exists between any two human persons.

In the trinitarian life, the acts of the begetting of the Son and of the procession of the Spirit stand at the origin of the relations of Person to Person, so that each of the hypostases is constituted by a relation with the two others. Here we encounter an ontological unity that is greater than any other imaginable, as well as a distinction of Persons in which each is singularly unique. Paternity and filiation as such are found first and foremost in the heart of the Trinity, and the human correspondents (paternity-maternity and filiation) are participations in these perfects modes of existence that are proper to God alone. Finally, divine paternity and filiation are both inseparable from the Holy Spirit, who originates eternally from the mutual affability of the Father and the Son and from the gratitude of the Son toward the Father. The Spirit manifests the perfection of the divine paternity and filiation, as love is indissociable from each of these persons. By contrast, we know all too well that in human experience, paternity and filiation need not always imply balanced and loving relations.

THE MYSTERY OF THE FATHER

Our systematic reflection can proceed beginning from a question that is not resolved, centered upon a medieval theological dispute that is of great importance: Is God a Father based upon his pure and simple primacy, or based upon his relation to the begotten Son? There are two contrasting theological answers in the Western theological tradition. The desire to identify how the unbegotten character of the Father is to be understood with respect to his relational character is also discussed by certain authors in the Eastern tradition, especially in the Cappadocians.[8]

The trinitarian theology of Bonaventure is centered upon the notion of a plenitude of source or origin (*fontalis plenitudo*), and the *innascibilitas* (innascibility or unbegottenness) of the Father is portrayed as something primary with respect to every secondary emanation, both those that are intradivine as well as those that are created. By contrast, in the trinitarian theology of Aquinas, positive content is not accorded to the innascibility of the Father, and his Person is positively envisaged principally in relation to the Son and the Spirit. The starting points of this medieval discussion are taken from Hilary of Poitiers and Augustine. In effect, reread by the Scholastics of the thirteenth century, Hilary witnesses to a positive conception of the unbegotten character of the Father, which includes the Father's primacy as source of all else (*auctoritas*).[9] Augustine, meanwhile, sees in the Father's innascibility simply a negative exclusion of any origin: the Father is he who does not proceed from another (*ingenitus*).[10]

For Bonaventure, then, the Father can be conceived of as a Person in virtue of his primacy alone, the fact that he is not begotten by another. Like pagan monotheists then, "we can conceive of the

8. See Basil of Caesarea, *Contra Eunomium* I.5.517a, I.15.545b-I.16.548c; Gregory Nazianzen, *Orationes* 29.16.

9. See Hilary of Poitiers, *De Trinitate* IV.32–35. For the aftermath, see Emmanuel Durand, "Généalogie de la typologie médiévale sur l'*innascibilitas* du Père. Pierre Lombard, Guillaume d'Auxerre et Alexandre de Halès," *AHDLMA* 74, no. 1 (2007): 7–26.

10. See Augustine, *De Trinitate* V.6–7.7–8.

divine nature and he who possesses it [that is to say, God as a subject], even if we do not conceive of a plurality of persons."[11] This affects our trinitarian theology, however, when we attempt to understand the Father in relation to the divine generation of the Son. To conceive of the Father as Father (eternally able to beget a consubstantial Son) no other property is available than that of innascibility, the fact that God does not receive his nature from another. This perspective leads to a trend that is prevalent in contemporary theology: the tendency to treat the Person of the Father and the divine essence as coextensive notions, thereby overlooking the fact that the relation to the Son is itself constitutive of the primary hypostasis of the Father.[12] Bonaventure's theory then poses a serious problem: if the simple fact that God possesses a nature that he does not receive from another suffices to give intelligibility to a notion of divine generation (unbegottenness implies fecundity), then knowledge of the existence of the Trinity could seemingly be deduced simply from a property of the divine essence, one accessible to philosophers and pagan monotheists. In any case, Bonaventure estimates that the primacy and innascibility render sufficient intelligibility to a concept of divine generation, which is subordinate to the notion of paternity. According to our manner of knowing, the Father is posited as first by virtue of his primacy (*primitas*); primacy is then qualified by reference to emanations (including generation and spiration). The relations of paternity and spiration are then subordinated to primacy and emanation. The *primitas* signals the inexhaustible plenitude of the divine mystery in its paternal origin, an origin that is superior to any emanation, whether divine or created.

By contrast, when Aquinas treats of the divine Persons, he envisages a reciprocal primacy of processions and relations as characterizing the very root intelligibility of the Persons. His theory has recourse to a conceptual distinction between the formal principle of a distinction of Persons *versus* the way the distinction of Persons

---

11. Bonaventure of Bagnoregio, *Sent.* I, d. 27, p. 1, a. un., q. 2, ad 3.
12. See Walter Kasper, *The God of Jesus Christ* (New York: Crossroad, 2002), 133–57.

comes to be known.[13] Processional origins are the way to understand Persons, but the intradivine relations (which are themselves founded upon the actions of procession) are, in reality, the formal principle of the distinction of Persons. Consequently, the negation of any origin in the Father, and his simple position as primary does not characterize his Person as such, properly speaking. Innascibility is a pure negation: it designates the fact that the Father is a principle who does not originate from another principle.[14] For us to conceive of the Father's innascibility, then, we must presuppose some prior, positive understanding of the Father as a principle, and this prior understanding is given in the notion of paternity. Innascibility is a strictly negative knowledge that must qualify our understanding of the Father as a principle, but this notion is not formally constitutive of the fatherhood of God as such.[15] Nevertheless, it remains a secondary property. Negation alone cannot express the characteristic dignity of a property, as every negation is founded upon a prior positive affirmation.[16] Innascibility presupposes, then, paternity. Innascibility can seem more perfect than paternity to the extent that it signifies something that is entirely incommunicable, while paternity is given in analogical fashion to creatures. But innascibility manifests in reality the incommunicable character of the divine paternity as such: it is entirely unique and transcendent. Only God the Father is perfectly and uniquely Father.[17]

Taking account of the medieval tradition, there are multiple ways in which we might further qualify our understanding of the first hypostasis of the Trinity. Four distinct strands of analysis can be distinguished. (1) With regard to the divine economy, the Father takes the initiative in the missions of the Son and the Holy Spirit. (2) With regard to the intra-trinitarian life of God, the Father is the first Per-

---

13. Aquinas, *De potentia*, q. 8, a. 3; *ST* I, q. 40, a. 2.

14. Aquinas, *Sent.* I, d. 28, q. 1, a. 1, ad 1; *ST* I, q. 33, a. 4.

15. Aquinas, *Sent.* I, d. 28, q. 1, a. 1, ad 4.

16. Ibid., ad 2.

17. For further analysis, especially on the Father as *auctor*, see John Baptist Ku, *God the Father in the Theology of St. Thomas Aquinas* (New York: Peter Lang, 2012), 149–69.

son and is innascible. (3) The Father eternally begets the Son and spirates the Holy Spirit. (4) He therefore maintains two original relations that are constitutive of his very identity. If one takes into account the *perichoresis*, or mutual indwelling, of the three Persons, it is impossible to understand the Father as holding the "first place" in the trinitarian life in a purely solitary fashion, independent of his relation to the Son and his relation to the Spirit. Rather, one must adopt from the beginning a relational conception of the Person, in conformity with the Thomistic conception of the divine Persons as "subsistent relations." If we proceed in this way, then once the relational identity of the Father is acknowledged, one must also reaccentuate the profound meaning of his innascibility as signifying a plenitude as the source of divine life in God.

In every divine work, the Father is he from whom divine initiatives originally proceed, including all that pertains to the divine welfare for creation and original plan of divine adoption by grace. This is fitting, due to who the Father is: the origin of the Son and the Spirit, and the first principle of the trinitarian mystery of God, who alone has existence without origin. This unoriginate status can only be envisaged in a rigorous fashion if one analogically refines two complex notions: that of an "order of nature" and that of an "origin." These notions must be purified of any connotation of compositional complexity in order for them to be applied to the inner life of the Trinity without (falsely) projecting onto that life any notion of anteriority and posteriority, or of supremacy and subordination. Indeed, it is necessary to conceive of the primacy of the Father without disfiguring his completely unique expression of primacy, in other words, without wedding to this an erroneous notion of the subordination of the Son and the Spirit.

On a first approach, in order to correctly consider the primacy of the Father, it is sufficient simply to begin with the missions of the Son and the Holy Spirit sent into the world and to "ascend" from these back up to the Father, at whose initiative they are sent. This starting point is both intuitive and theologically sound. It follows from the common biblical motifs of "sending" and "mission," by which the New Testament revelation turns our view from the mission of the Word and Son who is filled with the Spirit back to the Father who sent him.

Although the Father is assuredly first in the order of origin that exists between the three divine Persons, nonetheless he is not anterior to the two other Persons in such a way that they would come to be after him, either temporally or by means of an ontological degradation, nor even simply according to a logical posteriority.[18] In our ordinary range of experience, an order that is based upon one thing originating from another usually implies a temporal sequence: it is necessary that A progressively attains to a certain state in order to then produce B. Furthermore, that which issues from a reality distinct from itself does not always possess the same perfection of being as the first reality, that is, its maturity and stability. In this way, we spontaneously think of the concept of "origin" as implying logical anteriority in a reality with respect to that which proceeds from the original source. In so doing, we spontaneously conceive the origin as being logically anterior to that which stems from it, failing to see that both may also be inseparable and intrinsically logically connected. This is why in the case of relations such as "double" and "half," "neighbor" to "neighbor," and "father" and "son," the one term of the relation cannot exist without the other, even if in reality a man becomes a father at a certain moment in time, and is never simply identical in all that he is with his paternity. He was himself a son before he became a father, and if his own son dies before he does, he will no longer truly be a father, in relation to an actually coexistent son.

To consider the Trinity according to an order of origin without thereby implying any temporal development requires a sort of conceptual passage toward the limits of human thinking. From notions of local movement, qualitative change, or the generation of a new being, we can retain only the notion of a relation of the origin to the

---

18. See Basil of Caesarea, *Contra Eunomium* I.20.557ac, III.I.656a; Aquinas, *ST* I, q. 42, a. 3.

term that originates, that is to say, of the principle and that which proceeds from the principle. This notion should in no way imply subordination, dependence, diminishment, or ontological posteriority. Here we must distinguish then between "dependence" and "relation": dependence implies some imperfection on the part of the one who depends on what is prior to itself, while relation in itself implies no imperfection. It allows one to think of the mutual constitution of two correlative terms, yet without negating the order of origin that exists between them. Thus the Father and the Son are mutually self-constituting, even while the Son proceeds from the Father. While proceeding from the Father, and in fact precisely due to this proceeding, the Son constitutes the Father as Father.

After having considered the uniqueness of the relative primacy of the Father, we can consider the two immanent acts of the Father. God the Father eternally begets his Son who is also his Word (according to the language of the Johannine prologue), truly distinct from the Father (Jn 1:1, 14, 17). The eternal Word who is the principle of creation (Jn 1:3) has become manifest in the flesh of Christ, in such a way as to reveal to us his glory, the glory of an only-begotten Son, that is to say, who is the unique Son of the Father (Jn 1:14). When these two revealed names for Jesus Christ (Word/Logos and only-begotten Son) are considered theologically, they enable one to consider two complementary analogies for the mystery of divine generation: one derived from human generation and another from the conception of an inner word, a Logos that in God is efficient, loving, and creative.

Our understanding of divine generation would be incomplete if we did not take into account an analogy from love as well, based upon a comparison to the love that accompanies any human father that is worthy of the title. In the generation of the Son, like the procession of the Spirit, the Father acts by virtue of a formal principle which is the divine nature, and in so doing communicates the fullness of his nature to the Son. Against the Arians, who attempted to subordinate the Son to the Father by arguing that the Son was created through an act of the will by the Father, the Church Fathers distinguished between the "nature" of God and his "will," such that the Father generates the Son naturally. However, by making this distinction, they did not simply exclude willing from the eternal generation: even though he begets by nature, the Father also wills the act of begetting and loves his begotten Son. Subsequently we can say that love is not something foreign to this preeminently paternal act. The medieval theologians further reflected upon this truth. That the loving will of the Father is concomitant with the act of divine generation denotes the following: the procession of the Word is correlative to the procession of the Spirit, who is the love that proceeds from the Father through the Son. In a preeminent way, then, the eternal Word must be seen as the perfect Word, that is to say, as the Logos who is generated in the heart of the Father, spirating love, and efficient in the loving acts of God.[19]

Just as the Son is generated eternally as the *beloved* of the Father, so likewise the Spirit proceeds eternally as the Love of the Father for the Son. One must, however, carefully distinguish between love as an "operation" and love as a personal "terminus." The paternal operation of love that is present in the divine generation of the Son by the Father is not really distinct from the Person of the Father, who exists in and as this very act of generating. By contrast, the Person of the Spirit *proceeds from* this same paternal operation of love and is himself a Person who is love, distinct from the Father and the Son. The Spirit therefore proceeds eternally from the Father in order to "rest upon" the beloved Son. In virtue of his irreducible uniqueness as a person, the Spirit cannot be understood merely as the power of generation residing in the Father, nor as the paternal operation of love with which the Father acts in his divine generation of the Son. The Spirit must not be conceived of in uniquely functional terms or as a mere "indicator" of eternal filiation, both of which constitute a form of reductivist pneumatology.

19. See Aquinas, *ST* I, q. 43, a. 5, ad 2: "Filius ... est Verbum, non qualecumque, sed spirans Amorem"; *Sup. Io.* 6:45, ed. Marietti, no. 946.

At the heart of trinitarian life, the Son fully assumes his filial identity because he responds to the Father. In an act of eternal gratitude, he returns the love that he receives from the Father in his own generation. This return of the Son to the Father by way of filial love includes the return to the Father of the Spirit who is love. The Spirit proceeds from the Father and reposes eternally upon the Son, as the loving affability of the Father for the Son. However, he proceeds also in concomitant fashion from the loving response of the Son to the Father. The relation of origin of the Spirit necessarily implies, then, a movement of return to the Father, in which the Son is the principal agent of the Spirit's proceeding. The Spirit is thereby constituted as much by his return toward the Father (from the Son) as by his procession from the Father. In this sense, the Father is revealed in his primacy as both the principle and the end of the eternal rhythm of the divine life, through the "going out" of the Son from the Father, and through the procession of the Spirit who rests upon the Son and returns from the Son to the Father. The Father is the source or *alpha* of the divine life of the Son and Spirit, but this return of the Spirit toward the Father in the Son designates the Father as the *omega* of intradivine life as well.

This plentitude as source that characterizes the Father as a person also serves as the primary basis for the trinitarian mystery, and is expressed in the twofold fruitfulness of the divine generation and the procession of the Spirit. These two eternal acts are the only acts of the Father that perfectly express the riches of his divine goodness and power. All the vital plenitude of the Father is invested in the gift by which he begets the Son as his perfect image and loves him in communicating to him his Spirit. As principle and source, this paternal plenitude gives intelligibility to the notion of intradivine fruitfulness, but this being said, this plenitude only exists in and as the act of self-communication. It is always understood entirely in relation to the Son and the Spirit. Divine fruitfulness is not simply an attribute of the divine essence, one which could be inferred independently of one's knowledge of the divine processions. On the contrary, it is attributed properly to the Person of the Father, and signifies precisely these two eternal acts of the Father, that is to say, the generation of the Son and the spiration of the Spirit. These two immanent operations constitute the proper expression of the original plenitude of the Father, such that this notion of "plenitude" in the Father cannot be treated apart from them, except in an equivocal sense of the term. Thus, we must take care to avoid conceiving of the unoriginate singularity of the Father within the immanent Trinity as though the innascibility and primacy of the Father contained something more than that which is engaged in his twofold effective fruitfulness (as source of the Son and Spirit). The fontal plentitude cannot be envisaged as something outside of, or more than, the relation of the Father to the two processions that issue from him. This kind of superiority or transcendence of the Father does not exist within the divine life itself. The original plenitude of the Father is not a potentiality of the divine essence that would find some kind of partial actuation through the generation of the Son and in the procession of the Spirit. The plenitude and fruitfulness of the Father are perfectly actualized and are entirely manifested in these two eternal acts of the Father.

Nevertheless, the theological motif of the "eschatological reserve" of the Father with regard to man is an important dimension of revelation, something essential to a proper understanding of the economy of salvation. The original plenitude of the Father unfolds from eternity in the twofold intra-trinitarian processions of the Word and the Spirit, but this spiritual fecundity of the Father is in turn prolonged otherwise or echoed analogously in the act of creation and the gracious gift of salvation. This new activity of giving *ad extra* is not the result of any divine need for creation, and does not actuate in God some unexploited potentiality that was not realized through the generation of the Son and the procession of the Spirit. Rather, this divine communication *ad extra* proceeds from a completely free will that gives being to spiritual creatures in order to invite them into a covenant with God, and in order to lead them into the sharing of the life of the Trinity. But this unveiling of the Trinity remains partial *in via* for the duration of earthly existence, filtered through the light of faith, and mediated by the resurrected flesh of Christ. Thus, we await the fullness of the eschatological revelation in which the Father will allow us to see him face to face, in his Word and by his Spirit, by an eternal participation of creatures in the intra-trinitarian life of God. Thus, a twofold eschatological distance of the Father can be spoken of, one *in via* and the other *in patria*. While we are wayfaring pilgrims subject to the life of ecclesial faith, we await the final *parousia* of Christ and the eschatological revelation of the Father. However, even in the state of eschatological beatitude, the Father will always exist beyond that which we are given to see and receive of him in glory. The immediacy of the vision does not entail an exhaustive knowledge or total comprehension of the Father.

We still must underscore the originality of the Holy Spirit in the manifestation of the Father. God the Father cannot be designated as such uniquely in reference to the Son. Generation and paternity do not suffice in order to characterize his identity completely. A balanced expression of faith in the Trinity requires one to take account of the uniqueness of the relation of the Father to the Spirit as one of the decisive properties of any theology of the Father. The relation of the Father to the Spirit must not be subordinated to that which exists between the Father and the Son. The Father is just as much he from whom the Spirit proceeds as he by whom the Son is begotten. However, neither can the procession of the Spirit as love be separated from the eternal generation of the Son. Indeed, it is intimately connected to it. In the trinitarian mystery, then, the Father is in relation to the Son in the very act in which he spirates the Spirit. And reciprocally, the Spirit proceeds from the Father, who is always the Father of the Son by virtue of the ever-present act of divine generation. The Son is thus inseparable from the Father even when the Father is the origin of the Spirit, and yet the inner fecundity of God pertains principally to the Father, because he is the source of the divine life. This perspective concerning the primacy of the Father, and the simultaneous indissociability of the processions, allows for a more robust understanding of the mystery of the *perichoresis* of the Persons, and thereby facilitates a renewed treatment of the problem of the origin of the Holy Spirit: he proceeds from the Father who is always the Father of the Son.

However important a consideration of the *perichoresis* of the immanent acts of the trinitarian life might be, the procession of the Spirit cannot be treated only in terms of its relation with the divine generation. The Spirit manifests a unique dimension of the Person of the Father, distinct from his paternity with respect to the Son. This second fecundity of the Father is irreducible to the first, even though it is intrinsically related to it. The mysterious identity of the Spirit therefore manifests something of the original plenitude of the Father that is not exhaustively expressed in the generation of the Son. The first Person of the Trinity cannot be understood as the Father uniquely by consideration of his constitutive, reciprocal relation with the Son.

How then can we characterize this novel "visage" of the uncircumscribed Father that is manifested uniquely by his relation to the Spirit? Here we must consider the pneumatic dimension of the economy of salvation. The procession of the Spirit is accessible to us as the agent acting behind the scenes in multiple settings within the economy: in the inspiration of the prophets, in the decisive stages of Jesus' life and ministry, in the unfolding of the drama of the passion, and finally in the new order that issues from the resurrection, and which is fully unfurled at Pentecost. Through these historical moments in the economy, one can perceive more explicitly the universal extension of filial grace. In keeping with the universal influence of the resurrected Lord, the Spirit reveals himself as the one who causes creatures to participate in the unique eternal filiation of the Son in a multiplicity of ways. The identity of the person of the Father is not limited to his relation toward the Son, for he is open to new relations of Fatherhood, in the person of the Spirit.

In the trinitarian mystery, the eternal relation of the paternity toward the Son is conjoined to another that is more difficult to name: the relation of origin of the Spirit with regard to the Father. The paternal fruitfulness of God is realized in a properly trinitarian communion, by the eternal interplay of these two relations. In fact, the Spirit is indispensable to the perfection of the trinitarian communion of the Father and the Son. In trinitarian theology, then, the mysterious richness of the procession of the Spirit manifests that the inexhaustible plenitude of the Father is both the source of filiation and of communion. The communion in God is not restricted to the Father and the Son alone, even if this procession does provide the most fundamental or structural dimension of the inner life of God. There are other modes of relationality, love, and personal exchange in human existence that may be attributed analogically to the interior life of God, and which find better expression in a theology of the Holy Spirit. They nourish our hope to one day obtain to the multiform-yet-integrated trinitarian communion of God, a communion which is perfect and unfractured in a way that mere human solidarity and human communion is not. The ungraspable procession of the Spirit constitutes, in a certain sense, the ultimate eternal opening to the Father, and proceeds by mission toward all the creatures of God called to inclusion within the unique filiation of the Son, who are thus invited to partake without measure in the ineffable communion of the Trinity.

CHRISTOCENTRISM WITHIN

PATERNAL THEOCENTRISM

As we draw these systematic proposals to a close, let us briefly consider the conclusions at which we have arrived. Despite the conjectures of Bonaventure, it is not possible to maintain theologically that the hypostasis of the Father is "posited" in virtue of his primacy alone, nor that his plenitude as the source of all else potentially surpasses the two divine processions of the Son and the Spirit. Such a conception of God does not correspond to the God revealed in

Jesus Christ. The idea of a primacy that exists outside of the effective fecundity of the Father is only a vain projection without name or personal identity. This "unknown God" postulated under the influence of an undue philosophical influence of Neoplatonic provenance, is not the Father-God who has personally and mysteriously made himself known by way of Christian revelation.

By contrast, however, the primacy of the Father can play a decisive role in trinitarian theology in order to denote something in the first Person other than his relation to the Son. The plenitude of the Father as an unbegotten source of divine life is not expressed effectively only through the generation of the Word, but also in the procession of the Spirit. These two acts are "ontologically adequate" to the paternal source from whom they proceed. These immanent acts in God are in turn extended by emanation to the economy of filial adoption, in which creatures become the children of God, configured to the Son by the Spirit. Consideration of the primacy of the Father helps us recover a sense of the unfathomable depths of love that the Father disposes of in a superabundant way. The Spirit is the ineffable, eternal expression of the spiritual fecundity of the Father, a distinct reflection of his original plenitude. He is also the ultimate source of the offering of God's divine life to the world. He completes and accomplishes the relational unfolding in God of the uncircumscribed life of the Father.

In light of this consideration of the mystery of the Father, we can conclude that Christocentrism cannot have the final word in the interpretation of revelation, nor in theology. The Book of Revelation states things clearly: it is the eschatological paternity of the One who sits upon the throne and makes all things new that gives final meaning to the mediation provided by the Lamb, even while the Lamb also partakes fully of the divine sovereignty.[20] This is the endpoint of the revelation: the Father whom we anticipate seeing. Thus theology is ultimately submitted to a trinitarian theocentricism that is

20. Rv 5:6; 7:9–12; 21:5–7, 22–23; 22:1. See Bauckham, *The Theology of the Book of Revelation*, 23–65.

eschatological. By the Word and the Spirit, all spiritual creatures are led toward personal union with the Father.[21] The interrelated missions of Christ and of the Spirit will only be fully accomplished in the *eschaton* when the Son and the Spirit will introduce all of the redeemed into the eschatological presence of the Father. Already their missions attract and lead all things toward him. In our state here below as wayfaring pilgrims in faith, theology must acknowledge the perennial transcendence of the Father, and by its eschatological aspiration toward him, it must remain open to a paternal theocentrism.

21. See Aquinas, *Sent.* I, d. 14, q. 2, a. 2; d. 15, q. 4, a.1; *ST* I, q. 43, a. 4, ad 1.

16

Christ's Mission
Implies His Preexistence
A Scriptural Argument

The classical doctrine of Christ's real preexistence as the Son of God has fallen on hard times in recent days. The current debate concerning this topic takes place at once regarding the exegetical legitimacy of making such an "ontological" affirmation as well as regarding its implications for systematic Christology. Many contemporary theologians find it difficult to reconcile Christ's preexistence as the eternal Word with the proper consistency of his full humanity.

Let us attempt to avoid a common misunderstanding from the start of our discussion. In its classical form, the term "preexistence" designates Christ's transcendence over the created world. It translates the notion that the eternal Word has a kind of ontological "overhang" [*surplomb*] throughout the entire mission of the incarnate Word, both "before" the incarnation as well as "during" and "since" it. These temporal adjectives are related to the human perspective that hems in our formation of Christological expressions. However, we must not allow them to lead us into error. Christ's preexistence is not a mythological motif simply because the word "preexistence" has a temporal prefix.

In this analysis, we propose to develop a simple and efficacious argument on behalf of Christ's real preexistence, basing our discussion on the motif of sending or mission, a motif that is at once biblical as well as something belonging to the domain of systematic theology. However, in order to suitably undertake our proposed demonstration, we must first begin by discussing the state of the question concerning this matter.

THE STATE OF THE QUESTION: THE TYPOLOGY OF PREEXISTENCE IN SYSTEMATIC THEOLOGY

In a provocative study published in 1990, Karl Joseph Kuschel, Hans Küng's successor at the Ecumenical Institute of Tübingen, wished to completely demythologize the real preexistence of Christ as the Son and Word of the Father.[1] He primarily relies on the theses of Harnack and Bultmann. Closely analyzing their thought, he ultimately comes to invoke a new ecumenical consensus against "descending" Christology in its traditional form. He emphasizes the political variables involved in the primitive affirmation of Christ's preexistence, taking into account the great difficulties entailed by the acceptance of it within the context of religious pluralism. Finally, he registers a strong critique against contemporary theologians for their lack of a scriptural foundation on behalf of Christ's ontological preexistence, even when the latter is presented in way that is relative to Christ's resurrection.

According to the outlook proposed by Kuschel, one that is difficult to discern and even here is sketched out here in all too brief a form, Jesus Christ is the eternal Son because the eternal God determined in himself to be his Father and is thus revealed in him. Therefore, Jesus' person and destiny belong in a definitive manner to the determination of the eternal being of God, but this fact

---

1. See Karl-Josef Kuschel, *Geboren vor aller Zeit? Der Streit um Christi Ursprung* (Munich: Piper Verlag, 1990).

need not lead us to draw conclusions that are foreign to scriptural terminology.[2]

This stubborn rejection of metaphysical language is quite contestable, but nonetheless the tendency points to a real dissatisfaction or a kind of timidity regarding Christ's ontological preexistence as the eternal Word. In the academic world, in addition to a number of reviews of Kuschel's work, many vigorous and thorough responses to it reveal the fact that Christ's real preexistence plays a crucial role in Christian soteriology.[3] Among these studies, those of Douglas McCready[4] and Simon J. Gathercole have particularly drawn my attention.[5]

In his monograph *He Came Down from Heaven,* McCready undertakes a bold defense of the classical doctrine of Christ's preexistence. He handles a great abundance of documentation and sets forth excellent discussions of the *status quaestionis* on the level of exegesis as well as on that of systematic theology. In his synthetic undertaking, he does indeed examine the principal aspects of the problem and sifts through the various relevant biblical, patristic, modern, and contemporary texts. This sometimes leads the reader to feel a bit overwhelmed by the data that he has gathered together. However, as a kind of compensation for wading through these details, the

2. See ibid., 640–45. For a different evaluation of the relationship between Greek metaphysics and the biblical tradition, see Janet M. Soskice, "The Gift of the Name. Moses and the Burning Bush," *Gregorianum* 79, no. 2 (1998): 231–46; Soskice, "Athens and Jerusalem, Alexandria and Edessa," 149–62.

3. See Brendan Byrne, "Christ's Preexistence in Pauline Soteriology," *Theological Studies* 58, no. 2 (1997): 308–30. The author perfectly explains the importance of Christ's real preexistence for Pauline soteriology: it is God himself who came to earth in his Son in order to bring about our salvation.

4. Douglas McCready, *He Came Down from Heaven: The Preexistence of Christ and the Christian Faith* (Downers Grove, Ill.: InterVarsity Press, 2005). In the preface to this work, the author explains how he participated in a seminar on Christ's preexistence led by Karl-Josef Kuschel at Tübingen in 1985. His disagreement with Kuschel ultimately led him to write this book as a response to *Geboren vor aller Zeit?*

5. Simon J. Gathercole, *The Preexistent Son: Recovering the Christologies of Matthew, Mark, and Luke* (Grand Rapids, Mich.: Eerdmans, 2006). The author conducted his studies under James D. G. Dunn and disapproves of his claim that scriptural evidence for Christ's preexistence is limited the Johannine corpus, as well as Dunn's reading of Phil 2.

work offers the reader a wealth of carefully chosen information and references.

On the level of systematic theology, we must retain the fundamental typology that distinguishes the three meanings of "preexistence" that are held today:[6]

- Christ's "real preexistence" as eternal Son, in continuity with patristic and dogmatic tradition.
- "Ideal preexistence," holding that Christ only preexisted in his humanity in the divine foreknowledge, providence, or election. This conception is often connected to the doctrine of election held by Karl Barth in his *Kirchliche Dogmatik* II/2 or invokes a so-called Christology of the new Adam, one that was defended in particular by James Dunn on the level of exegesis.[7]
- Christ's "eschatological preexistence," projected backward by the first Christians on the basis of Jesus' resurrection, in order to justify his "post-existence" (i.e., his henceforth-exalted existence), as well as the permanence of his community. This is the "weak" version of eschatological preexistence defended by Kuschel, though a "strong" version of it also exists in the work of Pannenberg.

Kuschel holds that Christ's preexistence represents a mythical projection, one that has some use and legitimacy on the political level, though without an ontological foundation prior to the event of the

6. See McCready, *He Came Down from Heaven*, 15–19, 99–103, 243–45. Also see earlier, McCready, "He Came Down from Heaven: The Preexistence of Christ Revisited," *Journal of the Evangelical Theological Society* 40, no. 3 (1997): 419–32.

7. This line of interpretation for the hymn found in the Letter to the Philippians establishes a debatable correspondence between the *morphè* of Phil 2:6 and the word *eikôn* in the Septuagint text of Gn 1:26–27. It is also founded on the translation of *harpagmos* by *res rapienda*. See James D. G. Dunn, *Christology in the Making: A New Testament Inquiry into the Origins of the Doctrine of the Incarnation* (London: SCM Press, 1989), 113–25. Also see Dunn, *The Theology of Paul the Apostle* (Grand Rapids, Mich.: Eerdmans, 1998), 281–93. For an outlook opposed to Dunn's, one that is based upon solid argumentation, see Teresia Yai-Chow Wong, "The Problem of Preexistence in Philippians 2:6–11," *Ephemerides Theologicae Lovanienses* 62, no. 4 (1986): 267–82.

resurrection, even one that would be unveiled *a posteriori*. Thus, he differs from Pannenberg,[8] who holds that the "retroactive" effect of the resurrection holds not only on the level of our knowledge but also on that of ontology, so much so that the eschatological attestation of Christ's preexistence corresponds to a foundation existing from all eternity.

Pannenberg denounces the weakness of Kuschel's arguments refusing to admit that Christ ontologically preexisted and was consubstantial to God. Pannenberg believes that Kuschel above all wishes to avoid the trinitarian implications of Christ's preexistence. For his own part, Pannenberg readily acknowledges that the sending of the Son spoken of in Galatians 4:4 (also in Rom 8:3 and Jn 3:17) presupposes that he preexisted.[9] Finally, his interpretation of Philippians 2:6–11 is, ultimately, traditional in tone: the abasement spoken of there at once pertains to the movement coming from preexistence (which implies an equality with God), as well as to Christ's human journey to the cross.[10]

Within the framework thus established, Christ's eschatological preexistence and real preexistence ultimately overlap in Pannenberg's Christology.[11] This is not the case for Kuschel, whose version of "eschatological preexistence" ultimately seems to be reduced a kind of ideal preexistence of the man Jesus.[12]

Taking Thomas Aquinas as a guide, our own analysis intends to develop a scriptural argument on behalf of a so-called real preexis-

8. See the substantial critique of Pannenberg by Kuschel in *Geboren vor aller Zeit?*, 527–28. Also, see Pannenberg's resolute response in *Systematic Theology*, trans. Geoffrey W. Bromiley (Grand Rapids, Mich.: Eerdmans, 1991), 2:367n126 and 369–70n134. For a broader view of Pannenberg's thesis concerning preexistence, see *Systematic Theology*, 2:368–89.

9. See Pannenberg, *Systematic Theology*, 2:369n133.

10. See ibid., 2:375–77.

11. It is not always easy to understand how Pannenberg distinguishes ontological preexistence from ideal preexistence. He critiques Karl Barth for having duplicated the concept (see ibid., 2:368n127), but he himself makes use of the distinction in some places, while nonetheless at times seeming to treat them like one and the same thing in other places.

12. See McCready, *He Came Down from Heaven*, 286–91 (against Kuschel).

tence, that is, the ontological preexistence of the eternal Son. This argument, having an astonishing kind of simplicity and currency, is directly engaged in the central question at stake in the contemporary debate. Therefore, before rereading Aquinas, we should let ourselves be instructed by the contributions made by the most recent exegetical discussions.

MISSION AND PREEXISTENCE IN GATHERCOLE

In an original and creative study,[13] Simon Gathercole deploys a decisive argument for correctly understanding Christ's real preexistence as the eternal Son. The Cambridge exegete carefully shows that the formulas in the Synoptic Gospels where Jesus affirms that he came into the world for a precise end all presuppose his transcendence over the domain to which he was sent and imply his real preexistence as Son (and not only an ideal preexistence in God's thought). His demonstration is very convincing within the framework of the Synoptic Gospels and enables us to perceive how this same motif was received in other New Testament texts which are more readily sought out when attempting to define the theological theme of Christ's preexistence. Gathercole's methodology involves an analysis of the Greek texts of the Synoptic Gospels, reading them as they immediately present themselves to the reader as well as in terms of how their first readers would have understood them. His argumentation centers around the formulas wherein Jesus affirms, "I came for ..."

After briefly discussing the affirmations of Christ's preexistence that can be found in Paul, the Letter to the Hebrews, and the Letter of Jude, Gathercole considers various aspects of Christ's transcendence expressed in the Synoptic Gospels, most particularly through his dual belonging to heaven and earth, his activity in calling the people of God, his ability to pardon sins, his role in the sending of prophets, and the invocation of his name. According to Gathercole's

13. For my detailed review of this work, see *RSPT* 92, no. 1 (2008): 157–61.

argumentation, an examination of these motifs clearly reveals multiple attestations of Christ's transcendence within the Synoptic Gospels, particularly in Matthew. Therefore, we are justified in thinking that the texts of the Synoptic Gospels communicate the theme of Christ's preexistence in an utterly precise form.

The middle portion of the Gathercole's work (as well as the core of his very argument) is concerned with Jesus' advent and mission. If a broad consensus holds that preexistence is implied by the Johannine account of Christ's coming from on high from heaven or into the world, this is not the case for the motif of Christ's coming expressed in the Synoptic Gospels. Nonetheless, this corpus contains ten decisive attestations to Christ's coming, all of which are announced as summaries of Jesus' entire mission throughout his earthly ministry.[14] Despite certain minor variations, we find ourselves faced with a common structure in the formulas: "I have come + [the end of the mission]." The subject is always *Jesus* or *the Son of Man*. To come somewhere with a precise goal presupposes that it is a question of a deliberate act. To express the point in ordinary language: the task received was not previously incumbent upon the subject under consideration, and he comes somewhere in order to perform it. However, if the task refers to the complete scope of Christ's earthly activity, its origin is thus outside the human sphere.[15]

Within this delimited perspective, Gathercole devotes himself to undertaking an exegesis of the ten passages in the Synoptic Gospels where we find the expressions, "I have come," "You have come," or "The Son of man has come."[16] His foundational assertion is that Christ freely came into the world. With great care, he studies certain striking parallels between the texts under consideration and several parables drawn from the Synoptic Gospels. Finally, he holds that Hebrews and John contain, in part, an authentic reception of a motif

14. See Gathercole, *The Preexistent Son*, 85.

15. See ibid., 86.

16. See Mk 1:24 (see Lk 4:34); Mt 8:29; Mk 1:38 (see Lk 4:43); Mk 2:17 (see Mt 9:13, Lk 5:32); Mt 5:17; Lk 12:49; Lk 12:51 (see Mt 10:34); Mt 10:35; Mk 10:45 (see Mt 20:28); Lk 19:10.

drawn from the Synoptic Gospels and not only the elaboration of a completely different theological outlook.[17]

At the conclusion of his central analysis, Gathercole is quite clear that the emphasis of the formulas examined is *directly* concerned with the finality of Jesus' complete ministry. The fact that his complete ministry is embraced in this way by the formulas of "coming" presupposes that he preexisted. At this stage, he already specifies a first form of conceptual content for the notion of preexistence progressively elaborated through the course of his demonstration: "The key point here is that this preexistence consists not least of a *will* which is the basis of Christ's coming to the human realm in accordance with the will of the Father."[18]

He then emphasizes the importance of the formulas and parables of "coming" as lights for interpreting Jesus' mission in the Synoptic Gospels.[19] In themselves, the formulas of "sending" most often remain ambiguous regarding the precise identity of the sent person (a mere prophet, a messianic or heavenly figure, etc.), for they primarily designate him who sends. However, once they are placed next to the previously studied motif, their meaning is strengthened so that they can incorporate the heavenly preexistence of the Son without, for all that, dismissing his messianic identity.[20]

The final chapter of Gathercole's work deals with certain aspects of the contemporary theological debate surrounding the question of preexistence. Here, we can see that he is an exegete well apprised of the criticisms made in recent works by systematic theologians.[21] Thanks to his careful and detailed exegesis of the Synoptic Gospels, as well as by returning to the key texts of the Pauline corpus and of the Letter to the Hebrews, he briefly refutes several common objections, most notably:

17. See Gathercole, *The Preexistent Son*, 174–75.
18. Ibid., 176.
19. See Mt 15:24; Lk 4:18, 43; Mk 9:37 (Lk 9:48); Mt 10:40; Lk 10:16; Lk 14:17; Mk 12:6.
20. See Gathercole, *The Preexistent Son*, 188–89.
21. Already see Simon J. Gathercole, "Preexistence, and the Freedom of the Son in Creation and Redemption. An Exposition in Dialogue with Robert Jenson," *International Journal of Systematic Theology* 7, no. 1 (2005): 38–51.

- The supposed incompatibility between the Son's preexistence and the veracity of Jesus' humanity.[22] Instead, the Synoptic Gospels speak of preexistence as something presupposed for Jesus' human life and not as something devaluing or destroying it.[23]
- The affirmation of a simple, ideal preexistence in God's thought or plan. This kind of very attenuated preexistence simply refers to the divine foreknowledge or predestination which could well apply to nearly all the realities in the Jewish or primitive Christian mentality. A simply-ideal preexistence would have no meaningful relevance for Christological preaching in its primitive context.[24]

Constructively, Gathercole gathers together another major achievement of his study, one that is well-suited for positively founding and enriching a Christology of preexistence: as we have seen many times, the formulas having the form, "I have come for …," emphasize Christ's active role in his incarnation and shed light on fact that the Son's will is engaged in his coming among men.[25]

For my part, I above all retain the fact that the Synoptic motif concerning Christ's coming or being sent implies his preexistence as Son. Not only does the fact of coming from somewhere with a precise end in sight presuppose a deliberate act and active role for Christ in his incarnation, but moreover as the mission received embraces the whole of his earthly activity, it is revealed as having an origin that is external to the human sphere and transcendent over the world into which he comes.

As is almost always the case, such an argument is not completely novel. It quite felicitously combines the old and the new. Therefore, it can help reveal the continued relevance of ancient arguments which have been almost completely ignored in modern discussions

22. Also see McCready, *He Came Down from Heaven*, 28, 262–71, 307.
23. See Gathercole, *The Preexistent Son*, 285–86.
24. See ibid., 286–87.
25. See ibid., 289–90.

of these matters. In turn, such supports are invaluable for solidly re-deploying a systematic theology of preexistence, a theological task that unfortunately is neglected today.

Therefore, our analysis will now consider a particularly rich section of Aquinas's Christology, guiding the discussion by reflecting on his *Summa contra Gentiles* IV.34. There, with great insight, Thomas develops a series of scriptural arguments against Nestorius's Christological error. We will see that many of these arguments dovetail with Gathercole's exegesis, even if they are not applied to the same passages in the Synoptic Gospels, but rather draw from Pauline and Johannine texts. This combined medieval and contemporary contribution enables us to redefine Christ's real preexistence on the basis of the concept of mission—a notion that is at once biblical and dogmatic—without, for all that, separating the man Jesus from the Word of God. Much to the contrary, it makes clear the personal unity of him who was thus sent.

AQUINAS'S SCRIPTURAL ARGUMENTATION IN *SUMMA CONTRA GENTILES* IV.34

Our examination of Thomas's Christology will focus on the scriptural arguments that he develops in IV.34, where he defends the unity of Christ's unity as a single subject, namely, his arguments defending the claim that Christ and the Word are a single Person and hypostasis—a thesis held against Nestorianism and able to provide an utterly solid foundation within Thomas's Christology, which holds that there is only one subsistence in Christ. This argument makes use of a great number of key texts from the New Testament, placing them in high relief. This is particularly true for arguments that, in one form or another, assert Christ the Word's transcendence or preexistence, even in his descent or mission into the world. In order to make clear the theological outlook concerning Christ's preexistence underlying such arguments, let us enter into the pedagogy proper to this rather original Christological chapter in Aquinas's theological oeuvre.

We will prioritize our consideration of this matter from within the framework of IV.34, and when we can draw an important confirmation or supplementary illumination from other works, we will make recourse to Aquinas's scriptural commentaries on the verses mobilized in his argumentation or to its implications in the *Compendium theologiae, De unione,* and the *Tertia pars* of the *Summa theologiae.*

In the fourth book of the *Summa contra Gentiles,* Thomas reflects upon truths that are superior to what can be known by unaided human reason. After considering those that have God himself as their object (namely the Trinity, IV.2–26), Thomas then considers the works of God that exceed reason, among which the incarnation of the Son holds the first rank (IV.27–49). Aquinas introduces his Christological intention as follows:

It now remains to speak of the mystery of the Incarnation itself. Indeed, among divine works, this most especially exceeds reason; for nothing can be thought of which is more marvelous than this divine accomplishment: that the true God, the Son of God, should become true man. And because among them all it is most marvelous, it follows that toward faith in this particular marvel all other miracles are ordered, since "that which is greatest in any genus seems to be the cause of the others."[26]

Such a mystery is so astounding that man's heart could never imagine it on its own. Only the divine authority engaged in revelation enables us to confess the incarnation, just as only the scriptures are able to unveil its principal motive or finality.[27]

The two New Testament passages immediately appealed to by Thomas are John 1:14 and Philippians 2:6–7. In fact, in the sections of his scriptural commentaries devoted to these verses, he explains the matter at length, expressing a robust summary of his theology of the incarnation.[28] Therefore, these two passages provide us with sources

---

26. *SCG* IV.27.1. The text cited at the closing of the passage comes from Aristotle, *Metaphysics* I.993b24–26. Translation drawn from Thomas Aquinas, *On the Truth of the Catholic Faith* (*Summa contra Gentiles*), trans. Charles J. O'Neill (Garden City, N.Y.: Image Books, 1957).

27. See *ST* III, q. 1, a. 3, resp.

28. See *Sup. Io.* 1:14, ed. Marietti, nos. 165–78; *Super Epistolam ad Philippenses lectura* [hereafter *Sup. Phil.*] 2:6–7, ed. Marietti, nos. 53–62.

that clearly attest to the revealed datum which provides a foundation for faith in the mystery of the incarnation. We will again encounter these two key texts—shrewdly associated with Galatians 4:4—among the scriptural arguments that are decisive for analyzing the Son's mission and for extracting its presuppositions in terms of the preexistence, priority, and eternity of the single subject in Christ.

After having assured a first scriptural basis for his Christological reflections in this text, Thomas then proceeds to provide a lengthy exposition and refutation of the most important errors related to the topic of the incarnation (IV.28–36), most notably that of Photinus, that of the Manicheans, that of Valentine, the multiple errors of Apollinaris (certain of which are combined with that of Arius or that of Origen), the central error of Theodore of Mopsuestia and Nestorious, that of Eutyches, etc. The dossier of heresies presented here by Thomas is quite full,[29] offering a typology of errors sketching out the borders within which a correct understanding of the Christological faith can be developed.

Further on, in chapters 37 and 38, Thomas will take a position before two extreme medieval positions which delimit the immediate framework within which he will come to express his own elaboration concerning this matter. On the one hand, there was the *assumptus homo* theory, which envisioned the hypostatic union as being a union of the Person of the Word with a complete man endowed with an autonomous subsistence. On the other hand, there was what we could call the investiture theory (or the *habitus* theory), which held that an accidental union existed between Christ's soul and body—and, hence, between his humanity and the Word. Thomas considers both of these positions as representing resurgent forms of Nestorianism[30] and will himself develop a middle way between them by

---

29. See the supplementary remarks by Jean-Pierre Torrell, "Renseignements techniques," in his *Saint Thomas d'Aquin, Somme Théologique. Le Verbe incarné I* (IIIa q. 1–6) (Paris: Cerf, 2002), 298–306.

30. See *Compendium* I.209–11; *ST* III, q. 2, a. 6, resp. On the development of Thomas's thought on this subject, see Torrell, "Renseignements techniques," 311–19. Also see

means of his theory of the hypostatic union in the single subsistence of Christ the Word.

Chapter 34, where Thomas responds to Nestorius, deserves further examination. Here, Thomas assembles an impressive sequence of scriptural arguments on behalf of Christ's unity as a single subject. He thus seeks to show that the union of the Word and man in the incarnation is not a union that can be reduced to a superior form of indwelling through grace—something that would remain accidental—but rather is a union which is accomplished in the unique Person and hypostasis of the Word-Son.

After having exposited what he retains as paradigmatic from Nestorius's error, namely the accidental (though full) indwelling of God in Christ and the limitations that such a conception of the hypostatic union imposes upon the communication of idioms (§2), Thomas then draws out a well-furnished, manifold scriptural argument as a kind of counterpoint to Nestorius's argument (§§3–31).

Let us follow the developmental arc of chapter 34. The arguments in §§3–4 show that if the Word were united to man through an indwelling of grace, "God would have repeatedly been made flesh since the beginning of the world,"[31] indeed, each time that the Lord dwelt within in holy men (§3) or spoke through the prophets (§4). And one cannot merely invoke a superior degree of indwelling in the case of Christ as though this would properly qualify as an incarnation, for "greater and less do not diversify the species of union."[32] In other words, the very notion (*ratio*) of the incarnation is formally irreducible to that of indwelling.

In the next paragraph (§5), we find a new argument, here in support of a metaphysical interpretation of John 1:14: "The word was made flesh." It is already understood that "flesh" signifies, according to the very use made of the term in the scriptures, "the whole man,

Jason L. A. West, "Aquinas on Peter Lombard and the Metaphysical Status of Christ's Human Nature," *Gregorianum* 88, no. 3 (2007): 557–86.

    31. *SCG* IV.34.3 (trans. Pegis, 165).

    32. Ibid.

also, to express the weakness of the human nature which the Word of God assumed."[33] In order to give the words of John their full weight, Thomas makes use of a principle that formalizes the relations between being and becoming: "Whatever was made is what it was made; thus, what was made man is man, and what was made white is white. But God's Word was made man, as is gathered from the foregoing [discussion]. So God's Word is man." Now, one term cannot be attributed to another if they are not related to the same subject. Hence, "if 'the Word was made flesh,' that is, 'man,' as the Evangelist witnesses [Jn 1:14], it is impossible that there be two persons, or hypostases, or supposits of the Word of God and of that man."[34] This argument fixes the objective sought after in most of the arguments that will follow: it is a question of making use of numerous scriptural resources at Aquinas's disposal in order to show the unwavering unity of the hypostasis and person in the Christ the Word.[35]

A little later on, when he dismisses the *assumptus homo* theory (which, in the final analysis, is really just a form of Nestorianism), Thomas is quite clear about the necessity of maintaining Christ's unity: "Things which are many in supposit are many [beings] simply, and they are but incidentally one. If, then, in Christ there are two supposits, it follows that he is two [beings] simply and not incidentally. And this is 'to dissolve Jesus' [1 Jn 4:3], for everything, in so far as it is, is one."[36] Moreover, such an error would completely ruin the communication of idioms which is such a characteristic element of the very way that the scriptures speak of Christ.[37] In Thomas's estimation, only the assertion that there is a single subject in Christ enables us to maintain the scriptural data concerning the incarnation,

33. Ibid., 33.6 (trans. Pegis, 162). Thomas here cites Is 40:5: "All flesh together shall see that the mouth of the Lord has spoken."

34. *SCG* IV.34.5 (trans. Pegis, 166). The same argument is taken up in *Sup. Io.* 1:14, ed. Marietti, no. 170.

35. Aquinas's next argument is quite eloquent in the same sense as he exploits the use of the pronoun *ego* on Jesus' lips in Jn 8:58 ("Before Abraham was, I am") and Jn 10:30 ("The Father and I are one"). See *SCG* IV.34.6.

36. *SCG* IV.38.11 (trans. Pegis, 189).

37. See *SCG* IV.38.8.

data which regularly interchanges divine and human properties on account of the single subject of attribution that is Christ.[38]

All of the arguments of *Summa contra Gentiles* IV.34 arguing on behalf a single subject in Christ deserve our attention; however, we will limit our consideration to those that imply the dynamic motifs of the descent, coming, and sending ("mission") of Christ. The theological delimitation and qualification of these scriptural motifs represent a considerable contribution to a biblically-founded speculative Christology. Indeed, these notions possess quite a rich basis in the New Testament and must serve as points of contact between the confession of Christological faith and Christological elaboration in theology proper.

THE DESCENT AS AN ASSUMPTION OF A NATURE TAKEN FROM BELOW

A first set of arguments (§§7–8) are concerned with providing a correct interpretation of Christ's "descent." Thomas shows that neither Christ's body nor his soul can be held to descend from heaven. Only the Word really descended:

From our exposition one sees that the body of Christ did not descend from heaven as in Valentine's error [chap. 30], nor did his soul according to Origen's [chap. 33]. What is left is this: one can say pertinently of the Word of God that he descended [from heaven], not by some local motion, but by reason of the union to a lower nature. This was said above [chap. 30]. But that man [namely, Christ], speaking in his own person, says that he descended from heaven in John 6:51: "I am the living bread which came down from heaven." Necessarily, then, the person and hypostasis of that man must be the person of the Word of God.[39]

The argument forever strives to assure Christ's unity as a single subject. Valentine held that "Christ did not have an earthly body, but

___

38. See *SCG* IV.39.1–2.

39. *SCG* IV.34.7 (trans. Pegis, 166). Also, see *Sup. Io.* 6:51, ed. Marietti, no. 957 (*in fine*): "Per hoc excluduntur haereses dicentium Christum purum hominem, quia secundum hoc non descendisset de caelo."

brought one from heaven; that he received nothing from the Virgin Mother, but passed through her as through an aqueduct."[40] Once this error has been avoided, as well as that of Origen concerning the preexistence of Christ's soul,[41] we must recognize that Word himself is the subject of the descent in question. However, we still have more to reflect on so that we may understand aright the action in question: it would not be a question of a change or a mutation,[42] nor of a simple local movement.

This further precision finds an exact parallel in Thomas's exegesis of the Johannine texts attesting to Christ's descent. This point merits a brief detour through the *Lectura super Ioannem* so that we may have a better perception of the scope of the discussion in §7. Reflecting on the words of John 3:13, "No one has ascended into heaven but he who descended from heaven, the Son of man," Aquinas emphasizes the importance of the closing words in this verse: "For he came down from heaven without ceasing to be above, yet assuming a nature which is from below. And because he is not enclosed or held fast by his body which exists on earth, he was, according to his divinity, in heaven and everywhere."[43] Therefore, to descend does not mean to leave a lofty place in the strict and proper sense of these words. Rather, it means to lower oneself by taking an inferior nature onto oneself[44]—or, more precisely, by making it one's own.[45]

The distinction of Christ's two natures proves to be indispensable for us to form a correct notion of the paradox of his descent: "To descend from heaven is said of the Son of Man, not according to his human nature, but according to his divine nature, according to

40. *SCG* IV.30.1 (trans. Pegis, 154).

41. See the parallel text in *Sup. Io.* 3:13, ed. Marietti, no. 467, where Thomas argues against Valentine and Origen with the same argumentative concerns.

42. See *SCG* IV.31. Against the position of Apollinaris, Thomas argues that the incarnation is not a change of the Word, for he remains immutable and simple (i.e., non-composed).

43. *Sup. Io.* 3:13, ed. Marietti, no. 469; trans. Weisheipl, 198.

44. This interpretation of Christ's *kenosis* is constant in Augustine. See *Tractatus in Euangelium Iohannis* 23.6, 36.9, 67.1, 69.3, 78.1; *De Trinitate* I.7.14, VII.3.5.

45. John Damascene, *De fide orthodoxa* 47. This is partially cited by Thomas in *ST* III, q. 10, a. 1. Also see *Sup. Io.* 1:14, ed. Marietti, no. 172.

which it was appropriate to him to have been from heaven before the incarnation, as is said, "Heaven belongs to the Lord" (Ps 113:16).[46] Thus, we have a first way of envisioning the Son's preexistence in his divine nature: he existed in heaven before the incarnation and forever continues to remain there, even when he comes to assume our condition. It is an inalienable property of his divine, eternal, and uncircumscribed nature.

Faced with such an affirmation, we could well fear that a kind of duplication would be posited within Christ as a consequence of his dual belonging to heaven and earth. Indeed, this is the reproach registered by certain contemporary theologians against the descending sort of Christology which presupposes the Word's preexistence as an ontological preliminary to the incarnation.

So far as the *Summa contra Gentiles* is concerned, such a fear is completely unfounded, for the arguments advanced by Thomas all aim at affirming Christ's unity as a single subject. His twofold belonging pertains to the duality of his natures, but we cannot hold that this duality itself does damage to Christ's unity in any way. Here again, we rediscover the equilibrium of Chalcedonian Christology asserting that unity stands at the heart of Christological enunciations from start to finish, so much so that the duality of Christ's natures does not imply any division within the one, unique Person of Christ the Word. There is no separation between the Word and Christ. If we do not isolate either of the propositions from the full and complete movement of the Chalcedonian formula, we must acknowledge the equilibrium of the complete text, which goes from unity to unity by passing through distinction without separation.[47] Taken in its full and complete movement, we cannot reproach the Chalcedonian definition either with an excess of duality nor with a monophysite tendency.

The descent motif is correlative to that of ascent. This connec-

---

46. *Sup. Io.* 3:13, ed. Marietti, no. 468; trans. Weisheipl, 197.

47. See Bernard Sesboüé and Joseph Wolinsky, *Histoire des dogmes*, vol. 1: *Le Dieu du Salut* (Paris: Desclée, 1994), 408–11.

tion is already quite clear in John 3:13. The identity of him who ascends and him who descends already comes to the aid of the purposes of *Summa contra Gentiles* IV.24; §8 of that text negotiates this motif as follows:

> To ascend into heaven plainly belongs to Christ the man who "was raised up while the disciples looked on," as Acts [1:9] says. But to descend from heaven is proper to the Word of God. But the Apostle says: "He that descended is the same also that ascended above all the heavens" [Eph 4:10]. The very person and hypostasis of that man is, accordingly, the person and hypostasis of the Word of God.[48]

According to the scriptures' very manner of speaking,[49] Christ's unity as a single subject is implied by the concrete identity of the man who ascends and the Word who descends.

In the *Summa theologiae*, where he discusses how the assumption of human nature by the Word directly coincides with Christ's conception by the Virgin, Thomas orders the descent and ascent in relation to one another in a way that is consistent with the importance that he accords to the rejection of every form of accidental union between the Word and man in Christ: "The mystery of the Incarnation is not to be looked upon as an ascent, as it were, of a man already existing and mounting up to the dignity of the Union: as the heretic Photinus maintained. Rather is it to be considered as a descent, by reason of the perfect Word of God taking unto himself the imperfection of our nature; according to John 6:38: 'I came down from heaven.'"[50] Indeed, the rejection of Photinianism[51] and Nestorianism requires a Christology that gives priority to the Word's descent, one that is capable of illuminating the fact that Christ's humanity was assumed in the same act by which it was created, without needing any prior, progressive sanctification. The hypostatic union does not require a transformation or prior disposition in the assumed humanity, nor an intermediary quality which would bring about the conjunc-

---

48. *SCG* IV.34.8 (trans. Pegis, 166).

49. See *Sup. Eph.* 4:10, ed. Marietti, no. 209.

50. *ST* III, q. 3, a. 3, ad 3.

51. Also see *Compendium* I.202; *Sup. Rom.* 1:3, ed. Marietti, no. 30.

tion of Christ's humanity with his divinity. It is an immediate union.

In virtue of the very quality of being the image of God, particularly akin to the Word in his own Person-property as the image of the Father, human nature is in some way predisposed to the hypostatic union: "And although the Word of God by his power penetrates all things, conserving all, that is, and supporting all, it is to the intellectual creatures, who can properly enjoy the Word and share with him, that from a kind of kinship of likeness he can be both more eminently and more ineffably united."[52] Thomas thus sets aside the opinion holding that the union would require a *habitus* of grace, that is, an intermediary form or dispositive quality that would render this human nature apt to the hypostatic union.[53] Habitual (or, sanctifying) grace remains an accident, whereas the hypostatic union is not accidental.

THE SENDING OF THE SON INTO THE WORLD PRESUPPOSES HIS PREEXISTENCE

On the basis of the New Testament motifs of coming and sending, Thomas advances an utterly simple argument, one that is marked with the seal of common sense. It could be reformulated thus: the fact of coming anywhere presupposes a prior existence transcending the delimited domain into which one comes. A first form of this argument is developed in a negative manner:

That whose origin is in the world, which had no being before the world, does not properly "come into the world" [*ei quod originem habet ex mundo, et quod non fuit antequam esset in mundo, non convenit venire in mundum*]. But the man Christ in the flesh had his origin in the world, since he had a true, human, earthly body, as was shown. In his soul, as well, he had no being before he was in the world, for he had a true human soul in whose

52. *SCG* IV.41.13 (trans. Pegis, 197). Also, see the three arguments from suitability developed in IV.42.

53. See *ST* III, q. 6, a. 6, s.c. and resp. Moreover, ad 1 emphasizes the difference between our union with God by way of activity, which requires habitual grace, and the union of human nature to the Word in his personal being.

nature there is no being before it is united to the body. So, then, it does not belong to that man's humanity to "come into the world." He himself says, of course, that he came into the world: "I came forth from the Father," he says, "and I came into the world" [Jn 16:28].[54]

Once we have set aside unfounded speculations concerning the heavenly origin of Jesus' body or concerning the preexistence of his soul, we are still left with scripture's way of speaking: that which cannot be explained by his humanity (namely, his transcendent origin) is indeed said of Christ. In a new way, this confirms the fact that there is only one subject for the Word and Christ:

What belongs to the Word of God is truly said of that man. For, that it belongs to the Word of God to come into the world John the Evangelist clearly shows [1:10–11]: "He was in the world, and the world was made by him, and the world knew him not; he came unto his own." So, the person and hypostasis of the man speaking is the person and hypostasis of the Word of God.[55]

Bearing all of this in mind, let us now return to the initial affirmation made by the argument. It includes two key points: the subject's active engagement in his own coming and his anteriority in relation to the terminus of arrival. These two points can receive quite a precise translation into Christological terms, which we must now clarify.

The New Testament emphasizes the fact that Christ was not only sent or commissioned by the Father but, moreover, comes of his own will and is the proper subject of his own act of coming or of entering into the world. This is particularly emphasized in John, but it can also be found in Paul's writings, as well as in the Letter to the Hebrews. Moreover, within the internal arrangement of *Summa contra Gentiles* IV.34, the subsequent argument quite logically makes use of Hebrews 10:5: "Consequently, when Christ came into the world, he said, 'Sacrifices and offerings you have not desired, but a body have you prepared for me.'"

The anteriority pertaining to Christ's coming must be situated in

54. *SCG* IV.34.9 (trans. Pegis, 167).
55. Ibid.

relation to the terminus of the coming itself: he comes to the created world. From our perspective as observers existing in this world and submitted to its temporal progression, we naturally express transcendence in terms of temporal anteriority. To the degree that the incarnation occurs at a precise moment of the world's history, we must speak the subject who comes in function of that which preceded this event. However, this can only be expressed in terms that are formulated from our own human perspective. Thus, anteriority here expresses the idea of ontological preexistence: the Word already existed in a permanent and invariable manner "before" becoming incarnate in our time. This "before" respects scripture's own vocabulary, especially that used by the fourth Gospel. Indeed, even within that very Gospel, we can note an astonishing progression in the reference points used for indicating Christ's anteriority: he existed before John the Baptist (Jn 1:15 and 30); he existed before Abraham (Jn 8:58); he possessed glory before the world existed (Jn 17:5); and he was beloved by the Father before the foundation of the world (Jn 17:24).

Let us return to Thomas's exegesis of John 1:10–11. Here, looking at his interpretation of Christ's "coming," we find ourselves faced with the same kind of precaution that we already encountered in looking at explanation he offered for the "descent":

He came unto his own, in order to be known. The Evangelist says, unto his own, i.e., to things that were his own, which he had made. And he says this so that you do not think that when he says, he came, he means a local motion in the sense that he came as though ceasing to be where he previously was and newly beginning to be where he formerly had not been. He came where he already was. "I came forth from the Father, and have come into the world" [Jn 16:28].[56]

Here, Thomas relies on the theology of the so-called visible mission ordered to the recognition of Christ as the Son of God by believers.[57] Without ceasing to be with the Father, the creator Word en-

56. *Sup. Io.* 1:11, ed. Marietti, no. 143; trans. Weisheipl, 77. Also see *Sup. Io.* 16:28, ed. Marietti, no. 2162.

57. The Augustinian resonances here are clear. See Augustine, *De Trinitate* IV.20 and 29: "Just as when we say that the Son is born we mean that he is from the Father, so too

ters in a new way into the domain that is his own, that is, into the world that came forth from him. "For he was there, indeed, by his essence, power and presence, but he came by assuming flesh. He was there invisibly, and he came in order to be visible."[58] In addition to the Word's threefold presence in this world arising from the divine nature and its own proper manner of being engaged in the creative act,[59] there also is this new manner of being among us.

Note that the reference to John 1:10 also plays an important role in the *Summa theologiae* where Aquinas defines the very concept of mission. When he emphasizes the fact that a mission is constituted by a new manner of existing somewhere, thus prolonging the eternal *processio* by joining a new created effect to it, Thomas always takes care to recall that the Son already was in the world.[60]

Within the context of the *Summa theologiae*'s trinitarian theology, which comes to its completion with Thomas's discussion of the divine missions,[61] the Angelic Doctor does not feel that he must insist on Christ's preexistence, which is evident on the basis of his prior consideration of the eternal processions. However, within the context of the Christology found both in IV.34 and in the parallel texts of his commentary on John, Aquinas takes care to note not only that the Word was already in the world but also that he did not cease to be where he was before, from all eternity.

If we continue our study of IV.34, we find ourselves faced with a new scriptural argument in confirmation of these analyses. Indeed, Aquinas provides an even simpler formulation of what has been established up to this point. In conjunction with the Johannine texts concerning Christ's descent and coming, Thomas mobilizes Galatians 4:4 in order to combine Christ's mission and his birth:

---

when we say that the Son is sent we mean that he is known in his origin from the Father."

58. *Sup Io.* 1:11, ed. Marietti, no. 144; trans. Weisheipl, 77.

59. See *Compendium* I.135; *Sup. Io.* 1:9, ed. Marietti, no. 134.

60. See *ST* I, q. 43, a. 1, resp. (*in fine*).

61. See Gilles Emery, *The Trinitarian Theology of Saint Thomas Aquinas*, trans. Francesca A. Murphy (Oxford: Oxford University Press, 2007), 360–412; Emery, "*Theologia* and *Dispensatio*: The Centrality of the Divine Missions in St. Thomas's Trinitarian Theology," *The Thomist* 74, no. 4 (2010): 515–61.

The Apostle says further that "God sent his Son, made of a woman" (Gal 4:4). These words show us how to understand the sending of the Son of God: He is called sent thither, where he was made of a woman. This could not, of course, be true if the Son of God had not been before he was made of a woman, for that which is sent into another is understood to be previously to its being in that other to which it is sent [*quod in aliquid mittitur, prius esse intelligitur quam sit in eo quo mittitur*]. But that man, the Nestorian adoptive son, had no being before he was born of the woman. The Apostle's word, "God sent his Son," cannot, therefore, be understood of the adoptive son, but must be understood of the natural Son, that is, of God the Word of God. But if one is made of a woman, he is called the woman's son. Therefore, God the Word of God is the Son of a woman.[62]

When the fullness of time had come, Christ the man, born of Mary, was sent by the Father precisely by the very fact that he was born of her in this world.[63] Thus, as the subject of the action of giving birth, the man Jesus is the Son who is sent. Here, Thomas always has in his sight Christ's unity as a single subject. The Word of God can and must be said to be born of a woman.[64] Birth (not distinguished here from conception) does not imply any preexistence of him who thus comes into existence; by contrast, sending presupposes the preexistence of him who is sent in order to accomplish a specific mission in a precise place. This is advanced as a simple, honest statement: "that which is sent into another [place] is understood to [exist prior] to being in that other to which it is sent." To be sent somewhere is to enter into a given place or area. This presupposes that one first was not there. In the case of Christ, the ultimate sent Person, his sending coincides with his coming and entrance into the world. This logically implies his transcendence over the world.

Thus "when Christ came into the world, he said ... behold, I come."[65] Thomas's commentary on this *ingressus* begins by recall-

62. *SCG* IV.34.16 (trans. Pegis, 169).

63. Along the same lines, see *Sup. Io.* 1:14, ed. Marietti, no. 165, which mobilizes Gal 4:4 on behalf of its argument.

64. See *SCG* IV.34.20.

65. Cf. Heb 10:5–7, as used by *SCG* IV.34.10 in order to emphasize the unity of Christ who speaks with the Word who enters into the world.

ing as a kind of *sed contra* the words John 1:10: "He was in the world."
The *respondeo* simultaneously emphasizes the Son's threefold presence to the world and his exteriority in relation to it:

> I answer that it is true that he was in the world as ruling the whole world,
> inasmuch as he is said to be in all things by his essence, presence and power; but he is [also] outside the world [*extra mundum*], because he is not
> comprehended [*comprehenditur*] by the world, but has a goodness separated from the entire world, by which the goodness of the universe is caused.
> Yet, because he assumed a human nature for us, he is said to enter into the
> world, as was stated above: "And again when he brings in the first begotten
> into the world" [Heb 1:6].[66]

Without a doubt, this simple exteriority of him who enters into
the world through his mission is one of the best formulations of
Christ's preexistence. It thus designates the Son's permanent transcendence over the world "before," "during," and "since" his incarnation. Such transcendence in no way diminishes the fact that his
flesh wholly and completely belongs to the world. The Son's preexistence in no way alienates him from the humanity that he receives
from the world (through his birth) at the very same moment when
he created it (through his coming).

Contrary to the reasoning stating that being sent somewhere
presupposes that the sent person preexists prior to his coming, one
could perhaps object that the sent person could be created in the
very act of being sent. This is true for Christ's concrete human nature, but it does not befit his single and unique person and hypostasis, the sent Person *par excellence*, the Word the Son who is spoken of
in John 1:14 as well as in Hebrews 1:2 and Galatians 4:4.

Finally, as is specified in Thomas's commentary on the aforementioned verse from Galatians, if he was sent as a minister (*quasi ministrum*) this would imply an abandonment of his majesty (*depositio
maiestatis*), whereas he, instead, descended as Son through the as-

---

66. *Super Epistolam ad Hebraeos lectura* [hereafter *Sup. Heb.*] 10:5, ed. Marietti, no.
485. Aquinas, *Commentary on the Letter of Saint Paul to the Hebrews*, trans. Fabian R.
Larcher (Lander, Wyo.: Aquinas Institute, 2012), 213.

sumption of the flesh (*assumptio carnis*).[67] Otherwise, the incarnation would have represented a loss of the divinity or of given divine attributes—a rather strange (and, in truth, absurd) interpretation of Christ's *kenosis*.[68]

AN *EXINANITIO* WITH DIVINE GRANDEUR

In *Summa contra Gentiles* IV.34, §22, Thomas's interpretation of the "abasement" expressed in Philippians 2:6–7 is in the line with what the Church Fathers thought concerning this matter.[69] This intersects with the conception of the "descent" which Thomas explains as being a kind of assumption of the human nature to the Person of the Word. The key for reading Philippians 2:6–7 is to take seriously the unity of the subject engaged in the *forma divina* and in the *forma servi*:

The Apostle, once more, says of Christ Jesus that, "being in the form of God, emptied [*exinanivit*] himself, taking the form of a servant, being made in the likeness of men" [Phil 2:6–7]. Now, clearly, if, following Nestorius, we divide Christ into two—into that man who is the adoptive son, and into God's natural Son who is the Word of God—this text cannot be understood of that man. For that man, if he be pure man, was not first in the form of God, so as to be made later in the likeness of man; rather conversely: the existing man was made to share in divinity; in this he was not emptied, but exalted.[70]

---

67. See *Super Epistolam ad Galatas lectura* 4:4, ed. Marietti, no. 202, which mobilizes Jn 1:8, 1:14, 3:13 in its argumentation.

68. See the severe judgment formulated on this point by Barth, *Church Dogmatics*, IV.1, §59.1, 180–83. On the multiple meanings of the term *kenosis* in modern theology, see C. Stephen Evans (ed.), *Exploring Kenotic Christology: The Self-Emptying of God* (Oxford: Oxford University Press, 2006). The most useful contribution on this subject is that of Thomas R. Thompson concerning the novel insights of Gottfried Thomasius which have had lasting influence. It is also particularly interesting to see the care taken, out of ecumenical sensitivity, by Bruce L. McCormack, "Karl Barth's Christology as a Resource for a Reformed Version of Kenoticism," *International Journal of Systematic Theology* 8, no. 3 (2006): 243–51.

69. For a typology of the various interpretations of the *kenosis* discussed in Phil 2:6–7, see Jean-Noël Aletti, *St. Paul, Épître aux Philippiens* (Paris: Gabalda, 2005), 158–59.

70. *SCG* IV.34.22 (trans. Pegis, 171).

Once the Nestorian thesis has been ruled out, we must recognize that the Jesus Christ spoken of by the Apostle, he who is the subject of this abasement, is the Son the Word in person: "The text must, then, be understood of the Word of God who first was eternally in the form of God [*qui prius fuerit ab aeterno in forma Dei*], that is, in the nature of God, and later emptied himself, made in the likeness of man."[71] Even when he speaks of Christ, Paul's words quite obviously must be attributed personally, according to the hypostasis, to the Word of God. Christ's unity as a single subject is thus frequently attested to in the New Testament. A little further on, Thomas emphasizes an analogous phenomenon expressed in Colossians 1:16–18: "Now, clearly, the text, 'In him were all things created,' refers to the Word of God; whereas the text, 'first-born from the dead,' belongs to the man Christ. Therefore, God's Word and the man Christ are one supposit and, consequently, one Person; and whatever is said of that man must he said of the Word of God, and conversely."[72]

The principle of creation reveals himself as also being the first of the resurrected. Whereas creation falls to Christ inasmuch as he is God, he is resurrected inasmuch as he is a man. Beyond this particular attestation to Christ's unity, the communication of the eternal and temporal properties in Christ is frequently presented as being the privileged thematic way for discussing scripture's language speaking of Christ as a single subject.[73]

Now, let us return for a moment to the discussion of Christ's preexistence functioning as a presupposition for Thomas's exegesis of Philippians 2:6–7. The Word's anteriority and preexistence to the incarnation were rightly qualified by the *ab aeterno* of his *forma Dei*. His anteriority in relation to the assumed humanity, thus expressed from our perspective, is a simple ontological "overhang" on the side of the Word.

Thomas then shows once again that "by itself, the indwelling of

71. Ibid.

72. Ibid., 34.29 (trans. Pegis, 174).

73. The affirmation of the communication of idioms is a constant theme in *SCG* IV.34.

the Word in the man Jesus Christ does not enable us to understand this emptying," for merely on the basis of such indwelling we would describe something that would hold for all the saints, as well as for the Father and the Spirit just as much as it does for the Son—an utterly absurd claim.[74] Thus, Thomas finally defines the emptying in a positive manner: "namely, let the Word of God be called 'emptied' [*exinanitum*], that is, made small [*parvum vactum*], not by the loss of his own greatness [*non amissione magnitudinis*], but by the assumption of human smallness [*assumption humanae parvitatis*]."[75] Indeed, such smallness and weakness characterize the assumed nature in its condition of fragility and passibility, affected by the consequences of sins according to a disposition of Christ's saving work, even if Christ himself was without sin.[76] Thus, if he assumed human nature in the condition that is our own, he did so because it was befitting in view of restoring it.[77]

The *exinanitio* does not imply the abandonment of the divinity, nor the abandonment of any of the divine attributes. Indeed, this would imply a true alteration of the unique subject who is engaged in the incarnation. Christ's unity as a single subject completely rules out this foolish idea precisely because the Word of God cannot change without thereby ceasing to be God.[78] It is utterly absurd to think that such becoming could affect the Word and "momentarily" deprive him of certain properties of his divine nature, for this would

74. See *Sup. Rom.* 1:3, ed. Marietti, no. 35; *Compendium*, I.203; *De unione*, a. 1, resp.; *Sup. Io.* 1:14, ed. Marietti, no. 176. The second aspect of the argument is not formulated in *SCG* IV.34.

75. *SCG* IV.34.22 (trans. Pegis, 171). The same definition will be taken up in this form in *De unione*, a. 1, ad 14: "non quidem deponens magnitudinem formae Dei, sed assumens parvitatem humanae naturae."

76. See *Sup. Io.* 3:31, ed. Marietti, no. 527. Christ took on something from the three states of humanity, namely, a flesh that was undefiled (i.e., from our state of original justice), the capacity to suffer and die (i.e., from our sinful state, without himself being subject to sin), and the impossibility to sin, as well as the full development of the soul (i.e., from our glorified state in the hereafter).

77. See *Sup. Io.* 1:14, ed. Marietti, nos. 168–69.

78. See ibid. (no. 166). Against the thesis attributed to Eutyches, Thomas recalls that the Word was God and that God is immutable, therefore not being able to be changed into another nature.

not merely entail a modification of certain accidental properties of the divine nature—which, in any case, are not found in God—but, rather would in fact entail an alteration of the divine subject himself (a completely meaningless proposition).

The theological outlook of the Thomistic thesis holds that the hypostatic union is a mixed relation, one that is "real" on the side of the assumed human nature (for it holds its very existence from this relation) and "rationate" (*relatio rationis*) on the side of the divine subject (for it does not change in itself because of the incarnation).[79] However, this does not mean that the hypostatic union would be accidental. Indeed, the full strength of Aquinas's theological insight came to bear in order to show that this union was brought about in the unique subsistence of the Word-Son. See the first stage of the conclusion of the Christological section of *Summa contra Gentiles IV*:

For all that, just because the Word preexists from eternity [*ab aeterno praeexistit*], it does not follow that the human nature accrues to the Word accidentally [*accidentaliter adveniat*] ... For the Word assumed human nature so as to be truly man. But to be man is to be in the genus of a substance. Therefore, since by union with human nature the hypostasis of the Word has the being of man, this does not accrue to the Word accidentally. For accidents do not bestow substantial being.[80]

If the Son is said to have been emptied (*exinanitum*) or "made less" (*breviatum*), this is "not because something would have been subtracted [*subtractum*] from the plenitude or grandeur of the divinity itself but, rather, because he took on our weakness [*exilitas*] and smallness [*parvitas*]."[81] Indeed, he did not deliver over his divinity or empty himself of it, for "he remained what he was and assumed what he was not."[82]

---

79. See *ST* III, q. 2, a. 7; *Sup. Io.* 1:14, ed. Marietti, no. 172.

80. *SCG* IV.49.16, trans. Charles J. O'Neill (Notre Dame, Ind.: University of Notre Dame Press, 1975), 211 (slightly altered). Also see *De unione*, a. 1, resp. and ad 13; *ST* III, q. 2, q. 2, a. 5, ad 1; q. 2, a. 6, ad 2; q. 17, a. 2, resp. (*in fine*).

81. *Sup. Rom.* 9:28, ed. Marietti, no. 805.

82. *Sup. Phil.* 2:6–7, ed. Marietti, no. 57: "Quod erat permansit et quod non erat,

SOTERIOLOGICAL IMPLICATION: THE SAVING HUMANITY OF THE PREEXISTENT SON

We have not yet exploited one of the conclusions of Gathercole's study. He came to the conviction that while Christ's preexistence does not in any way detract from the priority that rightly falls to soteriology and eschatology in the New Testament, nonetheless we should maintain the very equilibrium of the Synoptic Gospels by recognizing the fact that the scandal of the cross precisely lies in the fact that he who was crucified had a heavenly identity. Such are Gathercole's closing words in his final chapter: "The heavenly preexistence of Christ then does not diminish the importance of his death, but rather is part of the reason for the scandalous paradox of that death."[83]

The development of the soteriological implications of Christ's preexistence does not fall within the central concerns of the chapter from Thomas that we have been using in this study. However, these implications are quite clearly developed in other places within Thomas's Christology as a kind of prolongation of Augustine's Christology. Here, we can recall one of them, namely, how the incarnation eloquently attests to the humility of the Son of God.

In the *Summa theologiae*, the consideration of the humility of the Son of God plays a particularly important role in the first question of Christology, which discusses the "reasons from suitability" on behalf of the incarnation. Such arguments are always *a posteriori* in character: given that the Word of God *in fact* became incarnate, what reasons can we marshal in our attempt to perceive the suitability and finality of this act?

---

assumsit." One may perhaps expect Thomas to interpret 2 Cor 8:9 in the same way as calling to mind the incarnation. However, this is not the case. In the latter text, he understands this impoverishment of Christ as being a neediness in relation to material goods whereas he was rich in spiritual goods. See *Super Secundam epistolam ad Corinthios lectura* 8:9, ed. Marietti, no. 294.

83. Gathercole, *The Preexistent Son*, 292.

Thomas first examines this question in relation to God and then in relation to our own condition.[84] The principal suitability is drawn from the very nature of God: he is the sovereign Good, and it is highly befitting to say that he would communicate himself to the creature in a sovereign manner. On our side, it will be a question of knowing whether the incarnation is, properly speaking, "necessary" for the restoration of our nature, that is, for the rehabilitation of our sinful condition. We need not envision an absolute necessity here. It is a question of a necessity that is relative to an end being aimed at, namely, salvation. Thus, this comes down to asking whether the incarnation is indeed the best, most apt way for bringing about our salvation.

The arguments offered here are multiple and inspiring. They principally come from Augustine's meditation on the scriptures. Without claiming that they are exhaustive, something impossible in the present case, Thomas closes his response with a comment that leaves room for the incomprehensibility of the mystery in its contingency and gratuity: "And there are very many other advantages which accrued [from the incarnation], above man's apprehension."[85]

Thomas uses two groupings for classifying the reasons retained from Augustine: that which fosters our progress toward the good and that which draws us away from evil. The attestation to God's humility in the incarnation is seen in this second register in the following manner: "'man's pride, which is the greatest stumbling-block to our clinging to God, can be convinced and cured by humility so great,' as Augustine says in the same place [*De Trinitate*, XIII.17]."[86] The Son's equality with God (Phil 2:6) represents a direct corollary of the Son's preexistence. Following this schema, the Son freely lowered himself according to the divine will which he entirely shared in and to which he consented by his very nature. This lowering can be described as a kind of humility and is presented to us an example (see Phil 2:5, Mt 11:27).

84. *ST* III, q. 1, aa. 1–2.
85. *ST* III, q. 1, a. 2, resp. (*in fine*): "Sunt autem et aliae plurimae utilitates quae consecutae sunt, supra comprehensionem sensus human."
86. Ibid.

Augustine's formula is pithy, lapidary, and eloquent. Thomas accepts it here as such. However, this treatment should be enriched and qualified by the specifications he expresses in *Summa contra Gentiles* IV.55. After having explained the arguments from suitability on behalf of the incarnation (IV.54), Thomas responds in chapter 55 to the objections made against the suitability of the incarnation in chapter 53. The objection raised against the idea of God's humility is quite pertinent:

But let a man say that this was necessary as a demonstration of humility, as the Apostle appears to say, that Christ "humbled himself, becoming obedient unto death" (Phil 2:8)—this reason is not suitable either, because, in the first place, one must commend humility in him who has a superior to whom he can be subject. This cannot be said of God. Therefore, it was not suitable for God's Word to be humbled unto death.[87]

Thomas responds to this strongly worded objection by making recourse not only to the distinction of the two natures but also to Christ's unity as a single subject:

In the same way, too, there is no awkwardness in saying that Christ willed the death on the cross as a demonstration of humility. To be sure, the humility does not touch God, as the seventeenth argument was proposing. Truly, the virtue of humility consists in this, that one keep himself within his own limits; he does not stretch himself to what is above him, but he subjects himself to his superior. Hence, clearly, God can have no proportionate humility, for he has no superior; he himself exists above all things. But, if a man at times subjects himself in humility to an equal or inferior, this is because the one who is his equal or inferior simply is held by the man as his superior in a certain respect. Therefore, although the virtue of humility was not fitting to Christ in his divine nature, it was fitting to him in his human nature, and his humility was tendered the more praiseworthy by his divinity. For the dignity of the person contributes to the praise humility deserves; for example, when out of some necessity a great man has to suffer something lowly. But there can be no dignity of man so great as this: that he be God. Hence, the humility of the God-man was praiseworthy in the extreme when he bore those abject things which he was called on to suffer for the salvation of men.[88]

87. *SCG* IV.53.18 (trans. O'Neill, 226).
88. Ibid., 55.20 (trans. O'Neill, 242).

As regards the single, unique subject who is Christ (i.e., the person who is the subject of this lowering), it is not only a question of the humility of the man Jesus or of the humility of Jesus' humanity but, rather and quite precisely, the humility of the eternal Son. The single, unique subject who is Christ is the eternal, transcendent, and preexisting Son, without for all that meaning that the humanity would be united to him in an accidental manner.

If we place parentheses around the Son's real preexistence, Christ's humility becomes nothing more than the greatest possible human humility, repaid by God in the resurrection. For certain thinkers, Christ's humility and obedience go so far that they reveal that he is the Son of God. According to Pannenberg, the identification of Jesus with the eternal Son of God is manifested and realized through his human relation to the Father.[89] One could say that this relation goes so far down the road of unconditional obedience that it reveals itself as being the very same relation as that which unites the eternal Son to the Father. Jesus is himself never equal to God but, on the contrary, lowered himself and allowed himself to be humiliated to the point of death in such a way that he lives as a man in a way that approximates the Son's "eternal submission" to the Father. This presupposes an archetypical form of submission, obedience, or humility in the eternal relation of the Son to the Father from whom he comes forth. This outlook is closely akin to a form of trinitarian theology that would risk expressing a deformed image of the reality of origination in the trinitarian relations in God, which we must reflect on without introducing any notion of subordination, something we have discussed elsewhere at greater length.[90]

From Thomas's perspective, Christ's humility contains much more than that. It is assuredly something exemplary for us.[91] However, given that it is the humility of the Son of God in person, it is

---

89. See Pannenberg, *Systematic Theology*, 2:308–11.

90. See Durand, *La Périchorèse des personnes divines*, 125–49.

91. See *ST* II-II, q. 161, a. 5, arg. 4 and ad 4. The objection claims that humility is the greatest of virtues, calling upon, as supposed witnesses to this assertion, Augustine, Mt 11:29, and Gregory the Great.

not a simple model for Christian action. It is also efficaciously salvific far beyond Jesus' exemplarity or the moral causality of his merits. This topic has been discussed in admirable studies by profound Thomistic writers.[92]

RESKETCHING CHRIST'S PREEXISTENCE

We will draw to a close by enunciating the principal acquisitions of our reading of Thomas's scriptural argumentation with the end of better characterizing Christ's preexistence. In this way, we can gather together the synergistic fruits we have brought forth from our reflection on Gathercole's exegesis and Aquinas's scriptural demonstration, spurred on by a strong dogmatic aim:

- Christ's preexistence is not only ideal, something laying merely within God's plan, but instead is something real inasmuch as he is the Son of the Father *ab aeterno*. A merely ideal preexistence would not do justice to the specific, bold claim made by the Christian faith.
- Christ's preexistence as the eternal Son enables us to understand his personal engagement and active role in the very act of being sent and of coming into the world. Christ is not passive in the fact of being sent, just as he is not passive in the fact of being begotten of the Father. His sending by the Father is a free coming into the world, just as his being begotten by the Father is also an eternal generation of which the Son is the active subject.[93] Here, we see that we can indeed say that the Son's *missio* prolongs his eternal *processio*.

92. See Theophil Tschipke, *L'humanité du Christ comme instrument de salut de la divinité* (Fribourg: Academic Press, 2003); Jean-Pierre Torrell, "La causalité salvifique de la résurrection du Christ selon saint Thomas," in his *Recherches thomasiennes* (Paris: Vrin, 2000), 214–41.

93. We have already elsewhere explained the active role of the Son in his eternal generation by the Father. See Emmanuel Durand, *Le Père Alpha et Oméga de la vie trinitaire* (Paris: Cerf, 2008), 245–74.

- Such a preexistence coincides with the transcendence implied in the very notion of a mission, at least if the latter is recognized as being the eschatological mission of the sent Person *par excellence*. Understood in this way, Christ's mission embraces Jesus' complete trajectory in his incarnation, death, resurrection, and ascension, having the world in its universality as the field in which it is exercised.

- Christ's preexistence thus designates his transcendence over the world into which he is sent. One can thus consider it as being the ontological permanence of the Son through Jesus' entire mission, as much "before" as "during" and "since" the incarnation. These temporal categories are legitimate in relation to the humanity assumed in our temporal condition and on account of the time-bound perspective embedded in the language we must use in our Christological discourse.

- Such an understanding of Christ's preexistence remains continually subordinate to the affirmation of the unity of Christ the Word as a single subject. In such a Christology, Christ's preexistence cannot be considered as though it were an infringement on Christ's unity nor as a forgetfulness of his full humanity. Such is indeed one of the conclusions of the Christological section of the *Summa contra Gentiles*: "For all that, just because the Word preexists from eternity, it does not follow that the human nature accrues to the Word accidentally."[94]

- Accessible on the basis of the soteriological concept of mission, Christ's real preexistence explains the depths and power of the salvific humility of the Son of God.

More broadly, regarding the *modus operandi* and resources available within Christological reflection, the notion of mission or sending here serves as a very useful platform for discussing these matters, for it naturally makes use of the point of contact between New

94. *SCG* IV.49.16 (trans. O'Neill, 211, slightly altered).

Testament Christology and systematic Christology. Just as much as the Pauline and Johannine bodies of literature, the Synoptic Gospels enable us to elaborate the New Testament motif of sending into a robust concept for use within Christological discourse. By so recognizing the fact that Christ's eschatological and universal mission implies his preexistence as Son, we thereby find ourselves faced with an articulation of Christ's full identity.

17

Aquinas on the
Incarnation as a "Conversation"
in Charity

Evangelization is achieved through a kind of conversation with God and with men and women, including those who come from different backgrounds or who hold different convictions from our own.[1] The Gospels provide us with the fundamental principles for such a task. There, we see Jesus himself often entering into conversation, especially with his disciples and opponents. Undoubtedly, Christ is the Master: "Neither be called masters, for you have one master, the Christ" (Mt 23:10).[2] And yet, in the Gospels, with the exception of the Sermon on the Mount and his paradoxical elevation upon the cross, we do not find Christ proclaiming the message of revelation as though he were announcing it from a pulpit on high. More often than not, he communicates this revelation on an even level with those to whom it is addressed, through the channels of dialogue,

---

1. The motif of conversation recurs in many of the letters of Master Bruno Cadoré, OP. In particular, see "Envoyés pour prêcher l'Évangile," *Ordre des Prêcheurs*, March 25, 2017; available at www.op.org.

2. Basically, Christ is the only Master because he is in Person the Word of God; he is also Master in his humanity because he has been sent to teach, as Jn 1:18 and 13:13 attest, according to Aquinas, *Sup. Mat.* 23:10, ed. Marietti, no. 1852; see also *Sup. Io.* 13:13, no. 1775. Regarding the development of this motif, see Klimczak, *Christus Magister*.

378

controversy, confrontation, and even that of his own trial. Christ's word elicits amazement, provokes rejections, arouses responses, unmasks prejudices, outmaneuvers traps set for him, and finally, finds itself placed before a court inquiry.

Through his prophets, God already spoke his word to his people in various ways: in commands, instructions, words of consolation, appeals, invective, reproaches, and so forth. Some of the words addressed to them came close to having a dialogic tone, either with the person of the prophet (or envoy) or with the entire people called to respond through their commitment and action.[3]

It would be fruitful to revisit the ancient motif of *conversatio*, which extends beyond the registers of speech and dialogue. Through the incarnation, God entered into a kind of multifaceted conversation with humanity. What kind of conversation are we faced with here? What is its breadth? What is its aim? Where does it begin, and who is involved in it? What are the registers on which such a conversation takes place? To respond to these questions, we can gain much by exploring the motif of *conversatio* in the works of Aquinas. This Dominican friar entered into the Order of Preachers against his family's wishes, spurning the abbacy of Monte Cassino for which he had been prepared in his youth. Such a choice seems to have been motivated by a personal discernment bent on living a life of Gospel perfection, one that is poor and itinerant, having close proximity with the way of life embraced by Christ himself.[4]

Question 40 of the *Tertia pars* of the *Summa theologiae* is concerned with "Christ's way of life" (*De modo conversationis Christi*). For Thomas, to present the way that Christ acted in the midst of his contemporaries, as well as the character of his life among them, prin-

3. Pope Paul VI, in his encyclical *Ecclesiam Suam*, and then the Second Vatican Council, in the constitution *Dei Verbum*, presented revelation and salvation as being an extensive dialogue (*colloquium*) of God with humanity. See Paul VI, *Ecclesiam Suam* (August 6, 1964), pars. 60–122; Vatican Council II, *Dei Verbum*, no. 8, §3; no. 21; no. 25, §1.

4. See Ulrich Horst, "Christ, *Exemplar Ordinis Fratrum Praedictorum*, according to Saint Thomas Aquinas," in *Christ Among the Medieval Dominicans*, ed. Kent Emery Jr. and Joseph Wawrykow (Notre Dame, Ind.: University of Notre Dame Press, 1998), 256–70.

cipally involves a profound Christological meditation on the concrete dynamic of revelation and likewise engages us in a defense of
the way of life adopted by the Dominican friars.[5]

**MEANINGS AND USES,
COUNTERPARTS, AND REGISTERS
OF *CONVERSATIO***

Before looking into the implications of *conversatio* in Aquinas's
works, let us consult the meaning of the term as it is presented to
us in two reference dictionaries. Here are two brief forms of such
entries for the noun *conversatio* and the verb *conversor, -ari*; Blaise
(1954)[6] and Oxford (1982),[7] respectively:

Conversatio: ¶1 action de se retourner, de retourner ¶2 (moral.) trans-
formation, conversion ¶3 genre de vie, manière de vivre, cité || notre cité,
notre vie || conduite, mœurs, vie ¶4 vie monastique ¶5 relations, familiar-
ité, intimité || commerce, conversation || relations sexuelles.

Conversor, -ari: vivre avec || vivre, se conduire, se comporter.

Conuersatio: 1 A turning round, revolution. b the action of moving
about in a place 2 Habitual association, familiarity, intimacy (with a person). b constant practical experience (of a thing), acquaintance. c frequent
resorting (to a place). 3 Conduct, behavior.

Conuersor, -ari: 1 To consort, associate (with). b to be a constant visi-
tor (to a place) 2 To conduct oneself, behave, act.

A number of the meanings for the noun *conversatio* and the verb
conversor, -ari are in line with how Thomas made use of the terms,

5. The contemplation of Christ's life in this context encountered two concrete issues
of ecclesial life and ecclesiastical rivalries. The underlying controversy was twofold in nature. On the one hand, the mendicant orders were put on trial by certain secular masters
in relation to the how those living a mendicant life could legitimately obtain university
chairs. On the other, the Dominicans and Franciscans differed in how they understood
the life of voluntary poverty in relation to Christian perfection.

6. Albert Blaise, *Dictionnaire latin-français des auteurs chrétiens* (Turnhout: Brepols,
1954).

7. P. G. W. Glare, *Oxford Latin Dictionary* (Oxford: Clarendon Press, 1982).

especially "a way life, conduct, or behavior" as well as "the frequenting of a place, commerce, and familiarity or intimacy." In order to do justice to the many valences that the term *conversatio* takes on in the Latin language and in Thomas's theology, from now on in this study, we will use the substantives "conversation" / "converse" and the verb "to converse" in the Latin senses of the terms, without restricting their scope solely to verbal dialogue.

Aided by the *Index thomisticus*, an inquiry into the various ways that Thomas used *conversatio / conversor, -ari* in his works enables us to specify the types of partners and kinds of interactions implied in the *conversationes* explored by Aquinas. As regards the kinds of partners involved in *conversatio*, we have identified the following:

- *Conversatio* between human beings in the context of interpersonal friendships or amicable sharing of life[8]
- *Conversatio* in other forms of association: those of members of the household, those of citizens, those of participants in religious activities and worship[9]
- *Conversatio* between human beings and the souls of the dead, which can only be exercised in the supernatural order[10]
- *Conversatio* between human beings and the angels, which is possible in the natural order through the life of the spirit[11]
- *Conversatio* between human beings and God, made possible by charity, at once *in via* and *in patria*[12]

As regards the kinds of interaction found between these partners, the following registers emerge as distinct, though not necessarily separable, kinds of interaction:

8. See Aquinas, *ST* II-II, q. 114, a. 1, resp. and ad 1.
9. See Aquinas, *ST* I-II, q. 101, a. 4, resp.; q. 104, a. 4, resp.; II-II, q. 50, a. 3, ad 1; and multiple uses of Phil 3:20: "nostra autem conversatio in caelis est."
10. See Aquinas, *ST* I, q. 89, resp.
11. See Aquinas, *ST* II-II, q. 25, a. 10, ad 3.
12. See Aquinas, *ST* I-II, q. 65, a. 5, resp.

- Bodily conversations[13]
- Spiritual conversations, whether natural or supernatural[14]
- Conversations performed in both words and deeds together[15]

Let us pursue our inquiry by starting our reflections within the domain of Christology in order to see how, according to Thomas, Christ's mode of conversation with his contemporaries represents an integral part of God's activities in manifesting himself and in bringing salvation to men. Then, by extending our horizons, we will see that the Christological conversation intersects with the conversational dynamic of charity. This will enable us to coordinate two conversations: that of Christ with his contemporaries and that of God with humanity. Let us begin by first exploring the biblical foundations of the Christological conversation.

THE BIBLICAL FOUNDATIONS OF
THE CHRISTOLOGICAL CONVERSATION

Baruch 3:38 and Daniel 2:11

When he begins his discussion of Christ's way of life, Aquinas plays two biblical verses off each other. The *Summa theologiae* raises the question, "Should Christ have led a solitary life or, instead, should he have had converse with men?" (III, q. 40, a. 1). The first objection argues that Christ's way of life should reveal that he was not only a man but also was God. This seems to exclude a life of ordinary commerce among men and to require a solitary life of contemplation. The objection in support of this claim summons two authorities: a verse from the Book of Daniel regarding the human limits of divination as well as a famed passage from Aristotle's *Politics* concerning

---

13. For example, between Hebrews and Egyptians; see Aquinas, *ST* I-II, q. 102, a. 3, ad 2.

14. For example, the attendance of Wisdom (Wis 8:16), according to Aquinas, *ST* I-II, q. 35, a. 5, s.c.

15. See Aquinas, *ST* II-II, q. 114, a. 1, resp.; q. 40, a. 1, ad 1; q. 42, a. 1, ad 2.

the solitary man's condition. The Philosopher holds that man is naturally a political animal, so much so that a solitary man having neither city nor community is either a beast or a god.[16] The quotation from Daniel 2:11 is worth considering, because the *sed contra* contrasts it with another biblical verse, one that is decisive for our inquiry, namely, Baruch 3:38.

Nebuchadnezzar, the king of Babylon, was tormented by dreams. Looking to obtain an interpretation for them, he summons his court magicians and seers, drawn from the "Chaldeans," to himself in the hopes of obtaining an interpretation of his dream. From the start, the king's request is both suspicious and threatening in tone. Feeling the pressure of these circumstances, the Chaldeans admit that they cannot provide a response to Nebuchadnezzar. Such a response would belong to the gods, who do not converse with men. Daniel 2:11 in the Vulgate reads: "Sermo enim, quem tu rex quaeris, gravis est; nec reperietur quisquam qui indicet illum in conspectu regis, exceptis diis, quorum non est cum hominibus conversatio" (in Douay-Rheims, "For the thing that thou asketh, O king, is difficult: nor can any one be found that can shew it before the king, except the gods, whose conversation is not with men"). While the Chaldeans are sent off to their death, Daniel inquires into their fate, asks that their execution be delayed, and pledges to provide the king with the interpretation that he awaits. To this end, Daniel mobilizes his companions in prayer. Himself benefitting from a "vision of the night" (Dn 2:19), Daniel receives an interpretation of the dream. In thanksgiving, he addresses himself to God as to him who alone reveals secrets and who knows what is hidden (Dn 2:20–23). The Chaldeans' claims regarding the converse between man and the gods was not utterly meaningless. Nonetheless, it is surpassed by Daniel's clairvoyance, for he knows whom he should address concerning such matters.

In any case, Daniel 2:11 is appended to the objection concerning Christ's way of life (that is, his converse with men). The objection

16. See Aristotle, *Politics* I.2.1253a29.

thus argues that, given the fact that Christ is God, he should not enter into such commerce with men but, rather, should lead a solitary life. The discrepancy between the citation and the objection is appreciable. With their questionable theology, the Chaldeans speak about the gods in pagan terms, in the sense of angels, spirits, or demons. It is quite inappropriate to apply this verse to Christ, who is not a god in that sense. The objection's supposed biblical foundation is, in fact, null and void.

By contrast, the verse drawn from Baruch and mobilized by Aquinas in the *sed contra* turns out to be Christologically relevant. It comes at the end of a series of verses praising Wisdom in the form of a lamentation over Israel. The people's exile is understood as being the consequence for having abandoned the source of Wisdom (Bar 3:10–12). In practical terms, this involves their abandonment of the Law and their adoption of evil ways. Wisdom is not known by the leaders of the nations and is not accessible to human enterprises. God alone, who knows all things, possesses it and shares it with his people. The Vulgate and Douay-Rheims editions read as follows, for Baruch 3:36–38:

Hic Deus noster, et non aestimabitur alius adversus eum. Hic adinvenit omnem viam disciplinae, et tradidit illam Iacob, puero suo, et Israel, dilecto suo. Post haec in terris visus est, et cum hominibus conversatus est.

This is our God, and there shall no other be accounted of in comparison of him. He found out all the way of knowledge, and gave it to Jacob his servant, and to Israel his beloved. Afterwards he was seen upon earth, and conversed with men.

The Jewish theology exemplified by the passage personifies Wisdom and incarnates it in some manner in the Law given to the people. According to some modern translations of the Bible, the subject who thus conversed with men here is Wisdom, which is then immediately and explicitly identified with the Law (Bar 4:1). In the Vulgate, by contrast, God himself is the subject of the final phrase: he himself was seen on the earth and conversed with men. Such a reading can be found, for example, in the Douay-Rheims English translation of the Sixto-Clementine edition of the Vulgate, a Latin edition whose text was close in form to the various biblical texts used by Aquinas. In the end, to present God, rather than Wisdom, as the object of vision and the subject of conversation remains consistent with the Jewish outlook concerning Wisdom, which is envisioned as one of the concrete modalities of God's presence to his people.

Whether the subject be Wisdom or God, Baruch 3:38 is perfectly suited for presenting an argument from authority in favor of the idea that Christ fully conversed with men instead of living a solitary life. The passage bears witness to a real anticipation of the logic of the incarnation. Whereas Daniel 2:11 is a bit like shifting sand on this point, Baruch 3:38 provides a solid foundation for justifying the idea that Christ had full converse with his contemporaries. The literal meaning of this verse from Baruch supports its integration into a Christological thesis. We will find that much is to be gained from exploring how Aquinas makes use of this verse throughout his various works.

BARUCH 3:38 IN THREE BIBLICAL EXEGESES CONCERNING THE INCARNATION

The verse from Baruch declaring that God conversed with men—in the full sense of living and remaining with them—orients our investigation toward the explanations elaborated by Aquinas regarding three key texts related to the incarnation: Matthew 1:25, Philippians 2:7, and Hebrews 1:1–2.

On Matthew 1:25

Matthew 1:18–25 recounts Christ's coming into the world from Joseph's perspective. In a dream, the latter receives a revelation from the angel of the Lord regarding Mary and the child who has been begotten in her. The evangelist discerns these events as being the fulfillment of the words of Isaiah 7:14 proclaiming that the Virgin would conceive and give birth. The prophetic message is brought to a close with the words: "And he shall be called Emmanuel" (Mt 1:23, citing Is 7:14). Immediately thereafter in the narrative, in accord with the nighttime revelation, Joseph gives the child the name Jesus. The discrepancy between the two names, Emmanuel and Jesus, raises a question to which Aquinas responds in his commentary. Given that the angel's words present Jesus as the savior, Thomas holds that the name Jesus proves to be identical to Emmanuel, which means "God with us" (*nobiscum Deus*).

Of greater importance for our inquiry, Thomas then explains the four ways that God is with us. Presupposing the aforementioned equivalence between the names Jesus and Emmanuel, these four ways are all related to the incarnation, God's multiform presence with men through Christ. God is with us in the following ways:

- Through his assumption of human nature in the incarnation (Jn 1:14: "And the Word became flesh")
- Through the conformity of this nature with ours, for it is like ours in all things (Phil 2:27: "He was made like unto men and was recognized as a man by his behavior")
- Through his bodily conversation with us (Bar 3:38: "after this, he was seen on the earth and conversed with men")
- Through his spiritual conversation with us (Mt 28:20: "and behold that I am with you forever until the consummation of the ages")[17]

This unfolding of the semantic scope contained in the name "Emmanuel" into four modes of being-with-us amplifies the meaning of the incarnation. Christ's assumption of human nature does not provide the full story regarding the incarnation, for the latter also, as it were, brings him into league with men through his proximity and commerce with them. It is striking that conversation here acquires a twofold meaning as something at once bodily and spiritual. Christ's

17. See Thomas Aquinas, *Sup. Mat.* 1:25, ed. Marietti, no. 141. The section, including this paragraph, is a *reportatio*, that is, notes gathered together by a student without being revised by Aquinas. Also, see *Sup. Mat.* 28:20, no. 2469, where Is 7:14 is read alongside Rv 21:3.

bodily conversation includes all of his relations with his contemporaries, whereas his spiritual conversation extends to all of the disciples whose mission from Christ extends through the ages.

On Philippians 2:7

The hymn written in Paul's Letter to the Philippians retraces the complete trajectory of Christ's in the flesh, first as a form of abasement, then as a form of exaltation. Thomas observes that Philippians 2:7 breaks the incarnation down into four moments corresponding to the underlined propositions below (Phil 2:6–8):

[Christus] qui cum in forma Dei esset, non rapinam arbitratus est esse aequalem Deo; sed semetipsum exinanivit, formam servi accipiens, in similitudinem hominum factus, et habitu inventus ut homo. Humiliavit semetispum, factus obediens usque ad mortem, mortem autem crucis.

Who [i.e., Christ] being in the form of God, thought it not robbery to be equal with God: But emptied himself, taking the form of a servant, being made in the likeness of men, and in habit found as a man. He humbled himself, becoming obedient unto death, even to the death of the cross.

The first three propositions are relatively clear, whereas the fourth includes a kind of semantic uncertainty:

- Christ freely abased himself
- He did not bring this about by losing the divine nature, which he possessed by full rights, but rather, by assuming a human nature with its servile condition, weakened by sin and subject to the Law
- He was made in the image of men
- Logically, he was considered a man

Here, we usually close the phrase by adding, "in his behavior" or "in his appearance." However, the key word given here in the Latin, *habitus* rendered in the ablative as *habitu*, can have several meanings. The first is the common one, and it corresponds to the translation that is familiar to us ("in his manner of being"), whereas the others are more technical.

In his commentary on this text, Aquinas successively discusses these two possible interpretations. The second is not important for our study. Nonetheless, let us provide a summary of the argument made in its regard. If *habitu* is understood as being derived from the technical meaning of *habitus*,[18] then it can be subdivided into four configurations depending on whether (1) the subject possessing it is or is not changed by such possession and (2) whether what is possessed does or does not change on account of the fact that it is possessed. The only case that can be suitably applied to the mystery of the incarnation is that wherein the possessing subject is not changed, with the thing thereby possessed itself being changed. The typical example of this kind of *habitus* is a piece of clothing. In Christ, human nature "was drawn" to the divine Person without this Person being changed, for if he were changed, Christ's divine identity would have been lost in the operation of drawing the human nature to himself. However, for its own part, the human nature is thereby made better, filled with grace and truth (Jn 1:14). Following this reading, Thomas holds that the expression *habitu inventus est ut homo* intends to make clear that the preceding expression, *in similitudinem hominum factus* [*est*], does not imply a change for Christ's divine Person, the subject of the incarnation.[19]

However, the first interpretation is more directly relevant for our purposes here, for it explains *habitus* in terms of the notion of *conversatio*.[20] Thomas holds that *habitu inventus est ut homo* alludes to the "conditions" of the human nature assumed by Christ. Thus, Aquinas makes this term express all the "weaknesses" and "properties" relative to mankind (e.g., hunger and exhaustion), with the exception of sin. Christ's "external conversation" with men bears witness to such characteristics. Through the regular, sustained commerce between Christ and his contemporaries, in particular with his disciples, it be-

---

18. See Aristotle, *Categories* IV.2a2 and IX.11b10–15. Here, Aquinas understands the word *habitus* by combining having (*echein*) and disposition (*hexis*) as ramifications of a single, fundamental meaning.

19. See Aquinas, *Sup. Phil.* 2:7, ed. Marietti, no. 61.

20. See ibid. (no. 60).

came obvious that beyond partaking in human nature's form and perfections, he also partook in its common condition and weakness, with the exception of sin. Along this line of interpretation, *habitus* includes Christ's behavior and external relations. Therefore, in order to completely recognize the full realism of the mystery of the incarnation, it was important that Christ lead his life in the midst of his contemporaries and be in conversation with them.

On Hebrews 1:1–2

Aquinas's first *lectio* in his commentary on the Letter to the Hebrews proposes a *divisio textus* for the entire letter. Addressed to Christian faithful of a Jewish background who maintained their observation of the Law's prescriptions alongside their devotion to the Gospel, the letter lays great emphasis on Christ's preeminent excellence. His primacy is the foundation for the fact of the New Testament's excellence, leading it to surpass the Old Testament. This fact is established in the first two verses of the letter:

Multifarie multisque modis olim Deus loquens patribus in prophetis, novissime diebus istis locutus est nobis in Filio, quem constituit hearedem universorum, per quem fecit et saecula.

God, who, at sundry times and in divers manners, spoke in times past to the fathers by the prophets, last of all, in these days, hath spoken to us by his Son, whom he hath appointed heir of all things, by whom also he made the world.

Thomas notes the contrast between the two tenses of the verb "to speak" (*loquor*) which has God as its subject in two different places in this selection: in verse 2, God "hath spoken" (*locutus est*) through the Son, and in verse 1, we have God "speaking" (*loquens*) through the prophets. To illuminate the difference between these two tenses, Thomas makes use of a likeness drawn from the three moments involved in the development of a word (*locutio*):

There are three things that are required for our word [*locutio*]. First, the conception of a word, by which is preconceived in the mind what is to be pronounced [*loquendum est*] by the mouth; secondly, the expression of the conceived verb, by which that which is conceived is introduced [*insinuetur*] [into the mind]; thirdly, the manifestation of the expressed reality [*res expressa*], by which is it made evident.[21]

If we make the appropriate analogical adjustments to our terminology, these three stages marking out the progressive movement from internal to external discourse also are suitably applied to God who speaks:

- First of all, God conceives his Word from all eternity: the eternal begetting of the Son
- Moreover, in three ways, God expresses his Word thus conceived:
- in the production of creatures made in the likeness of the Word
- through certain notions that are given to the minds of holy angels and men
- through his assumption of the flesh

Aquinas characterizes these stages of the divine expression as follows. The first expression, creation, results in the being of creatures. A first kind of knowledge of God is made possible on the basis of this creaturely being. The second expression, namely, the infusion of forms into angelic and human minds, intends to offer some kind of knowledge of the divine Wisdom. However, neither of these two expressions are equal to the proper sense of what a manifestation is. Only the incarnation implies an "express manifestation." This alone proves to be integral and complete, involving being, knowledge, and full manifestation:

However, the third [expression], which occurs through [his] assumption of the flesh, is ordered to being [*esse*], knowledge, and an express manifestation, for through the assumption of the flesh, the Word both became man and perfected us in the knowledge of God: "For this was I born …

21. Aquinas, *Sup. Heb.* 1:1–2, ed. Marietti, no. 15: "sciendum est, quod tria requiruntur ad locutionem nostram. Primo, verbi conceptio, qua scilicet praeconcipiatur in mente id quod ore loquendum est; secundo ipsius verbi concepti expressio, qua insinuetur quod conceptum est; tertio ipsius rei expressae manifestatio, qua res expressa evidens fiat."

that I should give testimony to the truth" [Jn 18:37]. And he expressly manifested himself to us: "Afterwards he was seen upon earth, and conversed with men" (Bar 3:38).[22]

The Word finds its fullest expression in his assumption of the flesh (i.e., the incarnation), which includes his existence in the world, the perfection of knowledge, and express manifestation. Nonetheless, it is striking that Thomas here envisions the Word's conversation with men as being the final stage of this movement of expression. Here, "conversation" is equivalent to the ultimate reality of the incarnation as an "express manifestation" of the Word in terms of a bodily presence in words and deeds. Elsewhere, Thomas has recourse to analogies which are quite akin to those developed here— the word that is first conceived then uttered, the word that is pronounced and then written—to illustrate how the incarnation makes the Word manifest, visible, and tangible, to such a degree that the conversation proclaimed in Baruch 3:38 here becomes a reality.[23] In a kind of clandestine manner, Aquinas's theology holds that conversation is the moment of the incarnation's full efficacy or, to put it more simply, its concrete fulfillment.

Aquinas is thus in a position to bring to a close his overall argument aiming to prove the superiority of the New Testament over the Old. The manifestation through the flesh goes beyond the ancient "revelations" bestowed on the minds of the prophets, just as distant views of things and promises are surpassed by an immediate sensible manifestation and through personal presence. The explicit manifestation of God was expressed through the Son in the flesh, and it has been transmitted through the ages up to our own days by the Apostles as eyewitnesses and by their successors.

22. Aquinas, *Sup. Heb.* 1:1–2, ed. Marietti, no. 15. The same verses come up elsewhere in connection with the Christological motif of the *verbum breviatum* in the flesh. See *Sup. Rom.* 9:28, no. 804.

23. See Aquinas, *In Symbolum Apostolorum*, a. 3, ed. Marietti (1954), no. 897; Augustine, *De doctrina christiana* I.13.12.

MANIFESTATION AND SALVATION AS
CONVERSATIO IN AQUINAS

In order to explain Christ's way of life, we must have recourse to theological arguments from fittingness. Christ lived and conversed with his contemporaries as was befitting to him on account of his identity and mission as well as in response to the situations that he faced and to the stances taken by his interlocutors. The four Gospels hand on reliable testimonies regarding the way that Jesus interacted with men and women of his era, especially his disciples, though also with other kinds of people (e.g., the sick, the possessed, the marginal, children, sinners, crowds of people, etc.). All of these details are available through the Gospel accounts of his speeches and the narratives telling of his actions.

Now, how are we to form a theology from interactions that are so circumstantial and particular? Aquinas's intention here is not to bring forward an *a priori* argument about the way that Christ should have behaved in all circumstances in light of his identity and mission. Rather, it is a question of recognizing *a posteriori* how Christ's way of life was befitting in light of what his mission was. Here, this mission finds itself specified by a threefold finality ascribed to the incarnation: to manifest the truth, to free men from sin, and to enable man to truly have access to God (q. 40, a. 1, resp.). The characteristics befitting Christ's way of life are determined by a kind of exercise in coupling notions together, that is, by connecting this or that feature of Christ's conversation to one of the finalities inscribed within the incarnation. In such cases, Thomas provides multiple biblical and patristic citations.

Let us review the structure of his argumentation by gathering his principal responses and supplementary details around the three aforementioned finalities. I do not intend to set forth question 40 in all of its details here. Instead, I only wish to continue fleshing out the idea of Christological conversation as a completion of the incarnation, doing so by meditating at greater length on Thomas's exegeses on this topic.

The first end aimed at by Christ's coming into the world is the manifestation of the truth, as he himself attests at his trial (see Jn 18:37). In line with this sort of finality, it would not have been appropriate for Christ to have remained hidden, leading a solitary life. Rather, it was fitting that he went about in public places, preaching out in the open, as we see him doing time and again in the Gospels (q. 40, a. 1, resp. [1]). This argument is confirmed by numerous texts wherein Thomas relies on Baruch 3:38 to argue that the incarnation would need to culminate in the Word's visibility through the flesh.[24]

In response to an objection which we already raised above, one that erroneously relies on Daniel 2:11 in arguing that Christ would have needed to live a solitary life, Thomas specifies what kind of truth is involved in this manifestation: what is to be manifested is his divinity. Christ freely manifests his divinity through his humanity (q. 40, a. 1, ad 1).

In Aquinas's comments on John 14:7, where Christ responds to Thomas the Apostle about the Father, "Henceforth you will know him," the Angelic Doctor spells out the same process in personal terms (i.e., "the Father") rather than essential ones (i.e., "the divinity"), considering matters from the perspective of those who benefit from the manifestation: the experience of seeing Christ in the flesh led the disciples to see the Word by faith, and in the Word they also saw the Father, though *per speculum et in aenigmate*. However, perfect knowledge of the Father will be accessible *in patria* once Christ's passion, resurrection, and ascension, as well as the sending of the Spirit, have all taken place.[25]

Let us return to question 40. *In via*, this manifestation is addressed to all (*omnibus*) by way of conversation. This assertion could seem surprising, for Christ's bodily conversation directly reached only his contemporaries and indeed, even among them, only a limited number of persons. Nonetheless, we must understand that in

24. See Aquinas, *SCG* IV.31.6; *ST* III, q. 4, a. 4, resp. [3]; *Sup. Psalmos* 17:11b–13, trans. Jean-Éric Stroobant de Saint-Éloy (Paris: Cerf, 1996), 1999.
25. See Aquinas, *Sup. Io.* 14:7, ed. Marietti, no. 1880.

going out to meet with his contemporaries, Christ in fact entered into conversation with the whole of humanity. Because Christ's conversation is addressed to the full breadth of society in his era, this conversation is the mediation and sign of the fact that his mission is directed to all people. Notwithstanding the priority that he gives to the children of Israel during his itinerant life, Christ's conversation extends beyond the geographical and temporal limitations inscribed upon his humanity.[26]

Concretely, the nature of Christ's conversation with his contemporaries finds its specific expression in two registers. On the one hand, we have his preaching and miracles. On the other, there is his innocence and righteous life lived among men. Thomas believes that we can see something quite revelatory not only in his explicit exercise of his mission in extraordinary words and deeds but also in the testimony proclaimed by an ordinary life which, in fact, had a uniquely expressive character.

The next objection argues that Christ's lofty perfection required a purely contemplative life (as opposed to an active life). In his response to this objection, Thomas provides a supplementary explanation concerning the character of Christ's preaching and teaching (q. 40, a. 1, ad 2). In the final analysis, the activity of preaching and teaching presupposes the contemplative life and flow from it, in accord with the adage: "To convey to others what one has contemplated" (*contemplata aliis tradere*).[27] Christ's activity manifesting the truth was exercised in many ways. His words drew their revelatory power from his intimate time alone with God in prayer.

The second end aimed at by Christ's coming into the world is to

---

26. Elsewhere, Thomas draws attention to the mediation of the Apostles as the connection of Christ's preaching to the Gentiles: *Sup. Io.* 12:21, ed. Marietti, no. 1633: "Christ personally preached only to Jews ... but he preached to the Gentiles through the apostles."

27. Also see the last argument in *ST* III, q. 40, a. 2, ad 3. On the relative perfection of an active life rooted in contemplation, see *ST* II-II, q. 182, a. 1; q. 188, a. 6. On the adage, *contemplata aliis tradere*, which became a brief description of the charism of the Order of Preachers, see *Encyclopédie Jesus le Christ chez Saint Thomas d'Aquin*, ed. Jean-Pierre Torrell, 1123–37.

free men from sin, as is expressed in 1 Timothy 1:15. To illustrate this aspect of Christ's mission, Aquinas is content to cite an expression attributed to John Chrysostom (q. 40, a. 1, resp. [2]). The latter notes that Christ could have drawn men to himself through his preaching by remaining in one place. However, he did not choose this course of action but, instead, chose to seek out the lost, like a shepherd seeking after his lost sheep or a doctor making a sick call. As for his precise activity freeing man from sin, this was accomplished through the passion, the efficacy of which will be treated in terms of five different modalities a few questions later in the *Tertia pars* (see *ST* III, q. 48).

The third end aimed at by Christ's coming into the world consists in making man's approach to God possible through him, as is said in Romans 5:2. To this end, it was fitting that Christ would converse with men in a familiar manner, so that he might encourage them to approach him and, through him, God (q. 40, a. 1, resp. [3]). This is especially borne out in Christ's sharing of table with tax collectors and sinners. Such people particularly stood in need of having their confidence (*fiducia*) restored and of being brought into communion with God. Here, Thomas cites Matthew 9:10, which recalls the unexpected table gathering following upon Matthew's own call. In his commentary on this verse, Aquinas describes the expressive nature of Christ's presence at the sinners' table: "Here, he shows how many were called to have an intimate relationship with him [*familiaritas*]."[28] Elsewhere, when he discusses how charity urges us to behave in relation to sinners, Thomas argues that conversation with them is something enjoined upon the "perfect," for the latter are not threatened by sin and can potentially convert sinners.[29]

---

28. Thomas Aquinas, *Sup. Mat.* 9:10, ed. Marietti, no. 758; see *Sup. Io.* 1:14, ed. Marietti, no. 178. *Familiaritas* is a still-unexplored motif connected to that of *conversatio*. Aquinas uses it in particular to describe Christ's relationship with his beloved disciple (see *ST* I, q. 20, a. 4, ad 3); or, in the negative, to explain the Baptist's ignorance in respect to Christ before the latter's baptism (see *Sup. Io.* 1:31, no. 263). On the specific application to the Apostles, see Serge-Thomas Bonino, "The Role of Apostles in the Communication of Revelation according to the *Lectura super Ioannem* of St. Thomas Aquinas," in *Reading John with St. Thomas Aquinas* (ed. Dauphinais and Levering), 318–46.

29. See *ST* II-II, q. 25, a. 6, ad 5. Here, the example of Christ merges somewhat with

Aquinas continues to explore Christ's manner of conversation in the next article (q. 40, a. 2) by answering a concrete question: Did Christ need "to lead an austere life as regards food, drink, and clothing, or could he have lived in an ordinary form of life akin to that lived by others?" (q. 40, prol.). His response is formulated in terms of fittingness in relation to the end of the incarnation, which in the preceding article was specified as having three aspects:

It was in conformity [*congruum*] with the end of the Incarnation that Christ would not lead a solitary life but would, instead, converse with men. Now, it is sovereignly befitting [*conventissimum est*] that he who converses with others would conform himself to their own conversation, according to the words of the Apostle [1 Cor 9:22], "I have made myself all things for all men." And therefore, it was sovereignly befitting [*convenientissimum*] that Christ would ordinarily behave as others did in matters of eating and drinking.[30]

Thus, Christ ate and drank in accord with the manners of the Jews of his day without practicing the same austerities as did John the Baptist. Fasting was not a priority for Christ, for through his divinity he had mastery over his flesh and therefore did not need to practice abstinence. The need to mingle with sinners at table and offer to purify them through his power to pardon sins took precedence over the distance that would have been introduced through austerity and fasting (q. 40, a. 2, ad 2).

A first reading of the first two articles of q. 40 shows us that Christ's mode of conversation is principally related to his mission, specified in terms of the incarnation's threefold finality: to manifest the truth, to free men from sin, and to enable man to truly have access to God. Christ's exemplarity also plays an important, though auxiliary, role in these two articles. His manner of conversation finds

---

that of St. Dominic who, in his compassion, did not fear to eat with sinners (in this case, with heretics) and converted one of them who was his host by means of a long, strenuous, and heated nighttime conversation. See Jordan of Saxony, *Libellus* §15.

30. *ST* III, q. 40, a. 2, resp. Also, see *Sup. Mat.* 11:16–19, ed. Marietti, nos. 938–40, for a comparison with John the Baptist. As regards Christ the high priest who would need to be holy, innocent, spotless, and separated from sinners, yet nevertheless in *conversatio* with them, see *Sup. Heb.* 7:26, ed. Marietti, no. 375.

a kind of secondary justification by its worth as an example either for all men or for certain categories of Christians. Let us briefly consider this important aspect of his conversation.

The third objection of the first article argues that Christ's way of life should have had a uniformly solitary character, instead of alternating between his presence to the crowds followed by solitary retreats for prayer. Thomas responds to this objection by making use of the adage, "Christ's action was our instruction" (*action Christi fuit nostra instructio*).[31] Christ's practice of retreating from the crowds shows preachers that they must not always give of themselves in public but must also incorporate times of retreat into their own lives. Aquinas recommends this so that the body may find rest, so that one may make room for prayer, and also to avoid human favor (q. 40, a. 1, ad 3). Here Christ's exemplarity has a specific value for those who have received the office of preaching, first and foremost the Dominicans.

The first objection of the second article holds that Christ should have led an austere life, for he preached the perfection of life, indeed even more than did the Baptist who lived his life in austerity. Thomas's response provides us with a priceless key for knowing how to apply Christ's exemplarity to the lives of others: "In his conversation, the Lord gave an example of perfection in all those things that have an essential [*per se*] relation to salvation" (q. 40, a. 2, ad 1). Now, abstinence from food and drink are not part of such essential components of activities related to salvation. With this qualification, Christ's exemplarity holds for all men inasmuch as all men are concerned with those things that are essentially related to salvation.

The third article deals with a matter that would have been quite important for Aquinas, for it is connected to his era's disputes concerning the mendicant orders: "Should [Christ] have lived lowly circumstances [*abjecte*] in this world or, rather, should he have lived

---

31. See Richard Schenk, "Exteriority and Interiority: Their Mutual Qualification in Thomas Aquinas's Reception of the Axiom *Omnis Christi actio nostra est instructio*," in Schenk, *Soundings in the History of a Hope: New Studies on Thomas Aquinas* (Ave Maria, Fla.: Sapientia Press, 2016), 31–68.

with riches and honor?" (q. 40, prol.). His response essentially turns on Christ's voluntary poverty. In a single stroke, Thomas justifies begging in relation to the office of preaching.[32] He holds that obedience is the most elevated of the three vows, for it orients the most intimate part of the disciple toward God, namely his will. Moreover, Aquinas holds that one can legitimately receive renumeration for the office of preaching and that the common possession of goods is befitting to Gospel poverty lived in community. These discussions grew to great length in other works by Thomas.[33] Here, however, we must limit ourselves to rereading those elements in this article which will help to enrich our understanding of Christ's converse with men.

The second objection registered against Christ living a life of poverty is quite pertinent for our considerations: given that Christ conformed his way of life to that of his contemporaries in matters of food and clothing, he also should have done so as regards poverty and riches, consequently eschewing extreme forms of poverty (q. 40, a. 3, obj. 2). Already, the preceding objection advanced an understandable, common-sense argument in favor of Christ living a life of moderation (obj. 1). Nonetheless, the *sed contra* reveals the fact that Thomas takes Christ's poverty very seriously and even holds that, far from being moderate, it was extreme. With the backing of texts from Jerome, Aquinas mobilizes two details drawn from the Gospels in relation to this subject: Christ's own remark attesting to the fact that he had no bed in which to sleep (Mt 8:20) and another text suggesting that he could not pay for an ordinary tax on his own (Mt 17:26).

The principal justification for Christ's poverty is that it allowed

32. In explaining this aspect of Christ's life, the Dominican theologian here responds, on the one hand, to the secular masters who attacked the mendicant orders regarding the latter's claims to be able to practice begging while also holding university chairs and, on the other hand, to the Franciscans who thought poverty was the way *par excellence* for obtaining the heights of Christian perfection. See Bonaventure of Bagnoregio, *Apologia pauperum contra calumniatorem*, chaps. 7–11.

33. See Aquinas, *Contra impugnantes* VI.6, nos. 14, 19; VII.7.7, no. 9; 8, nos. 1, 4–6; 12, no. 1; *Contra retrahentes*, chap. 15; *De perfectione spiritualis vitae*, chap. 8. Also, see the illuminating introduction in Aquinas, *"La perfection, c'est la charité." Vie chrétienne et vie religieuse dans le Christ*, ed. Jean-Pierre Torrell (Paris: Cerf, 2010).

him to be freed from worries concerning worldly affairs, thus helping to secure his preaching office.[34] Now, this task is numbered among the explicit finalities of the incarnation, as we can see in Mark 1:38: "Let us go on to the next towns, that I may preach there also; for that is why I came out." An important supplement to this point can be found in the response to the aforementioned second objection: "Someone can live like everyone with regard to food and clothing not only by possessing riches but also by receiving life's necessities from wealthy persons. This is what was the case for Christ, as is said in Luke 8:2–3, where we are told that certain women followed Christ, 'ministering to him out of their resources'" (q. 40, a. 3, ad 2).[35]

Another, highly theological, justification for Christ's poverty reconnects with what we found in the first article of the question where Christ's conversation was presented in terms of the logic of God's manifestation: "So that the power of his divinity may be revealed all the more to the degree that he seemed lowlier on account of his poverty" (*ut tanto maior virtus divinitatis eius ostenderetur, quanto per paupertatem videbatur abiectior*; q. 40, a. 3, resp.). Thomas then immediately cites a moving homily concerning Christ's concrete poverty, transmitted in the acts of the Council of Ephesus (431). There is a kind of direct proportion between the manifestation Christ's divinity and the utter humility of his condition. The brilliance of the divinity shines forth all the more brightly through the Son's voluntary abasement in the flesh, assumed in the humblest of conditions. This very paradox intensifies the manifestation of the divinity.

To reconstruct Christ's manner of conversation requires us to face a potential difficulty. There is indeed one domain wherein Christ seems to have distanced himself from his contemporaries: the observation of the precepts the Jewish Law. Therefore, did Christ's manner of conversation represent a kind of rupture with the Jews of his time? Against intriguing arguments going in this direction,

---

34. The same argument was advanced to justify the first Dominicans' resolution not to own any land holdings. See Jordan of Saxony, *Libellus* §42.

35. For the Dominican doctor of the church, such a line of conduct had an exemplary value for the Order of Preachers.

Aquinas shows in the last article of q. 40 that quite the contrary was the case. Christ did not come to abolish the Law but rather to fulfill it (Mt 5:17). Like every circumcision, Christ's implied a profession (*protestatio*) that he would fulfill the Law's requirements (q. 40, a. 4, resp.). By making the Law his own, Christ brought it to its fulfillment and completion in himself, for in his very person he was the fulfillment of the Law. According to Galatians 4:4–5, he moreover delivered those who were subject to the Law without themselves every being able to completely fulfill it themselves. Christ's relationship to the Law thus, in fact, simultaneously reveals Christ's uniqueness and mission. His apparent transgressions of the Law's Sabbath requirements or of other precepts in reality manifest the primacy of God's work and that of salvation's integral nature, which should always have governed these observances (q. 40, a. 4, ad 1–3). Therefore, Christ showed himself to be fully Jewish, and his way of life did not separate him from his people in any way.[36]

The fortieth question of the *Tertia pars* paints a picture of Christ as a poor and itinerant preacher, not living in solitude and austerity like John the Baptist, but instead embracing a daily form of converse with his contemporaries, including those living on the margins of society as well as sinners with whom he shared in table fellowship. These characteristic traits of Christ's way of life are well adapted to the finalities to be achieved by his coming among men. Thus, Aquinas bestows a rich physiognomy upon Christ's mode of life. Conversation is treated not only in principle as a fulfillment of the incarnation's goal but also in the concrete circumstances of Christ's life: food, drink, clothing, his itinerant manner of life, table company, economic life, and observances of the Law. In this way, Thomas provides us with a full, vibrant, and detailed portrait of Christ.

---

36. On Christ's *conversatio* with the Jews as his brothers and neighbors, likewise see Aquinas, *Sup. Psalmos* 34:14 (425).

CONVERSATION, A WAY OF BEING AMICABLE
ELEVATED BY CHARITY

Up to this point, we have been looking deeper into Aquinas's uses of the notion of conversation in his Christology as well as into the scope that the term takes on in his thought, seeing that this conversation represents a fulfillment of the incarnation as well as a deployment of its finalities. Nonetheless, there is another area in Thomas's *opera* where the language of conversation is singularly concentrated: the theology of charity. For our purposes, let us consider three significant occurrences of this theme in this context before asking ourselves about the potential meaning of this kind of semantic overlap.

When Thomas discusses the interconnection of the virtues, especially that which exists between charity and the other moral and theological virtues, he raises the question of knowing whether charity can exist without faith and hope (*ST* I-II, q. 65, a. 5). His response provides us with a singular compendium of the conditions required for friendship with God:

Charity does not only signify the love of God but also indicates a kind of friendship with him. Now, beyond love, such friendship implies a kind of mutual returning of love [*mutual redamatio*] along with a kind of mutual communication [*mutua communicatio*], as is said in *Nicomachean Ethics* 8.2. Now, it is quite clear that these characteristics belong to charity, given what is said in 1 John 4:16, "He that abideth in charity abideth in God, and God in him," and in 1 Corinthians 1:9, "God is faithful: by whom you are called unto the fellowship [*societas*] of his Son." Now, this fellowship [*societas*] of man with God, which is a kind of familiar commerce [*familiaris conversatio*] with him, does indeed begin here-below in the present life through grace, although it will come to perfection in the future life through glory. We hold both of these things through faith and hope. Thus, just as someone cannot have friendship with someone else if the possibility of some kind of fellowship [*societas*] or familiar converse [*familiaris conversatio*] with that person seemed unbelievable or utterly impossible, so too one cannot have friendship with God, which is charity, unless he has faith through which he believes in a fellowship [*societas*] of this kind and in man's commerce [*conversatio*] with God, as well as hope that he may come to attain this fellowship [*societas*]. Thus, charity can in no way exist without faith and hope.[37]

The notion of friendship provides the master analogy for Thomas's discussion of man's relationship to God in charity. Looking upon man, we are understandably led to think that the conditions for friendship with God cannot be found in this finite creature, for given the immeasurable difference separating their natures, the human being cannot sustain an intimate and familiar converse with God through his own connatural resources. Nonetheless, when God bestows grace upon man, the latter finds himself introduced into communication and communion with God. Charity is this friendship through grace, made up of mutual love and intimate conversation. Such a sharing in life will find its consummation in glory. In anticipation of this, however, because God remains imperceptible by our senses, making our conversation with him intangible, Thomas argues that charity's life of friendship presupposes faith and hope.

We find ourselves substantially faced with the same theological point when Thomas discusses charity in itself (*ST* II-II, q. 23, a. 1). Taking his cue from the fourth Gospel (Jn 15:15), Thomas envisions charity as being a kind of friendship. He takes up Aristotle's analysis in order to define friendship by three elements: *benevolence* and *reciprocity* to the degree that they are *recognized* by the partners in such a relationship. Friendship involves the friends in a common form of life and action.[38] Thomas designates this latter element of friendship by using the term *communicatio*, which he presents as being the foundation of friendship. Thus, charity is presented as being a mutual, benevolent love, founded on a kind of communication. God has the initiative in such communication to the degree that he communicates his own beatitude to men, as is attested in 1 Corinthians 1:9,

---

37. See *ST* I-II, q. 65, a. 5, resp.

38. See Aristotle, *Nicomachean Ethics* VIII.2, 10; Joseph Bobik, "Aquinas on *Communicatio*, The Foundation of Friendship and *Caritas*," *The Modern Schoolman* 64, no. 1 (1988): 1–18.

which was already mobilized in the selection cited above. Nonetheless, a foreseeable objection held that there is neither *convivere* nor *conversatio* between men and God or the angels, following what is said in Daniel 2:11 (which we encountered above). This is true from a given perspective, but by initiating the *commmunicatio* through his grace, God changes things radically:

Man's life is twofold. On the one hand, it is related to his sensitive and bodily nature, and with regard to this life there is no communication or conversation with God and the angels. However, on the other, there is man's spiritual life according to his mind. As regards this life, there is indeed a conversation both with God and with the angels. Granted, it is an imperfect conversation in our present state of life. Whence, it is written [Phil 3:20]: "Our conversation is in heaven." However, this conversation will be perfected *in patria* when "God's servants will serve him and will see his face" [Rv 22:3–4]. Therefore, our charity is imperfect here-below but will be made perfect *in patria*.[39]

We could continue to cite multiple statements discussing the notion of conversation within the framework of friendship, whether natural friendship or the supernatural friendship of the life of grace.[40] However, let us merely be content with a third example relative to the virtue of friendship or friendliness (*ST* II-II, q. 114, a. 1). In order to justify the idea that a special virtue is required in this domain of activity, Thomas explains: "However, man must suitably set himself in order in relation to other men in their common company [*in communi conversatione*], both in deeds and words, so that each may conduct himself toward others in a befitting manner."[41] Human relations must be ruled by the virtue of friendliness (or friendship). Without being equivalent to the perfect form of friendship, the acquired quality of friendliness draws on the external forms of the behavior expressed in friendship, which cannot take root and flourish without virtue (*ST* I-II, q. 114, a. 1, ad 1). The latter is found above all between two persons who love one another in a special manner.

---

39. *ST* II-II, q. 23, a. 1, ad 1.
40. See *SCG* IV.22.2.
41. *ST* II-II, q. 114, a. 1, resp.

Understood in its principal sense, friendship offers us the best analogy for charity.[42]

Whether it be at the heart of interpersonal human interactions or in the communion between man and God through grace, Thomas sees conversation as being one of the distinctive traits of friendship, understood in its various modalities. As the preeminent way of acting as a friend, intimate and familiar conversation finds itself assumed and elevated into charity, conceived of as a form of friendship between man and God thanks to self-communication made by the latter through the gift of grace.

CHRIST'S LIFE IN CONVERSATION WITH US, AN APPRENTICESHIP IN THINGS DIVINE

I now believe that we can reap the benefits of our investigation into Christ's conversation with men so that we can suggest that this mode of Christ's presence and interaction, a fulfillment of the incarnation, is the preeminent mediation of the friendship that exists between God and man in the gift of grace and charity. Thus envisioned as a form of converse between God and man, the incarnation can be integrated into a covenant theology, one that is sketched out by Thomas in terms of friendship and charity.

Two recurrent motifs in Aquinas's Christology are readily applied in the domain of Christ's converse with men. On the one hand, in relation to knowledge, Christ's close commerce with men fosters in them a kind of familiarization with God through that which is bodily and sensible, for the incarnation of the Son singularly draws God close to men and enables them to enter into intimate relations with him.[43] On the other hand, the extreme love testified to by Christ's coming in the flesh is suitable for arousing love by men in

---

42. See ibid., ad 1.

43. See *Sent.* III, d. 1, q. 1, a. 2, resp.; *SCG* IV.54.6 (regarding the intimacy and equality of friendship); *Compendium theologiae*, I.201 [first reason]; *ST* III, q. 1, a. 1, s.c.; a. 2, resp. [first reason] and ad 3.

return, for they love more easily when they first experience proofs of a love that is great.[44]

These two reasons for the fittingness of the incarnation are admirably joined together in a brief *opusculum* by Aquinas, entitled *De rationibus fidei*:

In order to arouse our love for God, there was no more powerful way to accomplish this than that the Word of God, through Whom all things were made, would take up our nature so that he might restore it, thus being both God and man. The first reason that this is true is because by willing to become man for the sake of the latter's salvation, the extent of God's love for man was thus demonstrated in the strongest manner possible; indeed, nothing arouses love more than knowing that one is loved by someone else. Next, given that man's intellect and desires are drawn down to bodily things, he was not able to easily elevate himself to things that are above him. However, all men find it easy to know and love another man. Now, in order to think upon the divine loftiness and be carried toward it through an affection of love that befits it does not fall to everyone but only to those who, through God's help, are lifted upward with great zeal and toil from bodily things to spiritual ones. Therefore, in order for the way to God to be opened for all, God willed to become man, so that even little ones would be able to know and love God as someone like themselves and thus, through what they are able to grasp, gradually make their way toward perfection.[45]

Christ's proximity with men is the key for their journey to God. More precisely, a life of conversation with Christ is a kind of apprenticeship in learning to have close converse with God. This makes Christ's mediating function in the covenant all the more concrete.

God holds the initiative in charity. He loves men without placing any prior conditions upon them. He offers them a share in his own beatitude. As long as we are wayfarers, we stand in need of faith and hope so that we may believe in such a friendship with God and hope that such intimacy is indeed truly accessible to us. Christ is, for us,

---

44. See *SCG* IV.54.5; *Compendium theologiae*, I.201 [third reason]; *ST* III, q. 1, a. 2, resp. [second and third reasons].

45. Aquinas, *De rationibus fidei*, chap. 5., ed. (Vatican City: Leonine, 1969), B62, ll. 101–23.

the way toward beatitude. This fundamental affirmation, one that is placed in the prologue to Aquinas's Christology[46] (*ST* III, prol.), becomes surprisingly concrete at the end of our study of the conversation in which Christ is the principal actor. Christ is the way in act, uniquely drawing us to the end of the journey and accommodating close converse with God to the cognitive and affective requirements of our human condition. Through his conversation with men, Christ gives a human face to the revelation of salvation: in his words and preaching, his gestures and actions, his innocent way of life, poverty, and itinerant form of life, as well as in his sharing a common table with sinners. In other words, Christ's humanity in his activity of conversation becomes a living and incarnate parable about God's proximity to man. According to Thomas's sensible realism, "There is an order in [the process of] conversion. First of all, man must see that to which he must be converted."[47] Here, Thomas specifically has the nativity in mind. For Christ's contemporaries, sight has passed through their eyes; for other generations, faith is the channel for seeing these realities. Next come, in the order of conversion, fear and then hope.

Through his proximity and conversation with men, Christ leads them to love God in return by passing through him. He fosters confidence in God and access to the Father, especially for little ones and sinners. In this way, Christ makes the reciprocity of charity between men and God possible. He is the agent, at once human and divine, of the reciprocity in friendship proper to God's covenant with humanity.

In semantic and conceptual terms, two assets emerge from our study. First, Christ's conversation with his contemporaries, even in commensality with sinners, corresponds to the full manifestation of

46. See Aquinas, *ST* III, prol.: "Quia Salvator noster dominus Iesus Christus, teste Angelo, populum suum salvum faciens a peccatis eorum, viam veritatis nobis in seipso demonstravit, per quam ad beatitudinem immortalis vitae resurgendo pervenire possimus, necesse est ut ..." See Augustine, *De civitate Dei* IX.15; *Confessiones* III.4.8, V.13.23, VII.5.7, 18.24; *De Trinitate* XIII.8.11–10.14.

47. Aquinas, *Sup. Psalmos* 39:4b.

the mystery of the incarnation, in terms of "express reality." Second-ly, the register of *conversatio* qualifies both the friendship between God and man, made possible by charity, as well as the type of relationships that Christ had with his contemporaries in the fulfillment of his mission.

18

The Universal Amplitude
of Christ's Singularity

"… being born in the likeness of men."
—Philippians 2:7

"Truly this man was the Son of God."
—Mark 15:39

In this chapter, I would like to reflect attentively on how a confessing Christology should not dismiss any aspect of the Nazarene's particularity or his singularity, even though such a Christology, illuminated by our Paschal faith, has the exalted Christ and his universal salvific action as its object. Indeed, the Christian proclamation holds that the existence of Jesus Christ, along with what he accomplished and what happened to him throughout his entire earthly existence, exercises a universal influence over the created world, addressing the gift of salvation to all men. However, such a pretension to universality is securely connected to the flesh of Christ, to the man Jesus—indeed, not only to him in his exalted condition after Easter, a condition which radically eludes us, but also to him in the prior conditions of his earthly existence, those of his birth, his life, and his death. The confession of the exalted Christ can never be separated from the memory of Jesus of Nazareth's life shared with men on earth, with the conviction that everything that he taught, accomplished, and lived through still today has a transformative efficacy which can be imputed to the risen One.

Our discussion of this topic calls for a merely provisional, brief clarification of the key terms involved in the tension facing us here. When speaking of a given person, we use the language of "particularity" in relation to factual data concerning him or her. The particular is encountered in everything that characterizes an individual inasmuch as he or she is concrete and distinct: for example, one's skin color, place of origin, nationality, gender, height and weight, the various places one has traveled to, and so forth. By contrast, we speak of "singularity" in order to signify the unique composition of the multiple particularities that distinguish a given man or woman from all others. However, here we are no longer concerned merely with objectifiable data that can be written down on an information form used by a department of immigration services. Rather, we are speaking about something much more profound, namely these characteristics considered insofar as they are taken up, so to speak, as his or her personal dwelling place, through which self-communication is made possible, aspects of the person which are developed as a kind of expressive physiognomy, as a spiritual quality and a true and proper personality. From this perspective, singularity does not appear like a kind of original privilege given from the start of one's existence but, rather, as something to be progressively acquired, something earned through a journey of appropriation and singularization.

Now, in trying to preliminarily define "universality," we find ourselves faced with a much more delicate situation. Nonetheless, we can certainly accept one essential characteristic of that which is universal: it maintains a relationship with all things in a given group, not exclusively by containing all individuals, as humanity embraces all men or as the universe contains all things. Universality has other characteristics too, which we will explore below. For example, let us think of the desire for peace which, although never fully realized concretely, nonetheless magnetizes a hope which likely works at the heart of every man, at least within some delimited field of endeavors. Thus, we now can see our current investigation's objective, set within the limits of Christology: to discern what kind of universality might be combined with Jesus Christ's singularity.

However great the extent of his radiance, as well as the universality of his salvific activity, Jesus Christ remains singular in the strongest sense. He is unique through his lineage, unique through his proximity to God, and unique through the amplitude of his solidarity with men. Beyond his individual, masculine particularity, his own physiognomy, his Jewish ancestry, his Galilean origins, and so forth, Jesus quite obviously must be numbered among the most singular figures of world history. To be convinced of this fact, we need only observe the lasting reverberation of his teaching, words, and deeds, as well as the continued resonance of his life and death throughout the ages. Granted, Jesus' destiny could well have seemed like a mere anecdote in the eyes of some of his contemporaries, whether those of the distant or disillusioned, as well as those of the official chroniclers of his age. However, looking upon this young Jewish rabbi who stood in prophetic dissent upon the margins of the religious system of his era, an intellectually honest and reasonable person will find it impossible to deny his proven existence or his crucifixion under Pontius Pilate as well as to overlook certain disconcerting characteristics of his preaching and activity.

Christians recognize and, indeed, believe that Jesus of Nazareth reveals and exemplifies the ultimate truth concerning humanity, viewed under God's own gaze. Indeed, the loftiest possibilities and the most extreme precariousness of the human condition before God are joined together in him. He became not only a man of the loftiest accomplishments but also a man living in accord with the limited, mortal condition of the flesh. The full extent of the human condition is revealed in the figure of Christ. This is why, in addition to its fundamental theological aim of understanding the incarnation itself, Christology can be considered as presenting us with a kind of anthropology brought to its completion, though not without being stretched out, converted, and, in the end, surpassed.

The object of a confessing Christology is Christ in his uniqueness, true God and true man, eternally living in glory with the Father, inseparable from Jesus of Nazareth who lived in Palestine and was put to death under Pontius Pilate. The first confession of the Christian faith was precisely concerned with the identity of the earthly Jesus and the resurrected Lord as a single existing subject: "God has made him both Lord and Christ, this Jesus whom you crucified" (Acts 2:36). Certainly, the resurrection represents a transformation of Jesus' earthly existence, but it is not, properly speaking, a change, in the sense of a change of nature, the creation of a new subject, or the overturning of one's own psychological self-identity. His resurrection by God is applied to a subject that endures through his coming, life, demise, and restoration. The three days of death do indeed involve a true rupture, but Christ's Paschal existence is not independent or disconnected from his earthly existence. The exalted Christ preserves and integrates the actions and passions of the earthly Jesus, with all their revelatory and salvifically efficacious sacramental power. How should we conceive of the continuity found in this discontinuity, in particular as it stands in line with Christ's universality?

THE APORIA OF UNIVERSALITY AND AVENUES OF EXCESSIVE DISCONTINUITY

The problematic assertion holding that the exalted Christ's universality in no way does away with Jesus of Nazareth's particularity and singularity[1] comes from a *lectio difficilior* of the successive states of Jesus' life and Pasch, from the annunciation to Pentecost. It requires us to set aside three disjunctive schemata which bypass the aporia:

1. The contemporary tendency to circumvent Christ's particularity is deciphered very well in Terrence Merrigan, "Saving the Particular: Incarnation and the Mediation of Salvation in the Theology of Religions," in *Orthodoxy: Process and Product,* ed. Lieven Boeve, Mathijs Lamberigts, and Terrence Merrigan (Leuven: Peeters, 2009), 299–322.

(a) by directly stating that some form of discontinuity exists between the earthly Jesus and the heavenly Christ, (b) by holding that Jesus and the Word have distinct influences on salvation, or (c) by decoupling Christ's mission from the Spirit's.

The easiest path to take here would likely be to conceive of Jesus' death as representing the end of his particularity, with his resurrection then marking the beginning of his universality. Thus, the overall movement of Christ's Pasch would involve a stark discontinuity between Jesus' earthly activity and his salvific action in glory. Now, this outlook does partially express a truth, for in his death, Christ does indeed lay down certain determinations of his bodiliness and physiognomy. However, remembering the unity of Christ's salvific mission in its pre-Paschal, Paschal, and post-Paschal phases, let us take care not to look upon Christ's two existential states (earthly and heavenly, abased and exalted) and there see a disjunction between a supposedly earthly particularity, followed by heavenly universality.

However, it would not be any more acceptable for us to hold that the universality of Christ's salvific action is related to the eternal Word while the flesh of the incarnate Word would only be involved in the Judeo-Christian economy of salvation. Were this the case, the salvific mediation brought about through Jesus would be a kind of restricted mediation addressed only to Jews and Christians, with the universal offering of salvation being related only to the Word without the flesh which he assumed in the incarnation. Nonetheless, in 1 Timothy 2:5, Jesus is presented as being the sole mediator. The humanity of the Word is revealed as being the unique, permanent, and definitive mediation of his universal salvific will.

Finally, no more can we find an effective answer in holding that Jesus' salvific work remains particular, whereas its universalization would be entrusted to the Spirit's universal activity. The universality of the Spirit has a much closer relationship with Christ's universality than this, for the Spirit's universal action assures the proclamation of Christ's own universality. Indeed, Pentecost fueled the universalization of Christ's salvific influence through his Spirit. This enlargement can be seen in the ever-expanding diffusion of the faith aroused in response to the apostolic preaching. The Christ who is thus preached does not become universal through an accumulation of foreign elements borrowed from this or that culture reached by his message. Rather, he can be universalized precisely on the basis of his own singular identity, for it contains his own, proper universality. It is not progressively affixed to him by way of composition and synthesis, even if the various cultures reached by his message do indeed bring their own materials to the fabric of evangelization which is continuously knit together through the passage of time. The Gospel's universality finds its primary foundation upon Jesus Christ's own, initial universality, somewhat like how a fully deployed whole is already contained in the central figure who determines the organic configuration of that whole.

In my opinion, these three ways of separating Christ's earthly particularity from his heavenly universality, his incarnate particularity from his divine universality, or Christic particularity from the Spirit's universality, are all unsatisfactory. Faith's conviction that Christ is fundamentally one, exercising a unified salvific activity, is not sufficiently honored if his universal salvific power is related either (a) solely to the eschatological event of his resurrection, (b) solely to the eternal preexistence of the Word, or (c) solely to the universalizing action of the Spirit.

HYPOTHESIS: THE COINCIDENCE OF THE SINGULAR AND THE UNIVERSAL IN JESUS

Distancing ourselves from these explanations through discontinuity, I would like to explore the hypothesis of a graduated continuity. The fundamental insight guiding our thought here is that the Paschal universalization itself proceeds from an antecedent universality which then must be deployed and diffused. The only action or event which is universalizable is that which already contains a configuration which itself is subject to universality. The universality of the risen One would thus be fundamentally identical with the universality of the crucified One, as well as the universality of the infant in Bethlehem. Nonetheless, the resurrection was necessary in order for this continuity from the annunciation to Pentecost to become discernible, thereby making Jesus' singularity appear, according to its own proper texture, within his universality, which was already present, though in a muted way, at his birth, a universality which then fully sounds forth from Pentecost onward. The universalization of the preaching of the Gospel follows the progressive dispensing of the salvific universality contained in the person of Jesus, in accord with the parameters of his mission and identity.

In order to make explicit the universality already present and precontained in the earthly Jesus, we will present the hypothesis that Jesus of Nazareth is the universal man on account of the unique suitability of his singularities, which can beckon to every, singular man, in whatever condition he finds himself in, either through affinity or provocation. The field of application for the challenge which he presents will be considerably increased through the Paschal proclamation and apostolic preaching, though it will forever recall the singular itinerary of Jesus Christ, his words and deeds, what he accomplished and lived. Certainly, the exalted Christ exercises his sovereignty with a radius of activity that is greater than that of the earthly Jesus. However, this same sovereignty was nonetheless able to be discerned *a posteriori* in the very passion of Jesus, as is revealed in the Johannine Gospel narrative. The superpositioning of Christ's exaltation and his abasement is made possible only through the real interpenetration of these two dimensions. The universality contained in the earthly Jesus was expressed in a way proportioned to the propitious events of his life and to his various interpersonal encounters, but it already bore the mark of its future Paschal unfolding, which itself will remain proportioned to its recipients.

Before examining Jesus' humanity in light of such a theological hypothesis, we should first thematically consider the anthropological possibility that the singular and the universal would coincide in a given human person. To this end, a contemporary philosophical reflection will provide us with precious contributions for the heuristic we are looking to articulate.

THE AMPLITUDE OF WHAT IS HUMAN: POSSIBILITY OF A UNIVERSAL SUITABILITY

I have found certain philosophical reflections by Pierre Magnard quite simulating for conceiving how singularity and universality could be conjoined in a single man.[2] Following in the wake of Montaigne and Pascal, he proposes that man must above all be considered for himself, as a singular being, in the utter variability of his given condition. Nonetheless, the element of universality in a given, singular man is measured by the degree that he is able to cross the differences, sentiments, and states of life which separate men and women from one another. The more a singular man shows that he can empathize with others and is submitted to the variations befalling his own condition, to that degree does he synthesize within himself the various differences befalling men in general, thus showing his capacity for universality. We will still need to see, however, whether the human universality thus aimed at will be primarily verified through accomplishments, at the risk of taking the form of a kind of accumulation of achievements, or rather, through humility, to the benefit of man's availability to others though also at the risk of exposing himself to vulnerability.

Let us begin by bringing together the decisive points of the philosophical argument that will then inspire our theological proposals, not without laying out a few counterpoints. To the trained eyes of a

---

2. See Pierre Magnard, *Questions à l'humanisme* (Paris: Presses Universitaires de France, 2000). The central argument of this text is taken up (with an even clearer affirmation of its Christological profile) in Magnard, "L'homme universel," *Revue de Métaphysique et de Morale* 61, no. 1 (2009): 19–32. Moreover, see Magnard, *Pourquoi la religion?* (Paris: Armand Colin, 2006); also, see his further reflections developed concerning this theme in Magnard, "Religion, chemin d'humanité," *Revue Théologique de Louvain* 39, no. 3 (2008): 315–28.

philosopher sensitive to concerns of humanism, the contemporary concern for human dignity is a matter of great importance. However, the many-sided advocacy on behalf of formalizable criteria for such dignity, often ones that are peripheral or mere artifacts in relation to man in his singularity, mutely signals a kind of defeat of man himself. The quest for clues or benchmarks for a preestablished dignity prove to be an exercise that is potentially dangerous for man in his concrete reality. Even the human advocacy which leans on the simple affirmation of a common and inalienable essence can be a two-edged sword. The need to reclaim this kind of ultimate belonging likely bears witness to the fact that it is no longer recognized by others. As a French disciple of Pascal states: "The human essence, in its empty universality, may well be the last recourse to be had by him who has lost everything, no longer having a family, nor a city, nor a station in life, nor a place of origin, left now to seek in the abstract universal the last determination which could be inalienable."[3] Now, we cannot hold that the meaning of the human person is revealed first and foremost in liminal situations through the loss of differences, arrived at by stripping away all of man's various potential qualities and capacities, for without these the humanity thus attained would be utterly fragile, and such a definition of humanity would potentially become "the most redoubtable cause of the trivialization of what it means to be human."[4] In contrast to every kind of totalitarian reduction, authentic humanism emerges in the quest for, recognition of, and journey through differences without desiring to standardize them or to liken them to oneself.

THE MIDDLE AGES AND MODERNITY: MAN RELATED TO HIS ESSENCE OR TO HIS SUBJECTIVITY

We can diagnose various kinds of risks befalling attempts to define a kind of benchmark standard for what humanity is. These varia-

3. Magnard, *Questions à l'humanisme*, 22.
4. Ibid., 23; see also 212–13.

tions differ throughout the different eras in the history of philosophy. In particular, we can detect significant differences in the dangers befalling such philosophical reflection in the Middle Ages and in modernity. Classical metaphysics was able satisfy itself by defining man by combining what he shares in common with other animals with what specifically distinguished him as a species in a given genus, in accord with his own distinctive properties. Thus, the singular man followed his essence, the form of humanity, which was marked out at a determinate ontological index. As a rational animal, he occupied the frontier between the sensible world and the spiritual world. Without a doubt, he was thus placed in an uncomfortable location in the scale of beings, set between these two quite different domains, but his location was nonetheless situated and certain. Thus, he found his distinctive and assured place in the midst of an outlook holding that natures are set at various ontological degrees, tracing out the hierarchies inventoried by Dionysius.[5] Nonetheless, the ladder of the degrees of being was never reduced to a simple, formal rating system, statically situating a given creature in its assigned place, for it likewise thematized an order of finality. Thus it was presupposed that, throughout this great scale, inferior grades were able to participate in characteristics of superior ones, all in accord with a movement whereby beings return (through a kind of conversion, we might say) to the One and to the Good, a return motion that corresponds to the order in which creatures come forth from God. However, such a way of defining things, where we find logic and cosmology mutually interpenetrating each other, inevitably leads to a kind of conceptual stalemate when we finally come to individual, singular beings. In order to reach the universal determinations of human nature, one must abstract from the contingent details befalling any given, individual man. Indeed, when one wishes to understand and define man in terms of his species, all of the distinctive properties which can be of use in coming to such a defini-

---

5. See Pierre Magnard, "Ordre et dignité," in *La dignité de l'homme*, ed. Magnard (Paris: Champion, 1995), 3–12.

tion must be able to be applied to any given individual human whatsoever.

As Montaigne and Pascal intensely perceived,[6] man cannot be defined on the basis of any kind of classification, for he brings together in himself all kinds of opposites, constituting a kind of enduring paradox. In order to consider him in his universal singularity, such soothing notions as species, nature, race, class, society, or even that of the cosmos must all be cast aside.[7] In comparison to the ancient vision of man, which held that man is a kind of microcosm having a central place in the midst of the macrocosm, the Copernican revolution asserts that humanity has a terrestrial framework, not the cosmic extent that it once had in the older view of things. "This radical change affects the very dignity of man, who no longer holds a place in a hierarchy, no more than a place within a chain or series, but instead, finds himself at a given latitude which places him in charge of himself, at whatever degree he may happen find himself on the scale."[8] Thus, from this perspective, man discovers the principle of his dignity in his distinctive trait of knowing that he is free, thereby wishing to take responsibility for himself. Whereas in earlier days human fulfillment was understood in terms of man's participation in the sovereign Good which, itself remaining eternal, could not be found to be wanting for him who perseveringly sought after it, poetry attests, by contrast, that "that which is perishable comes to take on an inestimable value, precisely because of its precarious nature."[9] Taking up his responsibility and tasting the sweetness of contingent reality, man henceforth intends to find his fulfillment in his own proper domain.

The medieval inclination toward a primacy of the abstract over the singular was nonetheless taken up again in modernity as thinkers sought to establish human dignity on the basis of an *a priori* subjec-

6. See Pierre Magnard, *Pascal ou l'art de la digression* (Paris: Ellipses, 1997), esp. 5–36.

7. See Magnard, *Questions à l'humanisme*, 3–20. See also Magnard, "La dignité de l'homme de Raymond de Sebond à Montaigne," in *La dignité de l'homme*, 161–72.

8. Magnard, *Questions à l'humanisme*, 38.

9. Ibid., 40.

tivity, doing so upon a transcendental foundation or upon a condition of possibility common to every possible subjectivity. Metaphysics becomes functional and domineering when the quest for an epistemological foundation plays the role of a notional substitute—something which is necessarily alienating—replacing one's attention for the real man, who has a concrete and thoroughgoing (and, indeed, demanding) originality, indeed one that often is unclassifiable.

By way of counterpoint, let us specify, however, that the inference of the transcendental subject is not a philosophical acquisition of small worth. Its discovery had the merit of saving the empirical man from the dismemberment he had suffered at the hand of the methodological scalpel, with which he was lacerated by the positive sciences or unidimensional anthropologies: medicine, history, economy, sociology, psychology, psychoanalysis, and so forth. None of these formalized analytical schemata can tell me what I am, even though each of them is insightful in its particular auscultation and proves to be efficacious in its conclusions. Certainly, the transcendental subject, rescued from all of these partial analyses, is never identical to myself, nor to any real man. Nonetheless, placed before possibilities which are infrahuman and destructive of the real man, we must maintain, at the foundation of every particular itinerary of personalization, the affirmation of a metaphysical subject which subsists through all changes or the affirmation of a transcendental subject having inalienable possibilities. Still, let us acknowledge the serious limitations befalling these two, certainly reductive, ways of understanding the singular man so that we may attempt to take another path, one that we believe has the further benefit of enabling us to have an even subtler grasp of Jesus' humanity.

THE HUMAN CONDITION IN ITS VARIETY
AND ELECTIVE AFFINITIES

Let us admit with Pierre Magnard, following Montaigne and Pascal, that man cannot be defined in what is proper and distinctive to him: he does not allow himself to be reduced to a species, for he is forever in search of differences which mark him out from his fellow men. In this regard, it is quite indicative that, in Montaigne, the term "condition" clearly takes precedence over that of "nature" for designating the human being in his utter variability. One is not declared to be a man because we have verified that an abstract nature exists in him, nor because one conforms to the norms of good health, nor because one has certain physical and intellectual abilities. No, on the contrary, according to the *Essais*, the infinite variability of human beings, sometimes concentrated in a single individual through the amplitude or versatility of his or her sentiments, assures the possibility of each person's elective affinity with all other men and women.[10] In Montaigne's opinion: "He is universal who embraces all the passing occupations, affections, and thoughts of an individual."[11] Such an intuition leads to an anthropological paradox of inestimable power:

This "full form of the human condition" which each person bears within himself, is not such through conformity to some archetype but, rather, is there because it embraces all states [of human existence]. Humanism is not integral because it would safeguard its integrity but, rather, because it is unconditional.—Nonetheless, do we not utter the most disconcerting of paradoxes when we say that each person bears within himself or herself "the full form of the human condition"? The human condition is lived in a fragmented, crumbled, and dispersed way. To hold that it has a form, even if it is a full form which would be suited to all men, is to wish to make that which is fragmentary representative of the totality, the particular expressive of the generic, and the singular capable of the universal. Each condition, however determined that it may be, does not fail to be fully human.[12]

10. See ibid., 43, 85, 96–97, 120, 210, 222.

11. Ibid., 85.

12. Ibid., 43–44, here citing Michel de Montaigne, *Essais* III.2 (Paris: Gallimard, 1962), 782.

Hence, the form of humanity follows man's infinitely variable condition, not vice versa. Such an intuition is not necessarily alien to the new vistas opened up by the Gospel, and truth be told, it likely draws upon the legacy of the Christian outlook. Whereas Greek culture glorified the beautiful, quasi-divine form of the human person, Christianity knew how "to discover man under the rags of the poor man, the misery of the leper, and the disfigured body of the crucified. However diminished he may be, a man forever remains a man. The form of the human condition is always fully there."[13] Concrete humanity is not determined through a kind of alignment with an abstract nature or through the verification of certain criteria but rather is determined in the form of a recognition of and elective affinity for differences.

Possible agreement with others, who are always singular and significantly dissimilar, does not depend on an identity of nature, but rather on an affinity which is experienced or consented to in a given, particular respect.[14] In order to prevail in the trial involved in arriving at some agreement, the humanist renounces any attempt at classification, all to the benefit of appreciating a wholly singular affinity:

Therefore, humanism only exists in the agreement between singularities, which agree through their very differences. Indeed, to wish for them to agree in some common term would ultimately mean, on the one hand, that we presuppose that in which they must agree and, on the other, that we give secondary importance to what is essential, namely, quite precisely the fact that he is irreplaceable, unique and inexpressible, in short, his singularity.[15]

Friendship surely offers a most excellent illustration of the recognition and affinity of singularities in agreement. Clearly, the medieval explanation of friendship by a mere resemblance within the species or through a likeness of form is outdated here, for it comes up short in relation to the experience of an immediate interpersonal match.[16]

13. Magnard, *Questions à l'humanisme*, 44.
14. On the historical antecedents in Duns Scotus see ibid., 142.
15. Ibid., 143.
16. When Aquinas shows that a given kind of likeness is a cause of love, he

In the new way opened up by humanism, "If [a man] deserves the name *uomo universale*, this is not because he would reunite in a single head all human perfections created by God but, rather, does so through his capacity to be all things for all men through the various facets of his personality."[17] One or another gifted humanist would be singularly set forth as the ideal of a unique and universal man who would have affinity with the singularity of all men and would offer them the possibility of being recognized in him. To attain the universal would require him to elevate his own, proper singularity until it comes to gather within itself an infinite number of relations. Conversely, to make an exclusive selection from among the appeals and expectations of others ultimately is akin to a kind of self-amputation of so many latent possibilities.[18] In potency, we are all universal men. However, while believing that we are preserving our singularity, we in fact mutilate it through our indifference and exclusion, for we in reality cut off a part of ourselves through our rejection of such differences.

AN IMPLICIT CHRISTOLOGICAL FIGURE

A Christological inspiration can be clearly espied here, at first in the form of a human exaltation which nonetheless wishes to be discrete, sober, and moderate. The accomplished man, endowed with

---

distinguishes between the love of friendship (or of benevolence) and the love of desire. The love of friendship comes about through an established likeness, according to which two subjects in act possess the same form and communicate in it, whereas the love of desire comes about through a lesser form of similarity, according to which "the one possesses in potency and through a kind of inclination what the other possesses in act" (*ST* I-II, q. 27, a. 3 resp.). Such a potentiality better accounts for the emergence of the feeling of love or for the birth of a friendship than does the affirmation of an actual likeness. A likeness of form can dispose one to either love or hatred, for it is easy to become exasperated with someone who is like ourselves. Certainly, it provides favorable conditions for the stabilization of a lasting friendship, but it does not provide a full explanation for the emergence of a love experienced for another, singular person, a love which is fundamentally inexplicable and contingent. However, this is the phenomenon that the immediate agreement of singulars attempts to explain.

17. Magnard, *Questions à l'humanisme*, 205.

18. Magnard, "Religion, chemin d'humanité," esp. 326.

a wide variety of qualities, the catalyst of their novel and balanced synthesis, can be nothing but magnanimous, without ever putting on airs of pride or superiority. In Raymond of Sebond, the Christological tenor of the *homo infinitus* is formally appealed to in order to sustain a nascent anthropology.[19] A wide diversity of variations, the capacity for empathy, the attraction of differences, the original composition of qualities, and relational aptitude thus all appear as being constitutive elements of the loftiest human singularity and determine its degree of openness to the universal. The humanists thought (or at least wagered) that it suffices that one reconnect with one's singularity in order to be receptively open to others. According to Montaigne, the singularity of each person is what sets him before the whole of humanity, for each man bears within himself "the full form of the human condition," realized in proportion to a limitless availability and even in proportion to a vulnerability capable of undergoing utter abasement.[20]

This Christological reversal seems to be the ultimate conclusion reached by Pierre Magnard's stimulating reflections. Authentic humanism cannot find its realization in the loftiest human excellence, for it would be useless to exalt man's grandeur if this led us to forget his misery and, as a result, to exclude those who cannot successfully hide this fact of the human situation. Man is not only (or even not so much) opened up to the universal and capable of a superior form of empathy through the fulfillment of a lofty level of humanity, endowed with all human qualities and synthesizing multiple differences. Rather, this is made possible through the availability which man acquires by traversing many states of human existence, not only from its depths to its heights, but likewise from its heights to its depths. As we will soon discuss, this was indeed the path embraced by the man Jesus Christ.

Finally, when we valorize the attraction of singularities and attachment to differences, let us not forget that overcoming differenc-

---

19. See Magnard, "L'homme universel," esp. 19–25.
20. See ibid., 28–32.

es and agreement among singular persons is rarely a peaceful affair. It gives rise to friendship only in exceptional cases, for it also can arouse fear, annoyance, or suspicion. The catalysts and witnesses to the universal are indeed those men and women who traverse human frontiers and synthesize differences, but they often do so under the constraint of force and in the form of exile. Crossing such borders, agreement with the differences of others thus constitutes a challenge that is all the greater as it is more often necessary to take up a memory distraught by past evils and to overcome the violence so endemic in human situations. The challenge and vulnerability of those who bear the universal expose them to the possibility of crystalizing not only interpersonal recognition but also exasperation, rejection, or death.

Thus balanced and already on the way toward further conceptual prolongations, the anthropological reflection of Pierre Magnard, inspired by a subtle appropriation of intuitions drawn from Montaigne, is conducive for new developments in Christology. We have set them forth and, indeed, accepted them in light of our own questions and in view of having them serve as a heuristic for theological reflection. From this point onward in this chapter, our principal objective will be to verify whether the hypothesis of a proportion between the loftiest singularity and the broadest universality also enables us to envision, at certain decisive stages of its trajectory, the universality of the man Jesus as being a property of his singularity. In order to elaborate our reflections on Jesus' humanity, as well as the degree of universality immanent within it, we will not immediately refer to Christ's divinity, although it is presupposed by the Paschal confession with which we began. Nonetheless, a full understanding of the phenomenon of Jesus will require us, in the final analysis, to thematize the divine element which provides the foundation for the salvific efficacy of the human elective affinities established through the recognition of who Christ is.

Setting aside for another venue the task of rereading certain moments in the Gospels which poignantly express the combination of singularity and universality in the man Jesus, we will here limit our-selves to taking two or three brief cues from the theological tradi-tion, considering authors who have already approximated a kind of Christological synthesis of the states or separations of man.

TRADITIONAL FOUNDATION:

INTENSIVE AND EXTENSIVE DIMENSIONS OF

THE INCARNATION

In the patristic tradition, Jesus' solidarity with all men was affirmed principally in terms of the incarnation of the eternal Word in our own perishable flesh. In other words, Jesus of Nazareth is the eter-nal Son, having assumed the fallen nature that we have been born into, one that is destined for death, though one in which we also aspire to restoration and eternal life. Such is the ontological foun-dation for the salvific exchange eloquently attested to within the framework of the passion. Looking upon the suffering Christ who makes the psalms his own, we can see the expression of such a uni-versal form of solidarity, founded on a sharing in our suffering hu-manity. Thus, the conviction that what happens to Jesus in his sin-gularity itself affects all men is fundamentally based on the divine Word of our own common nature in its obediential posture before God and its ability to undergo suffering up to the point of death.

Along these lines, Augustine and Leo the Great remarked that Christ casts a superior illumination upon each man, for he presents him with a new representation of human nature in its full nobility and dignity, such as it was willed by God.[21] Indeed, Christ exem-plifies and fulfills in himself the full splendor of what is possible for man, in the very work of restoring it and reunifying it in us, over-coming the fragmentation and dislocation from which it suffers. This became one of the traditional aspects of theological elaborations of the fittingness of the incarnation: in light of Christ, we are in a posi-tion to discover, though at an additional cost, the dignity of our own

21. See Augustine, *De vera religione* XVI.30; Leo the Great, *Sermones* I.3.

humanity, which was freely taken up by the divine Word in our own precarious condition. A lively awareness of this proximity should restrain our desire to sin, which would disfigure this same humanity found in ourselves.[22]

Such a foundational affirmation concerning the objective elective affinity between Christ and every man builds on the Word's appropriation of our own human nature. The fact that we share human nature with every man and with the Word provides the foundation for the possibility of its salvific challenge addressed *de iure* to all. The explanatory value of such a foundational affirmation is radical and powerful, though it is confined to thematizing the conditions for the possibility of a universal salvific solidarity in Jesus' humanity, joined to his divinity.

In order to give full credence to such a proposal, however, it does not suffice that we affirm that the Son of God became a true man for our salvation or that the Word assumed humanity in the condition which is our own, affected by sin and death. We also must recognize that the humanity thus assumed is complete only through the full unfolding of Jesus' life from start to finish, from conception to death. Thus, Christ embraced the totality of human becoming, from one extreme to the other in a human life composed of a great number of the existential states which can befall man.

Among the Church Fathers, Gregory of Nyssa, on account of his positive conception of change (as distinct from evil or vicious *pathos*), was keenly aware of the at once intensive and extensive dimensions of the incarnation: "Our position is that God was born subject to both movements of our nature; first, that by which the soul hastens to join the body, and then again that by which the body is separated from the soul."[23] Meanwhile, he knew all the stages and components of the natural development involved in our own human condition: birth, nursing, education, growth, progress toward

---

22. See *ST* III, q. 1, a. 2, resp.; *Compendium theologiae*, I.200.2.

23. Gregory of Nyssa, *Oratio catechetica* XVI, trans. William Moore and Henry Austin Wilson, in *Dogmatic Treatises*, ed. Henry Wace and Philip Schaff, in NPNF-II 5 (Oxford: Parker and Company, 1893), 489.

maturity, sleep and fatigue, sorrow and tears, etc.[24] Prior to Gregory, Irenaeus of Lyons had already affirmed, in relation to the ages of Christ's life: "Being a Master, therefore, he also possessed the age of a Master, not despising or evading any condition of humanity, nor setting aside in himself that Law which he had appointed for the human race, but sanctifying every age, by that period corresponding to it which belonged to himself."[25] Through the incarnation, Christ assumes humanity not only in its density and depths but also in its entire temporal character and full extent. This is why we can speak not only of the intensive dimension of the incarnation but also of its extensive dimensions.

With the human unfolding of Jesus' life coming to its end in the ordeal of his death, God, through the resurrection, reunited in his Christ what death had separated: "For when our nature, following its own proper course, had even in him been advanced to the separation of soul and body, he knitted together again the disunited elements, cementing them, as it were, together with the cement of his Divine Power, and recombining what has been severed in a union never to be broken."[26] In Gregory's Christology, the incarnation and the resurrection are engaged in the full extent of human experience, from conception to death. The full course traveled by Christ deploys and actualizes that which has been rendered possible by the union of the divine and the human (soul, body, and becoming) in the unique person of Christ, namely the universal salvific efficacy of his birth, human life, death, and resurrection. Their soteriological benefits can be applied to every man and to all men, for Jesus of Nazareth embraces all the states of the human condition, all the way to its bitter end in death.

Granted, he did not know every single possible state of the human condition. However, this was not absolutely necessary. Thus,

---

24. See Gregory of Nyssa, *Oratio catechetica* IX, SC 453:203–5; see also *Letters* III.17, SC 363:137.

25. Irenaeus of Lyons, *Adversus haereses* XXII, ed. Alexander Roberts and James Donaldson, in Ante-Nicene Fathers 1 (New York: Charles Scribner's Sons, 1899), 391.

26. Gregory of Nyssa, *Oratio catechetica* XVI, trans. Wace and Schaff, 489.

for example, he did not experience the embrace of conjugal love and, in comparison with Paul, he remains rather restrained and reserved in his teaching concerning male-female relations, apart from his condemnation of adultery. Moreover, by dying in the prime of his life, he was spared the experience of lengthy illness and old age. However, we have reason to think that as he approached his death and experienced the dereliction involved in it—granted, as experiences lived in a shortened and condensed timeframe—he was able to know quite well the various existential modalities occurring as death progressively unfolds its work in man. In any case, through his true and real experience of death, he takes up and rejoins the other paths ways that lead to death, even if only by experiencing the terminus to which they lead.

In order to better perceive the incarnation's intensive dimension, not only as a venture attempting to synthesize the various existential states of the human condition but also as an ongoing journey of being stripped of one's dignity, it is fitting that we here consider one aspect of Aquinas's teaching concerning the passion. Indeed, he shows that the universality of the offer of salvation can be deciphered if we pay attention to everything which, in the humanity which he assumed, is reached and, ultimately taken away from Christ through his trial and passion. In Thomas's opinion, the passion in fact possesses a universal character from the perspective of the human sufferings taken up by Christ.[27] Granted, he did not endure the full diversity of possible sufferings (as regards the various species of possible suffering), and his own were even shortened through a death that was more rapid than was expected, as is attested to by the fact that his legs did not need to be broken. However, he took up many kinds of sufferings (as regards the genera of possible suffering), all of which are of great significance for his salvific mission. This is first of all made manifest by the various agents inflicting such sufferings upon him: pagans and Jews, men and women, leaders and servants, the host which submerges and overwhelms him, and even his close

27. See *ST* III, q. 46, a. 5.

companions, men like Judas and Peter. This universality is also made manifest to the extent that the man Jesus suffered everything that can make a man suffer: in his friends who abandoned him, in his reputation and honor which are flouted, in his goods (all the way down to the final garment which is stripped from his body), in his soul which was affected by sadness and fear, and finally, in his body which was affected in all of its sense powers and members.

Such contemplation of the suffering Christ arguably does not find its source in a kind of excessive search for sorrowful emotional states[28] but, rather, finds its basis in a theological outlook that is clear-eyed about the way that the various evils which befall sinful men come to be consolidated in the man of sorrows. Indeed, Aquinas specifies that the least of Christ's sufferings would have sufficed for the redemption of mankind.[29] It was not absolutely necessary that he would assume every single kind of suffering, and we must indeed hold that the passion remains a contingent event from start to finish. Nonetheless, in being lived by Christ, its accidental and anecdotal modalities become particularly expressive of the universality of the offer of salvation made in Christ. Thus, this particular combination of events remains only something that is fitting, without thereby being bound by an *a priori* necessity.

THE HIDDEN DIVINE FACTOR

By recourse to a contemporary philosophical perspective, we have suggested that we can possibly think of Christ's universality as being a property of the very singularity of Jesus of Nazareth. In order to reveal the features and contours of a universality which is thus founded on Jesus Christ's singularity, it would then be suitable to

---

28. However, it is true that medieval piety did strongly influence the theology of that time, as is amply shown in Caroline W. Bynum, "The Power in the Blood: Sacrifice, Satisfaction, and Substitution in Late Medieval Soteriology," in *The Redemption: An Interdisciplinary Symposium on Christ as Redeemer*, ed. Stephen T. Davies, Daniel Kendall, and Gerald O'Collins (Oxford: Oxford University Press, 2004), 177–204.

29. See *ST* III, q. 46, a. 5, ad 3.

pay close attention to the emblematic scope of the multiple concrete and singular "details" which punctuate the narratives of Jesus' origins, life, and death. This would enable us to follow in a detailed manner how Jesus' singularity offers, in an exceptional manner, the possibility of a universal elective affinity. We already established that the fact that his singularity traverses through many of man's existential states confers it with a power of the greatest extent and challenging force, a power which operates as much by way of affinity as it does by opposition or provocation. Indeed, he encounters men not only through an elective affinity with their various existential states of life but also, as the innocent One, joins and challenges, through confrontation or compassion, not through mere likeness but, rather, by way of affinities surpassing all differences: "For we have not a high priest who is unable to sympathize with our weaknesses, but one who in every respect has been tempted as we are, yet without sin" (Heb 4:15; see 5:2).[30] Obviously, the fact that Christ makes no compromise with sin does not thereby place any limitation on his compassion for sinners. His proximity and solidarity with them, founded on the testing and temptation which he himself knew, can only be reinforced by his unadulterated innocence. Nonetheless, for the benefit of sinners, he will in some manner bear a likeness to sin, cast upon him to the degree that his body will be disfigured by the violence inflicted upon him by men.

The astonishingly universal elective affinity which the man Jesus was able to establish and indeed still sustains, through the fullness and amplitude of his human singularity, has a decisive divine element in its background: he is the unique Son of God sent in mission to the world. In the end, only this foundation can render account of his truly universal salvific power and efficacy. The potential accord of the man Jesus with all men is the privileged surface onto which is refracted the universal salvific will, whose primordial

---

30. On the difference between Christ's compassion and the sympathy possible for every other high priest, see Albert Vanhoye, *La lettre aux Hébreux. Jésus-Christ, médiateur d'une alliance nouvelle* (Paris: Desclée, 2002), 87–88, 93–94.

author and principal agent remains God. The bearer of an eschato-logical and universal mission, Jesus' concrete humanity was consti-tuted and it deployed all of its virtualities in a wholly unique fashion having a universal amplitude. The ultimate mission of Jesus of Naza-reth in God's salvific design bears witness to the utter coincidence of the greatest singularity and the widest universality, with both being found in his concrete humanity.

In light of such a mission, Jesus Christ presents us with a whol-ly unique character, and what he accomplished cannot be repeated, even if some of his disciples reproduce his powerful challenge and empathy, doing so in a way that is cut to their own measure, though with a truly universal scope. We merely need to think of the Apostle Paul, who himself confesses that he constantly strove to be all things for all men in order to save, at any cost, those for whom he had such solicitude: a Pharisee with the Pharisees, as one without the Law when among the pagans, poor with the needy, as one who is filled with those who are rich, at work with those who labor, and so forth. Through the power of grace, God was clearly able to deploy the full extent of Paul's own, singular humanity, according to the spiritual freedom and adaptive capacities which were inspired in him by the charity of Jesus Christ.

Select Bibliography

ANCIENT AND MEDIEVAL SOURCES

Aristotle. *The Complete Works of Aristotle*. Edited by Jonathan Barnes. Princeton, N.J.: Princeton University Press, 1995.

Athanasius of Alexandria. *Contra Gentes*. Edited by Pierre T. Camelot. SC 18 bis. Paris: Cerf, 1977.

———. *Contra arianos*. Edited by Charles Kannegiesser et al. 2 vols. SC 598–99. Paris: Cerf, 2019.

Athenagoras. *Apologia pro Christianis*. Edited by Bernard Pouderon. SC 379. Paris: Cerf, 1992.

Augustine of Hippo. *Confessiones*. Edited by Lucas Verheijen. Corpus Christianorum Series Latina [hereafter CCSL] 27. Turnhout: Brepols, 1981.

———. *Confessiones*. Translated by Maria Boulding. New York: New City Press, 1997.

———. *De civitate Dei*. Edited by Bernard Dombart. 2 vols. CCSL 47–48. Turnhout: Brepols, 1955.

———. *De civitate Dei*. Translated by William M. Green. Cambridge, Mass.: Harvard University Press, 1988–97.

———. *De correptione et gratia*. Edited by Jean Chéné and Jacques Pintard. Bibliothèque Augustinienne 24. Paris: Institut d'Études Augustiniennes, 1962.

———. *De diversis quaestionibus LXXXIII*. Edited by Almut Mutzenbecher. CCSL 44A. Turnhout: Brepols, 1975.

———. *De doctrina christiana*. Edited by Joseph Martin. CCSL 32. Turnhout: Brepols, 1962.

———. *De Genesi ad litteram*. Edited by Paul Agaësse and Aimé Solignac. 2 vols. Bibliothèque Augustinienne 48–49. Paris: Institut d'Études Augustiniennes, 1972.

———. *De ordine*. Edited by William M. Green. CCSL 29. Turnhout: Brepols, 1970.

———. *De praedestinatione sanctorum*. Edited by Jean Chéné and Jacques Pintard. Bibliothèque Augustinienne 24. Paris: Institut d'Études Augustiniennes, 1962.

———. *De Trinitate*. Edited by Pieter Smulders. 2 vols. CCSL 62–62A. Turnhout: Brepols, 1979.

———. *De Trinitate*. Translated by Arthur W. Haddan. Edited by Philip Schaff. NPNF-II 3. Buffalo, N.Y.: Christian Literature Publishing, 1887.

———. *De vera religione*. Edited by Joseph Martin. CCSL 32. Turnhout: Brepols, 1962.

———. *Eighty-Three Different Questions*. Q. 52. Edited by Hermigild Dressler et al. Transkated by David L. Mosher. Fathers of the Church 70. Washington, D.C.: The Catholic University of America Press, 2002.

———. *Letter 130 to Proba*. Edited by Kl. D. Daur. CCSL 31B. Turnhout: Brepols, 2009.

———. *Tractatus in Euangelium Iohannis*. Edited by Marie-François Berrouard. 7 vols. Bibliothèque Augustinienne 71–75. Paris: Institut d'Études Augustiniennes, 1969–2003.

Basil of Caesarea. *Hexaemeron*. Edited by Stanislas Giet. SC 26. Paris: Cerf, 1950.

———. *Contra Eunomium*. Edited by Bernard Sesboüé. 2 vols. SC 299 and 305. Paris: Cerf, 1982–83.

———. *Letters*. Edited by Yves Courtonne. 3 vols. Les Belles Lettres 132, 148, 149. Paris: Presses Universitaires de France, 2002–3.

Bernard of Clairvaux. *De gratia et libero arbitrio*. Edited by Françoise Callerot et al. SC 393. Paris: Cerf, 2010.

Bonaventure of Bagnoregio. *Commentaria in quatuor libros Sententiarum*. 4 vols. Quaracchi: Ex Typographia Collegii St. Bonaventurae, 1882–89.

———. *Apologia pauperum contra calumniatorem*. in *Opera Omnia*, vol. 8. Quaracchi: Ex Typographia Collegii St. Bonaventurae, 1898.

Clement of Alexandria. *Stromata* V. Edited by Alain Le Boulluec. SC 279. Paris: Cerf, 1981.

Cyril of Alexandria. "Second Letter of Cyril to Nestorius." In *Decrees of the Ecumenical Councils: Nicaea I to Lateran V*, edited by Norman P. Tanner. Washington, D.C.: Georgetown University Press, 1990.

Cyril of Jerusalem. *Catechetical Lectures*. Edited by Auguste Piédagnel. SC 126 bis. Paris: Cerf, 1988.

Dionysius Areopagite. *De divinis nominibus. De mystica theologia*. Edited by Ysabel de Andia. 2 vols. SC 578–79. Paris: Cerf, 2016.

———. *Pseudo-Dionysius: The Complete Works*. Edited by Colm Luibheid and Paul Rorem. Classics of Western Spirituality. New York: Paulist Press, 1987.

Duns Scotus. *Ordinatio*. Book I. Edited by Carolus Balić. Vatican City: Typis Polyglottis Vaticanis, 1963.

Gregory Nazianzen. *Orationes*, vol. 6: *Discours 27–31*. Edited by Paul Gallay. SC 250. Paris: Cerf, 1978. Vol. 7: *Discours 32–37*. Edited by Claudio Moreschini. SC 318. Paris: Cerf, 1985.

Gregory of Nyssa. *Letters*. Edited by Pierre Maraval. SC 363. Paris: Cerf, 1990.

———. *Oratio catechetica*. Edited by Raymond Winling. SC 453. Paris: Cerf, 2000.

————. *Oratio catechetica*. Translated by William Moore and Henry Austin Wilson, in *Dogmatic Treatises*, collected in NPNF-I 5.

Gregory the Great. *Moralia in Job*, vol. 1. Edited by Robert Gillet and André de Gaumaris. SC 32 bis. Paris: Cerf, 1975.

Hilary of Poitiers. *De Trinitate*. Edited by Jean Doignon et al. 3 vols. SC 443, 448, 462. Paris: Cerf, 1999–2001.

Irenaeus of Lyons. *Adversus haereses*. Edited by Adelin Rousseau. 5 vols. SC 263–64, 293–94, 210–11, 100–100*, 152–53. Paris: Cerf, 1965–82.

————. *Adversus haereses*. Edited by Alexander Roberts and James Donaldson. In Ante-Nicene Fathers 1. New York: Charles Scribner's Sons, 1899.

John Chrysostom. *Trois catéchèses baptismales*. Edited by Auguste Piédagnel. SC 336. Paris: Cerf, 1990.

John Damascene. *De fide orthodoxa*. Edited by Pierre Ledrux. 2 vols. SC 535, 540. Paris: Cerf, 2010–11.

————. *De fide orthodoxa*. Edited by Eligius M. Buyteart. New York: Franciscan Institute St. Bonaventure, 1955.

Jordan of Saxony. *On the Beginnings of the Order of Preachers*. Edited and translated by Simon Tugwell. Dublin: Dominican Publications, 1982.

Lactantius. *De ira Dei*. Edited by Christiane Ingremeau. SC 289. Paris: Cerf, 1982.

Leo the Great. *Sermones*, vol. 1: *Sermons 1–19*. Edited by Jean Leclercq. SC 22 bis. Paris: Cerf, 1964.

Nemesius of Emesa. *De natura hominis*. Translated by Burgundio of Pisa. Edited by G. Verbeke and J. R. Moncho. Leiden: Brill, 1975.

Origen. *Treatise on Principles*, vol. 1. Edited by Henri Crouzel. SC 252. Paris: Cerf, 1978.

————. *Homilies on Ezekiel*. Edited by Marcel Borret. SC 352. Paris: Cerf, 1989.

Philo of Alexandria. *De posteritate Caini*. Edited by Roger Arnaldez. Les œuvres de Philon d'Alexandrie 6. Paris: Cerf, 1972.

————. *Quod Deus sit immutabilis*. Edited by André Mosès. Les œuvres de Philon d'Alexandrie 7–8. Paris: Cerf, 1963.

————. *De specialibus legibus*, vol. 1. Edited by Suzanne Daniel. Les œuvres de Philon d'Alexandrie 24. Paris: Cerf, 1975.

Plato. *Complete Works*. Edited by John M. Cooper. Indianapolis, Ind.: Hackett, 1997.

Plotinus. *Enneads*. Edited by Lloyd P. Gerson. Cambridge: Cambridge University Press, 2017.

Raymond of Capua. *The Life of St. Catherine of Siena*. New York: P. J. Kenedy, 1960.

Richard of St. Victor. *De Trinitate*. Edited by Gaston Salet. SC 63. Paris: Cerf, 1999.

————. *On the Trinity*. Translated by Ruben Angelici. Eugene, Ore.: Cascade, 2011.

Theophilus of Antioch. *Ad Autolycum*. Edited by Gustave Bardy. SC 20. Paris: Cerf, 1948.

Thomas Aquinas. *Commentary on the Gospel of John.* Translated by Fabian R. Larcher and James A. Weisheipl. 3 vols. Washington, D.C.: The Catholic University of America Press, 2010.

———. *Commentary on the Letter of Saint Paul to the Hebrews.* Translated by Fabian R. Larcher. Lander, Wyo.: Aquinas Institute, 2012.

———. *Compendium theologiae.* Edited by Hyacinthe F. Dondaine. Rome: Commissio Leonina, 1979.

———. *Contra impugnantes. De perfectione spiritualis vitae. Contra retrahentes.* Edited by Hyacinthe F. Dondaine. Rome: Commissio Leonina, 1970.

———. *De rationibus fidei.* Edited by Hyacinthe F. Dondaine. Rome: Commissio Leonina, 1969.

———. *Expositio et lectura super Epistolas Pauli Apostoli.* Edited by Raphael Cai. 2 vols. Rome: Marietti, 1953.

———. *Expositio libri Peri Hermeneias,* vol. 1. Rome: Commissio Leonina, 1989.

———. *Expositio super Iob ad litteram.* Edited by Antoine Dondaine. Rome: Commissio Leonina, 1965.

———. *In Symbolum Apostolorum.* Edited by Raimondo M. Spiazzi. Rome: Marietti, 1953.

———. *"La perfection, c'est la charité." Vie chrétienne et vie religieuse dans le Christ.* Edited by Jean-Pierre Torrell. Paris: Cerf, 2010.

———. *Lectura super Ioannem.* Edited by Raphael Cai. Rome: Marietti, 1952.

———. *Lectura super Matthaeum.* Edited by Raphael Cai. Rome: Marietti, 1951.

———. *On the Truth of the Catholic Faith (Summa contra Gentiles).* Translated by Charles J. O'Neill. Garden City, N.Y.: Image Books, 1957.

———. *Postilla super Psalmos* [Ps 1–51]. Translated by Jean-Éric Stroobant de Saint-Éloy. Paris: Cerf, 1996.

———. *Postilla super Psalmos* [Ps 52–54]. Edited by Pietro A. Uccelli. In *S. Thomae Aquinatis In Isaiam prophetam, In tres psalmos David, In Boetium de Hebdomadibus et de Trinitate expositiones,* 214–54. Rome: Ex Typographia Polyglotta, 1880.

———. *Quaestio disputata de virtutibus.* Edited by P. Bazzi et al. 2 vols. Rome: Marietti, 1965.

———. *Quaestio disputata de unione verbi incarnati.* Edited by P. Bazzi et al. Rome: Marietti, 1965.

———. *Quaestiones de quodlibet I-XII.* Edited by René A. Gauthier. Rome: Commissio Leonina, 1996.

———. *Quaestiones disputatae de malo.* Edited by Pierre-Marie Gils. Rome: Commissio Leonina, 1982.

———. *Quaestiones disputatae de potentia.* Edited by P. Bazzi et al. Rome: Marietti, 1965.

———. *Quaestiones disputatae de veritate.* Rome: Commissio Leonina, 1970–76.

———. *Scriptum super libros Sententiarum.* Vols. 1–2 edited by Pierre Madonnet; vols. 3–4 edited by Marie F. Moos. Paris: Lethielleux, 1927–47.

———. *Sententia Libri Ethicorum.* Rome: Commissio Leonina, 1969.

———. *Sententia super Metaphysicam.* Edited by Raimondo M. Spiazzi. Rome: Marietti, 1950.

———. *Summa contra Gentiles.* Rome: Commissio Leonina, 1934.

———. *Summa contra Gentiles.* Translated by Anton C. Pegis. Notre Dame, Ind.: University of Notre Dame Press, 1975.

———. *Summa theologiae.* Leonine edition. Rome: Edizioni Paoline, 1988.

———. *Super Boetium De Trinitate.* Edited by Pierre-Marie Gils. Rome: Commissio Leonina, 1992.

———. *Super librum Dionysii De divinis nominibus.* Edited by Ceslaus Pera. Rome: Marietti, 1950.

Vetus Latina. Die Resteder altateinischen Bibel, vol. 2: *Genesis.* Edited by Bonifatius Fischer. Freiburg i.B.: Herder, 1951.

OTHERS SOURCES, WORKS, AND STUDIES

Aletti, Jean-Noël. *St. Paul,* Épître *aux Philippiens.* Paris: Gabalda, 2005.

Amit, Yairah. "'The Glory of Israël Does Not Deceive or Change his Mind.' On the Reliability of Narrator and Speakers in Biblical Narrative." *Prooftexts* 12, no. 3 (1992): 201–12.

Andia, Ysabel de. "Remotio-Negatio. L'évolution du vocabulaire de Saint Thomas touchant la voie négative." *AHDLMA* 68, no. 1 (2001): 45–71.

Ansaldi, Jean. "La toute-puissance du Dieu du théisme dans le champ de la per version." *Laval Théologique et Philosophique* 47, no. 1 (1991): 3–11.

Antoni, Gérald. *La prière chez saint Augustin. D'une philosophie du langage à la théologie du Verbe.* Paris: Vrin, 1997.

Arendt, Hannah. *The Human Condition.* Chicago: University of Chicago Press, 1958.

Balthasar, Hans Urs von. *Karl Barth. Darstellung und Deutung Seiner Theologie.* Cologne: J. Hegner, 1951.

———. "Kommentar." In Thomas von Aquin, *Besondere Gnadengabe und die zwei meschlichen Lebens.* Heidelberg: Die deutsche Thomas-Ausgabe, 1954.

———. "Der Heilige Geist als Liebe." *Skizzen zur Theologie, III: Spiritus Creator,* 106–22. Einsiedeln: Johannes Verlag, 1967.

———. "Mysterium Paschale." In *Mysterium Salutis. Grundriss Heilsgeschichtlicher Dogmatik. Das Christusereignis,* III.2, edited by Johannes Feiner and Magnus Löhrer, 269–81. Einsiedeln: Benziger Verlag, 1969.

———. *Herrlichkeit,* III.2. *Neuer Bund.* Einsiedeln: Johannes Verlag, 1969.

———. *The Glory of the Lord,* I: *Seeing the Form.* Translated by Erasmo Leiva-Merikakis. San Francisco, Calif.: Ignatius Press, 1982.

———. *The Glory of the Lord,* VII: *Theology: The New Covenant.* Translated by Brian McNeil. San Francisco, Calif.: Ignatius Press, 1989.

———. *Theo-Drama,* V: *The Last Act.* Translated by Graham Harrison. San Francisco, Calif.: Ignatius Press, 1998.

———. *Epilogue*. Translated by Edward T. Oakes. San Francisco, Calif.: Ignatius Press, 2004.

———. *Dare We Hope That "All Men Be Saved?": With a Short Discourse on Hell*. Translated by David Kipp and Lothar Krauth. San Francisco, Calif.: Ignatius Press, 2014.

Barbour, Ian G. *Religion in an Age of Science. The Gifford Lectures 1989–1991*. London: SCM Press, 1990.

Barth, Karl. *Church Dogmatics*. Edited by Geoffrey W. Bromiley and Thomas F. Torrance. 12 vols. London: T and T Clark, 2004.

Batut, Jean-Pierre. *Pantocrator. "Dieu le Père tout-puissant" dans la théologie prénicéenne*. Paris: Institut d'Études Augustiniennes, 2009.

Bauckham, Richard. *The Theology of the Book of Revelation*. Cambridge: Cambridge University Press, 1993.

———. *Jesus and the God of Israel*. Grand Rapids, Mich.: Eerdmans, 2008.

Bériou, Nicole, and Bernard Hodel, eds. *Saint Dominique de l'Ordre des frères Prêcheurs. Témoignages écrits*. Paris: Cerf, 2019.

Blaise, Albert. *Dictionnaire latin-français des auteurs chrétiens*. Turnhout: Brepols, 1954.

Blenkinsopp, Joseph. *Isaiah 1–39*. New York: Doubleday, 2000.

Bobik, Joseph. "Aquinas on *Communicatio*, The Foundation of Friendship and *Caritas*." *The Modern Schoolman* 64, no. 1 (1988): 1–18.

Bonhoeffer, Dietrich. *Letters and Papers from Prison*. New York: Touchtone, 1997.

Bonino, Serge-Thomas. "The Role of Apostles in the Communication of Revelation according to the *Lectura super Ioannem* of St. Thomas Aquinas." In *Reading John with St. Thomas Aquinas*, edited by Michael Dauphinais and Matthew Levering, 318–46. Washington, D.C.: The Catholic University of America Press, 2005.

———. "Providence et causes secondes. L'exemple de la prière." In *Saint Thomas d'Aquin*, edited by Thierry-Dominique Humbrecht, 493–519. Paris: Cerf, 2010.

———. *Dieu, "Celui qui est" (De Deo ut uno)*. Paris: Parole et Silence, 2016.

———. "Contemporary Thomism through the Prism of the Theology of Predestination." In *Thomism and Predestination: Principles and Disputations*, edited by Steven A. Long, 29–50. Ave Maria, Fla.: Sapientia Press, 2016.

———. "L'incompréhensible sagesse de Dieu dans l'*Expositio super Iob*." In *Études Thomasiennes*, 593–624. Paris: Parole et Silence, 2018.

———. "Vertus sociales et sens de Dieu." In *Études thomasiennes*, 423–37. Paris: Parole et Silence, 2018.

Boulnois, Olivier, ed. *La puissance et son ombre. De Pierre Lombard et Luther*. Paris: Aubier, 1994.

———. *Être et représentation*. Paris: Presses Universitaires de France, 1999.

Brocke, Michael D. "On the Jewish Origin of the Improperia." *Immanuel* 7 (1997): 44–51.

Bulgakov, Sergei. *The Lamb of God.* Translated by Boris Jakim. Grand Rapids, Mich.: Eerdmans, 2008.

Bultmann, Rudolf. "New Testament and Mythology." In *Kerygma and Myth: A Theological Debate,* edited by Hans W. Bartsch, 1–44. London: SCPK, 1953.

Bynum, Caroline W. "The Power in the Blood: Sacrifice, Satisfaction, and Substitution in Late Medieval Soteriology." In *The Redemption: An Interdisciplinary Symposium on Christ as Redeemer,* edited by Stephen T. Davies, Daniel Kendall, and Gerald O'Collins, 177–204. Oxford: Oxford University Press, 2004.

Byrne, Brendan. "Christ's Preexistence in Pauline Soteriology." *Theological Studies* 58, no. 2 (1997): 308–30.

Calvin, John. *Institutes of the Christian Religion.* Translated by Henry Beveridge. Grand Rapids, Mich.: Eerdmans, 1957.

Cappiapuoti, Pierluigi. *"Deus existentia amoris." Teologia delle carità et teologia della Trinità negli scritti di Riccardo di San Vittore († 1173).* Turnhout: Brepols, 1998.

Cavafy, Constantin P. *Collected Poems.* Translated by Edmund Keeley and Philip Sherrard. Edited by George Savidis. Princeton, N.J.: Princeton University Press, 1992.

Chergé, Christian de. *L'invincible espérance.* Paris: Bayard-Centurion, 1997.

Clavier, Paul. "Le jeune Sartre et le vieux Sertillanges: le chassé-croisé de la création." *RSPT* 96, no. 3 (2012): 493–511.

Clore, Gerald L., and Andrew Ortony. "Appraisal Theories: How Cognition Shapes Affect into Emotions." In *Handbook of Emotions,* 3rd ed., edited by Michael Lewis et al., 628–42. New York: Guilford Press, 2008.

Courtenay, William J. *Capacity and Volition: A History of the Distinction of Absolute and Ordained Power.* Bergamo: P. Lubrina, 1990.

Cuchet, Guillaume. "Une révolution théologique oubliée. Le triomphe de la thèse du grand nombre des élus dans le discours catholique du XIXe siècle." *Revue d'histoire du XIXe siècle* 41, no. 2 (2010): 131–48.

———. "Comment Dieu est-il acteur de l'histoire? Le débat Broglie-Guéranger sur le 'naturalisme historique.'" *RSPT* 96, no. 1 (2012): 33–55.

Daguet, François. *Théologie du dessein divin chez Thomas d'Aquin. Finis omnium Ecclesia.* Paris: Vrin, 2003.

Dahan, Gilbert. ed. *Le Brûlement du Talmud à Paris, 1242–1244.* Paris: Cerf, 1999.

———. *Lire la Bible au Moyen Âge. Essais d'herméneutique médiévale.* Geneva: Droz, 2009.

———. "Les émotions de Dieu dans l'exégèse médiévale." In *Émotions de Dieu. Attributions et appropriations chrétiennes (XVIe-XVIIIe siècle),* edited by Chrystel Bernat and Frédéric Gabriel, 97–121. Turnhout: Brepols, 2019.

Dalferth, Ingolf U. "God, Time, and Orientation. 'Presence' and 'Absence' in Religious and Everyday Discourse." In *The Presence and Absence of God. Claremont Studies in the Philosophy of Religion: Conference 2008,* edited by Ingolf U. Dalferth, 1–20. Tübingen: Mohr Siebeck, 2008.

Dauphinais, Michael, and Matthew Levering, eds. *Reading John with St. Thomas Aquinas: Theological Exegesis and Speculative Theology.* Washington, D.C.: The Catholic University of America Press, 2010.

———. *Reading Romans with St. Thomas Aquinas.* Washington, D.C.: The Catholic University of America Press, 2012.

Davidson, Donald. "What Metaphors Mean." *Critical Inquiry* 5, no. 1 (1978): 31–47.

Dearman, J. Andrew. *The Book of Hosea.* Grand Rapids, Mich.: Eerdmans, 2010.

Denzinger, Heinrich. *Enchiridion symbolorum, definitionum et declarationum de rebus fidei et morum. Compendium of Creeds, Definitions, and Declarations on Matters of Faith and Morals.* Edited by Peter Hünermann, Robert Fastiggi, and Anne E. Nash. 43rd ed. San Francisco, Calif.: Ignatius Press, 2012.

Devillers, Luc. "Le sein du Père. La finale du prologue de Jean." *Revue biblique* 112, no. 1 (2005): 63–79.

Dewan, Lawrence. "St. Thomas and the Ontology of Prayer." *Divus Thomas* 77, nos. 3–4 (1974): 392–402.

Dilthey, Wilhelm. *Weltanschauung und Analyse des Menschen seit Renaissance und Reformation.* Göttingen: Vandenhoeck and Ruprecht, 1964.

Diriart, Alexandra. "La dimension nuptiale des catéchèses baptismales. Entre similitude, circularité, et dissymétrie." *Nova et Vetera* 93, no. 1 (2018): 25–45.

Dodds, Michael J. *The Unchanging God of Love: Thomas Aquinas and Contemporary Theology on Divine Immutability.* Washington, D.C.: The Catholic University of America Press, 2008.

———. *Unlocking Divine Action: Contemporary Science and Thomas Aquinas.* Washington, D.C.: The Catholic University of America Press, 2012.

Dunn, James D. G. *Romans 1–8.* Dallas, Tex.: Word Books, 1988.

———. *Christology in the Making: A New Testament Inquiry into the Origins of the Doctrine of the Incarnation.* London: SCM Press, 1989.

———. *The Theology of Paul the Apostle.* Grand Rapids, Mich.: Eerdmans, 1998.

Durand, Emmanuel. "Au principe de l'amour: *formatio* ou *proportio*? Un déplacement revisité dans l'analyse thomasienne de la *voluntas.*" *Revue thomiste* 104, no. 4 (2004): 551–78.

———. *La Périchorèse des personnes divines. Immanence mutuelle, réciprocité et communion.* Paris: Cerf, 2005.

———. "L'innascibilité et les relations du Père, sous le signe de sa primauté, dans la théologie trinitaire de Bonaventure." *Revue thomiste* 106, no. 4 (2006): 531–63.

———. "Généalogie de la typologie médiévale sur l'*innascibilitas* du Père. Pierre Lombard, Guillaume d'Auxerre et Alexandre de Halès." *AHDLMA* 74, no. 1 (2007): 7–26.

———. "Le Père en sa relation constitutive au Fils, selon saint Thomas d'Aquin." *Revue thomiste* 107, no. 1 (2007): 47–72.

———. *Le Père Alpha et Oméga de la vie trinitaire.* Paris: Cerf, 2008.

———. *L'Offre universelle du salut en Christ.* Paris: Cerf, 2012.

———. "Note sur la théologie de l'histoire." *RSPT* 98, no. 2 (2014): 353–79.

———. "The Gospel of Prayer and Theories of Providence." *The Thomist* 78, no. 4 (2014): 519–36.

———. Évangile *et Providence. Une théologie de l'action de Dieu.* Paris: Cerf, 2014.

———. *L'Être humain, divin appel. Anthropologie et création.* Paris: Cerf, 2016.

———. *Les Émotions de Dieu, indices d'engagement.* Paris: Cerf, 2019.

Ekman, Paul. "Basic Emotions." In *Handbook of Cognition and Emotion,* edited by Tim Dalgleish and Mick J. Power, 45–60. Sussex: John Wiley, 1999.

Emery, Gilles. *La Trinité créatrice. Trinité et création dans les commentaires aux "Sentences" de Thomas d'Aquin et de ses précurseurs Albert le Grand et Bonaventure.* Paris: Vrin, 1995.

———. "Trinité et unité de Dieu dans la scolastique. XIIe-XIVᵉ siècle." In *Le christianisme est-il un monothéisme?,* edited by Gilles Emery and Pierre Gisel, 195–220. Geneva: Labor et Fides, 2001.

———. *The Trinitarian Theology of Saint Thomas Aquinas.* Translated by Francesca A. Murphy. Oxford: Oxford University Press, 2007.

———. "Trinitarian Theology as Spiritual Exercise in Augustine and Aquinas." In *Aquinas the Augustinian,* edited by Michael Dauphinais, 1–40. Washington, D.C.: The Catholic University of America Press, 2007.

———. "*Theologia* and *Dispensatio*: The Centrality of the Divine Missions in St. Thomas's Trinitarian Theology." *The Thomist* 74, no. 4 (2010): 515–61.

Evans, C. Stephen, ed. *Exploring Kenotic Christology: The Self-Emptying of God.* Oxford: Oxford University Press, 2006.

Eyzaguirre, Samuel F. "'*Passio caritatis*' according to Origen in *Ezechielem Homiliae* VI in the Light of *DT* 1, 31." *Vigiliae Christianae* 60, no. 2 (2006): 135–47.

Feuerbach, Ludwig. *The Essence of Christianity.* Translated by George Eliot. Amherst, N.Y.: Prometheus Books, 1989.

Flint, Thomas P. *Divine Providence: The Molinist Account.* New York: Cornell University Press, 1998.

Fretheim, Terence E. "Suffering God and Sovereign God in Exodus: A Collision of Images." *Horizons in Biblical Theology* 11, no. 1 (1989): 31–56.

———. "The Repentance of God: A Key to Evaluating Old Testament God-Talk." *Horizons in Biblical Theology* 10, no. 1 (1988): 47–70.

———. "The Repentance of God: A Study of Jeremiah 18:7–10." *Hebrew Annual Review* 11 (1987): 81–92.

Garrigues, Jean-Miguel. "La persévérance de Dieu dans son dessein universel de grâce." *Nova et Vetera* 77, no. 4 (2002): 35–59.

———. "La philosophie et la théologie dans l'exercice interactif de leurs sagesses chez S. Thomas et chez Jacques Maritain." *Bulletin de littérature ecclésiastique* 105, no. 3 (2004): 255–74.

———. "Miséricorde et justice dans le dessein divin sur les créatures spirituelles selon S. Thomas." *Nova et Vetera* 79, no. 4 (2004): 9–18.

Gathercole, Simon J. "Preexistence, and the Freedom of the Son in Creation and Redemption. An Exposition in Dialogue with Robert Jenson." *International Journal of Systematic Theology* 7, no. 1 (2005): 38–51.

———. *The Preexistent Son: Recovering the Christologies of Matthew, Mark, and Luke.* Grand Rapids, Mich.: Eerdmans, 2006.

Geach, Peter T. "Omnipotence." *Philosophy* 48, no. 183 (1973): 7–20.

Glare, P. G. W. *Oxford Latin Dictionary.* Oxford: Clarendon Press, 1982.

Godzieba, Anthony J. *A Theology of the Presence and Absence of God.* Collegeville, Minn.: Liturgical Press, 2018.

Gourgues, Michel. *Les deux lettres à Timothée. La Lettre à Tite.* Paris: Cerf, 2009.

Green, Lowell C. "Luther's Understanding of the Freedom of God and the Salvation of Man: His Interpretation of 1 Timothy 2:4." *Archiv für Reformationsgeschichte* 87 (1996): 57–73.

———. "Universal Salvation (1 Timothy 2:4) according to the Lutheran Reformers." *Lutheran Quarterly* 9, no. 3 (1995): 281–300.

Greggs, Tom. "'Jesus is victor': Passing the Impasse of Barth on Universalism." *Scottish Journal of Theology* 60, no. 2 (2007): 196–212.

Haddox, Susan E. *Metaphor and Masculinity in Hosea.* New York: Peter Lang, 2011.

Hallman, Joseph M. "The Emotions of God in the Theology of St. Augustine." *Recherches de Théologie Ancienne et Médiévale* 51 (1984): 5–19.

Hartshorne, Charles. *Omnipotence and Other Theological Mistakes,* 6–26. Albany: State University of New York, 1984.

Heschel, Abraham J. "The Meaning and Mystery of Wrath." In his *The Prophets,* 2:59–78. New York: Harper and Row, 1962.

Horst, Ulrich. "Christ, *Exemplar Ordinis Fratrum Praedictorum,* According to Saint Thomas Aquinas." In *Christ Among the Medieval Dominicans,* edited by Kent Emery Jr. and Joseph Wawrykow, 256–70. Notre Dame, Ind.: University of Notre Dame Press, 1998.

Humbrecht, Thierry-Dominique. *Théologie négative et noms divins chez saint Thomas d'Aquin.* Paris: Vrin, 2006.

Hume, David. *Dialogue concerning Natural Religion.* In *Dialogues concerning Natural Religion and Other Writings,* edited by Dorothy Coleman. Cambridge: Cambridge University Press, 2007.

Hwang, Alexander Y. "Augustine's Interpretations of 1 Tim. 2:4 in the Context of His Developing Views of Grace." *Studia Patristica* 43 (2006): 137–42.

Ide, Pascal. *Une Théologie de l'Amour. L'amour, centre de la "Trilogie" de Hans Urs von Balthasar.* Brussels: Lessius, 2012.

———. *Une Théo-logique du Don. Le don dans la "Trilogie" de Hans Urs von Balthasar.* Leuven: Peeters, 2013.

Jakobson, Roman. "Closing Statement. Linguistics and Poetics." In *Style in Language,* edited by Thomas A. Sebeok, 350–77. Cambridge, Mass.: MIT Press, 1960.

Jalbert, Guy. *Nécessité et contingence chez Saint Thomas et chez ses prédécesseurs.* Ottawa: University Press, 1962.

James, William. "What is an Emotion?" *Mind* 9, no. 34 (1884): 188–205.

Janowski, Bernd. *Arguing with God: A Theological Anthropology of the Psalms.*

Translated by Armin Siedlecki. Louisville, Ky.: Westminster John Knox Press, 2013.

Jeager, Werner. *The Theology of the Early Greek Philosophers*. Oxford: Clarendon Press, 1947.

Jeremias, Jörg. *Die Reue Gottes. Aspekte alttestamentlicher Gottesvorstellung*. Neukirchen-Vluyn: Neukirchener Verlag, 1975.

John Paul II, Pope. *Fides et Ratio*. Encyclical Letter. September 14, 1998. Available at www.vatican.va.

Jonas, Hans. "Is Faith Still Possible? Memories of Rudolf Bultmann and Reflections on the Philosophical Aspects of His Work." In *Mortality and Morality: A Search for the Good after Auschwitz*, edited by Lawrence Vogel, 144–64. Evanston, Ill.: Northwestern University Press, 1996 (1976).

———. "The Concept of God after Auschwitz: A Jewish Voice." *The Journal of Religion* 67, no. 1 (1987): 1–13.

Journet, Charles. *The Meaning of Grace*. Translated by Arthur V. Littledale. New York: Scepter, 1996.

———. *L'Église sainte mais non sans pécheurs*. Paris: Parole et Silence, 1999.

Jüngel, Eberhard. *God as the Mystery of the World*. Translated by Geoffrey Wainwright. Edinburgh: T and T Clark, 1983.

———. *God's Being Is in Becoming: The Trinitarian Being of God in the Theology of Karl Barth*. Translated by John Webster. Edinburgh: T and T Clark, 2001.

Kant, Immanuel. *Critique of Pure Reason*. Translated by Paul Guyer and Allen Wood. Cambridge: Cambridge University Press, 1998.

———. *Anthropology from a Pragmatic Point of View*. Translated by Robert B. Louden. Cambridge: Cambridge University Press, 2006.

Kasper, Walter. *The God of Jesus Christ*. New York: Crossroad, 2002.

Kierkegaard, Søren. "The God as Teacher and Savior." In *Philosophical Fragments*, edited by Howard V. Hong and Edna H. Hong. Princeton, N.J.: Princeton University Press, 1985.

Klimczak, Pawel. *Christus Magister. Le Christ Maître dans les commentaires évangéliques de saint Thomas d'Aquin*. Fribourg: Academic Press, 2014.

Ku, John Baptist. *God the Father in the Theology of St. Thomas Aquinas*. New York: Peter Lang, 2012.

Kuschel, Karl-Joseph. *Geboren vor aller Zeit? Der Streit um Christi Ursprung*. Munich: Piper Verlag, 1990.

Labbé, Yves. "Apologie philosophique de la réciprocité." *Nouvelle Revue Théologique* 131, no. 1 (2009): 65–86.

Lacoste, Jean-Yves. *The Appearing of God*. Translated by Oliver O'Donovan. Oxford: Oxford University Press, 2018.

Lecuit, Jean-Baptiste. "L'épreuve de la providence." *Recherches de Science Religieuse* 106, no. 2 (2018): 255–74.

Levering, Matthew. *Scripture and Metaphysics: Aquinas and the Renewal of Trinitarian Theology*. Oxford: Blackwell, 2004.

Levering, Matthew, Piotr Roszak, and Jörgen Vijgen, eds. *Reading Job with St. Thomas Aquinas*. Washington, D.C.: The Catholic University of America Press, 2020.

Lim, Bo H., and Daniel Castelo. *Hosea*. Grand Rapids, Mich.: Eerdmans, 2015.

Lindbeck, George A. *The Nature of Doctrine: Religion and Theology in a Postliberal Age*. Louisville, Ky.: Westminster John Knox Press, 2009 (1984).

Locke, John. *The Second Treatise of Government*. In *Two Treatises of Government*, edited by Peter Laslett. Cambridge: Cambridge University Press, 1994.

Ludlow, Morwenna. *Universal Salvation: Eschatology in the Thought of Gregory of Nyssa and Karl Rahner*. Oxford: Oxford University Press, 2000.

———. "Universalism in the History of Christianity." In *Universal Salvation? The Current Debate*, edited by Robin A. Parry and Christopher H. Partridge, 191–218. Carlisle: Paternoster Press, 2003.

Luther, Martin. *Disputatio Heidelbergae habita*. In *Weimarer Ausgabe* I. Weimar: Böhlau, 1883.

Mager, Robert. "Un enchantement de l'histoire?" In *Dieu agit-il dans l'histoire?*, edited by Robert Mager, 47–74. Montreal: Fides, 2006.

Magnard, Pierre. "Ordre et dignité." In *La dignité de l'homme*, edited by Pierre Magnard, 3–12. Paris: Champion, 1995.

———. *Pascal ou l'art de la digression*. Paris: Ellipses, 1997.

———. *Questions à l'humanisme*. Paris: Presses Universitaires de France, 2000.

———. *Pourquoi la religion?* Paris: Armand Colin, 2006.

———. "Religion, chemin d'humanité." *Revue Théologique de Louvain* 39, no. 3 (2008): 315–28.

———. "L'homme universel." *Revue de Métaphysique et de Morale* 61, no. 1 (2009): 19–32.

Marguerat, Daniel. "L'œuvre de l'Esprit." In his *La première histoire du christianisme. Les Actes des Apôtres*, 149–74. Paris: Cerf, 1999.

Marion, Jean-Luc. "L'impossibilité de l'impossible: Dieu." *Archivio di Filosofia* 78, no. 1 (2010): 21–36.

Maritain, Jacques. *Dieu et la permission du mal*. Paris: DDB, 1963.

———. "Réflexions sur le savoir théologique." In *Approches sans entraves*, from Œuvres complètes, 13:823–69. Fribourg: Éd. Universitaires, 1993.

Marrou, Henri-Irénée. *L'ambivalence du temps de l'histoire chez saint Augustin*. Paris: Vrin, 1950.

———. *Théologie de l'histoire*. Paris: Seuil, 1968.

Marshall, Bruce D. "The Dereliction of Christ and the Impassibility of God." In *Divine Impassibility and the Mystery of Human Suffering*, edited by James F. Keating and Thomas-Joseph White, 246–98. Grand Rapids, Mich.: Eerdmans, 2009.

McCormack, Bruce L. "Karl Barth's Christology as a Resource for a Reformed Version of Kenoticism." *International Journal of Systematic Theology* 8, no. 3 (2006): 243–51.

McCready, Douglas. "He Came Down from Heaven. The Preexistence of

Christ Revisited." *Journal of the Evangelical Theological Society* 40, no. 3 (1997): 419–32.

———. *He Came Down from Heaven: The Preexistence of Christ and the Christian Faith.* Downers Grove, Ill.: InterVarsity Press, 2005.

Merrigan, Terrence. "Saving the Particular: Incarnation and the Mediation of Salvation in the Theology of Religions." In *Orthodoxy: Process and Product,* edited by Lieven Boeve, Mathijs Lamberigts, and Terrence Merrigan, 299–322. Leuven: Peeters, 2009.

Mongillo, Dalmazio. "Les béatitudes et la béatitude. Le dynamisme de la *Somme de théologie* de Thomas d'Aquin. Une lecture de la Ia-IIae, q. 69." *RSPT* 78, no. 3 (1994): 373–88.

Montagnes, Bernard. "Les deux fonctions de la sagesse: ordonner et juger." *RSPT* 53, no. 4 (1969): 675–86.

Montaigne, Michel de. *Essais.* Bibliothèque de la pléiade. Paris: Gallimard, 1962.

Muller, Richard A. *Dictionary of Latin and Greek Theological Terms Drawn Principally from Protestant Scholastic Theology.* Grand Rapids, Mich.: Baker Academic, 2006.

Nancy, Jean-Luc. *Dis-Enclosure: The Deconstruction of Christianity.* Translated by Bettina Bergo. New York: Fordham University Press, 2008.

Narcisse, Gilbert. *Les raisons de Dieu. Argument de convenance et Esthétique théologique selon saint Thomas d'Aquin et Hans Urs von Balthasar.* Fribourg: Éditions universitaires, 1997.

Newman, John Henry. "Milman's View of Christianity." In his *Essays Critical and Historical* II. London: Longmans, 1897.

Nicolas, Jean-Hervé. "La volonté salvifique de Dieu contrariée par le péché." *Revue thomiste* 92, no. 1 (1992): 177–96.

Nihan, Christophe. "Excès et démesure de la colère divine dans la Bible hébraïque." In *Colère et repentirs divins,* edited by Jean-Marie Durand et al., 89–107. Göttingen: Vandenhoeck and Ruprecht, 2015.

Pakaluk, Michael. "Philosophy as a Path of Salvation in the Ancient World." In *San Tommaso et la salvezza,* edited by Serge-Thomas Bonino and Guido Mazzotta, 13–29. Rome: Urbaniana University Press, 2020.

Paluch, Michał. "Note sur la distinction entre les nécessités chez Thomas d'Aquin." *AHDLMA* 70, no. 1 (2003): 219–31.

———. *La profondeur de l'amour divin. Évolution de la doctrine de la prédestination dans l'œuvre de Thomas d'Aquin.* Paris: Vrin, 2004.

———. "The Salvific Will according to Aquinas: An Inspiration for Contemporary Theology?" *Religion and Religions,* nos. 1–2 (2016): 181–93.

Pannenberg, Wolfhart. *Systematic Theology.* 3 vols. Translated by Geoffrey W. Bromiley. Grand Rapids, Mich.: Eerdmans, 1991–2004.

Paul VI, Pope. *Ecclesiam suam.* Encyclical Letter. August 6, 1964. Available at www.vatican.va.

Perrier, Emmanuel. *La fécondite en Dieu. La puissance notionnelle dans la Trinité selon saint Thomas d'Aquin.* Paris: Parole et Silence, 2009.

Pinckaers, Servais T. "Recherche sur la signification véritable du terme 'spéculatif.'" *Nouvelle Revue Théologique* 81, no. 7 (1959): 673–95.

Pinnock, Clark H., et al. *The Openness of God*. Downers Grove, Ill.: InterVarsity, 1994.

Placher, William C. *The Domestication of Transcendence: How Modern Thinking about God Went Wrong*. Louisville, Ky.: Westminster John Knox Press, 1996.

Plantinga, Alvin. *Warranted Christian Belief*. Oxford: Oxford University Press, 2000.

———. "Two Dozen (or so) Theistic Arguments." In *Alvin Plantinga: God's Philosopher*, edited by Deane P. Baker, 203–27. Cambridge: Cambridge University Press, 2007.

Popper, Karl. *A World of Propensities*. Bristol: Thoemmes, 1990.

Porro, Pasquale. "*Lex necessitatis vel contingentiae*. Necessità, contingenza e provvidenza nell'universo di Tommaso d'Aquino." *RSPT* 96, no. 3 (2012): 401–50.

Pouivet, Roger. Épistémologie *des croyances religieuses*. Paris: Cerf, 2013.

Prétot, Patrick. *L'adoration de la croix. Triduum pascal*. Paris: Cerf, 2014.

Rahner, Karl. "Immanent and Transcendent Consummation of the World." In *Theological Investigations* X, 273–89, translated by David Bourke. London: Darton, Longman and Todd, 1973.

———. "The Hermeneutics of Eschatological Assertions." In *Theological Investigations* IV, 323–46, translated by Kevin Smyth. London: Darton, Longman and Todd, 1974.

———. *Foundations of Christian Faith*. Translated by William V. Dych. New York: Seabury Press, 1978.

———. "The One Christ and the Universality of Salvation." In *Theological Investigations* XVI, 199–224. Translated by David Morland. London: Darton, Longman and Todd, 1979.

Ramelli, Ilaria L. E. "Christian Soteriology and Christian Platonism." *Vigiliae Christianae* 61, no. 3 (2007): 313–56.

Ratzinger, Joseph. *Eschatology: Death and Eternal Life*. Second edition. Translated by Michael Waldstein. Washington, D.C.: The Catholic University of America Press, 2007.

Richard, Anne. *Cosmologie et théologie chez Grégoire de Nazianze*. Paris: Institut d'Études Augustiniennes, 2003.

Ricoeur, Paul. "Metaphor and the Main Problem of Hermeneutics." *New Literary History* 6, no. 1 (1974): 95–110.

———. "The Metaphorical Process as Cognition, Imagination, and Feeling." *Critical Inquiry* 5, no. 1 (1978): 143–59.

———. *Parcours de la reconnaissance*. Paris: Stock, 2004.

Rocca, Gregory P. *Speaking the Incomprehensible God: Thomas Aquinas on the Interplay of Positive and Negative Theology*. Washington, D.C.: The Catholic University of America Press, 2004.

Romano, Claude. *L'événement et le monde*. Paris: Presses Universitaires de France, 1998.

Römer, Thomas. "The Revelation of the Divine Name to Moses and the Construction of a Memory About the Origins of the Encounter Between Yhwh and Israel." In *Israel's Exodus in Transdisciplinary Perspective*, edited by Thomas E. Levy, 305–15. Heidelberg: Springer, 2015.

———. "Yhwh peut-il changer d'avis? Arbitraire, colère, repentir, compassion divins dans la Bible hébraïque." In *Colère et repentirs divins*, edited by Jean-Marie Durand et al, 313–24. Göttingen: Vandenhoeck and Ruprecht, 2015.

Roszak, Piotr, and Jörgen Vijgen, eds. *Reading Sacred Scripture with Thomas Aquinas: Hermeneutical Tools, Theological Questions and New Perspectives*. Turnhout: Brepols, 2015.

———. *Towards a Biblical Thomism: Thomas Aquinas and the Renewal of Biblical Theology*. Pamplona: EUNSA, 2018.

Russell, Robert J., ed. *Scientific Perspectives on Divine Action: Twenty Years of Challenge and Progress*. Vatican City / Berkeley, Calif.: Vatican Observatory / CTNS, 2008.

Saussure, Ferdinand de. *Cours de linguistique générale*. Paris: Payot, 1971.

Schenk, Richard. "The Epoché of Factical Damnation: On the Costs of Bracketing Out the Likelihood of Final Loss." *Logos* 1, no. 3 (1997): 122–54.

———. "Exteriority and Interiority: Their Mutual Qualification in Thomas Aquinas's Reception of the Axiom *Omnis Christi actio nostra est instructio*." In *Soundings in the History of a Hope: New Studies on Thomas Aquinas*, 31–68. Ave Maria, Fla.: Sapientia Press, 2016.

Schenker, Adrian. "De la validité de l'exégèse croyante de la Bible." *RSPT* 97, no. 4 (2013): 449–57.

Schillebeeckx, Edward. "The Non-Conceptual Intellectual Dimension in Our Knowledge of God according to Aquinas." In *The Collected Works of Edward Schillebeeckx*, vol. 2: *Revelation and Theology*, 207–38. London: Bloomsbury, 2014.

Schreiner, Thomas. *Romans*. Grand Rapids, Mich.: Baker Academic, 1998.

Schumacher, Michele M. *A Trinitarian Anthropology: Adrienne von Speyr and Hans Urs von Balthasar in Dialogue with Thomas Aquinas*. Washington, D.C.: The Catholic University of America Press, 2014.

Schwager, Raymund. "Der Zorn Gottes. Zur Problematik der Allegorie." *Zeitschrift für katholische Theologie* 105, no. 4 (1983): 406–14.

Sénéchal, Vincent. *Rétribution et intercession dans le Deutéronome*. Berlin: de Gruyter, 2009.

Sesboüé, Bernard. "L'enfer est-il éternel?" *Recherches de Science Religieuse* 87, no. 2 (1999): 189–206.

Sesboüé, Bernard, and Joseph Wolinsky. *Histoire des dogmes*, vol. 1: *Le Dieu du Salut*. Paris: Desclée, 1994.

Söhngen, Gottlieb. "La sagesse de la théologie par la voie de la science." In *Mysterium salutis. Dogmatique de l'histoire du salut*, 4:159–250. Paris: Cerf, 1969.

Sonnet, Jean-Pierre. "*Ehyeh asher ehyeh* (Exodus 3:14). God's 'Narrative Identity' among Suspense, Curiosity, and Surprise." *Poetics Today* 31, no. 2 (2010): 331–51.

———. "God's Repentance and 'False Starts' in Biblical History (Genesis 6–9; Exodus 32–34; 1 Samuel 15 and 2 Samuel 7)." In *Congress Volume Ljubljana 2007*, edited by André Lemaire, 469–94. Leiden: Brill, 2010.

———. "Dieu sauve l'histoire comme en sous-main. La rhétorique des amendements divins." In *Raconter Dieu. Entre récit, histoire et théologie*, edited by Christian Dionne and Yvan Mathieu, 173–96. Bruxelles: Lessius, 2014.

———. "Justice et miséricorde. Les attributs de Dieu dans la dynamique narrative du Pentateuque." *Nouvelle Revue Théologique* 138, no. 1 (2016): 3–22.

Soskice, Janet M. "The Gift of the Name: Moses and the Burning Bush." *Gregorianum* 79, no. 2 (1998): 231–46.

———. "Athens and Jerusalem, Alexandria and Edessa. Is There a Metaphysics of Scripture?" *International Journal of Systematic Theology* 8, no. 2 (2006): 149–62.

Spinoza, Baruch. *Ethics*. In *Complete Works*, translated by S. Shirley and edited by M. L. Morgan. Indianapolis, Ind.: Hackett, 2002.

Sweeney, Marvin A. *The Twelve Prophets*, vol. 1: *Hosea, Joel, Amos, Obadiah, Jonah*. Collegeville, Minn.: Liturgical Press, 2000.

Talstra, Eep. "Exile and Pain. A Chapter from the Story of God's Emotions." In *Exile and Suffering*, edited by Bob Becking, 161–80. Leiden: Brill, 2009.

Tanner, Kathryn. *God and Creation in Christian Theology: Tyranny or Empowerment?* Oxford: Blackwell, 1988.

Tarico, Valerie. "God's Emotions: Why the Biblical God is Hopelessly Human." In *The End of Christianity*, edited by John W. Loftus, 155–77. Amherst, N.Y.: Prometheus Books, 2011.

Te Velde. Rudi. *Aquinas on God: The Divine Science of the "Summa theologiae."* Burlington, Vt.: Ashgate, 2006.

Teresa of Avila. *Autobiography*. Translated by E. Allison Peers. Mineola, N.Y.: Dover, 2010.

Theological Dictionary of the Old Testament. Edited by G. Johannes Botterweck and Helmer Ringgren. Translated by John T. Willis. 16 vols. Grand Rapids, Mich.: Eerdmans, 1974–2018.

Tiessen, Terrance L. *Providence and Prayer: How Does God Work in the World?* Downers Grove, Ill.: InterVarsity Press, 2000.

Torrell. Jean-Pierre. "Le savoir théologique chez Saint Thomas d'Aquin." *Revue thomiste* 96, no. 3 (1996): 355–96.

———. *Le Christ en ses mystères. La vie et l'œuvre de Jésus selon saint Thomas d'Aquin*. Paris: Desclée, 1999.

———. "La causalité salvifique de la résurrection du Christ selon saint Thomas." In his *Recherches thomasiennes*, 214–41. Paris: Vrin, 2000.

———. "Renseignements techniques." *Saint Thomas d'Aquin, Somme Théologique. Le Verbe incarné I (IIIa q. 1–6)*, 298–306. Paris: Cerf, 2002.

————. "L'interprète du désir. La prière chez saint Thomas d'Aquin." *La Vie spirituelle* 752 (2004): 213–23.

————. *Encyclopédie Jésus le Christ chez saint Thomas d'Aquin.* Paris: Cerf: 2008.

Trego, Kristell. *L'impuissance du possible. Émergence et développement du possible, d'Aristote à l'aube des temps modernes.* Paris: Vrin, 2019.

Tschipke, Theophil. *L'humanité du Christ comme instrument de salut de la divinité.* Fribourg: Academic Press, 2003 (1940).

Turner, Denys. *Faith, Reason, and the Existence of God.* Cambridge: Cambridge University Press, 2004.

Ulrich, Ferdinand. *Leben in der Einheit von Leben und Tod.* In his *Schriften*, II, edited by Martin Bieler and Stefan Oster. Freiburg i.B.: Johannes Verlag, 1999.

Van Steenberghen, Fernand. *Le problème de l'existence de Dieu dans les écrits de saint Thomas d'Aquin.* Louvain-La-Neuve: Institut supérieur de philosophie, 1980.

Van Tongeren, Louis. "Les Improperia du Vendredi saint au banc des accusés." *Questions liturgiques* 83, no. 4 (2002): 240–56.

Vang, Carsten. "God's Love According to Hosea and Deuteronomy: A Prophetic Reworking of a Deuteronomic Concept?" *Tyndale Bulletin* 62, no. 2 (2011): 173–94.

Vanhoye, Albert. *La lettre aux Hébreux. Jésus-Christ, médiateur d'une alliance nouvelle.* Paris: Desclée, 2002.

Vatican Council II. Edited by Austin Flannery. Northport, N.Y.: Costello, 1998.

Vermeylen, Jacques. "Le fou dit dans son cœur: pas de Dieu! Comment le Premier Testament parle-t-il de l'incroyance?" *Mélanges de Science Religieuse* 63, no. 3 (2006): 7–20.

————. *Le Livre d'Isaïe. Une cathédrale littéraire.* Paris: Cerf, 2014.

Vetö, Etienne. *Du Christ à la Trinité. Penser les Mystères du Christ après Thomas d'Aquin et Balthasar.* Paris: Cerf, 2012.

Vial, Marc. *Pour une théologie de la toute-puissance de Dieu. L'approche d'Eberhard Jüngel.* Paris: Classiques Garnier, 2016.

————. "God's Almightiness and the Limits of Theological Discourse." *Modern Theology* 34, no. 3 (2018): 443–56.

Vogels, Walter. *Célébration et sainteté. Le Lévitique.* Paris: Cerf, 2015.

Webster, John B. "The Holiness and Love of God." *Scottish Journal of Theology* 57, no. 3 (2004): 249–68.

Weinandy, Thomas G., OFM Cap. *Does God Suffer?* Edinburgh: T and T Clark, 2000.

Wénin, André. "Au-delà des représentations, Dieu." In *Dieu à l'épreuve de notre cri*, edited by Adolphe Gesché and Paul Scolas, 25–44. Paris: Cerf, 1999.

West, Jason L. A. "Aquinas on Peter Lombard and the Metaphysical Status of Christ's Human Nature." *Gregorianum* 88, no. 3 (2007): 557–86.

White, Thomas Joseph, ed. *The Analogy of Being: Invention of the Antichrist or the Wisdom of God?* Grand Rapids, Mich.: Eerdmans, 2011.

———. *Exodus*. Brazos Theological Commentary on the Bible. Grand Rapids, Mich.: Brazos, 2016.

Wiesel, Elie. *Night*. Toronto: Bentam Books, 1986.

Willis, John T. "The 'Repentance' of God in the Books of Samuel, Jeremiah, and Jonah." *Horizons in Biblical Theology* 16, no. 1 (1994): 156–75.

Wippel, John F. *The Metaphysical Thought of Thomas Aquinas*. Washington, D.C.: The Catholic University of America Press, 2000.

Yai-Chow Wong, Teresia. "The Problem of Preexistence in Philippians 2:6–11." *Ephemerides Theologicae Lovanienses* 62, no. 4 (1986): 267–82.

Divine Speech in Human Words: Thomistic Engagements with Scripture
was designed in Arno and composed by Kachergis Book Design of Pittsboro,
North Carolina. It was printed on 60-pound Maple Eggshell Cream
and bound by Maple Press of York, Pennsylvania.